Kinship in Solitude
Perspectives on Notions of Solidarity

Artists Unlimited, Anna Jehle, Paul Buckermann

Contents / Inhalt

4
Anna Jehle and / und Paul Buckermann
Kinship in Solitude
Solidarity among the (Lumpen)cognitariat

Kinship in Solitude
Solidarität im (Lumpen-)Kognitariat

24
Nanna Heidenreich
"Do you think I could borrow some of your refugees?"
Art, Activism, Migration

„Kann ich mir mal deine Flüchtlinge ausleihen?"
Kunst, Aktivismus, Migration

62
Rahel Jaeggi
Solidarity and Indifference

Solidarität und Gleichgültigkeit

104
Jochen Becker
Fugitive Communities
Scale Work, Digital Solidarity and Cosmopolitan Politics After Politics

Flüchtige Gemeinschaften
Maßstabsarbeit, digitale Solidarität und eine kosmopolitane Politik nach der Politik

160
Arkadiusz Półtorak and / und Paul Buckermann
Hands-On Utopias and Rampant Complexity
Relational Aesthetics, Solidarity and Organized Art Worlds

Konkrete Utopien und ungeheure Komplexität
Über relationale Ästhetik, Solidarität und organisierte Kunstwelten

184
Marcus Steinweg
Nine Remarks on Art, Attentiveness, Contingency, Solidarity and Lightheartedness

Neun Bemerkungen zu Kunst, Aufmerksamkeit, Kontingenz, Solidarität und Heiterkeit

204
Alexander Koch
Mobilising Solidarity
Art, Vocabulary Politics and Resolidarisation after Richard Rorty

Solidarische Mobilmachung
Kunst, Vokabularpolitik und Resolidarisierung nach Richard Rorty

242
Ana Teixeira Pinto and / und Peter Hermans
Solidarity and Fashionism
Negating the Rhetoric of Submission as Destiny

Solidarität und Fashionism
Zur Negation der Schicksalshaftigkeit einer Unterwerfungsrhetorik

275
Contributors / Beitragende

284
Imprint / Impressum

KINSHIP IN SOLITUDE

SOLIDARITY AMONG
THE (LUMPEN)COGNI

ANNA JEHLE   PAUL

ARIAT

BUCKERMANN

Anna Jehle and Paul Buckermann

Kinship in Solitude
Solidarity among the (Lumpen)cognitariat

For all its deep roots in European modernity, solidarity, both as idea and ideal, has in recent years never seemed more outdated. Against the quasi-ritualised declarations and calls for solidarity that we're used to hearing from trade union bureaucrats and paternalistic aid workers, we aim to propose a different way of thinking about the concept. Given how bad things have got now, solidarity should seem to us a necessity, yet we still treat it entirely as a matter of choice. It can be, in the best meaning of the term, self-interested, just as it must be pragmatic. We speak here of solidarity among non-predetermined kinship relations, because these relations reject the specificity of blood lines or imposed regional collectivities. Yet at the same time, the framework of this notional network of relations and collaborative practices based on solidarity is formed by the apparently individual condition of solitude. Our view is that this state of being alone, of being-only-for-oneself, of having responsibility for oneself alone, is a phenomenon determined by the common life, work and affective conditions of a large group of creative workers and knowledge producers. We hope, however, to show in this text that new prospects for solidarity are emerging from conditions that an entire lumpencognitariat—freelancers, interns, temps—now finds itself facing. Solidarity, therefore—understood as a feeling of attachment and as the practices associated with that feeling—is not inescapably determined by biological nature, history or fate; rather it can only be expressed by a fundamental act of freedom.

This volume, an anniversary edition of the artists and residency initiative *Artists Unlimited,* has its origins in a context of collective cultural production. The fact that we are still dealing with the concept of solidarity thirty years after the association was founded in 1985 suggests that the debates, themes and jokes that came out of this institutional context have now become exhausted. What has remained relevant, however, is what has emerged from a general discourse on living and surviving conducted over three decades: the notion of a possibly submerged relation of kinship among lives that have been forcibly individualised—a kinship in solitude—which we think will be helpful in developing new debates and strategies.

No one these days is in any doubt that a globalised capitalism has in its various forms presided over fundamental and permanent changes in the world of work. And yet uncertainty, enforced creativity, and countless isolated truths do not only dominate the world of wage labour; they are also penetrating other areas of life, since earning a wage often now means spending the whole morning on your smartphone. The decay of the welfare state, global competition at every level, the migration of industrial production to regions of the world even more desperate to be exploited—or simply to automated production—together with the deregulation of workers' rights are merely among the most visible signs of such developments. Other causes and consequences include the expansion of higher education, the growth of the service and creative sectors, digital information streams and a growing pressure on individuals to manage their own personal responsibilities. Perhaps it is not so surprising that current analyses of these civilisational shifts ascribe a dominant role to art, and in particular to what seem to be the most autonomous areas of this field of production and discourse. Creativity and the restless and endless creation of the new are the semantic figures of a modern art, which since the emergence of a Bohemia has gone hand in hand with a myth of the artist as someone who earns an irregular income and pursues a hedonistic way of life.[1]

We have the course of our lives set out for us by education, cultural production and consumption opportunities: we are in control of our own careers, our individual characters, our own future. Today every individual is subjected not only to this freedom, but to the whole pressure of success or the promise of happiness. Individual creativity seems to have become an imperative that society as a whole places upon everyone, even non-artists. This indirect pressure to develop an ever more refined character then combines with immediate toxic work conditions, with an oppressive ethic of self-reliance, with soul-destroying temp work, brutal employment contracts and temporary research or cultural projects to produce solitude and exhaustion[2] on a vast scale. We are alone and without a gallery contact after finishing art school; alone and unemployed after completing the nth externally-funded academic project; alone between two deadening graphic design jobs for local micro-businesses; alone while writing the next text for some trivial journal; alone and frustrated while preparing the next pitch for some ridiculous soft drink campaign. Thrown back upon ourselves, responsible for constantly pretending to provide things that are new and exploitable[3], we work as if we were one-man or -woman corporations, or as if we were "freelance" writers / gallery technicians / consultants / photographers / graphic designers / artists, etc. Marx himself could have told us that this freedom must necessarily have a dual, and decidedly capitalist, character. It is true that the members of the new cognitariat[4] are free to offer their creative potential on the market of opportunities, but at the same time they are forced to do so because they are also free from any resources of their own with which to pursue their hopes.

Other, quite different freedoms have now combined with this freedom from the means to satisfy one's own needs. Following the so-called *end of history*, the *death of the author*, the repudiation of modern art and the decay—indeed the *de facto* perversion—of the grand narratives of reason or progress, the contemporary subject seems now to face a "freedom from everything".[5] These negative freedoms *from*—from oppressive social relations and societal norms, but also from basic welfare services or effective labour regulation—do not appear as the same phenomena to everyone across the world. And yet, this turn from a positive concept of liberty, from a freedom *to*—which is still at least formally guaranteed by human and civil rights—to a freedom from social and legal protections, is becoming increasingly evident across society. If we take a closer look at the large numbers of creative workers, artists and knowledge workers, this negative freedom appears glaringly obvious. Unpaid work, short-term projects and work placements are manifestations of a freedom from security, from the ability to plan for the future and from financial resources. These sources of personal and financial crisis then combine with the effects of a freedom from guiding principles, truths or planning—the pressure to innovate within a glittering discourse that legitimates countless styles, theories or artistic forms.

The solitude of which we write is produced precisely by these freedoms from security, orientation and social belonging. In our view this is especially true of the vast group of unpaid workers and freelancers that maintains the whole sector of cultural production, flowing through it in an almost invisible tide.[6] Thus a freedom from specific relationships—from family ties and other affiliations that are not the result of (voluntary) choice—is as much part of this picture as freedom from clear class positions. It is precisely this ambivalent nature of negative models of freedom that has inspired our ideas about the possibilities for new paradigms in forms of association. Having emerged following the decay of classical forms of collective organisation and distribution, these associative forms, these elective affinities, are both voluntary and highly pragmatic. This means that any understanding gained here into the cognitariat's mode of existence, into this fragmented mass of solitary existences, should not be taken as a step towards developing a new class consciousness. Instead what we mean to do is reflect on the specific features and potentials of a new way of thinking about solidarity. We suspect that the fields we present here contain very different possibilities for relations of solidarity and kinship.

What conclusions can be drawn from the developments we have outlined here? What can we appeal to if we are to avoid proposing some fictional or ideal condition of community? Doesn't solidarity always involve a form of thinking that relates the local to a larger scale? If art must constantly react to a "permanent condition of crisis", what consequences does that have for these speculations? Is it not precisely in these reactive gestures that art confirms its own inability to formulate possible futures, becoming instead a hyperbolic continuation of the present that oscillates between social relevance, sincerity and detachment? What spaces of possibility might open up in this manifold state of atomised horror, in this freedom from solidarity and presumed kinship in solitude?

In an age when the media relentlessly conveys this condition of crisis and catastrophe, an examination of potential new forms of kinship and the possibilities they contain seems in order. Art and the production of art would seem to be the obvious subject for research of this kind, since in recent years artists have increasingly been turning to social, political and educative practices that were traditionally located outside the field of aesthetics. We have already mentioned how art is ascribed a capacity to create the new or to offer creative solutions, and we have little cause to doubt it ourselves. However, we are also struck by the stark contrast between these claims and the hardships of the sector's own precarious work and living conditions. Critical engagement with institutions, ideologies and structures of discrimination is generally carried out within the very museums, journals, galleries, colleges, educational projects and festivals that perpetuate the grievances under criticism. What other alternatives do producers have, though, when it is so difficult for them to find audiences outside of this framework? What other forms now exist for creative workers facing the dilemma of making a living as fragmented *solo-entrepreneurs?*

We first intend to consider the framework and spaces for other forms of collaboration and cooperation. We know there are whole social fields of cultural and knowledge production which extend far beyond the discipline of the visual arts and which depend on a vast number of human creative machines. Both these fields share the notion that creative potential emerges from an inner drive, a notion derived from both the well-worn image of the lonely and impoverished artistic genius and from a new type of artist as start-up entrepreneur or creative consultant. Both poles of this opposition clearly depend on a normative myth of creativity as a spontaneous urge, in which life and work meld together into a notion of *life as venture capital.* A new insight can be gained into both the cultural proficiency of constant production for the sake of production ("devotion to one's art") and relentless (minimal) differentiation under pressure to produce the new: the internal composition of this expanding group of producers, who supposedly own nothing but their creative potential, shows that although each individual experiences a world that is private and enclosed, these worlds can be joined together precisely through a kinship in solitude. This insight can be a first step in thinking about intellectual and practical bases of solidarity in circumstances where a heartfelt call for people to become conscious of their class position will not, in our opinion, be enough. That is to say, any purely materialist analysis of a *creative class in* and *for itself* would fail to realise that the issue is not some chimera of an entirely new *digital bohemia* existing in a handful of global cities.

We cannot indulge ourselves by wishing into existence the ideal conditions for developing solidarity; rather, any chance of creating new forms or association must come from changing the way actually existing conditions are understood. In this sense, solidarity is the basis for being able to speak and act freely in association with others. This does not mean a form of community that demands we ignore differences and sees identity as the sole basis for association. It is why the basic units for creating and expressing united communities are primarily free, unilateral actions that are not the outcome of negotiations or historical necessity. In contrast to the idea of solidarity as the practice of speaking on behalf of the disadvantaged, the voluntary nature of this *kinship in solitude* rejects any fixed allocation of roles to individuals or groups. This kinship emerges from the realisation that many of us do not suffer from solitude itself, but rather from a particular solitude under common existing conditions. Last but not least, these thoughts on positive and negative forms of freedom show us that we imagine we are not subject to historical responsibility, despite the fact that existing conditions both demand and make possible that we accept this responsibility. It is for precisely this reason that any genuinely free solidarity would appear as something utterly "breathtaking".

---

1   See for example Andreas Reckwitz's conclusions in *The Invention of Creativity: Modern Society and the Culture of the New* (trans. Stephen Black), Cambridge, Polity 2017 [orig. 2012]. http://www.polity.co.uk/book.asp?ref=9780745697031

2   Alain Ehrenberg, *The Weariness of the Self: Diagnosing the History of Depression in the Contemporary Age* (trans. Enrico Cauette, Jacob Homel, David Homel), Montreal, McGill-Queen's University Press 2010 [orig. 1998]. http://www.mqup.ca/weariness-of-the-self--the-products-9780773546486.php?page_id=73&; See also Mark Fisher, *Capitalist Realism. Is there no Alternative?,* London, zero books 2009. http://www.zero-books.net/books/capitalist-realism

3   See also McKenzie Wark, *A Hacker Manifesto,* Cambrigde, Harvard University Press. http://www.hup.harvard.edu/catalog.php?isbn=9780674015432

4   Franco Bifo Berardi, "What does Cognitariat Mean?" in *Cultural Studies Review* 11 (2) 2005, http://epress.lib.uts.edu.au/journals/index.php/csrj/article/view/3656

5   Hito Steyerl, "Freedom from Everything: Freelancers and Mercenaries" in *e-flux* 41 2013. http://www.e-flux.com/journal/41/60229/freedom-from-everything-freelancers-and-mercenaries/

6   Hito Steyerl, "Politics of Art: Contemporary Art and the Transition to Post-Democracy" in *e-flux* 21 2010. http://www.e-flux.com/journal/21/67696/politics-of-art-contemporary-art-and-the-transition-to-post-democracy/

Anna Jehle und Paul Buckermann

Kinship in Solitude
Solidarität im (Lumpen-)Kognitariat

Der Begriff und die Idee von Solidarität ist tief im Mythos der europäischen Moderne verwurzelt und wirkt beizeiten genauso angestaubt wie jene. Den teilweise ritualisierten Solidaritätsbekundungen oder -einforderungen, die wir von technokratischen Gewerkschaftsfunktionär*innen genauso kennen wie von paternalistischen Entwicklungshelfer*innen, wollen wir ein anderes Nachdenken über Solidarität entgegenstellen. Diese Solidarität scheint aufgrund unzumutbarer Verhältnisse zwar eigentlich notwendig und doch ist sie heute in Gänze freiwillig. Sie kann nur im besten Sinne egoistisch sein, wie sie pragmatisch sein muss. Wir sprechen von Solidarität in Verwandtschaftsbeziehungen, die nicht vorbestimmt sind, weil sie den Partikularismus von Blutlinien und regionalen Zwangskollektivierungen ablehnt. Den Rahmen dieser spekulativen Beziehungsgeflechte und solidarischen Verschwörungen bildet dabei der scheinbar ganz individuelle Zustand der Einsamkeit. Dieses Alleinsein, ein Nur-für-sich-Sein, die auferlegte Eigenverantwortung ist unserer Annahme nach ein weit verbreitetes Phänomen, das auf bestimmten Lebens-, Arbeits- und Liebesverhältnissen einer großen Gruppe von Kreativen und Wissensproduzent*innen fußt. Aus diesen Verhältnissen, derer sich ein ganzes Lumpenkognitariat – Freischaffende, Praktikant*innen, Befristete – ausgesetzt sehen, entspringen jedoch, das soll der Text zeigen, Möglichkeiten zu neuen Perspektiven auf Solidarität. Dieses Gefühl der Verbundenheit und darauf bezogene Praxen sind dabei nicht zwangsläufig durch biologische Natur, Geschichte oder Schicksal festgelegt, sondern können nur durch eine grundlegende Freiheit hindurch zum Ausdruck gebracht werden.

Dieser Band ist aus einem Kontext kollektiver Kulturproduktion entstanden und liegt als Jubiläumspublikation der Künstler*innen- und Residency Initiative *Artists Unlimited* vor. Eine Beschäftigung mit Solidarität – als Begriff und Konzept – über dreißig Jahre nach der Gründung des Vereins im Jahr 1985 lässt vermuten, dass die Debatten, Themen und Witze dieses institutionellen Zusammenhangs eben in die Jahre gekommen sind. Gleichzeitig ist aber aktuell, was ein allgemeiner Diskurs um Leben und Überleben in den letzten drei Dekaden herauskristallisiert hat: Eine möglicherweise verschüttete Verwandtschaft von zwangsindividualisierten Existenzen – eine *Kinship in Solitude* –, welche uns für neue Debatten und Strategien hilfreich erscheint.

Niemand zweifelt heute mehr an einem grundlegenden und andauernden Wandel der Arbeitswelt in den verschiedenen Ausdrucksformen eines globalen Kapitalismus. Unsicherheit, ein Kreativitätsimperativ und unzählige isolierte Wahrheiten bestimmen dabei aber nicht nur die Sphäre der Lohnarbeit, sondern dringen ebenso in andere Bereiche ein, wenn sich die (Lohn-)Arbeit beispielsweise bereits allmorgendlich am Smartphone selbst herstellt. Die Zersetzung des Wohlfahrtsstaates, globaler Wettbewerb auf allen Ebenen, Abwanderung der industriellen Produktion in noch ausbeutungsfreudigere Regionen oder gleich in automatisierte Maschinenparks sowie die Deregulierung von Arbeitnehmer*innenrechten bilden so nur die sichtbarsten Grundlagen solcher Entwicklungen. Eine Bildungsexpansion, die Ausweitung des Dienstleistungs- und Kreativsektors, digitale Informationsströme sowie immer mehr Ansprüche an die selbstverantwortliche Verwaltung der eigenen Person sind die weiteren Gründe und Konsequenzen dieser Entwicklung. Dass in einschlägigen Analysen angesichts solcher zivilisatorischen Verschiebungen Kunst und besonders den scheinbar autonomsten Sphären dieses Produktions- und Diskursbereiches eine dominante Rolle zugeschrieben wird, vermag bei einem zweiten Blick nicht zu verwundern. Kreativität bzw. die rastlose und endlose Schaffung von Neuem sind semantische Figuren einer modernen Kunst, die Hand in Hand gehen mit einem Künstler*innenmythos, der seit dem Auftreten des Bohemiens von unregelmäßigen Einkommensverhältnissen und einem hedonistischen Lebensstil geprägt ist.[1]

Die Richtung wird uns in Ausbildung, Kulturproduktion und Konsummöglichkeiten vorgegeben: Wir haben unsere Karrieren, unsere ganze Individualität, unsere eigene Zukunft selbst in der Hand. Diese Freiheit, aber auch der ganze Druck von Erfolg oder das Versprechen von Glück sind heute auf jede*n Einzelne*n gelegt. Individuelle Kreativität scheint – auch für die*den Nichtkünstler*in – zum gesamtgesellschaftlichen Imperativ geworden zu sein. Dieser indirekte Druck zu einer immer ausgefeilteren Persönlichkeit verdichtet sich sodann mit ganz unmittelbaren, toxischen Arbeits(losigkeits)verhältnissen, erdrückender Selbstständigkeit, zerfressender Zeitarbeit, kruden Werkverträgen sowie befristeten Forschungs- und Kulturprojekten zu einer Gemengelage, die massenhafte Zustände der Einsamkeit und Erschöpfung[2] produziert: Einsam und ohne Galerieverbindung nach dem Abschluss an der Kunsthochschule; einsam und arbeitslos nach dem x-ten wissenschaftlichen Drittmittelprojekt; einsam zwischen zwei stumpfen Grafikjobs für nachbarschaftliche Kleinstunternehmen; einsam am nächsten Textmanuskript für irgendeine belanglose Zeitschrift; einsam und frustriert vor dem nächsten Pitch für eine peinliche Limonadenkampagne. Zurückgeworfen auf sich selbst, verantwortlich für das ständige Vortäuschen vom Neuem und Verwertbarem[3], arbeiten wir als Ich-AGs oder „freie" Autor*in / Aufbauhelfer*in / Berater*in / Fotograf*in / Grafiker*in / Künstler*in, usw. Dass diese Freiheit selbstredend immer noch einen dezidiert kapitalistischen Doppelcharakter haben muss, wusste schon Karl Marx. Die Mitglieder des neuen „Kognitariats"[4] können zwar ihre kreativen Potenziale frei auf dem Markt der Möglichkeiten anbieten; sie sind aber gleichzeitig dazu gezwungen, weil sie ebenso frei sind von den Ressourcen, um ihren eigenen Wünschen nachzugehen.

Zu dieser Freiheit von Mitteln zur Verfolgung der eigenen Bedürfnisse haben sich nun noch ganz andere Freiheiten gepaart. Nach dem sogenannten *Ende der Geschichte,* dem *Tod des Autors,* der Ablösung der Kunst der Moderne und der Zersetzung oder gar faktischen Pervertierung der großen Erzählungen von Vernunft oder Fortschritt scheinen die zeitgenössischen Subjekte vielmehr einer „Freiheit von allem"[5] ausgesetzt zu sein. Diese negativen Freiheiten *von* erdrückenden sozialen Beziehungen und gesellschaftlichen Normen, aber auch sozialstaatlichen Grundleistungen oder arbeitsrechtlicher Absicherung sind keine Phänomene, die sich global für alle Menschen gleich zeigen. Und doch, diese Wendung von einem positiven Freiheitsbegriff (Freiheit *auf*) – der sich noch in Menschen- und Bürgerrechten zumindest formal verdichtete – hin zu einer Freiheit von rechtlichen und sozialen Absicherungen fällt in immer mehr Bereiche der Gesellschaft. Blicken wir genauer auf die weiten Bereiche der Kreativen, Künstler*innen und Wissensarbeitenden, scheint diese negative Freiheit mehr als augenscheinlich. Umsonst-Arbeit, befristete Projektformate und Praktika sind die Oberfläche einer Freiheit von Sicherheit, Planungsmöglichkeiten oder finanziellen Ressourcen. Mit diesen biografischen und finanziellen Krisenmotoren paaren sich dann noch die Folgen einer Freiheit von Leitbildern, Wahrheiten oder Planung – der Neuheitsdruck in einem flimmernden Diskurs über unzählige legitime Stilrichtungen, Theorien oder künstlerische Formen.

Die Einsamkeit, von der wir schreiben, stellt sich gerade über diese Freiheiten von Sicherheit, Orientierung und sozialen Banden her. Besonders gilt dies unserer eigenen Einschätzung nach für die riesige Gruppe von Umsonst-Arbeiter*innen und Selbstständigen, die den gesamten Sektor der kulturellen Produktion fast unsichtbar durchfließen und stützen[6]. Eine Freiheit von partikularer (Familien- oder Stammes-)Verwandtschaft gehört dann ebenso zu diesem Bild, wie die Freiheit von klaren Klassenstandpunkten. Genau in dieser Ambivalenz von negativen Freiheitsbildern entstehen unsere Überlegungen über Potenziale für neue Verbindungsparadigmen. Diese Verbindungen, diese Wahlverwandtschaften, sind nach der Zersetzung klassischer Zuweisungs- und Kollektivierungsformen in höchstem Maße freiwillig und pragmatisch. Die Einsicht in die Existenz eines Kognitariats, dieser zersplitterten Menge von einsamen Existenzen, muss dabei nicht als ein Weg zu einem neuen Klassenbewusstsein interpretiert werden. Wir wollen hingegen über die Besonderheiten und Potenziale für eine neue Perspektive auf Solidarität nachdenken. Wir vermuten, dass in den von uns dargestellten Sphären ganz andere Möglichkeiten für Solidaritäts- und Verwandtschaftsbeziehungen stecken.

Welche Rückschlüsse lassen sich aus diesen skizzierten Entwicklungen ziehen? An was kann appelliert werden, wenn es nicht darum geht, einem fiktiven, idealen Zustand der Gemeinsamkeit nachzueifern? Beinhaltet Solidarität nicht immer die Möglichkeit, in flexiblen Größenverhältnissen zu denken? Was bedeutet eine stete zwanghafte Reaktion von Kunst auf einen „permanenten Zustand der Krise" für diese Spekulationen? Besiegelt die Kunst nicht genau in dieser reaktiven Geste ihre eigene Unmöglichkeit, Zukünfte zu formulieren, anstatt eine hyperbolische Erweiterung der Gegenwart zu sein, die zwischen sozialer Relevanz, Offenheit und Unverbindlichkeit changiert? Welche Möglichkeitsräume eröffnen sich in dem vielfachen Dasein in atomisiertem Horror, in der Freiheit von Solidarität und bei doch vermutlicher Verwandtschaft in Einsamkeit?

In einer Zeit, in der ein solcher Zustand der Krisen und Katastrophen permanent medial vermittelt wird, scheint eine Befragung potentieller Verwandtschaften und deren Potentiale angebracht. Kunst und Kunstproduktion kann dabei als erste Adresse für genau solche Erforschungen erscheinen, da Künstler*innen sich in den letzten Jahren vermehrt sozialen, politischen und edukativen Praxen zuwenden, die traditionell außerhalb ästhetischer Praxen verortet werden. Dieses zugeschriebene Potenzial für die Schaffung von Neuem, von kreativen Lösungen, haben wir bereits angesprochen und wir zweifeln selber wenig daran. Allerdings verwundert uns gleichermaßen die Reibungshitze von genau diesen Ansprüchen und dem gleichzeitigen Darben in prekären Produktions- und Lebensbedingungen. Die kritische Auseinandersetzung mit Institutionen, Ideologien und Diskriminierungsstrukturen findet eben meist in genau den Museen, Zeitschriften, Galerien, Hochschulen, Bildungsprojekten und Festivals statt, welche die Säulen der kritisierten Missstände sind. Aber welche andere Wahl bleibt Produzent*innen, die außerhalb dieses Rahmens nur schwer eine Öffentlichkeit herstellen können? Welche anderen Formen finden sich nun für die Kreativen am Abgrund der Existenzwahrung von zersplitterten *Selbstunternehmen?*

Zunächst wollen wir über den Rahmen und die Orte für andere Kollaborationen und Pakte nachdenken. Wir wissen, dass ganze gesellschaftliche Felder der Kultur- und Wissensproduktion, die weit über die Disziplin der bildenden Kunst hinausgehen, von einer Horde an Kreativmaschinen ermöglicht werden. Diese Felder vereint die Vorstellung, dass kreative Potenziale einem Mangel entspringen, was sich sowohl auf altbekannte Vorstellungen eines vereinsamten und verarmten Künstlergenius zurückführen lässt, als auch sich in einem neuen Typus von

(Künstler*innen als) Start-Up-Unternehmer*innen oder *Creative Consultant* ausdrückt. Die beiden Pole bedienen offensichtlich einen normativen Mythos der Kreativität als freiwillige Notwendigkeit, in dem Arbeit und Leben in einer Vorstellung *des Lebens als Risikokapital* verschmelzen.

Über die kulturelle Kompetenz der ständigen Produktion um der Produktion willen („weil aus Leidenschaft"), die unaufhörliche (minimale) Differenzierung durch den Zwang zum Neuen, kann eine neue Perspektive eröffnet werden: Die interne Verfasstheit dieser expandierenden Gruppe von Produzent*innen, die vermeintlich nichts als ihre kreativen Potenziale besitzen, zeigt, dass zwar eine ganz eigene und abgeschlossene Welt für jede*n Einzelne*n besteht, diese Welten sich aber gerade durch die Verwandtschaft in Einsamkeit verbinden lassen. Diese Einsicht kann ein erster Schritt sein, um über intellektuelle und praktische Fluchtlinien von Solidarität nachzudenken, wobei eine affektive Forderung nach dem Bewusstwerden einer Klassenverfasstheit unserer Meinung nach nicht ausreichen kann. Jegliche rein materialistische Analyse einer *kreativen Klasse an sich* und *für sich* würde nämlich von der Einsicht ablenken, dass es nicht nur um das Phantom einer gänzlich neuen *digitalen Boheme* in einer Handvoll globaler Städte geht.

Das Anliegen kann nicht sein, sich die idealen Bedingungen für Solidarisierungsprozesse herbeizuwünschen, sondern es muss auf einen Perspektivwechsel auf bereits vorhandene Bedingungen als Potential für Verbindungen abzielen. In Verbindung zu Anderen sieht Solidarität in diesem Sinne die Grundlage für die Möglichkeit freiwilligen Sprechens und Handelns. Damit ist keine Gemeinsamkeit gemeint, die ein Hinwegsetzen über Differenzen verlangt und nur Identisches als Grundlage von Verbindung sieht. Die kleinsten Einheiten, um verbundene Gemeinsamkeit herzustellen und auszudrücken, sind daher zuerst freiwillige, unilaterale Handlungen, die nicht durch Gegenseitigkeit und historische Notwendigkeit bestimmt sind. Die Freiwilligkeit dieser *Verwandtschaft in Einsamkeit* verweigert sich dabei einer festen Rollenzuschreibung für Einzelne oder Gruppen, wie sie in einem Verständnis von Solidarität als reines Fürsprechen für Benachteiligte praktiziert wird. Diese Verwandtschaft ergibt sich aus der Einsicht, dass viele nicht durch Einsamkeit an sich leiden, sondern wir alle durch eine besondere Einsamkeit unter den gegebenen, geteilten Bedingungen. Zu guter Letzt zeigen uns die Überlegungen zu positiven sowie negativen Freiheiten ja gerade, dass wir uns frei von einer historisch-zwingenden Verantwortung wähnen, obwohl die Verhältnisse eigentlich das Gegenteil verlangen und ermöglichen. Jede freiwillige Solidarität würde sich gerade deshalb als ganz „atemberaubend" darstellen.

1. So dann auch der Befund von Andreas Reckwitz, 2012, *Die Erfindung der Kreativität. Zum Prozess gesellschaftlicher Ästhetisierung.* Berlin: Suhrkamp.
2. Alain Ehrenberg, 2015, *Das erschöpfte Selbst. Depression und Gesellschaft in der Gegenwart* (frz. Original 1998). Frankfurt/Main: Campus. Siehe auch Mark Fisher, 2009, *Capitalist Realism. Is there no Alternative?.* London: zero books.
3. Siehe auch McKenzie Wark, 2004, *A Hacker Manifesto,* Cambridge, Harvard University Press.
4. Franco Bifo Berardi, 2005: What Does Cognitariat Mean?. *Cultural Studies Review* 11(2). http://epress.lib.uts.edu.au/journals/index.php/csrj/article/view/3656
5. Hito Steyerl, 2013, Freedom from Everything: Freelancers and Mercenaries. *e-flux* 41. http://www.e-flux.com/journal/41/60229/freedom-from-everything-freelancers-and-mercenaries/
6. Steyerl, Hito, 2010: Politics of Art: Contemporary Art and the Transition to Post-Democracy. *e-flux* 21. http://www.e-flux.com/journal/21/67696/politics-of-art-contemporary-art-and-the-transition-to-post-democracy/

Nanna He[...]

"DO YOU THINK I C[O...]
SOME OF YOUR REF[...]

Ar[t...]

Mi[...]

denreich

JLD BORROW

GEES?"

Activism,

ration

Nanna Heidenreich

"Do you think I could borrow some of your refugees?"
Art, Activism, Migration

Prologue
Summer 2015. The discourse of the "refugee crisis" is spreading. Then in September that year the *March of Hope* makes history: after the number of refugees arriving in Greece had steadily risen over the spring, increasing numbers of migrants had started heading north over the so-called *Balkan Route*. As what is effectively the most southerly Dublin/Schengen state, Hungary was at least in theory responsible for examining most asylum applications, but its government under Victor Orbán was notorious for its racism and ill-treatment of refugees. The migrants arriving there resisted the policy of confining and incarcerating them and set off further westwards towards Germany and Austria, whose borders were temporarily open. Special trains and buses were laid on from Budapest's main railway station, but the most common form of transport was private cars; migrants travelling by foot along motorways were given lifts to the border by ordinary people. Though quite a few of these people have been accused of being human smugglers, the event's political momentum cannot be effaced. At their site *bordermonitoring.eu,* Mark Speer and Bernd Kasparek note that "we need to bear in mind that the [...] episode from the long summer of migration underlines how porous the border regime already was, although attention was only drawn to this with the disruption of mobility."[1] Right now this is not a refugee crisis, a crisis of numbers, but a "crisis of the European project".[2] That is why they speak of a "long summer of migration", rather than of a "refugee crisis". And this not least because the Schengen/Dublin regime has for decades now

been framing migration in terms of disenfranchisement, illegalisation and flight. The "long summer of migration" did not begin in 2015, and nor will it be over quite so quickly.[3]

As I write this, there's a steady stream of new reports about refugees coming out under the hashtag #marchofhope. Although the borders of Macedonia, Serbia, Slovenia and Croatia have been closed since the autumn of 2015, refugees continue to leave the horribly overcrowded camp near the Greek border village of Idomeni, heading west or north in larger or smaller groups. At the same time, they are resisting forced resettlement and containment in "state-run camps" (which eyewitnesses have compared with prisons, and where the conditions are said to be no better than at Idomeni),[4] and are opposing police violence on both the Greek and Macedonian sides of the border.

Radicality and Consensus
Art is supposed to transcend boundaries. It is supposed to be radical, or at least radically new. Art is supposed be able to do anything. But despite all its paradigms of subversion and transgression, when art becomes too radical, when it goes too far, it is said to be "no longer art". It must be radical only *as art,* which means remaining within art's conventions.[5] The cultural theorist, musician and self-described "semi-artist" Zoran Terzić has developed the theory that redistributing—or in this case deporting—radicality, extremism and fundamentalism has caused thought to become structured around a new centre. This centre begs a number of questions about itself, the first of which is its own self-understanding as the consensus: "the democratic consensus has banished radicality beyond its own political borders, while nevertheless constantly producing radicality itself. This constellation becomes particularly clear in public furores and scandals."[6] To put it another way:

who or what is radical or extreme, and what is the "empty centre"—to quote the title of Hito Steyerl's 1998 film—that is formed by this distribution of thought? Another reason for mentioning the film is that Terzić's ideas were (not coincidentally) developed in the context of reflecting on the nation and nationalism.

When art proclaims the transcendence of boundaries, this poses the question of the centre around which these boundaries are organised. And: does the "empty centre" of the nation state have anything to do with the consensus on radicality?

So, Once Again: Art and Politics—Yes, No, Maybe?
Is this a fundamental question? The question of the relation between art and politics, between art and activism? There are, at any rate, no shortage of programmatic answers to the question of the relationship between art and politics, each backed up by claims to its own validity. At least as far as art goes. To take just two examples from all the twists and turns of the last few years: on the one hand the museumization of the great promise of the 1990s, that theory, art and activism would henceforth be inseparable, which was thematised in the exhibition *to show, to demonstrate, to inform, to offer*,[7] and on the other, the recent and unfortunately ultimately vacuous conference of *Artists Organisations International*,[8] which aimed to locate radicality in the replacement of the principle of authorship with that of the organisation (whether the association, the group, the party or the movement).[9]

Though these examples are somewhat randomly picked from a western European context, they are indicative of a recent growing trend in the field of art which has seen the emergence of a series of claims to represent the political avant-garde. My favourite quote here still has to be Franco Bifo Berardi's call for a "bunch of curators" who, he says, are urgently needed "for the European insurrection". The claim was made at the 2011 Venice Biennale in an essay commissioned for the Norwegian *Office for Contemporary Art,* and then reprinted in 2013 in the journal *e-flux,* approvingly and without a hint of irony.[10] The fact that *art* can mobilise artists against the current miserable post-political and post-democratic conditions is unquestionably a good thing. (And before this gets drowned out by the admittedly polemical tone of my text: I simply take it as given that there's a basic need for a connection between aesthetics and politics, between art and activism, and between form and content). Especially as so many artist-subjects take the slightest hint that they are being subjected to anything so degrading as politics as an outrageous personal affront and attack on the autonomy of art, particularly when this concerns the politics of the art world itself or the institutions in which she or he operates. This is one reason, for example, why so many art school professors consider university politics to be disrespectful, harmful to their own artistic practice and generally an imposition. It's true, of course, that other academics also consider university administrations an imposition, and many have done so long before the arrival of post-Fordism and the transformation of university management into a monstrosity that treats free thought, teaching and working as if they were efficiency valuation measures, before peddling them like a feeder machine to a supposedly ever-receptive labour market. The only thing is: people do need to strongly resist the post-Fordist restructuring of universities, since no one has ever started a revolution—let alone stopped anything from happening—by waiting things out on their own.[11] And given that's the case: if the system that is art now feels itself called on to lead the coming insurrection, then I say: go for it! The trouble is that right now this gesture is not grounded in action, it is not involved in forms of practical organisation, rather this self-definition remains firmly anchored in the modern intellectual tradition of the artistic avant-garde, including its self-declared radicality. And it's not as if this gesture isn't framed by contrary arguments, which point out art's complicity in stabilising geopolitical inequalities. As Hito Steyerl puts it: "contemporary art thus not only reflects, but actively intervenes in the transition towards a new post-Cold War world order. It is a major player in unevenly advancing semiocapitalism wherever T-Mobile plants its flag. It is involved in mining for raw materials for dual-core processors. It pollutes, gentrifies, and ravishes. It seduces and consumes, then suddenly walks off, breaking your heart. From the deserts of Mongolia to the high plains of Peru, contemporary art is everywhere. And when it is finally dragged into Gagosian dripping from head to toe with blood and dirt, it triggers off rounds and rounds of rapturous applause."[12] In her article Steyerl is primarily concerned with the politics of the art world itself, including its working conditions, and above all with criticising its tendency to always assume the political to be elsewhere—preferably in certain disadvantaged demographic groups that artists claim membership of as a means of self-distinction, allowing them to present themselves as authors of transgressive practices, for example, or the avant-garde of the precariat.

Jens Kastner has recently formulated the thesis that there are "all kinds of connections between art and social movements", but that these are not the norm, but rather the exception: "It is therefore neither a matter of ignoring them nor declaring them to be obvious, but rather of theorising them as something unusual".[13] Kastner also places his argument in the context of the large number of art contexts which have incorporated activism in recent years: events such as the *Berlin Biennale* and *Steirischer Herbst* 2012 have given the impression that (today) art and political activism form a natural unity.[14] He also argues that there are structural borders between art and activism, or more precisely that there is, in Pierre Bourdieu's words, a "structurally determined trench".[15] It's not just that what's considered to be politically successful and what's considered to be successful art are measured by different standards, but also that we judge the legitimacy of certain activities and actions differently. However, Kastner precisely does *not* argue that there's no meaning, history or justified concern to be found in the "and" of "art and activism": as one of the most prominent theorists, critics, historians and sociologists of art on the left, and as the coordinating editor of *Bildpunkt* (the journal of the leftist artists' union *IG Bildende Kunst*) and a translator of postcolonial theory,[16] he personally represents the productive combination of both. Kastner not only critiques art for declaring itself to be the political avant-garde, he also addresses art history's ignorance of the influence of social movements (as well as the correlative phenomenon of the history of social movements' blindness towards the role of artistic strategies in those movements). If we develop this argument further, we might simply infer from it that it is important to be as precise about political questions as about aesthetic decisions. Contemporary art's assumed political avant-gardism should at least entail a critical look at the temporalities at play in it. Critical investigations of the idea of the contemporaneity of art have already led to a critique of the time and place implied by such categories as *tradition* and *world art;* The critique of the very notion of "contemporaneity" which is based on an idea of a hegemonic present that is always ahead of its time has led to thinking in terms of asynchronicity, difference and interconnectedness. Might it be that the current sentimentalisation of the archetype of resistance in art is formed of a mixture of nostalgic longing for the past and elite speculation in future options—in theoretical *futures,* as it were—which, rather than opposing the "art of speculation" (the structural transformation of art described by Julia Voss),[17] is actually complicit in it? What would be left of contemporary art's claims to be spearheading the political if all of its criteria were to become negotiable; if lengthy collective negotiations were to undermine its established measure of value, and if "results" no longer amounted to catalogues, CV entries or cultural or economic capital?

Some time ago I made the argument that this is a question of attitude—namely of bringing art and politics together, which for me involves developing a position that combines "politics with art", and not one that is specifically inherent to art.[18] However: the approach lies in artistic and political activity; it does not involve setting conditions either for art or for activism, nor does it lie in the relation between these two fields.

"Do you think I could borrow some of your refugees?"
Back to the beginning. At the opening of an exhibition on the history of the artistic solidarity movements, based around the "international art exhibition for Palestine in 1978",[19] a friend of mine who is a performance artist, activist and sex worker tells me of several recent events where she overheard students at the contemporary dance school where she teaches encouraging each other to perform a particular movement "like the refugees on the boats".

A short while later I hear from a film maker, author and curator that two film projects that I know of have regularly to deal with requests from other artists to "lend us some of their refugees".

In October 2015 Tania Canas, the art director of *RISE,* "the first refugee and asylum-seeker organisation in Australia to be run and governed by refugees, asylum seekers and ex-detainees", published ten rules for art projects and artists who want to work with refugees.

They are straightforward, precise and—one would like to think—rather obvious; but it seems they don't go without saying, and that is why I quote them here in full:

> There has been a huge influx of artists approaching us in order to find participants for their next project. The artist often claims to want to show "the human side of the story" through a false sense of neutrality and limited understanding of their own bias, privilege and frameworks.
>
> 1. Process not product
> We are not a resource to feed into your next artistic project. You may be talented at your particular craft but do not assume that this automatically translates to an ethical, responsible and self-determining process. Understand community cultural development methodology but also understand that it is not a fool-proof methodology. Who and which institutions are benefiting from the exchange?
>
> 2. Critically interrogate your intention
> Our struggle is not an opportunity, nor our bodies a currency, by which to build your career. Rather than merely focusing on the "other" ("where do I find refugees"… etc.) Subject your own intention to critical, reflexive analysis. What is your motivation to work with this particular subject matter? Why at this particular time?
>
> 3. Realise your own privilege
> What biases and intentions, even if you consider these "good" intentions, do you carry with you? What social positionality (and power) do you bring to the space? Know how much space you take up. Know when to step back.
>
> 4. Participation is not always progressive or empowering
> Your project may have elements of participation, but know how this can just as easily be limiting, tokenistic and condescending. Your demands on our community sharing our stories may be just as easily disempowering. What frameworks have you already imposed on participation? What power dynamics are you reinforcing with such a framework? What relationships are you creating (e.g. informant vs. expert, enunciated vs. enunciator).
>
> 5. Presentation vs. representation
> Know the difference!
>
> 6. It is not a safe-space just because you say it is
> This requires long term grass-roots work, solidarity and commitment.

7. Do not expect us to be grateful
We are not your next interesting art project. Our community is not sitting waiting for our struggle to be acknowledged by your individual consciousness nor highlighted through your art practice.

8. Do not reduce us to an issue
We are whole humans with various experiences, knowledge and skills. We can speak on many things; do not reduce us to one narrative.

9. Do your research
Know the solidarity work already being done. Know the nuanced differences between organisations and projects. Just because we may work with the same community doesn't mean we work in the same way.[20]

10. Art is not neutral
Our community has been politicised and any art work done with/by us is inherently political. If you wish to build with our community know that your artistic practice cannot be neutral.

Working together. That means, very simply: taking into account the possibly different interests of the participants. Reflecting authorship. Taking the working process as seriously as the aesthetic decisions. Thinking about cultural/symbolic capital, about who, if anyone, has access to this; and when it really should be about money, that is, about economic capital. Here too the question is, who has a bank account, or rather: who has to remain below the radar and what does this mean for authorship, payment, and who it is that benefits from a project?

And: being deeply shocked has nothing to do with solidarity.

The *RISE* manifesto/manual draws a clear distinction between those artists who are involved in processes of flight, migration and asylum and those who are not. I would like to define the distinction more strongly, as an issue of attitude rather than of *being affected* (especially in the context of the ongoing and important discussions about the political relation between "refugees", "non-citizens", "supporters", about self-description and self-organisation and about solidarity versus support, etc.).[21] However, here the distinction refers precisely to the structural trench theorised by Kastner: it relates to the different logics operating in the fields of art and activism, and should not so much imply a totalising difference that places artists on one side and refugees on the other. Here I'd like to quote Hannah Ahrendt, who in an essay from 1943 puts it very succinctly: "In the first place, we don't like to be called 'refugees'. We ourselves call each other 'newcomers' or 'immigrants'."[22] Newcomers: the recently arrived, immigrants, those who belong. Which implies membership of a *political body,* not simply of a nation state (indeed *citizenship* itself needs to be reformulated—migration as a social and political movement is both making that clear and making it a fact).[23]

Or to put it another way: art and politics and migration do not mean art projects "about" migrants, nor even simply "with" them—rather they imply projects with and about and against the conditions that deprive migrants of their rights. And that means understanding migration as a total social fact, not as something supplementary or exceptional, nor as a transhistorical fact, but rather as a political and social movement: "Is it helpful to understand migration as a social movement? I think it is, as long as the concept is historically defined. In any case, it is better to understand migration this way than as an ontological constant, a form of ethnic movement or as an economic variable."[24]

And, since it can't be said often enough, perhaps the most important point is this: talking about migration means talking about racism. In a 1993 text entitled "Flüchtlingsbewegungen und Rassismus" (Refugee Movements and Racism), Eberhard Jungfer writes that "Aristide R. Zolberg has pointed out that the theoretical literature on migration has little to say about the policies of immigration control and deportation, and that psychological explanations of racism are ultimately tautologous because they reduce a cause to its symptoms, rather than looking for its wider structural determinants. For him, migration policy is the context in which racism should be discussed as the deliberate organisation of prejudices favourable to ideologies that justify the implementation of specific political aims. A connection exists between the immigration policy of the state and the racism of society which should actually be far easier to research than, for example, its psychological aspects."[25] In Germany people still prefer *not* to speak about racism (but rather, for instance, about xenophobia), and if they do, they tend to talk about it not as a structural issue but to psychologise it instead. (It is no coincidence that the CERD, the United Nations' expert committee responsible for ensuring that the convention against racism is implemented and observed, has demanded that Germany, a signatory to the convention since 1969, formulate a new definition of racism).

This is another reason why "refugees" are not simply "others", neither for a film nor an art project nor in terms of politics.

The Art of Migration
Ten years ago, Tom Holert and Mark Terkessidis published their book *Fliehkraft* (Centrifugal Force),[26] which analysed the relations between migration and tourism. They considered the points of intersection, parallels and connections between these two apparently different forms of mobility, which up until then had been seen as quite separate phenomena, with the aim of revising prevailing ideas about migration and tourism. Both forms of movement—tourism as one of the world's largest economic sectors, and migration as a transnational reality—are not properly understood as factors that are transforming societies (migration for example is largely perceived as a danger and a threat): "When

a society is in movement, relations between majority and minority also enter a state of flux. New collectivities, new lifestyles, and new communities emerge at transit points and along migration and tourist routes. At the same time, individuals are increasingly transformed into subjects of mobility. People move in translocal networks. And their attachment to a certain place is determined by the possibilities that that place offers for them to realise their own projects. Inevitably these changes bring social transformations. It's just that the public reacts to them very slowly. This book was written during a period of fierce debates over German *Leitkultur* and integration. But a glance at the real conditions in a society in movement makes these debates seem not only provincial, but almost absurd."[27] Mobility must also be organised. It is not just that tourism has always been an organisational form of migration (even during the so-called "Gastarbeiter era", many travel agents specialised in package deals and other forms of travel arrangements).[28] Holert and Terkessidis see the widely condemned and criminalised "human smugglers" that operate today as something like the clandestine counterparts to regular travel agencies, organising logistics, transport and to a certain extent also travel accommodation.[29]

One reason I conclude this article by referring to this study is because the (discredited, or rather discrediting) talk of a refugee crisis that I referred to at the beginning is symptomatic of a wider historical amnesia, one that not only ignores actual migration movements but also the research into critical migration and border regime studies (which is always activism-based),[30] the work of refugee activists and anti-racism activism, and the latter's artistic expressions. Holert and Terkessidis' book is also representative here of a whole series of other, older publications whose arguments have lost nothing of their relevance. However, what I want to emphasise is that the interconnection between tourism and migration as two different forms of movement is also—or should also be—relevant to art and migration. The system of international biennales and large-scale *art events* is not only a system of cosmopolitan, privileged global travellers; the system that is *art* is also one that organises, or at least makes possible, migration on a wide variety of different levels. Tanja Ostojić's work *Looking for a Husband with an EU Passport* (2000–2005), and Petja Dimitrova's *Staatsbürgerschaft/ Nationality* (2003) are both examples of artistic works that simultaneously exhibit, address and enact the art of migration.[31] They perform, embody and document as an artistic process their own struggles to gain the legal right to remain in the EU. However, both projects also show that the inventiveness of migration strategies can be understood as being part of the art of migration. The fact that art projects can also come out of this inventiveness has less to do with the dynamics of artistic creation and more with the dynamics of movement. This makes the project initiated by two French artists, Patrick Bernier and Olive Martin all the more compelling. The project aims at developing a migration strategy based on French laws on copyright, authorship and intellectual property, which the artists publicly stage as a theatre of legal argumentation.[32] In 2001 Bernier started working for *GASPROM* ("Groupement Accueil Service Promotion du Travailleur Immigré"), an organisation that offers legal advice to immigrants and fights for their rights. He began as a kind of ghostwriter, writing letters to the authorities on behalf of migrants. This practice laid the basis for *X.c/ Préfet de …, Plaidoirie pour une jurisprudence* (X and Y vs. France: the Case for a Legal Precedent, 2007 – ongoing), in which two lawyers present the case of X to an audience given the role of a judicial authority. Their argument is based on the notion that X, who is a migrant with a precarious residency status, is the author of her-/himself as an immaterial site-specific work, which, should X be deported or expelled from the country, could no longer exist. The work explores Hannah Arendt's famous dictum of the "right to rights": the deprivation of migrants of their rights (by the law of nation states) is confronted by an active setting-to-rights. It is the activation of law's performativity and, like other, similar tribunals,[33] presents a theatre of the law that actively rewrites and develops new legal arguments and understandings of rights.

To reformulate a well-known slogan of migrant struggles: "we have not committed an offence against the law, the law has committed an offence against us."[34]

Coda

The "long summer of migration" is not over, and it is not without history. Its time, however, is the Now of futurity. The struggles for migrants' right of entry, against the deprivation of their rights, against detention and deportation and for the right to radical equality have been fought for a long time. But it is now time to put an end to the finality of the present and the ideas that govern it, and to seriously consider the foundational failures of the nation state diagnosed by Hannah Arendt almost seventy years ago, failures that began with the minority treaties after the First World War and have continued from the Second World War to this day in processes that render individuals stateless and illegal.[35] We need to reconfigure in a new and radically different way: law, politics, citizenship, belonging, legitimacy, dignity, the right to be heard and to have a voice. A radical imagination is needed. And that in turn needs art. The art of migration, for example.

1 http://bordermonitoring.eu/ungarn/2015/09/of-hope/, last accessed on 15 March 2016.
2 Ibid.
3 Politicians' reaction to the crisis, an absurd and historically amnesiac pretence at being surprised, also failed to address the fact that the migration movements didn't suddenly appear from nowhere nowhere. (This was immediately followed by talk of being "overwhelmed": since the far-right Republikaner party—actively supported by media organisations like Der *Spiegel* and the *Frankfurter Allgemeine Zeitung*—revived the "boat is full" argument in the 1990s, natural disaster metaphors have become *de rigeur*. The argument was first used by Switzerland in the 1940s as a way of justifying their policy of closing borders to refugees.) It is interesting to compare this with a recent article in *Spiegel* Online on the closing of the "Balkan route", and on claims that this could lead to a revival of the route through the Adriatic. On the face of it, the article is critical of current attempts to "deal" with migration by shutting people out or deporting them; however, it contains a number of links to another, much older, *Spiegel* article from the "dangerous summer" of 1991, which presents mass migration from Albania as an apocalyptic disaster scenario. This was *Spiegel's* editorial policy at the time, and one that it assiduously promoted for many years by means of front-page headlines and pictures. The link appears without any kind of (self-)critical commentary. See Hans-Jürgen Schlamp, "Neue Flüchtlingsroute. Angst in der Adria" in *SPON (Spiegel Online)*, 27 January 2016, http://www.spiegel.de/politik/ausland/adria-route-italien-fuerchtet-zehntausende-fluechtlinge-a-1074224.html; last accessed on 10 April 2016. (Update from 5 May 2016: the link is still visible in the article, but no longer active. Is this for technical reasons, or is there some other explanation? At any rate, the article from 1991 can now no longer be found on the *Spiegel Online* site.)
4 See for example this entry in the Idomeni liveticker at bordermonitoring.eu: http://livertickereidomeni.bordermonitoring.eu/2016/04/30/26-4-2016-idomeni-flyer-by-greek-authorities/, last accessed on 28 April 2016.
5 On artistic radicality and political radicality, see Zoran Terzić, "Nation & Exzess IV: Extrem! Überlegungen zur Logik der Darstellung radikaler Phänomene in Kultur und Politik", a talk held in Leipzig in November 2009; see http://www.halbkunst.de/halbkunst/nex4.html, last accessed on 30 April 2016. On the consensus, see also Irmgard Emmelhainz, "Art and the Cultural Turn: Farewell to Committed, Autonomous Art?" in the journal *e-flux*, no. 42, February 2013, http://www.e-flux.com/journal/art-and-the-cultural-turn-farewell-to-committed-autonomous-art/, last accessed on 30 April 2016.
6 Antonia Baum's opinion piece in the *Frankfurter Allgemeine Zeitung* of 10 April 2016 on the case of Jan Böhmermann, the television presenter whose reading of a poem on his ZDF programme about the Turkish president Erdogan entitled *Schmähkritik* (Satirical Criticism) led eventually to a court case, makes a similar argument. Baum describes Böhmermann as a "model citizen who devoutly believes in the state" and as a "representative of the new Establishment", who will always find himself on the right side of things and who performs distinction instead of producing critique. That is, he is precisely not to be seen a as a "rebel": "The fact is that the Erdogan affair has revealed one thing above all, namely how smoothly this Germany – its government, its laws, its 'culture of debate' and public service television, Böhmermann included—collaborates and ultimately con-

curs when faced with an episode of this kind. A paid rebel is reprimanded by the institution that pays him and first installed him as a rebel, after the individual in question is said to have done something wrong, something one should not do in the Federal Republic of Germany. At this point, the government publicly says that this particular rebel really has done something wrong and, since he is alleged to have done something wrong, the public prosecutor's office gets involved, while the press use their press freedom to argue about whether the rebel really has done something wrong. And what is more, the young people of Germany (ZDF's target audience) get for a mere 17.50 euros the feeling, so important as a rite of passage to adulthood, that they are confronted with a real rebel. Everything here plays out seamlessly." (http://www.faz.net/aktuell/feuilleton/medien/spiessbuerger-nervensaege-wer-ist-jan-boehmermann-14169789.html, last accessed on 30 April 2016).

7 See the exhibition *to show, to demonstrate, to inform, to offer. Künstlerische Praktiken um 1990* at the Museum moderner Kunst Stiftung Ludwig Wien (mumok), curated aby Matthias Michalak (10 October 2015 – 14 February 2016), https://mumok.at/de/events/expose-show-demonstrate-inform-offer; last accessed on 5 May 2016.

8 AOI, a conference/performance/event "initiated" in January 2015 by Florian Malzacher, Jonas Staal and Joanna Warsza at the Hebbel Theater am Ufer in Berlin; see http://www.artistsorganisationsinternational.org/, last accessed on 5 May 2016. The idea was that the event would only involve organisations founded by artists. This distinction was consistently observed, despite the fact that the organisations' aim to "really" change the world through "daily political struggle" was conceived purely in terms of their activities *as artists*. From the event's statement about itself on its website: "Artist Organisations International brings together over twenty representatives of organisations founded by artists whose work confronts today's crises in politics, economy, education, immigration and ecology. Artist Organisations International explores a current shift from artists working in the form of temporary projects to building long-term organisational structures. What specific artistic value and political potential do such organisations have? How do they perform? What could be their concrete impact on various social-political agendas and possible internationalist collaborations?" And: "Artist Organisations International brings together organisations that that have been initiated by artists and advocate a specific understanding of art within a social and political context by using the subversive and transformative potential of visual literacy, modes of re-contextualisation and performativity." But also: "In their work artist organisations bring forward a social/political agenda that connects the field of ethics with aesthetics. Rather than a medium merely 'questioning' and 'confronting' the world, the artist organisation situates itself in the field of daily political struggle. Rather than questioning the world, it makes a world."

9 Obviously the question of authorship implicitly draws a structural distinction between art and activism: art collectives are under constant pressure to offer the names of individual members and, as Jens Kastner has also argued (see note 12), giving prominence to individual people in political collectives always requires some explanation. At the Vienna *mumok's* exhibition on art in the 1990s mentioned in note 7, every group and action suddenly became associated with

particular names, most of them names that are well-known in the art world. Thus for example, of the forty or so women who participated *in when tekkno turns to sound of poetry,* an exhibition and research project on biocommunication and information technology, feminism and (conceptual) art held at the Shedhalle Zürich and at the Kunst-Werken in Berlin in 1994–95, only two of its participants were named: Juliane Rebentisch and Sabeth Buchmann. This undoubtedly has to do with the fact that these women are the speakers in a video of a tour of the exhibition shown at the *mumok,* and no doubt also because they were involved in coming up with the idea for the project. But it also has to do with the fact that there appears to be no list of names of the other women participating. None of this, however, is mentioned in the exhibition, which contains only the names of a few particular participants, and where the political context—which motivated the various actions and projects shown in the exhibition—is never explained in quite as much detail as the artistic methods employed. By contrast, the writer Monika Rinck, who was part of the "sub-group" *Übung am Phantom* (see http://werkleitz.de/ubung-am-phantom-revisited-i-projection-sound; last visited on 5 May 2016), wrote in an article in the FKW (*Frauen Kunst Wissenschaft* no. 14 1994) that was primarily about group processes and how it was important to keep "the group" open till the last instance. The only list of names that was circulated as part of *tekkno* was of those artists whose work was shown in it.

10   Franco Bifo Berardi, "Pasolini in Tottenham", in *e-flux* no. 43, March 2013, http://www.e-flux.com/journal/pasolini-in-tottenham/; last accessed on 5 May 2016.

11   To do that, their refusal would have to assume Bartleby-sized proportions. On this see, among other things, Sabeth Buchmann, "Rain is a cage you can walk through. Zu einigen Arbeiten von Judith Hopf", http://eipcp.net/transversal/0601/buchmann/de; last accessed on 6 June 2016. Or it would have to become an exodus.

12   Hito Steyerl, "Politics of Art: Contemporary Art and the Transition to Post-Democracy", in *e-flux* no. 21, December 2010, http://www.e-flux.com/journal/politics-of-art-contemporary-art-and-the-transition-to-post-democracy/; last accessed on 30 April 2016. On this see also Julia Voss' book *Hinter weissen Wänden / Behind the White Cube,* Berlin 2015, in which she writes on the art system's trade secrets—how it deliberately obscures its own operations, speculative activities, and strategies for inflating the value of works—and in which she also develops the theory that art has become an image of new global inequalities (other writers have also proposed this, among them Georg Seeßlen). Last year *e-flux's* "conversations" platform quoted Ben Davis and the question he posed on Artnet: "Do you have to be rich to make it as an artist?" Davis' answer was: "Economics remains a blind spot at the heart of the discourse" (quoted in http://conversations.e-flux.com/t/do-you-have-to-be-rich-to-make-it-as-an-artist/3106; last accessed on 30 April 2016). There are actually very few reliable figures, partly because no studies (or at least very few) have been made on this subject, but also because there is a determined effort to remain silent on the issue.

13   Jens Kastner, "Über strukturelle Grenzen (hinweg). Was Kunstproduktionen und soziale Bewegungen trennt und verbindet", in Alexander Fleischmann and Doris Guth eds., *Kunst. Theorie. Aktivismus,* Bielefeld 2015, pp. 23–58, here p. 26.

14   See ibid.

15   Ibid.

16 On Kastner's various different activities, see http://www.jenspetzkastner.de, last visited on 3 May 2016.
17 Julia Voss, *Hinter weissen Wänden / Behind the White Cube,* Berlin 2015, p. 78.
18 Nanna Heidenreich, "Die Perspektive der Migration aufzeichnen/einnehmen/ausstellen/aktivieren", in Fleischmann and Guth eds., pp. 113–145.
19 *Zeit der Unruhe,* curated by Kristine Jhouri and Rasha Salti, 19 March – 9 May 2016, HKW Berlin. http://hkw.de/de/programm/projekte/2016/zeit_der_unruhe_start.php, last accessed on 5 May 2016.
20 http://riserefugee.org/10-things-you-need-to-consider-if-you-are-an-artist-not-of-the-refugee-and-asylum-seeker-community-looking-to-work-with-our-community/, last accessed on 5 May 2016.
21 On this, see for example Vassilis S. Tsianos and Bernd Kasparek, "'Too much love'. Von 'Non-Citizens' und ihren 'Supportern'. Über problematische neue Begriffe im deutschen antirassistischen Diskurs", in *Jungle World* no. 30, 25 July 2013, http://jungle-world.com/artikel/2013/30/48137.html; last accessed on 5 May 2016.
22 Hannah Arendt, "We Refugees", first published in the *Menorah Journal,* reprinted in Marc Robinson ed., *Altogether Elsewhere: Writers on Exile,* Boston and London 1994, pp. 110–119, here p. 110.
23 Of the numerous publications on this subject see first of all Ilke Ataç and Étienne Balibar in the *Tranversal* edition entitled "Flee, Erase, Territorialise", which deals with the actual struggles of the sans papiers and refugees in Vienna and Paris, March 2013: http://eipcp.net/transversal/0313, last accessed on 5 May 2016. Also on this see the new journal *Movements,* which has come out of critical research into migration and border control regimes: http://movements-journal.org/, last accessed on 5 May 2016.
24 Eberhard Jungfer, "Migrationen im Sozialen Weltkrieg" in the Komitee für Grundrechte und Demokratie ed., *Jenseits der Menschenrechte. Die europäische Flüchtlings- und Migrationspolitik,* Münster 2009, pp. 16–27, here quoted from the PDF available at http://archiv.labournet.de/diskussion/grundrechte/asyl/festungeu.html, last accessed on 6 June 2016. Understanding migration as a social and political movement is one of the central concerns of critical research into migration and border control regimes. On this see, among others, Sandro Mezzadra, "Autonomie der Migration. Kritik und Ausblick", transcription of a lecture held on 28 January 2010 in Vienna, http://wwww.grundrisse.net/grundrisse34/Autonomie_der_Migration.htm#_ednref3; last accessed on 6 June 2016.
25 Eberhard Jungfer, "Flüchtlingsbewegung und Rassismus. Zur Aktualität von Hannah Arendt, 'Die Nation der Minderheiten und das Volk der Staatenlosen'", in *Beiträge zur nationalsozialistischen Gesundheits- und Sozialpolitik* 11 (1993), pp. 19–49; quoted in a PDF circulating on the net, no pagination (here the 9th page of 28 in the PDF, in section "3"), available at http://www.materialien.org/texte/migration/fluebewrass.html, last accessed on 30 April 2016.
26 Tom Holert and Mark Terkessidis, *Fliehkraft. Gesellschaft in Bewegung – von Migranten und Touristen,* Cologne 2006.
27 Ibid., p. 15.
28 Gastarbeiter, or guest workers, was the term used to describe migrants who came to West Germany between the 1950s and 1970s. In these post-war years Germany experienced both rapid economic growth and a labour shortage, leading it to sign

a series of bilateral recruitment agreements with other countries, among them Spain, Turkey, Greece, Portugal, and Yugoslavia. Although the treaties permitted increased levels of migration, they also need to be seen also as attempts to regulate already existing migration movements. And although the agreements aimed at making migration temporary, many migrants settled permanently in their new country despite policies of "rotation" and "return". East Germany's migration policy was quite similar, despite using a different terminology: the recruited labourers were referred to as "Vertragsarbeiter", or contract workers.

29 On the art projects *Bundesverband Schleppen&Schleusen,* see http://www.faridaheuck.net/2_5_1/c_d.php, as well as the *2. Internationale Schlepper- und Schleusertagung* (ISS), which was organised by the Munich Kammerspiele in October 2015 as part of the activist-inspired "Open Border Kongresses" (Munich Welcome Theater); see http://iss2015.eu/. Both events deliberately blurred the borders between reality and fiction in order to bring about an actual "image shift". Another result was that the Bavarian minister of the interior Joachim Herrmann (CSU) judged the ISS not to be "a successful cultural project", but rather "a misguided piece of political propaganda". Quoted in http://www.sueddeutsche.de/muenchen/theater-kammerspiele-provozieren-mit-tagung-ueber-schleuser-1.2664985. All URLs last accessed on 5 May 2016.

30 On this see among other things http://kritnet.org/ as well as http://bordermonitoring.eu/; both URLs last accessed on 6 May 2016.

31 See www.petjadimitrova.net/works/Staatsbuergerschaft.html, and

32 See Audrey Chan's portrait of the two artists in *Afterall* 2009, http://www.afterall.org/online/bernier-martin.essay#.Vy3T76YWGD7; last accessed on 3 May 2016.

33 See for example the activist tribunal "NSU-Komplex-Auflösen", which will take place at the Schauspielhaus Köln in the spring of 2017, or the Congo Tribunal initiated by the "International Institute of Political Murder", also known as Milo Rau (http://international-institute.de/das-kongo-tribunal/); both URLs last accessed on 5 May 2016.

34 "We didn't cross the border, the border crossed us."

35 Hannah Arendt, "The Decline of the Nation-State and the End of the Rights of Man", in *The Origins of Totalitarianism,* New York 1951, pp. 267–302.

Nanna Heidenreich

**„Kann ich mir mal deine Flüchtlinge ausleihen?"
Kunst, Aktivismus, Migration**

Prolog

Sommer 2015. Die Rede von der „Flüchtlingskrise" verbreitet sich. Im September des Jahres schreibt dann der *March of Hope* Geschichte: Nachdem im Frühjahr die Zahl der ankommenden Geflüchteten in Griechenland beständig angestiegen war, machten sich immer mehr Migrant*innen über die sogenannte *Balkan-Route* auf den Weg nach Norden. In Ungarn, dem faktisch südlichsten Dublin/Schengen-Staat, der damit zumindest auf dem Papier für die Durchführung der meisten Asylverfahren zuständig ist und zugleich unter der Regierung Victor Orbáns notorisch ist für Rassismus und die schlechte Behandlung von Geflüchteten, widersetzen sich Migrant*innen der Politik der Einsperrung und der Stillstellung und machen sich auf den Weg: weiter nach Westen, nach Deutschland und Österreich, die vorübergehend ihre Grenzen öffneten. Es werden Sonderzüge aus Keleti eingesetzt, Busse, aber vor allen Dingen private PKW beginnen, den Menschen, die zu Fuß u. a. entlang von Autobahnen marschieren, einen Teil des Weges abzunehmen. Nicht wenige dieser Wegeshelfer*innen sind zwar als Schleuser angeklagt worden, das Wissen um das politische Momentum lässt sich dadurch nicht ausradieren. Marc Speer und Bernd Kasparek notieren auf *bordermonitoring.eu:* „Uns ist es wichtig festzuhalten, dass die […] geschilderte Episode aus dem langen Sommer der Migration unterstreicht, wie durchlässig das Grenzregime schon vorher war, es aber erst die Störungen der Mobilität waren, die die Aufmerksamkeit darauf lenkten."[1] Es handelt sich eben gerade nicht um eine Flüchtlingskrise, um eine Krise der Zahlen, sondern um eine „Krise des europäischen Projekts."[2] Sie sprechen daher von einem „langen Sommer der Migration", statt von einer „Flüchtlingskrise". Zumal die Formatierung von Migration unter den Vorzeichen von Entrechtung, Illegalisierung und Flucht durch Schengen und Dublin ein seit Jahrzehnten beständiges Thema ist. Der „lange Sommer der Migration" hat weder erst 2015 angefangen, noch wird er so schnell vorüber sein.[3]

Während ich dies schreibe, verbreiten sich unter dem Hashtag *#marchofhope* beständig neue Nachrichten über Geflüchtete, die sich aus den elenden Verhältnissen im restlos überfüllten Auffanglager im griechischen Idomeni immer wieder in kleinen und größeren Gruppen auf den Weg nach Westen bzw. Norden machen, trotz der Grenzschließungen durch Mazedonien, Serbien, Slowenien und Kroatien seit Herbst 2015. Auch sie wehren sich gegen die Zwangsumsiedlung und Einsperrung in andere „state run camps" (die von Augenzeugen mit Gefängnissen verglichen werden und in denen die Verhältnisse auch nicht besser sein sollen als in Idomeni)[4] und gegen die Polizeigewalt auf griechischer und mazedonischer Seite.

Radikalität und Konsens

Kunst muss, ja sie soll Grenzen überschreiten. Sie soll radikal sein, mindestens radikal neu. Kunst soll alles dürfen. Aber: Ist Kunst zu radikal, geht sie zu weit, sei „das keine Kunst mehr", trotz Subversions- und Transgressionsparadigma. Sie muss eben kunstradikal sein: innerhalb der Ordnungen der Kunst verbleiben.[5] Zoran Terzić, Kulturwissenschaftler, Musiker und „Halbkünstler" formuliert die These, dass mit der Zu- oder vielmehr Ausweisung von Radikalität, Extremismus und Fundamentalismus ein Zentrum des Denkens gebildet wird, das Fragen aufwirft, zuallererst nach dessen Selbstverständigung, die die des Konsens ist: „Der demokratische Konsens hat die Radikalität außerhalb seines politischen Umfangs verbannt, produziert sie aber dauernd selbst. An Eklats und Skandalen wird diese Konstellation besonders deutlich."[6] Anders formuliert: Wer oder was ist radikal, oder extrem, und welche „leere Mitte" – um den Titel eines Films von Hito Steyerl von 1998 zu zitieren – bildet sich durch diese Zuweisungen? Das Filmzitat auch deswegen, weil Terzićs Überlegungen nicht zufällig im Kontext von Überlegungen zur Nation und zum Nationalismus stehen.

Wenn Kunst Grenzüberschreitungen proklamiert, dann stellt sich die Frage, um welches Zentrum herum diese organisiert sind. Und: Hat die „leere Mitte" des Nationalstaats etwas mit dem Radikalitätskonsens zu tun?

Also nochmal: Kunst und Politik, ja, nein, vielleicht?

Ist es eine Grundsatzfrage? Die Frage nach der Relation von Kunst und Politik, von Kunst und Aktivismus? Die Frage nach dem Verhältnis von Kunst und Politik wird jedenfalls gerne programmatisch beantwortet und mit entsprechenden Geltungsansprüchen verknüpft. Zumindest die Kunst betreffend. In den ganzen Drehungen und Wendungen der letzten Jahre, zu der die Musealisierung des großen Versprechens der 1990er Jahre, dass Theorie, Kunst und Aktivismus von nun an nicht mehr zu trennen seien, ebenso gehört[7], wie die letztlich doch inhaltsleere Versammlung von *Artists Organisations International*[8], die in der Ersetzung des Prinzips der Autor*innenschaft durch das der Organisation (des Vereins, der Gruppe, der Partei, der Bewegung) schon Radikalität verortet, um einfach mal zwei Beispiele herauszugreifen.[9] Dieses nicht nur sehr westeuropäische Herausfischen dient mir aber auch als Hinweis auf den im Kunstfeld in den letzten Jahren so gerne wieder behaupteten politischen Avantgarde-Anspruch. Mein Lieblingszitat in diesem Zusammenhang ist und bleibt Franco Bifo Berardis Ruf nach einem „bunch of curators", die „for the European insurrection" dringend nötig seien, den dieser 2011 bei der 54. Biennale von Venedig in einem vom norwegischen *Office for Contemporary Art* in Auftrag gegebenen Essay verlauten ließ. Der Essay wurde 2013 im *e-flux journal* wieder abgedruckt – affirmativ und völlig ironiefrei.[10] Dass sich *die Kunst* bzw. Künstler*innen als Akteur*innen gegen die Misere postpolitischer und postdemokratischer Verhältnisse in Stellung bringt, ist ohne Frage eine gute Sache. (Und bevor das im doch sehr polemischen Ton meines Textes untergeht: Ich setze die grundsätzliche Notwendigkeit der Verbindung von Ästhetik und Politik, von Kunst und Aktivismus, von Form und Inhalt hier einfach voraus). Zumal so manches Künstler*innensubjekt ja jede Anwehung, von den Niederungen der Politik heimgesucht zu werden, als unmöglichen persönlichen Affront und Angriff auf die Autonomie der Kunst empfindet, gerade wenn es die Politik des Kunstbetriebs selbst betrifft, oder die Politik der Institutionen, in denen es sich bewegt. So beispielsweise gerne zu finden bei vielen Professor*innen an Kunsthochschulen – die Hochschulpolitik als despektierlich, der eigenen künstlerischen Praxis abträglich und generell als Zumutung empfinden. Gut, die Hochschulselbstverwaltung wird auch von anderen Akademiker*innen als Zumutung begriffen – und das nicht erst seitdem der Postfordismus Einzug hält und Administration zum Monster wird, das freies Denken, Lehren, Arbeiten als Evaluationen von Zweckmäßigkeit missversteht und diese dann als Fütterungsmaschine für einen vermeintlich stets aufnahmebereiten Arbeitsmarkt verkauft. Allein: Zwar wäre Widerstand gegen die postfordistische Umstrukturierung der Hochschulen dringlich geboten – aber durch individualisiertes oder eher subjektiviertes Aussitzen hat noch niemand einen revolutionären Blumentopf gewonnen, oder irgendetwas verhindert oder verändert.[11] Insofern: Wenn sich das System Kunst jetzt zum Anführen des kommenden Aufstands berufen fühlt, unbedingt: Los geht's! Aber dieser Gestus ist eben gerade nicht im Aktivismus verortet, es geht nicht um Aktionen, ums tätige Handeln, sondern diese Selbstbeschreibung steht vielmehr fest verankert in der modernen Ideentradition künstlerischer Avantgarden, inklusive selbst erklärter Radikalität. Und es ist ja nicht so, dass dieser Gestus nicht auch von gegenläufigen Argumentationen flankiert wird, mit denen gerade auf die Verwicklung von Kunst in die Verfestigung geopolitischer Ungleichheiten abgestellt wird: „Contemporary art thus not only reflects, but actively intervenes in the transition towards a new post-Cold War world order. It is a major player in unevenly advancing semiocapitalism wherever T-Mobile plants its flag. It is involved in mining for raw materials for dual-core processors. It pollutes, gentrifies, and ravishes. It seduces and consumes, then suddenly walks off, breaking your heart. From the deserts of Mongolia to the high plains of Peru, contemporary art is everywhere. And when it is finally dragged into Gagosian dripping from head to toe with blood and dirt, it triggers off rounds and rounds of rapturous applause", so Hito Steyerl.[12] In diesem Artikel geht es ihr jedoch vor allen Dingen um die Politik des Kunstbetriebs selbst, um die Arbeitsbedingungen, aber vor allem um die Kritik daran, das Politische immer anderswo zu vermuten, bevorzugt bei benachteiligten Bevölkerungsgruppen, zu denen man sich als Künstler*in nur dann zählt, wenn es um Distinktionsgesten geht, also beispielsweise darum, sich als Hort der Transgression zu präsentieren oder als die Avantgarde des Prekariats.

Jens Kastner hat vor kurzem die These aufgestellt, dass es „vielfältige Verknüpfungen zwischen Kunst und sozialen Bewegungen" gäbe, dass diese aber nicht selbstverständlich seien, sondern die Ausnahme: „Es gilt also, sie weder zu ignorieren noch für selbstverständlich zu erklären, sondern sie als Besonderes zu konzeptualisieren."[13] Kastner verortet sein Argument ebenfalls im Kontext der Vielzahl aktivistischer Manifestationen im Kunstkontext: Der angesichts von Artikulationen wie der *Berlin Biennale* und des *Steirischen Herbsts* 2012 entstehende Eindruck, dass Kunst und politischer Aktivismus (heute) eine selbstverständliche Einheit bilden, trüge.[14]

Im selben Text, in dem er diese These vertritt, führt er aus, dass zwischen Kunst und Aktivismus strukturelle Grenzen bestünden, genauer, mit Pierre Bourdieu ein „strukturell bedingter Graben."[15] Was als politisch erfolgreich gilt, wird mit anderen Maßstäben gemessen als erfolgreiche Kunst, aber auch die Legitimität von Handlungen und Aktionen wird unterschiedlich beurteilt. Kastners Argument besagt nun aber gerade *nicht,* dass im „und" von „Kunst und Aktivismus" weder Sinn, Geschichte noch begründete Anliegen zu finden sind – als einer der profiliertesten linken Kunsttheoretiker und -kritiker, Kunsthistoriker und Soziologe, koordinierender Redakteur der *Bildpunkt* (die Zeitschrift der linken Künstler*innengewerkschaft *IG Bildende Kunst*) und Übersetzer postkolonialer Theorie[16] steht er mit seiner Person ja gerade für die produktive Verknüpfung von beidem. Seine Argumentation weiterführend – die neben der Kritik an der Selbstversicherung, *in der Kunst* die politische Avantgarde zu bilden, auch auf die Ignoranz der Kunstgeschichte sozialen Bewegungen gegenüber abstellt (ebenso wie auf die Ausblendung künstlerischer Strategien aus der Bewegungsgeschichte) – ist daher vielleicht schlicht festzuhalten, dass es darauf ankommt, gegenüber der Frage des Politischen ebenso präzise zu sein wie hinsichtlich ästhetischer Entscheidungen. Gerade die *contemporary* Selbstverständigung im Kunstfeld politisch und kritisch Ton angebend oder wegweisend zu sein, sollte ihre Zeitlichkeiten auch in politischer Hinsicht kritisch betrachten: Die in den Diskussionen um das Konzept der Zeitgenossenschaft von Kunst aufgeworfene Problematisierung der Einteilungen von Ort und Zeit durch Begriffe wie *Tradition* und *Weltkunst* haben die Zeit der Avantgarde und ihre Zukunftsentwürfe als Extensionen der Gegenwart durch Betrachtungen von Ungleichzeitigkeit, Ungleichheit und Verwobenheit ersetzt. Stellt die gegenwärtige Sentimentalisierung des widerständigen Archetyps in der

Kunst hier dann nicht eher eine Mischung aus nostalgischem Vergangenheitsbezug mit elitären Zukunftsoptionen dar, theoretische *Futures* sozusagen, die der „Kunst der Spekulation",[17] also dem von Julia Voss beschriebenen Strukturwandel der Kunst eher zu- als gegenspielt? Was bleibt übrig vom politischen Avantgardeanspruch, wenn die Maßstäbe ebenfalls zur Verhandlung stehen, wenn langwierige Aushandlungen in Gruppenprozessen Geltungsanspruch unterwandern, wenn *Ergebnisse* nicht in Katalogen, Einträgen in CVs oder kulturellem oder ökonomischem Kapital bestehen?

Ich habe selbst vor einiger Zeit argumentiert, dass es um eine Frage der Haltung geht – wenn Kunst und Politik miteinander verknüpft werden, wobei es mir vor allen Dingen um eine Bestimmung aus der Perspektive von „Politik mit Kunst" ging und eigentlich nicht um eine spezifisch kunstimmanente Perspektive.[18] Aber: die Haltung liegt im künstlerischen und politischen Handeln, nicht als Setzung der Verhältnisse, weder die Kunst noch den Aktivismus betreffend, auch nicht in der Relation dieser beiden Felder/Ökonomien/instituierenden und instituierten Praktiken.

„Kann ich mir mal deine Flüchtlinge ausleihen?"
Zurück zum Anfang. Bei einer Ausstellungseröffnung – zur Geschichte der künstlerischen Solidaritätsbewegungen anhand der „Internationalen Kunstausstellung für Palästina in 1978"[19] – berichtet eine befreundete Performancekünstlerin, Aktivistin und Sexarbeiterin von mehreren Ereignissen der jüngeren Vergangenheit, Begegnungen, bei denen sie u. a. im Kontext eines Ausbildungsortes für zeitgenössischen Tanz Kommentare aufschnappt, wie sich Studierende gegenseitig auffordern, eine Bewegung auszuführen „wie die Refugees auf den Booten".

Wenig später höre ich von einer Filmemacherin, Autorin und Kuratorin, dass zwei Filmprojekte, die mir beide vertraut sind, regelmäßig mit der Anfrage umgehen müssen, ob man sich denn mal „deren Flüchtlinge ausleihen könne", man brauche noch welche – für einen Film, ein Interview, eine Ausstellung, ein Projekt.

Im Oktober 2015 publiziert Tania Canas, Arts Director von *RISE,* „Refugees, Survivors and Ex-detainees", „the first refugee and asylum seeker organisation in Australia to be run and governed by refugees, asylum seekers and ex-detainees" zehn Regeln für Kunstprojekte und Künstler*innen, die mit Geflüchteten arbeiten wollen.

Sie sind so präzise wie naheliegend schlicht, aber offensichtlich nicht selbstverständlich, sodass ich sie hier vollständig zitiere:

There has been a huge influx of artists approaching us in order to find participants for their next project. The artist often claims to want to show "the human side of the story" through a false sense of neutrality and limited understanding of their own bias, privilege and frameworks.

1. Process not product
We are not a resource to feed into your next artistic project. You may be talented at your particular craft but do not assume that this automatically translates to an ethical, responsible and self-determining process. Understand community cultural development methodology but also understand that it is not a full-proof methodology. Who and what institutions are benefiting from the exchange?

2. Critically interrogate your intention
Our struggle is not an opportunity, or our bodies' a currency, by which to build your career. Rather than merely focusing on the "other" ("where do I find refugees"… etc.) Subject your own intention to critical, reflexive analysis. What is your motivation to work with this particular subject matter? Why at this particular time?

3. Realise your own privilege
What biases and intentions, even if you consider these "good" intentions, do you carry with you? What social positionality (and power) do you bring to the space? Know how much space you take up. Know when to step back.

4. Participation is not always progressive or empowering
Your project may have elements of participation but know how this can just as easily be limiting, tokenistic and condescending. Your demands on our community sharing our stories may be just as easily disempowering. What frameworks have you already imposed on participation? What power dynamics are you reinforcing with such a framework? What relationships are you creating (e.g. informant vs. expert, enunciated vs. enunciator)

5. Presentation vs. representation
Know the difference!

6. It is not a safe-space just because you say it is
This requires long term grass-roots work, solidarity and commitment.

7. Do not expect us to be grateful
We are not your next interesting arts project. Our community are not sitting waiting for our struggle to be acknowledged by your individual consciousness nor highlighted through your art practice.

8. Do not reduce us to an issue
We are whole humans with various experiences, knowledge and skills. We can speak on many things; do not reduce us to one narrative.

9. Do your research
Know the solidarity work already being done. Know the nuanced differences between organisations and projects. Just because we may work with the same community doesn't mean we work in the same way.[20]

10. Art is not neutral
Our community has been politicised and any art work done with/by us is inherently political. If you wish to build with our community know that your artistic practice cannot be neutral.

Zusammenarbeiten. Also ganz schlicht: die möglichen unterschiedlichen Interessen der Beteiligten zur Kenntnis nehmen. Autor*innenschaft reflektieren. Den Arbeitsprozess ebenso wichtig nehmen wie die ästhetischen Entscheidungen. Über kulturelles/symbolisches Kapital nachdenken, wer dafür überhaupt ein Konto besitzt, und wo es um Geld, also ökonomisches Kapital gehen muss, und auch hier zu beachten ist: Wer besitzt ein Konto, oder vielmehr: Wer muss unter dem Radar der Erfassung bleiben?

Und: Betroffenes Schockiertsein hat nichts mit Solidarität zu tun.

Das Manifest/Manual von *RISE* zieht eine klare Trennlinie zwischen Künstler*innen mit und ohne Involvierung in Flucht, Migration und Asyl. Ich würde zwar die Trennschärfe stärker in der Frage der Haltung und nicht nur in der *Betroffenheit* verorten wollen (zumal im Kontext der anhaltenden und wichtigen Diskussionen um die politische Relation von „Refugees", „Non-Citizens", „Unterstützer*innen", um die Selbst-/ Bezeichnungen, um Selbst-/Organisation, um Solidarität vs. Support usw.[21]), aber die Unterscheidung verweist hier auf genau jenen strukturellen Graben, den Kastner thematisiert hat: die unterschiedlichen Feldlogiken Kunst und Aktivismus betreffend – und soll hier weniger eine totalisierende Differenz einbeziehen: hier die Kunstschaffenden, dort die Geflüchteten. Hier gebe ich gerne Hannah Arendt das Wort, die 1943 so prägnant formuliert hat: „In the first place, we don't like to be called ‚refugees'. We ourselves call each other ‚newcomers' or ‚immigrants'."[22] Newcomers: Ankommende, Einwandernde, Dazugehörende. Was heißt: Zugehörigkeit zum *Politischen Körper,* nicht einfach zum Nationalstaat (ja, *Citizenship* muss reformuliert werden – Migration als soziale und politische Bewegung macht das deutlich und tut dies auch.[23]).

Und noch mal anders: Kunst und Politik und Migration heißt nicht Kunstprojekte „über", aber auch nicht einfach „mit" – sondern mit und über und gegen die Verhältnisse, die Migrant*innen entrechten. Und Migration als gesamtgesellschaftliche Tatsache begreifend, nicht als Addendum, Ausnahme, überhistorische Tatsache, sondern als politische und soziale Bewegung: „Hilft es uns, Migration als soziale Bewegung zu begreifen? Ich glaube, ja, wenn der Begriff historisch definiert wird. Jedenfalls ist Migration so besser zu verstehen, als wenn sie als ontologische Konstante, als völkische Bewegungsform oder ökonomische Variable aufgefasst wird."[24]

Und weil es gar nicht genug benannt werden kann, vielleicht der wichtigste Punkt: Über Migration reden heißt, über Rassismus sprechen. So schrieb der schon zitierte Eberhard Jungfer 1993 in einem Text mit dem Titel „Flüchtlingsbewegungen und Rassismus": „Aristide R. Zolberg hat darauf verwiesen, daß die theoretische Literatur zur Migration über die Politik der Zuzugsbegrenzung und der Abschiebungen wenig zu sagen weiß und daß in den psychologisierenden Erklärungen des Rassismus eine Tautologie steckt, weil von den Phänomenen auf die Ursache rückgeschlossen wird. Für ihn ist die Migrationspolitik der Rahmen, in dem der Rassismus diskutiert werden sollte als zweckvolle Organisation von Vorurteilen zu Ideologien, auf deren Basis spezifische politische Ziele durchgesetzt werden konnten. Zwischen der Migrationspolitik des Staats und dem Rassismus in der Gesellschaft besteht ein Zusammenhang, welcher der Forschung eigentlich viel leichter zugänglich sein müßte, als etwa dessen tiefenpsychologische Aspekte."[25] In Deutschland wird immer noch bevorzugt *nicht* von Rassismus gesprochen (sondern beispielsweise von Fremdenfeindlichkeit), und wenn, dann zumeist nicht als strukturelle Frage, sondern eben psychologisierend. (Nicht umsonst verlangt der CERD, der UN-Fachausschuss, der die Umsetzung und Einhaltung der Antirassismus-Konvention kontrolliert, von Deutschland, welches die Konvention 1969 mit unterzeichnet hat, eine neue Definition von Rassismus).

Auch deswegen sind „die Flüchtlinge" nicht einfach „die Anderen", weder für einen Film, ein künstlerisches Projekt und schon gar nicht politisch.

Die Kunst der Migration
Vor zehn Jahren analysierten Tom Holert und Mark Terkessidis in *Fliehkraft*[26] die Beziehungen zwischen Migration und Tourismus. Sie betrachteten die Überschneidungen, Parallelitäten und Verknüpfungen dieser scheinbar unterschiedlichen Mobilitätsformen, die bis dato als isolierte Kräfte betrachtet wurden, um dabei insbesondere die Vorstellungen zu revidieren, die über Migration und Tourismus kursieren. Beide Bewegungsformen, Tourismus als einer der weltweit größten Wirtschaftszweige und Migration als transnationale Realität, werden nicht ausreichend als gesellschaftsverändernde Faktoren wahrgenommen (und im Falle von Migration höchstens als Gefahr und Bedrohung): „In der Gesellschaft in Bewegung geraten außerdem die Verhältnisse von Mehrheit und Minderheit in Bewegung. An den Orten des Transits, auf den Wegen von Migration und Tourismus entstehen neue Kollektive, neue Lebensstil- und Schicksalsgemeinschaften. Zugleich verwandeln sich die Individuen mehr und mehr in Subjekte der Mobilität. Die Menschen bewegen sich in translokalen Netzwerken. Und ihre Bindungen an einen Ort sind von den Möglichkeiten abhängig, die der jeweilige Ort bereitstellt, um die eigenen Projekte zu realisieren. Zwangsläufig ziehen diese Veränderungen gesellschaftliche Veränderungen nach sich. Nur reagiert die Öffentlichkeit darauf sehr langsam. Eine Begleitmusik bei der Entstehung dieses Buches waren heftige Debatten um Leitkultur und Integration. Doch der Blick auf die realen Verhältnisse in einer Gesellschaft in Bewegung lässt diese Debatten nicht nur provinziell, sondern geradezu absurd erscheinen."[27] Und Mobilität muss organisiert werden. Nicht nur, dass Tourismus immer schon eine Organisationsform von Migration war (bereits zu Zeiten der sogenannten „Gastarbeitermigration" war so mancher

Reiseunternehmer auf inoffizielle Pauschalangebote und andere Mobilitätsarrangements spezialisiert), auch Holert und Terkessidis sehen in den heute so bekämpften und kriminalisierten „Schleusern" so etwas wie die verdeckt arbeitenden Gegenstücke zur regulären Reisebüros, die Logistik, Transport und teils auch Unterkünfte während der Reise organisieren.[28]

Der Grund, warum ich mit dem Verweis auf diese Studie schließe, liegt zum einen daran, dass die eingangs zitierte (und diskreditierte) Rede von der Flüchtlingskrise geschichtsvergessen ist, die die Bewegungen der Migration ebenso wie die Arbeit der kritischen Migrations- und Grenzregimeforschung (die immer auch aktivistisch ist[29]), der Flüchtlingsaktivist*innen, des antirassistischen Aktivismus, und ihrer künstlerischen Artikulationen ignoriert. Das Buch von Holert und Terkessidis ist hier also auch Statthalter für eine ganze Reihe weiterer älterer Publikationen, die Argumente aufgemacht haben, die nichts an ihrer Aktualität eingebüßt haben. Es geht mir aber vor allen Dingen auch darum, dass die Verschaltung der beiden Bewegungsformen Tourismus und Migration auch für Kunst und Migration Sinn macht oder machen würde: das System der internationalen Biennalen und großen *Kunstereignisse* ist nicht nur ein System kosmopolitischer, privilegierter, globaler Reisender, das System *Kunst* ist auch eines, das Migration auf den unterschiedlichsten Ebenen organisiert oder zumindest ermöglicht. Tanja Ostojić „Looking for a Husband with EU Passport" (2000–2005) und Petja Dimitrovas „Staatsbürgerschaft/Nationality" (2003) sind Beispiele künstlerischer Arbeiten, die die Kunst der Migration gleichzeitig zeigen, thematisieren und implementieren.[30] Sie inszenieren, realisieren und dokumentieren ihren jeweiligen Kampf um einen legalen Aufenthaltsstatus in der EU als künstlerischen Prozess. Die beiden Projekte zeigen aber auch, dass unter der Kunst der Migration die Findigkeiten von Migrationsstrategien zu verstehen sind. Dass daraus auch Kunstprojekte werden, ist also etwas, das weniger den Dynamiken künstlerischen Schaffens entspringt, sondern aus den Bewegungsdynamiken hervorgeht. Umso plausibler erscheint das Verfahren der beiden französischen Künstler*innen Patrick Bernier und Olive Martin, das französische Recht zu Copyright/Autor*innenschaft/*intellectual property* als Migrationsstrategie in öffentlichen Rechtsauslegungstheatern zu verhandeln.[31] Bernier begann 2001 für *GASPROM* zu arbeiten („Groupement Accueil Service Promotion du Travailleur Immigré"), einer Organisation, die für die Rechte von Migrant*innen kämpft und diese berät. Er begann dort als eine Art *Ghostwriter* Schreiben an Behörden für Migrant*innen zu verfassen. Aus dieser Praxis ging „X. c/ Préfet de ..., Plaidoirie pour une jurisprudence (X and Y vs. France: The Case for a Legal Precedent, 2007 – ongoing)" hervor. Darin vertreten zwei Rechtsanwält*innen den Fall von „X" gegenüber dem Publikum, das als rechtsprechende Instanz eingesetzt wird. Die Argumentation basiert darauf, dass X, die/der Migrant*in mit prekärem Aufenthaltsstatus ist, als Autor*in einer immateriellen ortspezifischen Arbeit präsentiert wird, die, sollte X abgeschoben/ausgewiesen werden, nicht mehr existieren könnte. Das berühmte Diktum von Hannah Arendt vom „Recht auf Rechte" wird hier zur Aushandlung gebracht: Der Entrechtung in der Migration (durch den Nationalstaat) wird eine aktive Ins-Recht-Setzung entgegengestellt. Die dem Recht eignende Performativität wird aktiviert und, wie in anderen ähnlichen Tribunalen[32] auch, als Theater des Rechts zur aktiven Neufassung, zum Entwickeln von Argumenten und Auslegungen zur Aufführung gebracht.

Um einen bekannten Slogan der migrantischen Kämpfe neu zu formulieren: „Wir haben das Recht nicht verletzt, das Recht hat uns verletzt."[33]

Coda

Der „lange Sommer der Migration" ist nicht vorüber und er ist nicht geschichtslos. Aber seine Zeit ist das Jetzt der Zukünftigkeit. Die Kämpfe um das Recht auf Ankunft, gegen Entrechtung, gegen Inhaftierung und Deportation, für das Recht auf radikale Gleichheit werden schon lange gekämpft. Aber jetzt ist die Zeit, die Endgültigkeit der Gegenwart und ihre Begriffe über den Haufen zu werfen und das von Hannah Arendt vor 70 Jahren diagnostizierte Scheitern des Nationalstaats, das mit den Minderheitenverträgen nach dem Ersten Weltkrieg beginnt und sich in Staatenlosigkeit und Illegalisierung nach dem Zweiten Weltkrieg bis heute fortsetzt[34], in neue Denkbarkeiten zu überführen: Das Recht, das Politische, Bürgerschaft, Zugehörigkeit, Geltung, Würde, Gehör finden, eine Stimme haben – es muss neu und radikal anders instituiert werden. Dazu bedarf es radikaler Einbildungskraft. Und dazu bedarf es der Kunst. Die Kunst der Migration, beispielsweise.

---

1   http://bordermonitoring.eu/ungarn/2015/09/of-hope/, zuletzt aufgerufen am 15.03.2016
2   Ebd.
3   Dass die Migrationsbewegungen nicht plötzlich da waren, wird auch von dem geschichtsvergessenen Getue vieler Politiker*innen, überrascht worden zu sein, nicht richtig (um dann gleich daran zu hängen: überrollt worden zu sein – ohne Naturgewaltenmetaphern geht seit dem Revival der „Das Boot ist voll"-Argumentation in den 1990er Jahren durch den Republikanerwahlkampf und in der Folge des massenmedialen Schulterschlusses von *Spiegel, FAZ* und Co., die in den 1940er Jahren von der Schweiz erstmalig lanciert wurden, um die Politik der Grenzschließung zu legitimieren, gar nix). Interessant ist an dieser Stelle auch der rückverlinkende Verweis in *Spiegel Online* in einem Artikel jüngeren Datums zur Schließung der Balkan-Route, die, so das Argument, zur Wiederbelebung der Adria-Route führen könne. Eingebettet in diesen Artikel, der sich explizit kritisch zu den aktuellen Versuchen, Migration durch Abschottung und Abschiebung „beizukommen", äußert, sind Links zu jenem „Gefährlichen Sommer" Artikel im *Spiegel* 33/1991, in dem die Massenflucht aus

Albanien als apokalyptisches Drohszenario präsentiert wurde und der Teil der jahrelang gehegten „Das Boot ist voll"-Schlagzeilen und Schlagbilder Redaktionspolitik des *Spiegel* war. Die Rückverlinkung kommt ohne jegliche (Selbst-)Kritik aus. Siehe Hans-Jürgen Schlamp: Neue Flüchtlingsroute. Angst an der Adria, in: *SPON* 27.01.2016, http://www.spiegel.de/politik/ausland/adria-route-italien-fuerchtet-zehntausende-fluechtlinge-a-1074224.html; zuletzt abgerufen am 10.4.2016. (Update 05.05.2016: Die Verlinkung ist in dem Artikel noch sichtbar, aber nicht mehr aktiv. Technische oder doch andere Gründe? Der Artikel von 1991 ist jedenfalls jetzt gerade nicht mehr auf der Seite von *SPON* zu finden.)

4   Siehe dazu u. a. diesen Eintrag im Liveticker Eidomeni auf bordermonitoring.eu: http://livetickereidomeni.bordermonitoring.eu/2016/04/30/26-4-2016-idomeni-flyer-by-greek-authorities/, zuletzt abgerufen am 28.04.2016.

5   Zu Kunstradikalität und Politradikalität siehe Zoran Terzić: Nation & Exzess IV: Extrem! Überlegungen zur Logik der Darstellung radikaler Phänomene in Kultur und Politik, Präsentation in Leipzig im November 2009, http://www.halbkunst.de/halbkunst/nex4.html, zuletzt abgerufen am 30.04.2016. Zum Konsens siehe auch: Irmgard Emmelhainz: Art and the Cultural Turn: Farewell to Committed, Autonomous Art?, in: *e-flux* 42, 02/2013, http://www.e-flux.com/journal/art-and-the-cultural-turn-farewell-to-committed-autonomous-art/, zuletzt abgerufen am 30.04.2016.

6   Sehr schön hier Antonia Baums Kommentar in der *FAZ* am 10.04.2016 zur Causa Jan Böhmermann, der in seiner Sendung im ZDF ein Gedicht namens *Schmähkritik* auf den türkischen Präsidenten Erdogan vortrug, was in der Folge zu einem Justizfall wurde. Baum beschreibt Böhmermann als „absolut staatsgläubigen Vorzeigebürger" und als „Vertreter des neuen Establishments", der immer auf der richtigen Seite stehe und statt Kritik reine Distinktion betreibe. Also eben gerade nicht als „Rebell" zu sehen sei: „Tatsächlich hat die Erdogan-Sache aber vor allem eines gezeigt, nämlich: wie perfekt dieses Deutschland, seine Regierung, seine Gesetze, die ‚Debattenkultur' und das öffentlich-rechtliche Fernsehen, inklusive Böhmermann, angesichts einer solchen Affäre zusammenarbeiten und letztlich harmonieren. Ein bezahlter Rebell wird von einer Institution, die ihn bezahlt und als Rebell installiert hat, gemaßregelt, nachdem dieser, mit Ansage, etwas falsch gemacht hat, das man in der Bundesrepublik Deutschland nicht falsch machen soll. Woraufhin die Regierung öffentlich sagt, dass jener Rebell da wirklich etwas falsch gemacht habe, die Staatsanwaltschaft, weil er mutmaßlich etwas falsch gemacht hat, aktiv wird und die Presse von ihrer Pressefreiheit Gebrauch macht, indem sie darüber streitet, ob der Rebell nun tatsächlich etwas falsch gemacht hat. Und die jungen Menschen Deutschlands (die Zielgruppe des ZDFs) zusätzlich und für nur 17,50 Euro das für das Erwachsenwerden so wichtige Gefühl geschenkt bekommen, ihnen stehe ein echter Rebell vor. Es läuft alles einwandfrei hier." (http://www.faz.net/aktuell/feuilleton/medien/spiessbuerger-nervensaege-wer-ist-jan-boehmermann-14169789.html, zuletzt abgerufen am 30.4.2016).

7   Siehe die Ausstellung *to show, to demonstrate, to inform, to offer. Künstlerische Praktiken um 1990,* am Museum modern Kunst Stiftung Ludwig Wien (mumok), kuratiert von Matthias Michalak (10.10.2015–14.02.2016), https://www.mumok.at/de/events/expose-show-demonstrate-inform-offer; zuletzt abgerufen am 05.05.2016.

8   AOI, eine von Florian Malzacher, Jonas Staal und Joanna Warsza „initiierte" Konferenz/Performance/Veranstaltung im Hebbel Theater am Ufer in Berlin im Januar 2015, siehe: http://www.artistorganisationsinternational.org/; zuletzt abgerufen am 05.05.2016: Das Konzept basiert darauf, dass es nur um Organisationen geht, die von Künstler*innen gegründet wurden. Diese Distinktion wird konsequent durchgezogen, obwohl der Anspruch der nach *realer* Veränderung der Welt ist: die Verortung ist innerhalb von „daily political struggle", aber stets als Künstler*innen. Aus dem „About"-Statement der Webseite: „Artist Organisations International brings together over twenty representatives of organisations founded by artists whose work confronts today's crises in politics, economy, education, immigration and ecology. Artist Organisations International explores a current shift from artists working in the form of temporary projects to building long-term organisational structures. What specific artistic value and political potential

do such organisations have? How do they perform? What could be their concrete impact on various social-political agendas and possible internationalist collaborations?" und „Artists Organisations International brings together organisations that have been initiated by artists and advocate a specific understanding of art within a social and political context by using the subversive and transformative potential of visual literacy, modes of re-contextualisation and performativity." Aber eben auch: „In their work artist organisations bring forward a social/political agenda that connects the field of ethics with aesthetics. Rather than a medium merely ‚questioning' and ‚confronting' the world, the artist organisation situates itself in the field of daily political struggle. Rather than questioning the world, it makes a world."

9   Selbstverständlich liegt in der Frage der Autor*innenschaft ein strukturelles Unterscheidungsmerkmal zwischen Kunst und Aktivismus: Kunstkollektive werden vom Zwang zum individuellen Namen heimgesucht, während die Herausstellung einzelner Personen in politischen Kollektiven stets erklärungsbedürftig ist, wie auch Jens Kastner ausführt (siehe Anm. 12). In der in Anm. 7 genannten Ausstellung im *mumok* zur Kunst der 1990er Jahre sind plötzlich alle Gruppen und Aktionen mit bestimmten Namen verknüpft, zumeist Namen, die im Kunstkontext bekannt sind. So werden von den ca. 40 Frauen, die an *when tekkno turns to sound of poetry,* einem Ausstellungs- und Rechercheprojekt zu Bio-, Kommunikations- und Informationstechnologien, Feminismus und (Konzept-)Kunst von 1994/95 in der Shedhalle Zürich und in den Kunst-Werken in Berlin beteiligt waren u. a. Juliane Rebentisch und Sabeth Buchmann als Protagonistinnen benannt. Was sicher auch daran liegt, dass diese in dem im *mumok* gezeigten Video einer Ausstellungsführung die Sprecherinnen sind, und natürlich auch an ihrer Rolle in der Konzeptualisierung des Projekts. Und daran, dass es scheinbar keine Namensliste der beteiligten Frauen gibt. Aber das wiederum findet keine Erwähnung in der Ausstellung, ebenso wie der politische Kontext, die Beweggründe für viele der ausgestellten Aktionen und Projekte, nicht mit ebenso viel Detailliertheit ausgeführt wird, wie die künstlerischen Verfahrensweisen – und bestimmter beteiligter Namen. Die Autorin Monika Rinck, die Teil der „Untergruppe" *Übung am Phantom* war (siehe dazu http://werkleitz.de/ubung-am-phantom-revisited-i-projection-sounds; zuletzt abgerufen am 05.05.2016), schrieb in einem Artikel in der FKW (*Frauen Kunst Wissenschaft* 18, 1994) dagegen vor allen Dingen von Gruppenprozessen, von „der Gruppe", die bis zuletzt offengehalten werden sollte. Die einzige Namensliste, die im Kontext von *tekkno* zirkulierte war die der Künstler*innen, deren Arbeiten gezeigt wurden.

10 Franco Bifo Berardi: Pasolini in Tottenham, in: *e-flux* 43, 03/2013, http://www.e-flux.com/journal/pasolini-in-tottenham/; zuletzt abgerufen am 05.05.2016.

11 Dazu müsste die Verweigerung schon Bartleby-Ausmasse annehmen. Siehe dazu u. a. Sabeth Buchmann: Rain is a cage you can walk through. Zu einigen Arbeiten von Judith Hopf, http://eipcp.net/transversal/0601/buchmann/de; zuletzt abgerufen am 06.06.2016. Oder zum Exodus werden.

12 Hito Steyerl: Politics of Art: Contemporary Art and the Transition to Post-Democracy, in: *e-flux* 21, 12/2010, http://www.e-flux.com/journal/politics-of-art-contemporary-art-and-the-transition-to-post-democracy/; zuletzt abgerufen am 30.04.2016. Siehe dazu auch Julia Voss' Buch *Hinter weißen Wänden,* Berlin 2015, in der sie über die Betriebsgeheimnisse des Kunstsystems schreibt, das gezielt seine Einsätze, Wertsteigerungsstrategien und Spekulationen verschleiert und in der sie die auch von anderen (u. a. Georg Seeßlen) formulierte These vertritt, dass die Kunst Abbild der neuen globalen Ungleichheiten sei. *e-flux* zitierte in ihren „conversations" vor einem Jahr Ben Davis und dessen auf Artnet gestellte Frage: „Do you have to be rich to make it as an artist?" Davis' Antwort: „Economics remain a blind spot at the heart of the discourse" (zitiert in http://conversations.e-flux.com/t/do-you-have-to-be-rich-to-make-it-as-an-artist/3106; zuletzt abgerufen am 30.04.2016). Es gibt tatsächlich wenig belastbare Zahlen, weil keine Studien dazu gemacht werden (bzw. wenige) aber auch, weil eben dezidiert geschwiegen wird.

13 Jens Kastner: Über strukturelle Grenzen (hinweg). Was Kunstproduktionen und soziale Bewegungen trennt und verbindet, in: Alexander Fleischmann und Doris Guth (Hg.): *Kunst. Theorie. Aktivismus,* Bielefeld 2015, S. 23–58, hier S. 26.
14 Vgl. ebd.
15 Ebd.
16 Zu den vielseitigen Tätigkeiten Kastners siehe seine Webseite http://www.jenspetzkastner.de, zuletzt abgerufen am 03.05.2016.
17 Julia Voss: *Hinter weißen Wänden / Behind the White Cube,* Berlin 2015, S. 78.
18 Nanna Heidenreich: „Die Perspektive der Migration aufzeichnen/einnehmen/ausstellen/aktivieren", in: Fleischmann und Guth, a.a.O., S. 113–145.
19 *Zeit der Unruhe,* kuratiert von Kristine Jhouri und Rasha Salti, 19.03.–09.05.2016, HKW Berlin. http://hkw.de/de/programm/projekte/2016/zeit_der_unruhe/zeit_der_unruhe_start.php, zuletzt abgerufen am 05.05.2016.
20 http://riserefugee.org/10-things-you-need-to-consider-if-you-are-an-artist-not-of-the-refugee-and-asylum-seeker-community-looking-to-work-with-our-community/, zuletzt abgerufen am 05.05.2016.
21 Siehe dazu beispielsweise Vassilis S. Tsianos und Bernd Kasparek: Too much love. Von „Non-Citizens" und ihren „Supportern". Über problematische neue Begriffe im deutschen antirassistischen Diskurs, in: *Jungle World* 30/2013, 25.07.2013, http://jungle-world.com/artikel/2013/30/48137.html; zuletzt abgerufen am 05.05.2016.
22 Hannah Arendt: We Refugees, zuerst veröffentlicht im *Menorah Journal,* hier zitiert aus dem Wiederabdruck in: Marc Robinson (Hg.): *Altogether Elsewhere. Writers on Exile,* Boston/London 1994, S. 110–119, hier S. 110.
23 Aus den zahlreichen Publikationen zum Thema siehe hier zunächst nur Ilke Ataç und Étienne Balibar in der „Flee, Erase, Territorialize" Ausgabe von *Transversal,* die sich auf konkrete Kämpfe von Sans Papiers bzw. Refugees in Wien und Paris beziehen, 03/2013: http://eipcp.net/transversal/0313; zuletzt abgerufen am 05.05.2016. Siehe dazu auch das noch neue *Movements*-Journal, das aus der kritischen Migrations- und Grenzregimeforschung hervorgegangen ist: http://movements-journal.org/; zuletzt abgerufen am 05.05.2016.
24 Eberhard Jungfer: Migrationen im Sozialen Weltkrieg, in: Komitee für Grundrechte und Demokratie (Hg.): *Jenseits der Menschenrechte. Die europäische Flüchtlings- und Migrationspolitik,* Münster 2009, S. 16–27, hier zitiert aus dem PDF, verfügbar unter: http://archiv.labournet.de/diskussion/grundrechte/asyl/festungeu.html; zuletzt abgerufen am 06.06.2016. Migration als soziale und politische Bewegung zu verstehen ist eine der zentralen Thesen der kritischen Migrations- und Grenzregimeforschung. Siehe dazu u. a. Sandro Mezzadra: Autonomie der Migration. Kritik und Ausblick, Transkription eines Vortrags, gehalten am 28.01.2010 in Wien, http://www.grundrisse.net/grundrisse34/Autonomie_der_Migration.htm#_ednref3; zuletzt abgerufen am 06.06.2016.
25 Eberhard Jungfer: Flüchtlingsbewegung und Rassismus. Zur Aktualität von Hannah Arendt, „Die Nation der Minderheiten und das Volk der Staatenlosen.", in: *Beiträge zur nationalsozialistischen Gesundheits- und Sozialpolitik* 11, 1993, S. 19–49, zitiert aus einem im Netz zirkulierenden PDF o. S. (hier Blatt 9 von 28 des PDFs, im Abschnitt „3"), verfügbar unter http://www.materialien.org/texte/migration/fluebewrass.html; zuletzt abgerufen am 30.4.2016.
26 Tom Holert und Mark Terkessidis: *Fliehkraft. Gesellschaft in Bewegung – von Migranten und Touristen,* Köln 2006.
27 Ebd., S. 15.
28 Zu den Kunstprojekten *Bundesverband Schleppen&Schleusen* siehe http://www.faridaheuck.net/2_5_1/c_d.php, sowie die 2. *Internationale Schlepper- und Schleusertagung* (ISS), die im Oktober 2015 von den Kammerspielen München veranstaltet wurde, als Teil des politischen/aktivistischen *Open Border Kongresses* (Munich Welcome Theater) siehe http://iss2015.eu/. In beiden Fällen wurde gezielt die Grenze zwischen Realität und Fiktion verwischt, um einen realen „Imagewandel" herbei zu führen. So sah der bayerische Innenminister Joachim Herrmann (CSU) in ISS dann auch „kein gelungenes Kulturprojekt",

sondern „fehlgeleitete Politpropaganda", zitiert in: http://www.sueddeutsche.de/muenchen/theater-kammerspiele-provozieren-mit-tagung-ueber-schleuser-1.2664985. Alle URLs zuletzt abgerufen am 05.05.2016.

29 Siehe dazu u. a. http://kritnet.org/ sowie http://bordermonitoring.eu/; beide URLs zuletzt abgerufen am 06.05.2016.
30 Siehe www.petjadimitrova.net/works/Staatsbuergerschaft.html und
31 Siehe Audrey Chans Portrait der beiden Künstler*innen in *Afterall* 2009, http://www.afterall.org/online/bernier-martin.essay#.Vy3T76YWGD7; zuletzt abgerufen am 03.05.2016.
32 Siehe z. B. das aktivistische Tribunal „NSU-Komplex" auflösen (http://nsu-tribunal.de/), das im Frühjahr 2017 im Schauspielhaus Köln stattfinden soll, oder das vom „International Institute of Political Murder", respektive Milo Rau initiierte Kongo-Tribunal (http://international-institute.de/das-kongo-tribunal/); beide URLs zuletzt aufgerufen am 05.05.2016.
33 „We didn't cross the border, the border crossed us."
34 Hannah Arendt: Der Niedergang des Nationalstaats und das Ende der Menschenrechte, in: *Elemente und Ursprünge totaler Herrschaft*, Frankfurt/M. 1986, S. 422–470.

RAHEL

JAEGGI

Solidarity and

Indifference

Rahel Jaeggi

Solidarity and Indifference

"One thing will remain from socialism: It has sharpened our awareness that solidarity is more than a moral sentiment."
Warnfried Dettling (*Die Zeit,* December 27, 1996 – trans. R.J.)

The concept of solidarity is omnipresent, at least in the public discourse. It is in danger of becoming ambiguous, to turn into a wishy-washy concept that tries to evoke a vague sense of belonging, a readiness to help, or the value of social responsibility.

What exactly, then, is at stake when we talk about solidarity? Is it possible to defend a non-essentialist concept of solidarity—and in which sense is the concept of solidarity related to the discussion about the "cement of society" or new social bonds?

What are the implications of referring to the notion of solidarity when it comes to welfare arrangements or our duties towards, for example, refugees? In what follows I will defend a non-essentialistic, symmetrical notion of solidarity. While taking into account the precarious character of solidarity, solidarity is then understood as a certain kind of cooperation that *realizes* (in the sense of becoming aware as well as bringing about) the social connectedness and interdependencies we are confronted with as inherently social beings.

The first part of my chapter is an attempt to analyse the concept and the phenomenon of solidarity. Therefore, I examine the specific character of solidaristic associations and attitudes by relating them to other forms of social relations. Above all I am concerned with pointing out the differences between solidarity and attitudes like readiness to help or compassion on one hand, and other kinds of communality, on the other. As a result, I will argue in the second part of the chapter, that we should understand solidarity as a certain kind of cooperation that can be related to Hegel's concept of "ethical life" (Sittlichkeit) (Hegel, 1987). The precarious character of solidarity here leads us to inquire into the social and ethical basis of solidarity. My thesis is that solidarity *is neither given nor invented.* Even if it relies on the fact of *being associated,* this fact still has to be *realised*—in the double sense of being aware of something and putting something into being—in order to lead to solidaristic action. This leads to a certain view of the problem of de-solidarisation discussed in part four. Following up on my discussion of solidarity and processes of solidarisation in the first part, I will argue that the problem of de-solidarisation, the *downfall of solidarity* in modem societies (that troubles some recent social theorists) should be distinguished from phenomena like the *loss of communality/community* or individualisation as such; neither is it properly understood as the loss of the *moral infrastructure* or as the *demoralisation* of society.

1. What is solidarity?

What, then, is solidarity? Corresponding to its etymological origins in the Latin *solidus,* meaning solid, tight, dense, whole, or united, the notion of solidarity evokes the idea of a certain kind of connectedness. The historical evolution of the term from the juridical idea of joint liability (the liability of every single debtor for the entire debt in a shared enterprise) is still present in its present day association with social security systems. The idea of *standing in for each other* thus seems to cover the central aspect of this notion: "That everyone has to stand in for the others and that these have to stand in for every single one is the basic content of solidarity" (Amengual, 1990). The usage of the notion in social theory goes back to these origins. Linked to the problem of social integration, solidarity refers to the social bond that holds society together. As the sociologist Émile Durkheim explains in *The Division of Labor (De la division du travail social):* "Solidarity is what prevents the breakdown of society" (Durkheim, 1893/1978). Solidarity here has a descriptive meaning. It refers to a state of affairs within a group of people or society that is characterised by mutual attachment, connection or simply (objectively given) dependency. On the other hand, solidarity is also a disposition to act in a solidaristic way. As such it has a normative meaning.

When we appeal to solidarity we expect a certain behaviour and a certain attitude from each other; further, we think of this as something we somehow *owe to each other,* something we should do and expect each other to do—at least within particular relations and in specific situations. It is this second, normative aspect that leads to the most controversial questions.

What exactly is it, then, that we expect when we ask for solidarity? What kind of connectedness or relatedness is it that provides the basis for this specific sort of *standing in for each other?*

Everyday use of the concept
A first approach to answering these questions may be taken from our everyday understanding of solidarity as it evolves when we compare solidarity to other kinds of social relations.

Like friendship, solidarity can be based on a feeling of (affective) attachment and some sort of connection. Nevertheless, when it comes to friendship we wouldn't speak of acting out of solidarity. Feeling solidarity for someone or acting out of solidarity for someone is not specific enough to entail being their friend. Friendship is not only a *stronger* emotional bond, relying on unconditional feelings and *resemblances of the heart* (as expressed in the romantic concept of friendship); it is also necessarily restricted to a limited number of people. Friendship is a face-to-face relation, whereas we can form solidaristic bonds with distant people and even with strangers. Think of solidarity as it evolves in solidarity campaigns. The desire to express one's solidarity with political or social movements in foreign countries has nothing to do with knowing the people involved, nor even necessarily with knowing some of them. Here solidarity is mediated through a common cause (or what we think of as a common cause). We are solidaristic with a group of people or a political movement because it stands for something we ourselves identify with. Perhaps they are fighting for something that we ourselves consider worth achieving; perhaps as we often suspect—we simply have the same enemy. (But even having the same enemy is not a simple fact, as will be argued below, but relies on taking a certain position with regard to something.) The notion of identification here points to an important feature and another distinction: solidarity should not be equated with the shallower common interest of a coalition. On the one hand, solidarity may be based on common interest, a *common fate* and certain interdependencies, for example the common interest of workers during a strike. On the other hand, solidarity seems to express a *deeper* commitment than is necessary for a coalition, which is only formed in order to achieve a certain goal. One doesn't change solidaristic commitments the way one changes sides in coalitions once a certain constellation of interests has altered. Moreover, many of the attitudes that we consider solidaristic don't seem to be directed to the realisation of simple self-interest—we can even think of them as characterised by a willingness to make sacrifices. Relations of solidarity therefore should not be seen as strategic. They seem to transcend a narrow conception of individual interests. This suggests an affinity between solidarity and loyalty. But although both seem to be based on identification with a common cause (a nation, an institution or an idea), there are also significant differences between them. Solidarity is a nonhierarchical relation; loyalty can have a hierarchical structure. It would be, for example, peculiar to speak of the mafia as calling for solidarity. The loyalty demanded and sometimes enforced in this context requires unconditional dedication that may go along with subordination. Solidarity, in addition to that, seems to be related to a sense of legitimacy. It often evolves out of the sense that a certain claim, for example of the workers' movement, is justified. It often disappears once we lose our confidence in the justification.

Therefore one might be tempted to define solidarity as support of common goals considered worthwhile and legitimate. A solidaristic group would then be characterised by a specific self-image that distinguishes it from other groups. It is not just a group as such, fighting for its own dominance, but a group that considers itself legitimate (that is not to say that it is legitimate). Whether we could distinguish between regressive and non-regressive forms of solidarity with respect to this feature is an open question. Should we call the connectedness and identification among a group of violent hooligans solidarity at all? On the other hand, wouldn't our definition be too narrow if we excluded these cases?

Solidarity should thus be redefined: it doesn't refer to connectedness per se and it shouldn't be identified with community/communality. Emphasising the importance of a common goal and not only of a somehow common background, face-to-face relations as such, as we find them in tight-knit communities, do not guarantee a basis for solidarity. On the contrary, small communities can be unsolidaristic. On the other hand, there are many instances of the *solidarity of strangers*. The decisive question is under which conditions the *we* of a certain community is able to relate to each other and to act in a solidaristic way. As will be argued below, there are two crucial distinctions between solidarity and communality: solidarity does not evolve *naturally,* it is in some respect an artificial bond between individuals, one that is not given but created. As such it is a relation between individuals, it does not presuppose the unconditional fusion of individuals into a community.

This leads to another problem. Is a solidaristic group defined by the particularity—which is to say the exclusivity—of its common cause? Is solidarity always the solidarity of one particular group against others? As far as loyalty is concerned, this seems to be clear. We think of loyalty as a relation to a particular institution, directed at something exclusive; it is the commitment to a particular institution, nation or group as opposed to another one. To call for *international loyalty* would therefore be absurd.

Instead, the notion of solidarity has a remarkable history as a compound of *international solidarity.* And even if this was meant as the international solidarity of the working class opposing their oppressors, it is not to be understood as genuinely particularistic. Think of the universalism in the idea that the international movement of the working class fights for human rights. The underlying idea—however flawed—seems to be that of a solidaristic mankind. But then, isn't there some truth in Richard Rorty's remark, that a "we" that includes whole mankind would be somewhat too general in order to create solidaristic bonds. The very nature of solidaristic bonds—and their possible limits—thus remains to be discussed.

These questions return when we address the difference between solidarity and compassion. Having distinguished solidarity from friendship, loyalty and other forms of coalitions, we should also tell apart solidarity from the less particular disposition of being ready to help. Confusing these attitudes—as is the tendency in current discussions—means ignoring important connotations of the concept. Readiness to help and compassion are not always expressions of solidarity—and vice versa. And even if altruistic conduct and helpfulness often are part of a solidaristic practice, they are not what is constitutive of its specifically solidaristic aspect. That is to say, being moved by the suffering of others and even practising charity is not to be identified with acting out of solidarity. Offering help to anyone who is in a difficult situation—the homeless in the cities or the victims of natural disasters—or offering solidarity and acting out of solidarity has to be understood as something different. If we think of solidaristic motivations as an expression of common goals, shared projects or a common fate they are opposed to compassion in two significant aspects. First, solidarity, relying on inclusion, demands the realisation of a certain kind of connection that relates one's situation to the situation of the others. Acting out of solidarity means standing up for each other because one recognises *one's own fate in the fate of the other.* Pity or compassion for the other, in contrast, do not necessarily relate the other's to one's own situation, except in the very vague sense of being a vulnerable human being oneself. Altruism, compassion and readiness to help can even go along with distance and separateness. Second, compassion signifies an asymmetrical relation, solidarity a symmetrical one. Compassion and altruism are likely to mark the relation between unequals, the relation between those who need and those who provide help. They create a one-sided dependency and therefore an asymmetrical relation. Opposed to this, solidarity is, at its core, asymmetrical, mutual and reciprocal relation. Solidarity means cooperation.

The distinction between (political) solidarity and humanitarian help that is often discussed in solidaristic movements might indicate how to make sense of this feature. Humanitarian aid should be offered to human beings who suffer, no matter who they are and what they are doing, whereas the solidarity of solidaristic movements is expressed with respect to people (organised in social or political movements or not) with whom we share (political) goals. Of course, the transition may be fluent. Organising, for example, the victims of an earthquake against the municipal authorities and their institutional deficits, posing fundamental questions of urban planning and poverty can lead from humanitarian aid to solidarity. But even this counts for the validity of the distinction. By addressing the situation of the earthquake victims, political activists (not made homeless by the earthquake themselves) were criticising the very political and social order they themselves are concerned with. Thus, while being united behind the same political goals (at least for a while) what might have begun as humanitarian help turns into a common struggle. Thus the relation between the activists and the victims becomes symmetrical and reciprocal. We can see the significance of the distinction between solidarity and compassion when we look at the long history of oppressed groups calling for (and building on) solidarity. Obviously, being treated as a *comrade* as opposed to being treated as a helpless victim affects the self-esteem of those concerned. See for example the history of relations between blacks and Jews in the United States. In this context bell hooks (1995) remarks that "solidarity between blacks and Jews must be mutual. It cannot be based on a notion of black people as needy victims that white Jews 'help'".

2. Non-instrumental cooperation and ethical life

But then again, to characterise solidarity as a symmetrical and reciprocal relation generates certain problems: to conceptualise it as symmetrical may be quite convincing in cases such as a strike movement in a labour struggle; here solidarity means to stand by each other, to give each other mutual support in a joint activity. In this context solidarity is, indeed, a symmetrical relation.

But in some of the cases mentioned above symmetry is less obvious. Solidarity with the Zapatistas or social movements in the global south may be perceived as one-sided. And how can social care for helpless people be seen as symmetrical and as a form of cooperation at all? In these cases, there is no mutual support and the achieved engagement cannot expect any immediate payoff. However, as I will argue, the reciprocity of solidaristic relations is not meant to be a simple exchange relation. There is a kind of *enlarged reciprocity* at work. The reason for solidarity is the belief that the success and wellbeing of others is important to ensure the flourishing of projects with which I myself identify. But even then, emphasising the symmetrical and reciprocal character of solidarity could mean underestimating its altruistic dimension. Rather the argument is, that the most challenging feature of solidarity is that in a certain way it seems to transcend the opposition between altruistic and egoistic motivations. That is to say, despite its reciprocity, the motivation for solidarity cannot be reduced to the enlightened self-interest of rationally calculating individuals. Seeing *one's own fate in the fate of the other* not only refers to the possibility that one is or could be confronted with the same situation as the other, it means that his fate affects me in a significant way.

How should we understand, then, the symmetry- and reciprocity that is characteristic for this notion of solidarity with reference to welfare state arrangements? Of course, one could easily understand it as the symmetry and reciprocity of an insurance model where everyone tries to lower his own risk by sharing it with others. But this would underestimate the extent to which the public support of welfare institutions depends on an idea of connectedness, especially when it comes to the affirmation of the redistribution-aspect that is linked to welfare systems.

Thus, here again a kind of *enlarged reciprocity*—referring to a certain idea of social integration—seems to be required. How can we understand solidarity as a relation that is neither to be equalled with asymmetrical attitudes, as in compassion and pity for the vulnerable groups in society, nor with well-calculated self-interest that leads to the formation of pressure groups? These motives will be examined in the next section, suggesting that we can understand the characteristics of solidarity as a form of non-instrumental cooperation that can be linked to Hegel's notion of "Sittlichkeit" (ethical life). Solidarity, it is argued, is based on a non-instrumental understanding of cooperation that contrasts sharply with the instrumental conception of cooperation we find in most cases of commonality of interest.

Two models of cooperation
Let me spell out the implications of these two models of cooperation. In the first case of instrumental cooperation, cooperation with others is a pure means to achieve individual ends: each individual has certain interests that are more likely to be achieved by acting together with others. The motivation for cooperation in this case has to be understood as arising out of "enlightened self-interest." In some cases it is simply rational to act together in order to achieve a certain goal. This is why we may call this type of cooperation instrumental; cooperation here is not a value in itself. It is easy to see that this kind of motivation will

not lead to strong commitments. In most cases, the actors will cease to cooperate when the cooperation fails to serve their individual interests. The second model applies when the goals to be achieved are common goals themselves. Interests are common interests. That is to say: I cannot even describe my interests and goals apart from the goals of the others. These are intrinsically common goals because they are constituted only in common. The cooperation is non-instrumental insofar as one does not merely use the others in order to achieve an individual goal. The individual's interest has to be understood as "interest in the interest of the others." A strike can serve as an example for both models, instrumental as well as non-instrumental cooperation. Imagine a scenario in which a certain group—in a labour struggle—is being made an offer and is tempted to end the strike. In this case, their comrades may appeal to solidarity by saying: "we have started the struggle in order to achieve fair salaries for all—as a common goal." They may also continue to appeal to their self-interest: de-solidarisation will weaken our power for the next conflict. But if one determines the very purpose of the strike as achieving fair salaries for all, the problem is not only that one should not abandon one's comrades in a difficult situation, but also that the real goal of the strike would not have been reached.

The case of common goals is even stronger when we can attribute an intrinsic value to the process of cooperation itself, so to say a second order interest in not only achieving the common goal but in achieving it in a cooperative way. See for the structure of this relation the often-used example of playing in a music band where one is interested not only in the outcome but in the process of playing together itself. An argument for limiting the concept of solidarity to non-instrumental relations would be that the model of instrumental cooperations based on enlightened self-interest fails to grasp the willingness to move beyond self-interest, to do sacrifices which characterises much of what we perceive as solidarity. It would be simply irrational (and therefore incomprehensible) from this point of view. On the contrary, from a rational choice perspective everyone entering into cooperative projects has an interest in enjoying the advantages of these projects without contributing his or her own share to them (the well-known free-rider problem). Thus, the understanding of solidarity based on instrumental cooperation could turn out not only to be too weak a basis for what we need, but it would also fail to understand certain types of social relations that already exist.

Talking about solidarity as a *fundamental value* therefore means thematising this willingness and the character of this connection as the basis of solidarity. How can this relatedness that is characterised by an interpenetration of self-interest and the interests of the other, undermining the very distinction between egoism and altruism, be understood? To go back to the dimension to which Hegel referred as "ethical life" may be helpful here.

Emphasising its formal structure, Michael Theunissen characterises "ethical life" as "those conditions in which the individual first and foremost finds his own self" (Theunissen, 1981). That is to say, individuals "realise" themselves by committing to those kind of relations that are "intersubjective conditions of self-realisation" (Axel Honneth). The "Other" is, as Marx argued, not the limitation but the precondition of my own freedom. These ideas obviously refer to a social (as opposed to an atomistic) conception of human life and personal identity. In this conception human beings are socially constituted on a fundamental level. This leads to a non-instrumental understanding of basic social relations. As Charles Taylor argues against atomistic theories: "what man derives from society is not aid in realising his good, but the very possibility of being an agent seeking that good" (Taylor, 1985). Embedded in a certain culture, acting within an already present structure of social cooperation, it would be mistaken to see them as *using* these relations in order to promote their own good. Rather it is only the very background conditions that provide him with the possibility to articulate his own good. To share a common life form (however *thin* this may be described in a post-traditional situation) in this perspective is essential—not only with regard to the problem of social integration but also with regard to the individual's possibility for self-realisation. Applied to this account of, solidarity and the "enlarged reciprocity", this means: as far as we share a common form of life, solidaristic support has to be understood as an engagement that is related not only to the other but to the preservation of this common form of life. In this respect it is *neither egoistic nor altruistic?* Solidarity thus is an ethical concept; being solidaristic might be understood an expression of one's own identity, as it is related to others (to communal life).

The particularity of "Ethical Life"
Referring to *identity* and *common forms of life* now brings us back to an issue mentioned above. If solidarity is an expression of a common form of life it seems to be exclusive, particularistic. It would include only those who share this form of life. This is true, even if we hold that one can share common goals and form cooperative relations with strangers (as is discussed in the examples of international solidarity), where a common form of life doesn't exist as a fact but as an idea (or as an anticipation). But even if we use the notion of cooperation in a wide sense; and even if we try to understand solidarity—under *post-traditional* conditions—as a connection that estimates the individuality of persons, as Durkheim does with his concept of "organic solidarity" and as Axel Honneth does by defining solidarity in terms

of mutual recognition with respect to the individual's contribution to a common praxis, we still have the problem that these contributions can't be recognised then against the background of shared values or a shared "project". Should we understand the *ethical duty* to act out of solidarity—a set of obligations towards a specific group—as opposed to moral duties, that we are supposed to have towards all human beings? Forming solidaristic associations, so it seems, we *owe something to each other,* we have certain obligations as far as we are involved in these relations and with respect to their preserving. But how could we be obliged to enter these relations at all, how could we be obliged to include certain groups or individuals into the *we* of solidaristic bounds? We could suggest here a kind of a *moral division of labour:* there are moral duties towards all human beings; ethicalduties towards specific relations, groups and projects. Nevertheless, with respect to solidarity the particularity remains problematic. Even if we have solidaristic duties only in regard of those with whom we share something specific or with whom we are bound up in some sort of cooperation, it can easily be argued that we are connected in a significant way to much more people than we may expect to be. Habermas' quest for a new cosmopolitic solidarity in this respect draws consequences out of the fact of growing interdependencies in a globalised world (Habermas, 1998).

If we then want to examine the possibilities for extending solidarity (a problem that is also posed within the institutional framework of the EU), we have to inquire the social and ethical basis of solidarity. Interested in the capacity for inclusion that can be ascribed to solidarity we have to ask for the character of identities that are linked with solidarity. What exactly means *sharing a common form of life?* How is the basis of cooperative relations to be understood? My thesis here will be, that the *we* of solidarity is not necessarily fixed. It is open (and expansible) with respect to the different contexts of dependency and of cooperation that individuals are involved in. The capacity to form solidaristic associations then is related to the capacity to act within these contexts.

3. The precarious basis of solidarity

In her novel *None to Accompany Me* Nadine Gordimer characterises the motivation of one of her protagonists—a white South African—for working in solidarity campaigns as following: "Vera read newspapers and reports [...] She did come to know. She went to work at the foundation, not because of the white guilt people talked about, but out of a need to take up, to balance on her own feet the time and place to which, by birth, she understood she had no choice but to belong" (Gordimer, 1994). Important in our context is the relation that is been made here between self-understanding and the effort to relate to the social conditions and circumstances she is confronted with. Solidarity for Gordimer's activist seems to mean relating consciously to the situation and conditions in which she finds herself (to which she belongs)—which also implies a better understanding of herself. Seen in this light, developing solidarity means realising a context of dependencies in the double sense of recognising and actualising. We are always already *in* the social world and we are thus part of a net of social interdependencies. That is, our own situation is—voluntarily or involuntarily—connected to the situations of others. This explains the meaning of the statement by Leon Bourgeois, founder of the nineteenth-century French intellectual movement of *solidarisme:* "In understanding that one is an associated being one acts in solidarity." Thus, solidarity points to the ability to relate actively and positively and to shape the social bonds and interdependencies, in which the individual is, as a matter of fact, always already involved. But, even if solidarity is based on the fact of being associated, its emergence always seems to be precarious and to some extent contingent.

The problem of unemployment or neoliberal attacks on the welfare state existed for many years when at a certain point a student movement in France thematised it; French and German workers during World War I would have had good reasons to promote working class solidarity instead of fighting each other on the battlefield (one of the first great defeats the idea of *international solidarity* had to suffer); it took a long time before the women's liberation movement could raise the collective consciousness of women as suffering the same destiny, a process still going on in various kinds of ethnic or social minorities. At any given time, there seem to be many more good reasons for solidarity than actual outcomes of solidaristic action. This points not only to features related to the problems of collective action and the theory of social movements. The readiness to act out of solidarity, it seems, cannot be traced back directly either to a person's origins or circumstances alone.

In this regard, there would seem to be no fixed or certain foundation for solidarity, be it the cultural or historical origins of an individual or a group, their social, geographical, or organisational proximity, or even their objectively shared interests. Thus, even the statement "we're all in the same boat" is a matter of interpretation. This is partly the case because we are never *associated* in just one respect. We are at the centre of various relations, which link us to a nation, a class, to gender, a sexual orientation, or to various forms of life, and it is not at all clear out of which of these commonalities a basis for solidarity will emerge. Being a black lesbian professor in the United States, for example, should one relate to the black community all over the world (the *African diaspora*), to women as such (black and white, gay and straight), to homosexuals (including men), to the upper-middle class, or to the academic community? Each of these classifications characterises a possible source of identification, but none of them compels someone to actually act on it.

There could be reasons to identify with one of these groups, for example because she realises that she has been discriminated as a black or as a woman even though she has been professionally successful. But the pure fact of belonging does not create a compelling reason for solidarity. That is to say, there is no hidden essence of collective identity out of which solidarity will automatically arise.

Appeals to solidarity that relate to characteristics like being a woman, being black or whatever, *create* what they are appealing to as much as they *discover* previously latent characteristics. Even then, the social fact of someone being treated as a woman or as a black person—e.g. being oppressed—is more powerful than the mere biological fact of it. *Consciousness raising* doesn't appeal an awareness of biological but of social facts.

That is even true for the old problem of class-consciousness: obviously parts of the working class chose to identify with the nation of France or Germany instead of identifying with class struggle during World War I. In a classical Marxist perspective, this would count as a *failure* in achieving *class consciousness,* not getting to move from class *in itself* to class *in itself and for itself.* But we have no way to argue like this, once we don't assume there is a hidden *essence* of identity that goes without question. Thus, the fact of being associated, which even might exist *behind the individual's back,* has to be actualised as a willingness to identify with a certain situation (a *common lot*) and to act out of solidarity. The *we* of the solidaristic group must first constitute itself in order to be. That is to say, solidarity only actualises itself as a common practice and it is this practice in which the ability to *stand in for each of her* emerges. Common projects or common goals are therefore not limited to the *common lot* of a group as it may be apparently given by existing social circumstances and then narrowly interpreted on this basis. The most interesting question with respect to solidarity then is, how to get from a *common lot* to *common goals.*

This has some consequences for the questions discussed above. The very fact that the *we* of solidaristic action is not simply given but has to be constituted leads to a potential for enlargement, for extending solidaristic relations. Mediated via a sense of cooperation or common goals, the very process of solidarisation sometimes provides the possibility for an inclusion of others. See for example the construction workers' strike in Berlin in 1998 that started with claims for the exclusion of foreign loan workers and—at its height—ended up with demands for better wage and social security for all. The openness for inclusion here again seems to be depending on the ability to see the own situation as changeable. That is not to deny that the same process does very often lead to exclusions. But yet, even if it is true that solidarity has no fixed foundation and that there is a potential for enlargement, solidarity is not a voluntaristic option. Solidarity in this regard is neither given nor invented. You might get your own situation wrong in rejecting certain solidarities. Acting out of solidarity might imply realising interdependencies between one's own circumstances and those of others that one can deny only for the price of powerlessness with regard to these circumstances. Think of the need for international social legislation or labour laws that might be a consequence of the construction worker's experience. Realising international interdependencies might enable them to react to a situation that would otherwise leave them helpless. Referring to our analysis above: the enlargement of solidarity does not rely on the deepening of our powers of empathy alone, as Rorty (1989) seems to suggest, but on the becoming aware of and relating to the "fact of being associated." Nevertheless, objective trends seem to make this kind of solidarity more difficult even as they make it more necessary.

4. De-Solidarisation

What can be learned from this for our understanding of solidarity and its possible decline in modem societies? If solidarity depends on the ability to be aware of the interdependencies and relations which connect us with others, the *decline* of solidarity—its possible loss—has to be described as the inability to make this connection. More interesting than individual deficits here, are the social and structural obstacles, which prevent people and social groups from attaining this awareness. De-solidarisation then means not simply *not being connected*, being indifferent or *atomised*, but is an expression of a disconnection between individuals who actually are involved with or dependent on each other and have good reasons to form solidaristic bonds. This is to say that the independence here is somewhat delusional. This sense of de-solidarisation can be criticised as social *alienation*, as estrangement from something you actually are or should be involved with. A situation where important aspects of the social structure are *hidden* or nontransparent, implying that people are unable to relate to it or to identify with it, can be seen as *alienating*. Turning to the social diagnosis of a *downfall of solidarity*, the question we have to pose in order to examine our present resources for solidarity is not so much how much we have *in common*. More specifically, the question is whether what we have in common will enable us to see ourselves as acting subjects with respect to the social institutions that shape our lives.

Bibliography

Amengual, G.: 1990, "Gattungswesen als Solidarität. Die Auffassung vom Menschen in der Bestimmung des Gattungswesens als Begriff und Grundlegung der Solidarität", in: H.-J. Braun et al. (Hrsg.), *Ludwig Feuerbach und die Philosophie der Zukunft,* Akademie-Verlag, Berlin, p. 345–367.

Brudney, D.: 1999, *Marx' Attempt to Leave Philosophy,* Harvard University Press, Harvard.

Durkheim, É.: 1893, *De la division du travail social,* Presses Universitaires de France, Paris. Deutsch: 1992, *Über soziale Arbeitsteilung. Studie über die Organisation höherer Gesellschaften,* Suhrkamp: Frankfurt am Main, übers. v. L. Schmidts (durchges. v. M. Schmid).

Gordimer, N.: 1994, *None to accompany me,* Bloomsbury, London.

Habermas, J.: 1998, *Die Einbeziehung des Anderen,* Suhrkamp, Frankfurt am Main.

Hegel, G. W. F.: 1987, *Vorlesungen zur Philosophie des Rechts,* Suhrkamp, Frankfurt am Main.

Honneth, A: 1993, "Posttraditionale Gemeinschaften", in H. Brunkhorst and M. Brumlik (eds.), *Gemeinschaft und Gerechtigkeit,* Fisher, Frankfurt am Main, p. 260–270.

hooks, b.: 1995, *Killing rage: ending racism,* Holt, New York.

Radin, M. J.: 1996, *Contested Commodities,* Harvard University Press, Harvard.

Rorty, R.: 1989, *Contingency, Irony, Solidarity,* Cambridge University Press, Cambridge.

Sartre, J.-P.: 1960, *Critique de la Raçon Dialectique,* Gallimard, Paris.

Taylor, C.: 1985, "The Nature and Scope of Distributive Justice", in: ders., *Philosophy and the Human Sciences. Philosophical Papers 2,* Cambridge University Press, Cambridge, p. 289–317.

Theunissen, M.: 1982, *Selbstverwirklichung und Allgemeinheit. Zur Kritik des gegenwärtigen Bewußtseins* (1981), De Gruyter, Berlin/New York.

Tugendhat, E.: 1994, *Vorlesungen über Ethik,* Suhrkamp, Frankfurt am Main.

Walzer, M.: 1983, *Spheres of Justice,* Basic Book, New York.

Wildt, A.: 1992, "Solidarität", in J. Ritter and K.-F. Gründer (eds.), *Historisches Wörterbuch der Philosophie,* 8, Wissenschaftliche Buchgesellschaft, Darmstadt, p. 1004.

Wildt, A.: 1995, "Zur Begriffs- und Ideengeschichte von Solidarität", in K. Bayertz, Solidarität. Begriff und Problem, Suhrkamp, Frankfurt am Main, p. 202–216.

Rahel Jaeggi[1]

Solidarität und Gleichgültigkeit

„Vom Sozialismus wird eines bleiben: Er hat das Bewußtsein dafür geschärft, daß Solidarität mehr ist als ein moralisches Gefühl."
Warnfried Dettling (*Die Zeit,* 27. Dezember 1996)

Der Begriff der Solidarität ist allgegenwärtig, zumindest im öffentlichen Diskurs. Und er läuft Gefahr uneindeutig zu werden, zu einem kraftlosen Begriff zu geraten, der ein vages Zugehörigkeitsgefühl, Hilfsbereitschaft und den Wert gesellschaftlicher Verantwortung zu beschwören sucht.

Worum handelt es sich also genau, wenn wir von *Solidarität* sprechen? Ist es möglich, ein nicht-essentialistisches Solidaritätskonzept zu vertreten – und in welchem Verhältnis steht der Solidaritätsbegriff zur Diskussion über den „sozialen Kitt" der Gesellschaft und neue gesellschaftliche Bindungen?

Welche Implikationen hat die Bezugnahme auf die Vorstellung von Solidarität im Zusammenhang mit Sozialleistungen und auch mit unseren Pflichten, etwa gegenüber Flüchtlingen? Im Folgenden vertrete ich einen nicht-essentialistischen, symmetrischen Solidaritätsbegriff. Während dem brüchigen Charakter von Solidarität Rechnung zu tragen sein wird, ist Solidarität zugleich zu begreifen als eine bestimmte Art der Kooperation, die den gesellschaftlichen Zusammenhalt und die wechselseitigen Abhängigkeiten *realisiert* (*Realisieren* sowohl im Sinne der Bewusstwerdung als auch der Verwirklichung), mit denen wir als zutiefst gesellschaftliche Wesen konfrontiert sind.

Der erste Teil meines Essays ist der Versuch, Solidarität als Begriff und Phänomen zu analysieren. Daher untersuche ich den spezifischen Charakter solidarischer Vereinigungen und Haltungen, indem ich sie mit anderen Formen gesellschaftlicher Beziehungen in Verbindung setze. Mir geht es vor allem darum, die Unterschiede zwischen Solidarität und Einstellungen wie Hilfsbereitschaft und Mitgefühl einerseits und anderen Arten der Gemeinschaftlichkeit andererseits herauszustellen. Folglich führe ich im zweiten Teil des Essays aus, dass Solidarität zu verstehen wäre als eine bestimmte Art der Kooperation, die sich mit Hegels Begriff der „Sittlichkeit" (Hegel, 1987) in Verbindung setzen lässt. Das brüchige Wesen der Solidarität führt mich dann dazu, die gesellschaftliche und ethische Basis der Solidarität zu untersuchen. Meine These lautet, dass Solidarität *weder (vor-)gegeben noch erfunden* ist. Selbst wenn Solidarität auf der Tatsache des *Assoziiert-Seins* basiert, muss diese Tatsache – um zu solidarischem Handeln zu führen – immer noch *realisiert* werden, in dem doppelten Wortsinne sich etwas bewusst zu sein und etwas zu erschaffen. Dies führt, in Teil vier, zu einem bestimmten Blick auf das Problem der Entsolidarisierung. An meine Ausführungen zu Solidarität und Solidarisierungsprozessen im ersten Teil anschließend, werde ich darlegen, dass das Problem der Entsolidarisierung, des *Untergangs der Solidarität* in modernen Gesellschaften (welcher jüngst einige Gesellschaftstheoretiker beunruhigt) zu unterscheiden wäre von Phänomenen wie dem *Verlust von Gemeinschaft(-lichkeit)* bzw. der Individualisierung an sich; auch als Verlust der *moralischen Infrastruktur* oder als *Demoralisierung* der Gesellschaft ist das Problem der Entsolidarisierung nicht richtig verstanden.

1. Was ist Solidarität?

Was also ist Solidarität? Seinem etymologischen Ursprung im lateinischen *solidus* entsprechend – was so viel bedeutet wie fest, eng, dicht, ganz bzw. vereint –, evoziert der Begriff Solidarität den Gedanken einer gewissen Verbundenheit. Die historische Entwicklung der Begrifflichkeit, ausgehend von der juristischen Vorstellung der Gesamthaftung (die Haftung jedes einzelnen Schuldners für die Gesamtschuld eines gemeinsamen Unternehmens), ist im heutigen Zusammenhang der sozialen Sicherungssysteme noch immer gegenwärtig. Die Idee des *Füreinander-Eintretens* scheint denn den zentralen Aspekt dieses Konzeptes abzudecken: „Dass einer für alle und alle für einen verantwortlich sind und einzutreten haben, bleibt der Grundsinn von ‚Solidarität'" (Amengual, 1990: 345). Die Verwendung des Begriffs in den Gesellschaftswissenschaften geht auf diese Ursprünge zurück. Verbunden mit dem Problem der gesellschaftlichen Integration, verweist Solidarität auf das soziale Band, welches die Gesellschaft zusammenhält. So erklärt der Soziologe Émile Durkheim in *Über soziale Arbeitsteilung (De la division du travail social)*: „Solidarität verhindert den Zusammenbruch der Gesellschaft" (Durkheim, 1893/1992). Solidarität hat hier eine deskriptive Bedeutung und verweist auf den Zustand einer Menschengruppe oder Gesellschaft, der gekennzeichnet ist durch eine gegenseitige Bindung, Verbindung oder einfach eine (objektiv gegebene) Abhängigkeit. Andererseits bezeichnet Solidarität auch die Bereitschaft zu solidarischem Handeln. Als solche hat sie eine normative Bedeutung.

Wenn wir an die Solidarität appellieren, so erwarten wir voneinander ein bestimmtes Verhalten und eine bestimmte Haltung; des Weiteren begreifen wir sie als etwas, das wir einander gewissermaßen *schulden:* etwas, das wir leisten und voneinander erwarten können – dies zumindest in spezifischen Beziehungen und in bestimmten Situationen. Dieser zweite, normative Aspekt wirft äußerst kontroverse Fragen auf.

Was genau also erwarten wir, wenn wir Solidarität fordern? Welche Art Verbundenheit oder Bezogenheit bildet die Grundlage für diese spezifische Art des *Füreinander-Eintretens?*

Der Alltagsgebrauch des Begriffs

Ein erster Ansatz zur Beantwortung dieser Fragen lässt sich aus unserem Alltagsverständnis von Solidarität ableiten, das sich zeigt, wenn wir Solidarität mit anderen Arten sozialer Beziehungen vergleichen.

Ebenso wie Freundschaft, kann Solidarität auf einem Gefühl der (affektiven) Bindung und einer gewissen Verbindung gründen. Dennoch würden wir im Zusammenhang mit Freundschaft nicht von solidarischem Handeln sprechen: Mit jemandem solidarisch zu sein oder zu handeln, ist zu unbestimmt, um notwendig ein Freundschaftsverhältnis zu begründen. Freundschaft ist nicht nur eine *stärkere* emotionale Bindung, die sich auf unbedingte Gefühle und *Wesensähnlichkeiten* stützt (wie sie im romantischen Freundschaftsbegriff ihren Ausdruck finden); Freundschaft ist notwendigerweise auch beschränkt auf eine begrenzte Anzahl von Menschen. Freundschaft ist eine direkte Beziehung, während wir solidarische Bande mit fernstehenden Menschen und sogar mit Fremden knüpfen können: etwa mit der Solidarität, wie sie sich in Solidaritätskampagnen entfaltet. Der Wunsch, die eigene Solidarität mit politischen oder sozialen Bewegungen in anderen Ländern auszudrücken, hat nichts damit zu tun, die beteiligten Menschen zu kennen – ja, man muss nicht einmal notwendigerweise einige von ihnen kennen. Hier ist Solidarität vermittelt durch eine gemeinsame Sache (oder was wir als gemeinsame Sache ansehen). Wir sind mit einer Gruppe von Menschen oder einer politischen Bewegung solidarisch, weil sie für etwas steht, mit dem wir uns identifizieren. Vielleicht kämpfen sie für etwas, das wir selbst für erstrebenswert halten; vielleicht auch haben wir, wie wir oft ahnen, einfach nur dieselbe*denselben Gegner*in. (Aber selbst dieselbe*denselben Gegner*in zu haben, ist – ich komme darauf zurück – keine bloße Tatsache, sondern abhängig von einer bestimmten Positionierung zu einer Sache.) In diesem Zusammenhang verweist der Begriff der Identifizierung auf ein wichtiges Merkmal, ein weiteres Kennzeichen: Solidarität darf nicht gleichgesetzt werden mit dem weniger weitreichenden gemeinsamen Interesse eines Bündnisses, einer Koalition. Einerseits kann Solidarität auf einem gemeinsamen Interesse gründen, einem *gemeinsamen Schicksal* und bestimmten wechselseitigen Abhängigkeiten, zum Beispiel dem gemeinsamen Interesse der Arbeiter*innen in einem Streik. Andererseits drückt Solidarität anscheinend eine *tiefere* Verpflichtung aus, als sie für eine Koalition notwendig ist, die nur zur Erlangung eines bestimmten Zieles gebildet wird. Man löst solidarische Verpflichtungen nicht in derselben Weise wie man in Bündnissen die Seiten wechselt, sobald sich eine bestimmte Interessenkonstellation verändert. Zudem scheinen viele derjenigen Haltungen, die wir als solidarisch begreifen, nicht auf die Realisierung bloßen Eigeninteresses abzuzielen – die Bereitschaft, Opfer zu bringen, lässt sich gar als ein Kennzeichen solidarischer Haltungen auffassen. Solidarbeziehungen sollten daher nicht als strategische Beziehungen angesehen werden, scheinen sie doch eine Konzeption individueller Interessen im engeren Sinne zu übersteigen. Dies lässt auf eine Verwandtschaft zwischen Solidarität und Loyalität schließen. Doch obwohl scheinbar beide auf der Identifizierung mit einer gemeinsamen Sache (einer Nation, Institution oder Idee) gründen, weisen sie auch bedeutende Unterschiede auf: Solidarität ist eine nicht-hierarchische Beziehung; Loyalität hingegen kann eine hierarchische Struktur aufweisen. Es wäre beispielsweise ungeheuerlich zu sagen, die Mafia fordere Solidarität. Die in diesem Zusammenhang verlangte und bisweilen erzwungene Loyalität erfordert eine bedingungslose Hingabe, die mit Unterordnung einhergehen kann. Darüber hinaus scheint Solidarität verbunden mit einem Sinn für Legitimität: Sie entwickelt sich oftmals aus dem Gefühl heraus, dass eine bestimmte Forderung – beispielsweise der Arbeiterbewegung – berechtigt ist. Und sie verschwindet häufig, sobald unser Glauben an diese Berechtigung schwindet.

Daher mag man versucht sein, Solidarität als Unterstützung für gemeinsame Ziele zu definieren, welche man als lohnend und legitim erachtet. Eine solidarische Gruppe würde sich dann durch ein bestimmtes Selbstbild auszeichnen, das sie von anderen Gruppen unterscheidet: Sie ist nicht nur eine Gruppe an sich, die um ihren Einfluss kämpft, sondern eine Gruppe, die sich als legitim betrachtet (was nicht heißt, dass sie legitim ist). Ob sich im Hinblick auf diese Eigenschaft unterscheiden lässt zwischen repressiven und nicht-repressiven Formen der Solidarität, ist eine offene Frage. Kann man den Zusammenhalt und die Identifizierung in einer Gruppe gewalttätiger Hooligans überhaupt als Solidarität bezeichnen? Wäre unsere Definition andererseits nicht zu eng, würden wir solche Fälle ausschließen?

Solidarität muss also anders definiert werden: Sie verweist nicht auf eine bloße Verbundenheit an sich, und sie darf nicht gleichgesetzt werden mit Gemeinschaft/ Gemeinschaftlichkeit. Hervorzuheben ist die Bedeutung eines gemeinsamen Zieles, nicht bloß eines irgendwie gemeinsamen Hintergrunds, denn direkte Beziehungen an sich – wie wir sie in verschworenen Gemeinschaften finden – bieten allein noch keine Basis für Solidarität. Ganz im Gegenteil, kleine Gemeinschaften können unsolidarisch sein. Andererseits gibt es viele Beispiele für *Solidarität unter Fremden*. Die entscheidende Frage lautet, unter welchen Bedingungen das *Wir* einer bestimmten Gemeinschaft sich zueinander solidarisch verhalten und entsprechend agieren kann. Wie ich im Weiteren ausführen werde, gibt es zwei zentrale Unterscheidungskriterien zwischen Solidarität und Gemeinschaftlichkeit: Solidarität entwickelt sich nicht *ganz natürlich,* sie ist gewissermaßen ein künstliches Band zwischen Einzelnen, das nicht (vor-)gegeben ist, sondern geschaffen wird. Als solche ist sie eine Beziehung zwischen Individuen und setzt nicht die bedingungslose Verschmelzung der Einzelnen in einer Gemeinschaft voraus.

Das führt zu einer weiteren Fragestellung: Definiert sich eine solidarische Gruppe durch die Besonderheit – das heißt, die Exklusivität – ihrer gemeinsamen Sache? Ist Solidarität immer die Solidarität einer spezifischen Gruppe im Gegensatz zu anderen: gegen andere? In Bezug auf Loyalität, ist das wohl klar. Wir begreifen Loyalität als eine Beziehung zu einer bestimmten Institution, eine auf etwas Exklusives gerichtete Beziehung; Loyalität ist die Verpflichtung gegenüber einer bestimmten Einrichtung, Nation oder Gruppe im Gegensatz zu einer anderen. Die Forderung nach *internationaler Loyalität* wäre daher absurd.

Der Begriff der Solidarität hingegen hat, in der Zusammensetzung *internationale Solidarität*, eine bemerkenswerte Geschichte: Auch wenn sie gemeint war als die internationale Solidarität der Arbeiterklasse gegen ihre Unterdrücker, ist sie nicht als eigentlich partikularistisch zu verstehen. Man denke nur an den Universalismus in dem Gedanken, dass die internationale Bewegung der Arbeiterklasse die Menschenrechte erkämpft. Der zugrundeliegende Gedanke – so unvollkommen er sein mag – scheint der einer solidarischen Menschheit zu sein. Liegt aber nicht auch ein Körnchen Wahrheit in Richard Rortys Bemerkung, dass ein die gesamte Menschheit umfassendes „Wir" zu allgemein wäre, um solidarische Bande schaffen zu können (Rorty, 1989)? Das Wesen solidarischer Bande – und die Möglichkeit ihrer Beschränkung – sind noch zu erörtern.

Diese Fragen tauchen wieder auf, wenn wir uns dem Unterschied zwischen Solidarität und Mitgefühl zuwenden. Nach der Unterscheidung der Solidarität von Freundschaft, Loyalität und anderen Bündnisformen, sollten wir auch Solidarität und die weniger spezifische Disposition der Hilfsbereitschaft auseinanderhalten: Beide Haltungen miteinander zu verwechseln – eine Mode in den aktuellen Debatten – hieße, wichtige Konnotationen des Begriffs zu übergehen. Hilfsbereitschaft und Mitgefühl sind nicht immer Ausdruck von Solidarität, und *vice versa*. Auch wenn altruistisches Verhalten und Hilfeleistung oftmals ein Bestandteil solidarischer Praxis sind, sind sie nicht konstitutiv für deren spezifisch solidarische Dimension. Das heißt, vom Leiden Anderer bewegt zu sein und gar praktische Nächstenliebe zu üben, ist nicht gleichzusetzen mit solidarisch motiviertem Handeln. Als voneinander verschieden zu verstehen sind das Hilfsangebot für Menschen in schwieriger Lage – für Obdachlose in den Städten oder für Opfer von Naturkatastrophen – und das Angebot von bzw. das Handeln aus Solidarität. Wenn wir solidarische Beweggründe als einen Ausdruck gemeinsamer Ziele, kollektiver Projekte oder eines gleichen Schicksals begreifen, stehen sie mit dem Mitgefühl in zwei wichtigen Punkten im Widerspruch: Erstens verlangt Solidarität, da sie auf Inklusion beruht, die Realisierung einer gewissen Verbindung, welche die eigene Situation mit der Situation der Anderen in Beziehung setzt. Das Handeln aus Solidarität heraus bedeutet, für einander aktiv zu werden, weil man *das eigene Schicksal im Schicksal des Anderen* erkennt. Im Gegensatz dazu beziehen Mitleid oder Mitgefühl die Situation des Anderen nicht notwendigerweise auf die eigene Situation, wenn man von dem sehr schwammigen Bezug absieht, dass man selbst ein verletzliches, menschliches Wesen ist. Altruismus, Mitgefühl und Hilfsbereitschaft können sogar einhergehen mit Distanz und Abtrennung. Zweitens bedeutet Mitgefühl eine asymmetrische Beziehung und Solidarität eine symmetrische. Mitgefühl und Altruismus markieren nicht selten das Verhältnis zwischen Ungleichen: die Beziehung zwischen denen, die Hilfe brauchen, und jenen, die sie gewähren. Mitgefühl und Altruismus schaffen eine einseitige Abhängigkeit und daher eine asymmetrische Beziehung. Im Gegensatz dazu ist Solidarität, in ihrem Kern, eine symmetrische, gegenseitige und wechselseitige Beziehung. Solidarität bedeutet Kooperation.

Die Unterscheidung zwischen (politischer) Solidarität und humanitärer Hilfe, wie sie in den Solidaritätsbewegungen häufig diskutiert wird, verweist auf den Sinngehalt dieser Qualität: Humanitäre Hilfe sollte leidenden Menschen angeboten werden, ganz egal wer sie sind und was sie tun, wohingegen die Solidarität von Solidaritätsbewegungen ihren Ausdruck gegenüber Menschen findet (ob sie nun in sozialen bzw. politischen Bewegungen organisiert sind oder nicht), mit denen wir gemeinsame (politische) Ziele teilen. Selbstverständlich ist der Übergang mitunter fließend. Zum Beispiel können die Organisierung von Erdbebenopfern gegen die örtlichen Behörden und deren institutionelle Defizite und/oder das Aufwerfen grundsätzlicher Fragen der Stadtplanung und Armut von der humanitären Hilfe hin zur Solidarität führen. Aber auch das spricht für die Gültigkeit der Unterscheidung: Indem sie die Lage der Erdbebenopfer thematisieren, würden die politischen Aktivist*innen (die selbst durch das Erdbeben nicht obdachlos geworden sind) eben die politische und gesellschaftliche Ordnung kritisieren, von der sie selbst betroffen sind. So verwandelt die Tatsache der (zumindest zeitweiligen) Vereinigung hinter denselben politischen Zielen in einen gemeinsamen Kampf, was unter Umständen als humanitäre Hilfe begonnen hat. Die Beziehung zwischen den Aktivist*innen und den Opfern wird in der Folge symmetrisch und wechselseitig. Wir erkennen die Bedeutung der Unterscheidung zwischen Solidarität und Mitgefühl, wenn wir uns die lange Geschichte derjenigen unterdrückten Gruppen ansehen, die Solidarität fordern (und auf Solidarität gründen). Als *Genossin*Genosse* behandelt zu werden – anstatt, im Gegenteil, als hilfloses Opfer – berührt das Selbstwertgefühl der Betroffenen. Man betrachte beispielsweise die Geschichte der Beziehungen zwischen Schwarzen und Juden in den USA. In diesem Zusammenhang merkt bell hooks (1995) an, die „Solidarität zwischen Schwarzen und Juden muss gegenseitig sein. Auf einer Vorstellung von schwarzen Menschen als bedürftige Opfer, denen weiße Juden ‚helfen', kann sie nicht gründen".

2. Nicht-instrumentelle Kooperation und Sittlichkeit

Aber: Solidarität als eine symmetrische und wechselseitige Beziehung zu charakterisieren, wirft auch bestimmte Probleme auf. Sie als symmetrisch zu begreifen, ist ganz überzeugend, wenn es um Fälle wie die Streikbewegung in einem Arbeitskampf geht: Hier bedeutet Solidarität, füreinander einzutreten und einander in einer gemeinsamen Aktion gegenseitig zu unterstützen. In diesem Zusammenhang ist Solidarität tatsächlich eine symmetrische Beziehung.

In einigen der oben genannten Fälle aber ist die Symmetrie weniger offenkundig: Die Solidarität mit den Zapatisten und sozialen Bewegungen im globalen Süden kann als einseitig wahrgenommen werden. Und wie lässt sich Sozialfürsorge für Hilfsbedürftige als symmetrisch, ja überhaupt als Form der Zusammenarbeit ansehen? In diesen Fällen gibt es keine gegenseitige Unterstützung und es ist nicht damit zu rechnen, dass sich das erbrachte Engagement unmittelbar auszahlt. Indes, so meine These, die Reziprozität solidarischer Beziehungen ist nicht als einfache Tauschbeziehung zu verstehen; hier ist eine Art *erweiterter Wechselseitigkeit* am Werk. Der Grund für die Solidarität ist die Überzeugung, dass Erfolg und Wohlergehen der Anderen für die Entfaltung derjenigen Projekte wichtig sind, mit denen ich mich selbst identifiziere. Aber auch dann könnte die Betonung des symmetrischen und gegenseitigen Charakters der Solidarität bedeuten, ihre altruistische Dimension zu unterschätzen. Der Punkt ist vielmehr folgender: Die schwierigste Eigenschaft der Solidarität ist es, dass sie den Gegensatz zwischen altruistischen und egoistischen Beweggründen gewissermaßen zu transzendieren scheint. Das heißt, trotz ihrer Gegenseitigkeit, lässt sich die Motivation für Solidarität nicht auf das aufgeklärte Eigeninteresse rational berechnender Individuen reduzieren. Das *eigene Schicksal im Schicksal der Anderen* zu erkennen, verweist nicht nur auf die Möglichkeit, dass man mit derselben Situation wie der Andere konfrontiert ist oder konfrontiert sein könnte, sondern bedeutet auch, dass dessen Schicksal mich signifikant betrifft.

Wie also ist die Symmetrie und Reziprozität zu verstehen, die charakteristisch ist für diesen Solidaritätsbegriff, wenn es um sozialstaatliche Modalitäten geht? Freilich könnte man sie leichthin als die Symmetrie und Gegenseitigkeit eines Versicherungsmodells begreifen, in dem jeder das eigene Risiko zu senken sucht, indem man es mit Anderen teilt. Dies aber würde unterschätzen, in welchem

Ausmaß der öffentliche Rückhalt für den Sozialstaat abhängig ist vom Gedanken des Zusammenhalts, insbesondere wenn es um die Zustimmung zum Umverteilungsaspekt geht, der mit den Sozialsystemen verbunden ist.

Abermals scheint hier also eine Art *erweiterter Wechselseitigkeit* erforderlich zu sein, die auf eine bestimmte Vorstellung von gesellschaftlicher Integration verweist. Wie lässt sich Solidarität als eine Beziehung begreifen, die weder gleichzusetzen ist mit asymmetrischen Haltungen (wie dem Mitgefühl und Mitleid für schutzbedürftige Gesellschaftsgruppen) noch mit dem genau kalkulierten Eigeninteresse, das zur Bildung von Interessengruppen führt? Diese Überlegungen werden im nächsten Abschnitt untersucht: unter der Annahme, dass wir die Eigenschaften der Solidarität als eine Form nicht-instrumenteller Zusammenarbeit verstehen können, die sich mit Hegels Sittlichkeitsbegriff in Verbindung setzen lässt. Solidarität, so meine These, gründet auf einem nicht-instrumentellen Kooperationsverständnis, das sich deutlich abhebt von dem instrumentellen Kooperationsbegriff, den wir in den meisten Fällen der Interessengemeinschaft vorfinden.

Zwei Kooperationsmodelle
Wir wollen die Implikationen beider Kooperationsmodelle ausbuchstabieren. Im ersten Fall, der instrumentellen Kooperation, ist die Zusammenarbeit mit Anderen ein reines Mittel zum Erreichen individueller Ziele: Jede*r Einzelne hat bestimmte Interessen, deren Realisierung wahrscheinlicher wird durch das gemeinsame Handeln mit Anderen. Die Motivation zur Zusammenarbeit muss in diesem Falle verstanden werden als ein Auswuchs des „aufgeklärten Eigeninteresses". In einigen Fällen ist es einfach vernünftig, zusammen zu agieren, um ein bestimmtes Ziel zu erreichen. Deshalb können wir diesen Typus der Kooperation als instrumentell bezeichnen – die Zusammenarbeit ist hier kein Wert an sich. Es ist leicht einsichtig, dass diese Motivation nicht zu starken Verpflichtungen führt. In den meisten Fällen werden die Akteur*innen die Kooperation einstellen, wenn die Zusammenarbeit ihren individuellen Interessen nicht (mehr) dienlich ist. Das zweite Modell hat Gültigkeit, wenn die verfolgten Ziele selbst gemeinsame Ziele sind, die Interessen gemeinsame Interessen sind und ich also gar nicht in der Lage bin, meine Interessen und Ziele losgelöst von den Zielen der Anderen zu beschreiben. Es sind wesentlich gemeinsame Ziele, weil sie sich nur gemeinsam konstituieren (lassen). Die Zusammenarbeit ist insofern nicht instrumentell als man die Anderen nicht bloß benutzt, um ein persönliches Ziel zu erreichen. Das Interesse der*des Einzelnen muss verstanden werden als „Interesse im Interesse der Anderen". Ein gutes Beispiel für beide Modelle, eine instrumentelle als auch nicht-instrumentelle Kooperation, ist der Streik. Stellen wir uns ein Szenario vor, in dem eine bestimmte Gruppe – in einem Arbeitskampf – ein Angebot erhält und

in Versuchung gerät, aus dem Streik auszusteigen. In diesem Falle können ihre Kolleg*innen an die Solidarität appellieren und sagen: „Wir haben den Kampf begonnen, um gerechte Löhne für alle zu erreichen – das ist unser gemeinsames Ziel." Sie können weiterhin an das Eigeninteresse der Gruppe appellieren: „Eine Entsolidarisierung wird uns in der nächsten Auseinandersetzung schwächen." Wenn man aber den eigentlichen Zweck des Streiks als die Erwirkung gerechter Löhne für alle definiert, dann besteht das Problem nicht nur darin, dass man seine Kolleg*innen in einer schwierigen Situation nicht im Stich lassen sollte, sondern auch darin, dass das eigentliche Ziel des Streiks nicht erreicht ist.

Das Argument der gemeinsamen Ziele wiegt noch schwerer, wenn wir dem Kooperationsprozess selbst einen intrinsischen Wert zuschreiben können – sozusagen als Sekundärinteresse, bei dem es nicht nur darum geht, das gemeinsame Ziel überhaupt, sondern dieses Ziel auch auf kooperative Weise zu erreichen. Zur Struktur dieser Beziehung betrachte man das häufig verwendete Beispiel des Musizierens in einer Band: hier ist man nicht nur am Ergebnis interessiert, sondern auch am Prozess des Zusammenspielens selbst. Ein Argument dafür, den Solidaritätsbegriff auf nicht-instrumentelle Beziehungen einzuschränken, wäre, dass es das Modell der instrumentellen Kooperation auf der Basis aufgeklärten Eigeninteresses nicht vermag, die Bereitwilligkeit zu erklären, mit der man über das Eigeninteresse hinausgeht und Opfer bringt – was einen Großteil dessen kennzeichnet, was wir als Solidarität wahrnehmen: Vom Standpunkt des Eigeninteresses wäre Solidarität einfach irrational (und daher unverständlich). Im Gegensatz dazu hat – aus der Perspektive der *rational choice* (rationalen Entscheidung) – jede*r bei der Beteiligung an kooperativen Projekten ein Interesse daran, in den Genuss der Vorteile dieser Projekte zu gelangen, ohne einen eigenen Teil zu ihnen beizutragen (das berühmte Trittbrettfahrer-Problem). Ein Solidaritätsverständnis, das auf instrumenteller Zusammenarbeit beruht, könnte sich also nicht nur als zu schwache Grundlage für unsere Anforderungen erweisen, sondern auch daran scheitern, bestimmte Typen schon bestehender sozialer Beziehungen zu verstehen.

Über Solidarität als *Grundwert* zu sprechen, bedeutet daher, diese Bereitwilligkeit und das Wesen dieser Verbindung als Fundament der Solidarität zu thematisieren. Wie ist diese Verbundenheit zu verstehen, die gekennzeichnet ist durch eine gegenseitige Durchdringung von Eigeninteresse und den Interessen des Anderen, und also die Unterscheidung zwischen Egoismus und Altruismus selbst untergräbt? Hier kann es hilfreich sein, auf die Dimension zurückzukommen, die Hegel als „Sittlichkeit" bezeichnete.

Mit einem Schwerpunkt auf deren formale Struktur, charakterisiert Michael Theunissen die „Sittlichkeit" als Allgemeinheit, „in der die einzelnen sich allererst als solche finden" (Theunissen, 1982: 20). Das heißt, Individuen „verwirklichen" sich selbst, indem sie sich jener Art von Beziehungen verschreiben, die „intersubjektive Bedingungen der Selbstverwirklichung" sind (Honneth, 1993). Der „Andere" ist, wie Marx ausführte, nicht die Schranke, sondern die Voraussetzung meiner Freiheit. Diese Gedanken verweisen offenkundig auf ein gesellschaftliches (im Gegensatz zum atomistischen) Konzept des Menschen und der persönlichen Identität. In dieser Begrifflichkeit sind die Menschen grundsätzlich sozial konstituiert. Dies führt zu einem nicht-instrumentellen Verständnis der grundlegenden gesellschaftlichen Beziehungen. So führt Charles Taylor gegen atomistische Theorien aus: „was der Mensch aus der Gesellschaft gewinnt, ist nicht Unterstützung bei der Verwirklichung seines jeweiligen Guten, sondern die Möglichkeit überhaupt, ein Handelnder zu sein, der dieses Gute anstrebt" (Taylor, 1985; 1988: 150). Es wäre verfehlt, die Einzelnen – die eingebettet sind in eine bestimmte Kultur und in einer schon bestehenden Struktur sozialer Zusammenarbeit agieren – derart zu betrachten, als würden sie diese Beziehungen *benutzen,* um für ihr eigenes Gutes zu wirken. Vielmehr sind es allein diese Verhältnisse im Hintergrund, die der*dem Einzelnen erst die Möglichkeit bieten, sein eigenes Gutes zu artikulieren. Aus diesem Blickwinkel ist es wesentlich, eine gemeinsame Lebensform zu teilen (als wie *dünn* man diese auch beschreiben mag, in einer posttraditionellen Situation) – wesentlich nicht nur im Hinblick auf das Problem der gesellschaftlichen Integration, sondern auch hinsichtlich der Selbstverwirklichungsmöglichkeit des Individuums. Bezogen auf dieses Verständnis von Solidarität und *erweiterter Wechselseitigkeit* heißt das: Sofern wir eine gemeinsame Lebensform teilen, ist solidarische Unterstützung zu verstehen als eine Verpflichtung nicht nur gegenüber dem Anderen, sondern auch gegenüber der Bewahrung dieser gemeinsamen Lebensform. Insofern ist Solidarität *weder egoistisch noch altruistisch.* Solidarität ist folglich ein sittlicher, ein ethischer Begriff; Solidarisch-Sein kann verstanden werden als ein Ausdruck der eigenen Identität in ihrem Verhältnis zu den Anderen (zum gemeinschaftlichen Leben).

Die Besonderheit der „Sittlichkeit"

Der Bezug auf *Identität* und *gemeinsame Lebensformen* führt uns nun zurück zu einem bereits erwähnten Thema: Wenn Solidarität Ausdruck einer gemeinsamen Lebensform ist, scheint sie doch exklusiv und partikularistisch zu sein. Sie schließt nur diejenigen ein, die diese Lebensform teilen. Dies gilt auch, wenn wir meinen, dass man auch mit Fremden gemeinsame Ziele haben und kooperative Beziehungen ausbilden kann (wie in den Beispielen internationaler Solidarität angeführt), mit denen eine gemeinsame Lebensform nicht als Tatsache, sondern als Idee (oder Projektion) existiert. Aber selbst wenn wir den Kooperationsbegriff im weiteren Sinne verwenden; auch wenn wir Solidarität – unter *posttraditionellen*

Bedingungen – als eine Verbindung zu verstehen suchen, welche die Individualität der Personen wertschätzt (so wie Durkheim es mit seinem Begriff der „organischen Solidarität" tut, oder Axel Honneth mit seiner Definition von Solidarität als gegenseitige Anerkennung des je individuellen Beitrags zu einer gemeinsamen Praxis); auch dann stehen wir immer noch vor dem Problem, dass diese Beiträge nur vor dem Hintergrund gemeinsamer Werte oder eines gemeinsamen *Projektes* Anerkennung finden können. Müssen wir die *ethische Pflicht* aus Solidarität zu handeln – eine Reihe von Verpflichtungen gegenüber einer bestimmten Gruppe – als Gegensatz zu moralischen Pflichten verstehen, die wir mutmaßlich gegenüber allen Menschen haben? Wenn wir solidarische Vereinigungen bilden, scheint es, sind wir *einander etwas schuldig* und haben wir gewisse Verpflichtungen, sofern wir in diese Beziehungen eingebunden sind und sie bewahren wollen. Was aber kann uns nötigen, diese Beziehungen überhaupt einzugehen; was kann uns nötigen, gewisse Gruppen oder Individuen in das *Wir* solidarischer Verbindungen aufzunehmen? Es lässt sich hier von einer Art *moralischer Arbeitsteilung* ausgehen: Es gibt moralische Pflichten gegenüber allen Menschen, und ethische Pflichten gegenüber besonderen Beziehungen, Gruppen und Projekten. Nichtsdestotrotz bleibt das Partikulare im Kontext der Solidarität problematisch. Selbst wenn wir Solidarpflichten nur gegenüber jenen haben, mit denen wir etwas Bestimmtes teilen oder mit denen wir in irgendeiner Art Zusammenarbeit verbunden sind, ließe sich leichthin argumentieren, dass wir mit sehr viel mehr Menschen signifikant verbunden sind, als wir es erwarten würden. Habermas' Suche nach einer neuen kosmopolitischen Solidarität zieht diesbezüglich die Konsequenzen aus der Tatsache der zunehmenden gegenseitigen Abhängigkeiten in einer globalisierten Welt (Habermas, 1998).

Wenn wir nun die Möglichkeiten der Ausweitung der Solidarität untersuchen wollen (ein Problem, das sich auch im institutionellen Rahmen der EU stellt), müssen wir die gesellschaftliche und ethische Grundlage der Solidarität ergründen. Wer an der Integrationsfähigkeit interessiert ist, die sich der Solidarität zuschreiben lässt, muss nach dem Wesen solidarischer Identitäten fragen. Was genau heißt es, *eine gemeinsame Lebensform zu teilen?* Wie ist die Grundlage kooperativer Beziehungen zu verstehen? Meine These lautet hier, dass das solidarische *Wir* nicht notwendigerweise fixiert ist: Es ist offen (und dehnbar) im Hinblick auf die verschiedenen Abhängigkeits- und Kooperationszusammenhänge, in die die Einzelnen involviert sind. Die Fähigkeit zur Bildung solidarischer Vereinigungen steht also in Verbindung mit der Fähigkeit, innerhalb dieser Zusammenhänge zu agieren.

3. Die brüchige Grundlage der Solidarität

In ihrem Roman *Niemand, der mit mir geht* beschreibt Nadine Gordimer die Motivation eines ihrer Protagonisten – einer weißen Südafrikanerin – für die Mitarbeit in Solidaritätskampagnen folgendermaßen: „Vera las Zeitungen und Berichte […] Sie wusste mehr und mehr davon [von Frustration und Elend]. Sie begann in der Stiftung zu arbeiten, nicht aufgrund der weißen Schuld, von der die Leute redeten, sondern aus der Notwendigkeit heraus, sich der Zeit und dem Ort zu stellen, denen sie sich durch Geburt, wie sie es verstand, zugehörig fühlte. Sie hatte keine Wahl" (Gordimer, 1994; 2007: 28). Wichtig in unserem Kontext ist die Beziehung, die hier hergestellt wird, zwischen Selbstverständnis und dem Bemühen um einen Bezug zu den gesellschaftlichen Verhältnissen und Umständen, denen sie sich gegenübersieht. Solidarität scheint für Gordimers Aktivistin zu bedeuten, sich bewusst zu der Situation und den Verhältnissen zu verhalten, in denen sie sich befindet (denen sie sich zugehörig fühlt) – was auch ein besseres Verständnis ihrer selbst nach sich zieht. In diesem Lichte betrachtet, bedeutet das Entwickeln von Solidarität, einen Zusammenhang von Abhängigkeiten zu realisieren (im doppelten Wortsinne des Erkennens und Verwirklichens). Wir sind immer schon *in* der gesellschaftlichen Welt, und folglich sind wir Teil eines Netzwerks wechselseitiger sozialer Abhängigkeiten. Das heißt, unsere eigene Lage ist – frei- oder unfreiwillig – verbunden mit den Situationen der Anderen. So erklärt sich der Sinn einer Äußerung von Léon Bourgeois, dem Begründer des *solidarisme,* einer französischen Geistesbewegung im 19. Jahrhundert: „Wer versteht, dass er ein assoziiertes Wesen ist, handelt solidarisch." Solidarität verweist also auf die Fähigkeit, sich aktiv und positiv in Verbindung zu setzen und die gesellschaftlichen Bindungen und wechselseitigen Abhängigkeiten zu formen, in die die*der Einzelne faktisch immer schon eingebunden ist. Aber auch wenn die Solidarität auf der Tatsache der Eingebundenheit, des Assoziiert-Seins gründet, scheint ihre Entstehung immer brüchig und in gewissem Maße kontingent, nicht notwendig zu sein.

Das Problem der Arbeitslosigkeit oder auch die neoliberalen Angriffe auf den Sozialstaat gab es schon jahrelang, als sie in einem gewissen Moment von einer studentischen Bewegung in Frankreich thematisiert wurden; die französischen und deutschen Werktätigen hätten im Ersten Weltkrieg gute Gründe gehabt, die Arbeitersolidarität hochzuhalten, anstatt sich gegenseitig auf dem Schlachtfeld zu bekämpfen (eine der ersten großen Niederlagen, die die Idee der *internationalen Solidarität* zu verkraften hatte); und es dauerte sehr lange, bis die Frauenemanzipationsbewegung das kollektive Bewusstsein der Frauen soweit entwickelt hatte, dass diese ihr gemeinsames Schicksal erkannten – ein Prozess, der für verschiedene ethnische bzw. soziale Minderheiten noch im Gange ist. Zu jeder Zeit scheint es viel mehr gute Gründe für Solidarität zu geben als tatsächliche Ergebnisse solidarischen Handelns. Dieser Umstand verweist nicht nur auf Gegebenheiten, die mit der Problematik kollektiven Handelns *(collective action)* und der Theorie sozialer Bewegungen zu tun haben. Die Bereitschaft zu solidarischem Handeln lässt sich scheinbar nicht direkt allein auf die Herkunft oder Lebenslage einer Person zurückführen.

In dieser Hinsicht scheint es keine fixierte, feste oder sichere Grundlage für Solidarität zu geben, weder in den kulturellen oder geschichtlichen Ursprüngen einer Person oder Gruppe, noch in ihren sozialen, geografischen oder organisatorischen Ähnlichkeiten oder gar ihren objektiv gemeinsamen Interessen. Folglich ist sogar der Ausspruch „Wir sitzen alle im selben Boot" Gegenstand der Interpretation. Teilweise ist das so, weil wir niemals in nur einer Hinsicht *assoziiert* sind. Wir sind für uns der Mittelpunkt verschiedener Beziehungen, die uns verbinden: mit einer Nation, einer Klasse, einem Geschlecht, einer sexuellen Orientierung oder verschiedenen Lebensformen – und es ist überhaupt nicht klar, aus welcher dieser Gemeinsamkeiten eine Grundlage für Solidarität entstehen wird. Soll man sich als schwarze lesbische Professorin in den Vereinigten Staaten, beispielsweise, auf die schwarze Gemeinschaft in der ganzen Welt beziehen (auf die *afrikanische Diaspora*), auf Frauen an sich (schwarze und weiße, lesbische und heterosexuelle), auf Homosexuelle (also auch Männer), auf die gehobene Mittelklasse oder auf die akademische Gemeinschaft? Jede dieser Kategorien steht für eine mögliche Identifikationsquelle, aber keine davon zwingt jemanden, tatsächlich dementsprechend zu handeln. Es kann Gründe geben, sich mit einer dieser Gruppen zu identifizieren; etwa weil die Professorin realisiert, dass sie trotz ihres beruflichen Erfolgs als Schwarze oder als Frau diskriminiert worden ist. Aber die bloße Tatsache der Zugehörigkeit schafft noch keinen zwingenden Grund für Solidarität. Das heißt, es gibt keinen verborgenen Wesenskern kollektiver Identität, aus der Solidarität automatisch erwachsen würde.

Solidaritätsappelle, die sich auf Eigenschaften wie das Frau-Sein, Schwarz-Sein oder etwas Anderes beziehen, *erschaffen* das Subjekt ihrer Anrufung ebenso sehr wie sie zuvor latent bestehende Eigenschaften *entdecken*. Ja, die gesellschaftliche Tatsache, dass jemand als Frau oder als Schwarze*r behandelt – etwa unterdrückt – wird, ist wirkmächtiger als das bloße biologische Faktum. *Bewusstseinsbildung* ruft ein Bewusstsein nicht von biologischen, sondern von sozialen Tatsachen hervor.

Dies trifft selbst für das alte Problem des Klassenbewusstseins zu: Offenkundig entschieden sich Teile der Arbeiterklasse im Ersten Weltkrieg, sich mit der französischen bzw. deutschen Nation zu identifizieren, statt mit dem Klassenkampf. Aus einem klassisch-marxistischen Blickwinkel gälte dies als *Scheitern* auf dem Weg zum *Klassenbewusstsein*, auf dem Weg von der Klasse *an sich* zur Klasse *an sich und für sich*. So aber können wir unmöglich argumentieren, sofern wir nicht annehmen, dass es einen außer Frage stehenden, verborgenen *Wesenskern* der Identität gibt. Folglich ist die Tatsache des Assoziiert-Seins – die sogar *hinter dem Rücken der*des Einzelnen* bestehen mag – zu aktualisieren als die Bereitwilligkeit, sich mit einer bestimmten Situation (einem *gemeinsamen Schicksal*) zu identifizieren und solidarisch zu handeln. Das *Wir* der solidarischen Gruppe muss sich erst konstituieren, um zu sein. Das heißt, Solidarität verwirklicht *(aktualisiert)* sich nur als gemeinsame Praxis und in dieser Praxis entsteht die Fähigkeit *für einander einzutreten.* Die gemeinsamen Projekte bzw. Ziele beschränken sich daher nicht auf das *gemeinsame Schicksal* einer Gruppe, wie es augenscheinlich durch die bestehenden gesellschaftlichen Umstände (vor-)gegeben sein mag und dann auf dieser Grundlage streng interpretiert wird. Die interessanteste Frage hinsichtlich der Solidarität lautet also, wie man von einem *gemeinsamen Schicksal* zu *gemeinsamen Zielen* gelangt.

Daraus ergeben sich einige Konsequenzen für die oben behandelten Fragen. Die Tatsache, dass das *Wir* des solidarischen Handelns nicht einfach (vor-)gegeben ist, sondern konstituiert werden muss, eröffnet ein Potenzial der Erweiterung, der Ausdehnung solidarischer Beziehungen. Vermittelt durch einen Sinn für Zusammenarbeit bzw. durch gemeinsame Ziele, bietet der Solidarisierungsprozess bisweilen die Möglichkeit einer Integration und Inklusion von Anderen. Nehmen wir zum Beispiel den Berliner Bauarbeiterstreik von 1998, der mit Forderungen nach dem Ausschluss ausländischer Leiharbeiter*innen begann und – auf seinem Höhepunkt – mit Forderungen nach besseren Löhnen und Sozialversicherung für Alle endete. Abermals scheint hier die Offenheit für Inklusion von der Fähigkeit abhängig gewesen zu sein, die eigene Lage als veränderbar wahrzunehmen. Damit soll nicht geleugnet werden, dass derselbe Prozess sehr häufig zu Ausschlüssen führt. Aber auch wenn es stimmt, dass die Solidarität keine feste Grundlage hat und dass es ein Potenzial ihrer Erweiterung gibt, so ist Solidarität doch keine voluntaristische Option. Insofern ist Solidarität weder (vor-)gegeben noch erfunden. Man kann die eigene Lage falsch erfassen und bestimmte Solidaritäten ablehnen. Solidarisches Handeln kann die Realisierung wechselseitiger Abhängigkeiten zwischen den eigenen Umständen und denen der Anderen zur Folge haben, welche man nur um den Preis der Ohnmacht gegenüber diesen Umständen verleugnen kann. Nehmen wir die Notwendigkeit internationaler Sozialgesetzgebung bzw. Arbeitnehmer*innenrechte, die eine Konsequenz jener Erfahrungen der Bauarbeiter*innen sein kann: Die Realisierung wechselseitiger internationaler Abhängigkeiten kann die Arbeiter*innen zur Reaktion auf eine Situation befähigen, der sie andernfalls hilflos gegenüberstünden. Bezugnehmend auf die obige Analyse: Die Erweiterung von Solidarität ist nicht ausschließlich angewiesen auf die Vertiefung unserer Empathiefähigkeit, wie Rorty (1989) zu behaupten scheint, sondern auch darauf, sich der „Tatsache des Assoziiert-Seins" bewusst zu werden und sich dazu zu verhalten. Jedoch scheinen objektive Trends diese Art von Solidarität zu erschweren, und zugleich auch notwendiger zu machen.

4. Entsolidarisierung

Welche Lehren für unser Verständnis von Solidarität und ihres möglichen Niedergangs in den modernen Gesellschaften lassen sich daraus ziehen? Wenn Solidarität von der Fähigkeit abhängt, sich der wechselseitigen Abhängigkeiten und Beziehungen bewusst zu sein, die uns mit Anderen verbinden, dann muss der *Niedergang* der Solidarität – ihr möglicher Verlust – beschrieben werden als die Unfähigkeit, diese Verbindung herzustellen. Interessanter als individuelle Defizite sind hier die gesellschaftlichen und strukturellen Hindernisse, welche die Menschen und sozialen Gruppen daran hindern, dieses Bewusstsein zu erlangen. Entsolidarisierung meint nicht einfach das *Nicht-verbunden-sein,* meint nicht einfach gleichgültig oder *atomisiert* sein; sondern sie ist ein Ausdruck einer Unverbundenheit zwischen Einzelnen, die wirklich miteinander zu tun haben bzw. abhängig voneinander sind und gute Gründe hätten, solidarische Bande zu knüpfen. Das heißt, dass diese ihre Unabhängigkeit gewissermaßen illusorisch ist. Dieses Entsolidarisierungsgefühl kann als soziale *Entfremdung* kritisiert werden: als Entfremdung von etwas, mit dem man tatsächlich zu tun hat oder zu tun haben sollte. Eine Situation, in der wichtige Dimensionen der Gesellschaftsstruktur *verborgen* oder undurchsichtig sind (sodass die Menschen folglich nicht in der Lage sind, sich dazu zu verhalten bzw. mit ihr zu identifizieren), kann als *entfremdend* angesehen werden. Angesichts der gesellschaftlichen Diagnose eines *Untergangs der Solidarität* stellt sich bei der Untersuchung unserer gegenwärtigen Kapazitäten für die Solidarität nicht so sehr die Frage, was wir *gemein* haben. Die Frage ist spezifischer, nämlich: ob unsere Gemeinsamkeiten uns befähigen, uns gegenüber den gesellschaftlichen Institutionen, die unser Leben prägen, als agierende Subjekte anzusehen.

Bibliografie

Amengual, G.: 1990, Gattungswesen als Solidarität. Die Auffassung vom Menschen in der Bestimmung des Gattungswesens als Begriff und Grundlegung der Solidarität, in: H.-J. Braun et al. (Hrsg.), *Ludwig Feuerbach und die Philosophie der Zukunft,* **Akademie Verlag, Berlin, S. 345–367.**

Brudney, D.: 1999, *Marx' Attempt to Leave Philosophy,* **Harvard University Press, Harvard.**

Durkheim, É.: 1893, *De la division du travail social,* **Presses Universitaires de France, Paris. Deutsch: 1992,** *Über soziale Arbeitsteilung. Studie über die Organisation höherer Gesellschaften,* **Suhrkamp: Frankfurt am Main, übers. v. L. Schmidts (durchges. v. M. Schmid).**

Gordimer, N.: 1994, *None to accompany me*, Bloomsbury, London. Deutsch: 2007, *Niemand, der mit mir geht*, Süddeutsche Zeitung Bibliothek: München, übers. v. F. Kuhn (1995).

Habermas, J.: 1998, *Die Einbeziehung des Anderen*, Suhrkamp, Frankfurt am Main.

Hegel, G. W. F.: 1987, *Vorlesungen zur Philosophie des Rechts*, Suhrkamp, Frankfurt am Main.

Honneth, A.: 1993, Posttraditionale Gemeinschaften, in: H. Brunkhorst und M. Brumlik (Hrsg.), *Gemeinschaft und Gerechtigkeit. Ein konzeptueller Vorschlag*, Fischer, Frankfurt am Main, S. 260–270.

hooks, b.: 1995, *Killing Rage: Ending Racism*, Holt, New York.

Radin, M. J.: 1996, *Contested Commodities*, Harvard University Press, Harvard.

Rorty, R.: 1989, *Contingency, Irony, Solidarity*, Cambridge University Press, Cambridge. Deutsch: 1989, *Kontingenz, Ironie und Solidarität*, Suhrkamp, Frankfurt am Main, übers. v. Christa Krüger.

Sartre, J.-P.: 1960, *Critique de la Raison Dialectique*, Gallimard, Paris. Deutsch: 1967, *Kritik der dialektischen Vernunft*, Rowohlt, Reinbek bei Hamburg, übers. v. Traugott König.

Taylor, C.: 1985, The Nature and Scope of Distributive Justice, in: ders., *Philosophy and the Human Sciences. Philosophical Papers 2*, Cambridge University Press, Cambridge, S. 289–317. Deutsch: 1988, Wesen und Reichweite distributiver Gerechtigkeit (1985), in: ders., *Negative Freiheit? Zur Kritik des neuzeitlichen Individualismus*, Suhrkamp, Frankfurt am Main, übers. v. H. Kocyba, S. 145–187.

Theunissen, M.: 1982, *Selbstverwirklichung und Allgemeinheit. Zur Kritik des gegenwärtigen Bewußtseins* (1981), De Gruyter, Berlin/New York.

Tugendhat, E.: 1994, *Vorlesungen über Ethik*, Suhrkamp, Frankfurt am Main.

Walzer, M.: 1983, *Spheres of Justice*, Basic Book, New York.

Wildt, A.: 1992, Solidarität, in: J. Ritter und K.-F. Gründer (Hg.), *Historisches Wörterbuch der Philosophie*, Bd. 8, Wissenschaftliche Buchgesellschaft, Darmstadt, S.1004.

Wildt, A.: 1995, Zur Begriffs- und Ideengeschichte von Solidarität, in: K. Bayertz, *Solidarität. Begriff und Problem*, Frankfurt am Main, S. 202–216.

---

1   Anmerkung des Übersetzers: Eine frühere Fassung dieses Aufsatzes erschien in: R. ter Meulen, W. Arts, R. Muffels (Hg.), *Solidarity in Health and Social Care in Europe*, Kluwer, Dordrecht 2001, S. 287–308.

JOCHEN BECKER

Fugitive Co
Scale Wo
Solida
Cosmopol
After

mmunities.
rk, Digital
ity and
an Politics
olitics

Jochen Becker

Fugitive Communities
Scale Work, Digital Solidarity and Cosmopolitan Politics
After Politics

In 2012 a group of refugees led a long protest march across Germany and held hunger strikes at the Brandenburg Gate, before setting up a protest camp on Oranienplatz in Berlin's neighbourhood of Kreuzberg. The refugees' demands and actions need to be understood as part of a broad movement of urban activism. Their struggle for what Henri Lefebvre called the "right to the city" generated spaces of political resonance and new practices for a future urban society—and not only this.

The refugees' actions and their moving sites of protest need to be understood as one aspect of the production of the cosmopolitan city that Berlin repeatedly claims to be. The refugees' militant appropriation of public space and their new forms of politicisation and mobilisation have implications for the whole city, and for all Berliners. They are exemplary attempts at developing strategies for an urban society that actively promotes an urban citizenship, in the sense of equal rights shared by all.[1]

Those who have played a crucial role in shaping the city and its atmosphere[2] can see that their scope for participating in the city they have helped produce is now steadily diminishing. Gentrification is driving them from their homes by making them unaffordable. As the urban theorist David Harvey puts it, "The population of Turkish descent, have suffered many indignities, and have largely been forced out of the city centre. Their contribution to Berlin as a city is ignored."[3] The initiative

Kotti&Co[4] has successfully fought for the right to the city, housing and work places under the slogan "Wir bleiben Innenstadt" (we remain the inner city). It operates as a networked field of (re-)production that includes jobs and wages, housing and work. Thus the right to the city covers every aspect of urban life.

Though their influence on the national or even the global space should not be exaggerated, it is fair to say that these struggles have consequences that go far beyond the limits of the cities themselves. The urban setting is a strategically limited testing ground, though one that has long been permeated by transnational movements, currents, interests and concerns. Great urban centres are testing grounds offering spaces of resonance. What is discussed and decided in Berlin, the "capital of the most powerful of the states that dominate the construction of Europe"[5]—or in a comparable city-state like Hamburg—can have significance far beyond its own borders. The basis of the "summer of migration"—that autonomous movement of migration across the so-called *Balkan route* in 2015—was a decision by the federal government in Berlin to temporarily suspend the binding powers of the EU's Dublin Regulation, a decision that had rhizomatic links with urban activism beyond the city's government.

Interweavings
Berlin today is seeing networked urban initiatives win local referendums, rewrite laws, overturn planned development projects, negotiate handwritten agreements with politicians and generally manage to change how the city's administration routinely functions. The urban activism of the various local initiatives has recently broadened its scope, joining forces in intercultural alliances to mobilise votes in referendums. Profound frustration with the behaviour of local government has led

them to weave together their activities to form a new urban citizenship: a citizenship of the inhabitants of Berlin, prepared to put in the time to work out complex subjects, and stubbornly determined enough to implement their demands both in the political realm and in practice.[6] Here is it worth considering the experiences of Hamburg's PlanBude,[7] which has assumed a degree of responsibility over planning control in the city's neighbourhood of St. Pauli, testing new ways of "producing desires" and forcing planning authorities and owners to accept their proposals.[8]

For some time now, the struggle has no longer been about the particular interests of refugees, the elderly or tenants affected by gentrification, but rather the collectively fought right to the city: "my right is your right"[9] instead of "not in my backyard". An urban network is developing through a process of social and structural interweaving and spreading through both the social and media world, with the effect—as the French philosopher Étienne Balibar puts it—"of producing a hybrid political agent, located in a particular place where, on a transnational (and in this sense 'cosmopolitan') scale, global conflicts encounter each other in a singular way and are capable of having real consequences."[10]

In what follows, this article will examine this process of digitally supported interweaving and the fugitive communities involved in it. How can urban activism be thought and practiced on a "cosmopolitan scale", beyond the tranquil field of local politics? Can social media, codes and programming help translate and bridge the different scales between the local and the global? Answering these questions will involve examining shifts in hacker cultures, which following an initial period of euphoria have turned into an integral part of cognitive capitalism. At the same time, new actors, as the French philosopher Geoffroy de Lagasnerie describes them, are reaching beyond the narrow confines of hacker cultures that aim merely at optimising systems. In so doing, they may be opening up a new space of fugitive communities, embedded in the digital world and continually constituting themselves anew.

Scale Work

The "question of the European public" is primarily posed at the local level: how can the policies of small groups, initiatives or neighbourhood associations organise locally, while simultaneously thinking of themselves as—for example—part of a European project and democratically realising their aims at a higher level? At least at the national level, collaboration between the Spanish neighbourhood assemblies and the newly emerged political party Podemos has offered a model for practice that has been closely followed from Berlin to Athens. This means constantly rethinking the role of administration in local and national government: David Harvey quotes the urban theorist Andrew Sancton when he writes, "municipalities are more than just providers of services. They are democratic mechanisms through which territorially based communities of people govern themselves at a local level."[11]

Who or what, then, can emerge as intermediaries without walking into the trap of representative and deputised politics? How should the experiences and practices of the street be translated onto the level of the whole city, the state or even the European continent? After all, as Harvey observes, it is "much easier […] to organise and enforce collective and cooperative action with strong participation of local inhabitants in smaller jurisdictions".[12] He raises here the central question of scale, that is, of the size of the social unit we are operating in: "as we 'jump scales' […] so the whole nature of the commons problem […] changes dramatically. What looks like a good way to resolve problems at one scale does not hold at another scale […] patently good solutions at one scale (the 'local', say) do not necessarily aggregate up (or cascade down) to make for good solutions at another scale (the global, for example)."[13]

It is even difficult to imagine how we would negotiate the "right to the city": how, for example, would Berlin's 3.5 million inhabitants negotiate this right among themselves? How, writes Harvey, "does one organise a city? This, it seems to me, is one of the key questions the left will have to answer if anti-capitalist struggle is to be revitalised in the years to come".[14] He comes to the open conclusion: "the honest answer to this question […] is: we simply do not know".[15]

Digital Solidarity

It may be that some prospect of solving the problem of scale will emerge by means of converting politics into algorithms, establishing technology-supported networks and embedding protocols. In 2013 the Zurich media theorist Felix Stalder published a pamphlet entitled *Digital Solidarity,* in which he considered new forms of digitally-supported solidarity that broke new ground in terms of social scalabilities: "something like a common culture is emerging: a culture of autonomy and solidarity".[16] From this he develops the idea that the new forms of digital solidarity are characterised by participation, and less by the representative structures of parliamentary politics or party affiliation. "This does not mean that there is no leadership at all, but it is based on the ability to gain supporters, participants and advisers and disappears as soon as this ability fails."[17]

Stalder classifies these new forms of solidarity, based on increasingly complex technologies, into four basic types: "commons, assemblies, swarms and dark networks".[18] This autonomous culture of solidarity grows in parallel with the spread and complexity of the Internet and its computer-supported capacity. It is clearly technology-based, but on the other hand also draws on social skills that lie beyond the net. "Manuel Castells summarises these values as 'trust, tolerance and coexistence'. It might make sense to define them somewhat more precisely, as sharing, cooperation, individuality, participation and variety."[19] Action taken in solidarity with others is therefore not always a good thing per se; socially it is narrowly defined and is still in its early stages: "the new institutions […] are still in their infancy. And they are still being supported by a relatively small part of the population, above all by globalised young people."[20]

Work and everyday life are increasingly appearing in ever more social, communicative, complex and networked structures. The market is engulfing the social, just as the social is incorporating the market. "By the mid-nineties the sociologist Manuel Castells was already able to affirm that the real unit of production was no longer the firm but the network, consisting of firms or parts of firms of different sizes."[21] As a medium of communication, control and coordination, the Internet appears to be omnipresent. A "new and specifically cultural environment" is developing out of it, which strengthens, interconnects and integrates "partly marginalised practices which formerly bore no relation to each other".[22]

Anna Roth also points to the fact that the technological complex is socially and individually produced: "to critique domination and power on the assumption that technology is appropriating and exploiting (or in this case, using and controlling) 'us'—human beings, creativity, subjectivity, communication, society or simply 'life' itself—is to miss the point. It overlooks the fact that technology first has to constitute and generate what it appropriates and exploits."[23] In November 2016 Roth, a member of the communist group ...umsGanze!, helped organise the Hamburg congress reproduce(future): digital capitalism and the communist wager. "Should we disrupt the logic of the new technologies? Should we sever the interfaces, sabotage the technology and withdraw from them completely? Or should we appropriate the commons that has been assembled in technology, do we first need to take it over and redeem it?"[24] The Janus-faced nature of every new technology is apparent in the fact that liberation and enslavement can often barely be distinguished from each other.[25]

You'll be free
"Join us and share the software / You'll be free, hackers, you'll be free / Hoarders can get piles of money / That is true, hackers, that is true / But they cannot help their neighbours / That's not good, hackers, that's not good."[26]

The hacker pioneer Richard Stallman wrote this "Free Software Song" as a kind of "moral code" for the open source scene. In 1991 he even haltingly sang a version of it in $7/8$ time to the tune of a Bulgarian folk song. According to the song, self-liberation does not consist in making piles of money but in helping your neighbour, who in the age of the Internet should not be imagined in purely spatial terms. Up until the late 1980s, the small and scattered software community spontaneously collaborated and shared their source codes across long distances. Access to data—whether codes, information or digital objects—was to be free and fair, adaptable, constantly developing and unimpaired.[27] The production of proprietary software by companies such as Microsoft enclosed this commons, turning it into a commodity that could be licensed, monopolised and sold in a form that cannot be adapted.

At the same time, Stallman's 1984 GNU software, the new operating system called Linux popularised by Linus Torvalds in 1991, and the general accessibility of the Internet all helped promote the use of non-corporate software known as "open source", whose rapid spread enabled data and codes to continue to circulate freely. New versions of Linux were published in weekly, sometimes daily instalments, and were tested and improved by hundreds of users and programmers. In 2008 there were already over 150,000 software projects with over 1.5 million developers and hundreds of millions of users.

In his text, *The Cathedral and the Bazaar,* the hacker, programmer and part-time anthropologist Eric Raymond treats the differences between proprietary and free software as alternative blueprints for the organisation of production and even society. "Linux is subversive. […] It coalesced out of part-time hacking by several thousand developers scattered all over the planet, connected only by the tenuous strands of the Internet."[27] His widely-regarded text, written from the perspective of his own profession, is, as the writer and legal expert Janet Hope puts it, "perhaps even the cradle of a new social order".[28] Raymond's reflections on the subject, first published in 1997, describe the differences this way: "the 'cathedral' model of most of the commercial world versus the 'bazaar' model of the Linux world. I show that these models derive from opposing assumptions about the nature of the software-debugging task."[29]

Debugging is the often painstaking process of removing errors from a programme code, which is now carried out by a scattered swarm of user/programmers.[31] These users, whom Raymond also calls "co-developers", will "if given a bit of encouragement […] diagnose problems, suggest fixes and help improve the code far more quickly than you could unaided". According to Raymond, Linus Torvalds' pioneering achievement was not so much writing the Linux kernel as the programme's core as it was the invention of the Linux model: "Linus was treating his users as co-developers in the most effective possible way."[32] It was primarily the social dynamics[33] that it released (or instrumentalised) and the largely unpaid commitment by the "co-developers" that created a collective software system. The bazaar of user/developers shares the work among its members. In contrast to the (old) corporate hierarchies and the orientation towards profitability, the Linux community appears "to be a large, bewilderingly chattering bazaar of different aims and approaches".[34]

According to Janet Hope, open source production is characterised by "transparency, exploitation of peer review and feedback loops, low cost and ease of engagement, and a mixture of formal and informal governance mechanisms, built around a shared set of technical goals".[35] Open source is based on voluntary engagement and the spontaneity of the market. It is a loosely coordinated puzzle, put together by peers. Since there are no formal thresholds for entry and exit, people come and go. Each user finds his own place on the basis of his abilities and preferences. The weaknesses of the bazaar principle are ultimately also its strengths;[36] they are precisely such elements as "long-term relationships", "reciprocal fairness" and "books being kept open",[37] as well as its horizontal organisation and the "collective".[38] The "invention-inducement"[39] is faster, more robust, more reliable and cheaper,[40] and the "usefulness"[41] of open source software is capable of producing use values instead of exchange values. In addition, the principle of the bazaar produces a new way of living together: "in the open source software context, empirical research indicates that these include fun, learning [...] and the sense of belonging to a community".[42]

In his vivid contrast of the cathedral with the bazaar, Raymond links questions of software production to models of a future society and economy: "the development of a leadership style and set of cooperative customs that could allow developers to attract co-developers and get maximum leverage from the medium."[43]

Raymond's impassioned and illuminating[44] text has since been followed by sobering analyses that describe this "open source world" as—to use the words of Maurizio Lazzarato—"cognitive capitalism". Even the Android operating system, introduced by Google in 2008, is based, albeit with certain qualifications, on open source codes.[45] What Luc Boltanski and Ève Chiapello call the "new spirit of capitalism" of the "creative industries" (apart from programming, John Howkins' concept covers advertising, architecture, art, craft, design, fashion, film, music, visual art, publishing, research and development, toys and games, television, radio and video games)[46] has given rise to a thoroughly heterogeneous "creative class".[47] Grotesque inequalities and working conditions often reminiscent of early capitalism are now leading to struggles within the "creative class" itself. Here it is worth mentioning the successful campaign "Mediaspree versenken" (sink the Mediaspree), which not only managed to prevent the construction of a cluster of buildings, part of the so-called creative industry settlement, along the river Spree in Berlin, but in so doing also brought to attention the conflict between the data jobbers who are being pushed out by gentrification and a class of creative industrialists backed by capital. The campaign resulted in a local referendum entitled "Spreeufer für alle" (Spree for everyone), which in 2008 was supported by 87 percent of local residents.

"Bazaar Governance"

"Even at a higher level of design, it can be very valuable to have the thinking of lots of co-developers random-walking through the design space near your product. Consider the way a puddle of water finds a drain, or better yet how ants find food: exploration essentially by diffusion, followed by exploitation mediated by a scalable communication mechanism."[48]

Hope develops from Raymond's design the concept of "bazaar governance", "a governance structure with incentives and control mechanisms distinct from those of markets, firm hierarchies, and networks".[49] Ideas about how to optimise software are read as techniques by the "bazaar governance structure" to manage states or enterprises in a different way. This "non-market form of governance"[50] would not build any hierarchical cathedrals that are "centrally coordinated through the authoritative directions of managers or leaders".[51] Using the model of "bazaar governance", Hope aims to scale the bazaar principle up from the relatively closed milieu of the hacker world to the level of everyday life and how it is governed. And she anticipates—in contrast to her hypothesis of a "non-market form of governance"—at least the commodification of intellectual work in current processes of value creation as part of a regime of "cognitive capitalism". But does this hypothesis also apply to political action?

Protocols shape standards of programming as well as of politics. "A bazaar-style or open source approach to technology development promotes the adoption of useful standards because the transparency of open source tools means it is obvious which technology is best for any given platform function."[52] As Andra Bonaccorsi and Cristian Rossi have shown, "software itself is a convention or a common language in which errors can be identified and corrected by the mechanism of compilation".[53] The inherent transparency of open codes makes the prospect of transferring them to political systems very seductive. Technological standards can even support and shape non-virtual cooperation: "protocols are therefore not merely available at the technical level, but also structure perspectives, rules and patterns of behaviour at all levels by functioning as interpretative frameworks. In this way, they provide a certain cultural homogeneity, a set of shared features which primarily lend these formations their common character."[54] On the whole there is a consensus about using protocols (and generally also the English language). The Simple Mail Transfer Protocol (SMTP), for example, has been accepted and used as an open email protocol by billions of people since it was developed in 1982.

Participation in traditional social networks offering purely physical or unilateral possibilities for contacting others was always limited to a relatively small number of individuals. Once this got beyond a certain number, finding a consensus became practically impossible. "These experiences gave rise to the worldview that propagated 'smallness' as a central value ('small is beautiful')."[55] Data processing by computers has made finding a consensus appreciably easier, even among large numbers of participants.[56] "In fact, pretty well all of us in the open-source world drastically underestimated how well it would scale up with number of users and against system complexity."[57] In addition, a social reality and social practice that were increasingly embedded in the digital world formed a laboratory for social experiments and the discovery of new social alliances. There is also the fact that technically-adept communities tend to develop a pronounced pragmatism. "We reject: kings, presidents and elections. We believe in: broad consensus and running codes."[58] This is how the computer scientist David D. Clark formulates the basic assumption of a pragmatic and technically adept (counter-)culture based on horizontal and voluntary cooperation, diverse social relations and general trust. Individuals cannot entirely block decisions, concrete solutions are generally sought, and everyone takes for granted a socially, ethnically and sexually homogeneous group[59] in which differences can be resolved.

Here the debates are held through mailing lists, newsgroups and chat systems in which many people can communicate with many others flexibly and incorporating time delays. "In this way, digital technologies and the social activism of individual users become intermeshed to an unprecedented degree."[60] The introduction of smartphones has made microcomputers constantly available. In the West, Internet access and, still more, envelopment by digital clouds have now become taken for granted, like water or electricity.

The invention of open source enabled programming to become a collective task carried out by scattered agents, and allowed programme codes to be understood as a form of commons. The development of archives, filters and search functions enabled programmers to both organise large quantities of data and exchange and develop software over the Internet. At the same time, a great deal of work was saved by algorithms[61] that automatised, filtered, aggregated, weighed and translated material, helping individuals to create ever larger networks. They did this not only by their "ability to search, filter and extract […] and to ignore the rest without entirely suppressing it, and keeping it available for possible future consideration."[62]

Blockchain technologies, such as the Bitcoin currency, can be used to set up collaborative trust protocols which can be anonymously regulated by their own users, thereby eliminating the need to involve either the state or corporations. By contrast, Google still helps people keep an overview of the billions of websites that can no longer be taken in at a glance.

But what is also clear—as the editors of this publication have rightly observed—is that Google's search machines use a non-transparent algorithm to select the results of keyword searches.

Most people know about the system's darker sides, since data companies like Google stockpile and commercially exploit "their" codes and pre-processed information in closed or secret systems. By contrast, shared data systems such as Wikipedia, DuckDuckGo or Open Street Map have only been able to gain acceptance within a narrow context. "Open data are an important precondition to being able to use the power of algorithms democratically. They are a precondition to the effective diversity of algorithms, since anyone can write his own algorithm or assign someone else to process data in a different way and with respect to different research or activity interests."[63]

Meshing together
By digitalising all areas of life (social networks) and soon also individual objects (Internet of things), "Big Data" is getting close to offering data that is increasingly dispersed and not systematically available through any library or publishing house. Feedback systems enable the corporate systems to progressively learn from their users' searches, and they are already able to communicate with us in everyday language through programmes such as "Siri", Apple's digital speech assistant. At the same time, these digital realities based on algorithms have started to be translated into social practices. So for example, methods of digitally organising and structuring communication are carried over into physical contacts. In this way, the physical and digital worlds are becoming

integrated and mutually influencing each other. In effect, people today have many more friends, followers or comrades in solidarity who can be mobilised in at the shortest notice, who can receive information more quickly, and who can coordinate with each other across wide differences of scale in matters both large and small.

In the initial stages of a movement or initiative, digital technologies can be used to leave the issue of space and time scales open. "Building up long-term institutional structures is always difficult. But it is often unnecessary, at least at the beginning."[64] Calling neighbourhood meetings and real space occupations at short notice enables participants to discuss and share experiences, which they can then spread, develop and distribute through the digital world.

"Weak networks" such as Facebook can be useful here. "They are often called the 'social Internet' or 'Web 2.0'. These labels are unfortunate, since the important part of them are not their technologies but the social formations and cultures that have developed through their use. The immense popularity of 'weak networks' has made them a new basis of what (inter)personal communication means today […]. They are the new normality."[65] These "weak networks" enable diverse groups to interconnect in easy-to-learn ways, allowing information to travel quickly from one mesh to another. "They create 'small worlds', because they create the structural conditions for efficiently sharing information across large social distances."[66] At the same time, the danger arises that pre-set, personalised filters will trap people in these closed and automatised "small worlds".

While the administration of large networks was once the preserve of elites, with their international conferences, clubs and assistants, this privilege became "quantitatively speaking, democratised. You no longer need a personal secretary who remembers the birthdays of five hundred people."[67] By using new forms of operability and visualisation, politics can more easily zoom in and out between individual people and masses assembled in front of computer screens or in public squares. "The order of scale can be adjusted for a particular purpose, and not only on maps."[68]

Not in Our Name

The French philosopher Geoffroy de Lagasnerie suggests that "Snowden and Assange could be the starting points of a refoundation of a radical political philosophy that would be about subjecting as many realities as possible to open consideration."[69] Like Stalder, he assigns the Internet an important role in reshaping social relations. So for example, he asks "whether the Internet is capable of effecting a break with the influence of the general conditions of socialisation, which are both imposed on us and taken for granted."[70] Thus the Internet might offer an "alternative space of socialisation"[71] and the option of a "*voluntary* socialisation".[72]

In contrast to Stalder's hope for a new, technologically supported politics of the street, square and forum, which would help socially established forms of politics achieve a greater scale, de Lagasnerie sees in the acts of Edward Snowden, Julian Assange and Chelsea Manning a form of singular politics that initiates a break with previous forms of the public. The three whistleblowers, all of whom had used the power of the Internet to spread information, break with many of the standards of (network) politics that have existed up until now.

Established politics demands physical involvement, requiring activists to use both their voices and faces. "To subjectivate yourself as a political subject means committing yourself to and publicly involving yourself in the game; it means entering the public space and making a declaration or expressing a protest or a concern *in front of everyone*."[73] By linking up together and publicly appearing in formations at strikes, blockades or demonstrations, bodies become understood as a form of political expression. "The political stage is one on which bodies assemble and occupy a place. By coming together, bodies make themselves visible and in so doing make visible the formation of a 'political body'".[74]

Becoming politically engaged is seen as an act of risk-taking that demands from the individual a certain price. In this way "a form of political pathos is established: the protest would demand that you show your body, that you reveal your identity."[75] When in the summer of 2014 refugees threatened to leap from the roof of the Gerhart-Hauptmann-Schule in Berlin's neighbourhood of Kreuzberg, this was a very public demonstration of the extreme self-sacrifice of the body and of what Giorgio Agamben calls "bare life". In the arena of normative politics, it is only when the demonstrator becomes a victim that he is really taken seriously.

Breaking with the Stage
By contrast, Snowden, Assange and Manning do not want to "sacrifice" themselves for their cause, but seek rather to evade the threat of a trial and state intervention by taking refuge in anonymity or asylum. At issue, then, is escaping the "problems of entering the public space" and "developing the struggle by laying claim to a practice of anonymity and non-appearance."[76] Here de Lagasnerie finds political subjects who articulate new forms of subjectivation:[77] *"they call into question the political stage itself"*, and in so doing develop a "radicality of destabilisation".[78]

The stage of public space—whether a public square, a parliament, a court of law or a medium—is considered the classic scene of protest. De Lagasnerie asks, "which implicit notion of politics and resistance do we adopt when we spontaneously ascribe more 'value' to large-scale mobilisations in public spaces than to the solitary actions of a hacker?"[79] He would like to make us consider the possibility that "a singular movement is highly unlikely to be recognised as such", unless it makes use of "a language that already exists".[80] It is only when a political action fits within a pre-existing framework of protest that it is generally recognised as such. "Doing politics means taking up pre-existing forms, adapting oneself to sedimented structures and working with them to achieve a concrete result by a particular point in time."[81] This has the consequence that either new forms are not recognised, or that a familiar pattern becomes imposed upon them .

De Lagasnerie distinguishes civil disobedience as a classic form of political action from a "critique of the operations of the law and of the political order".[82] Instead of inventing a new form of politics, the public dissident of the old school remains a subject of the state. "Despite its apparently unique and radical character, civil disobedience stands in continuity with the most traditional democratic forms. Its prime quality is to be public. The disobedient subject or collective must quite deliberately be disobedient publicly and in front of everyone."[83] Chelsea Manning, however, only became a public person against his/her own will and after being denounced to the security services. He/she would have very much preferred if the leaked information on the brutal US war in Iraq had gone out into the world without his/her name attached to it.[84]

Anonymity vs. Solidarity

Solidarity—understood as an attitude of sympathy and support for the ideas, activities and aims of others—presupposes visibility, identifiability and a public presence. Wikipedia defines "solidarity" as "cohesiveness among like-minded individuals and groups acting on equal terms, and their commitment to common values". Solidarity unifies people in the public moment, in a widely shared and broadly understood sense of togetherness. Though "international solidarity" is highly abstract, it is not based on anonymity but rather upon symbols, names and representations. Given the increasingly complex and global nature of human relations, individuals in solidarity with others must now be prepared to form contacts and become involved over great distances.

By contrast, Manning could have quite happily done without the greetings of solidarity from what Che Guevara called the "kindness of peoples" that have been sent to his military prison. Had his/her identity not been revealed, he/she might still be working today within the military apparatus. "Manning *acted politically, but without any public support.*"[85] He/she is therefore not to be defined as an outsider: "the function of anonymity is to give insiders the means of getting information out of the institution and to the public."[86] It was above all anonymity that made it possible for Manning to "constitute him/herself as a politically protesting subject"[87] Standing in solidarity with someone you don't know would not have been possible.

Beyond Accountability

"These people were and are dispersed. They do not act together as a concentrated unit, but in isolation. Nevertheless, the virtual collective they embody constitutes one of the crucial sites for reformulating contemporary politics and reformulating the demand for democracy."[88] De

Lagasnerie sees in the actions of Snowden, Assange and Manning "the fault line that contains the novelty of what is emerging through them, while simultaneously making possible this novelty."[89] While the dissenter appeals to the just law, accepts norms as given and even goes to court for the sake of them, the new protagonists evade and escape this consensus: "Snowden, Assange and Manning [...] *embody a challenge to the law itself.*"[90]

Here the court of law is no longer the favoured public forum where dispute is publicly and demonstratively sought. While dissidents commonly think of themselves as being more law-abiding than the state, and on this basis offer themselves as a punishable subject for show trials, the act of systematically breaking with the system by withdrawing from it constitutes a new politics: "they put in question the very concept of a legally accountable subject".[91] Although, in contrast to Manning, Snowden and Assange deliberately entered the public arena, they nevertheless defected to "the solitary practice of exile. [...] They haven't let themselves be peacefully and passively arrested [...] any more than Manning has, for that matter. Their politics consisted in flight."[92] In this way they challenge the notion of the "legally accountable subject".

"it" hacks

The members of Anonymous act still more clandestinely; although their protest is articulated collectively, it never actually involves "gathering together in a group".[93] Like Assange's WikiLeaks project—which has set itself the aim of *"enabling the multiplication of political subjects that act anonymously"*[94]—Anonymous opens up clandestine or encrypted spaces. Sites should be created which "guarantee that the people using them cannot be followed [...] thereby enabling them to act covertly".[95] Before he/she was exposed, Manning never defined him/herself as an outsider: guaranteed anonymity gives insiders a means of bringing information to the public from within the institution. The "practice of anonymity"[96] recognises neither the law nor allegiance to the legal order, and therefore offers alternative spaces of action that are hidden, encrypted and anonymising (such as whistleblowing).

Groupings—or labels—such as Anonymous are not organised around a political line as a "diverse and structure less movement", but rather "around this new form of anonymous action".[97] They exercise power, but are not identifiable: they erase their own traces, and do not operate either by making conventional admissions of accountability, or using spokespeople or representatives. Rather it is an "it" that hacks, blocks and brutally reveals the truth to the light of the media public. It is this that distinguishes its "process of redistributing and dispersing places of protest"[98] from that of the criminal world, which also shuns the light of the state. Conversely, it also has nothing in common with hired system optimisers, who offer governments, services or companies their expertise as hackers.

Fugitive Communities

Borrowing from Foucault, de Lagasnerie encourages us "to think in terms of singularity, exception and therefore also of rupture".[99] The break effected by the three central figures of his book undermines the basic arrangements of the nation state, its sovereign power and the borders it has established. The deliberately dispersed actions of Snowden, Assange and Manning and the other hackers and whistleblowers challenges the very concept of the law, the nation and citizenship. "At issue was not statelessness but rather citizenship. Not the state of exception, but the rule and the normal functioning of constitutional state."[100] De Lagasnerie therefore suggests that we "imagine new, plural, heterogeneous and fugitive communities—and therefore also how to realise them".[101] By using existentially charged vocabularies such as statelessness, exile, "migration practice"[102] or flight, he brings together diverse projects into a common politicised arena, "in order to link the art of revolt with the practice of exile and flight".[103]

De Lagasnerie links the actions of "classic" refugees crossing the "Balkan route" or the Sahara to the political practice of the three whistleblowers: "Interpretations of migrant movements often depoliticise them. They are generally presented as movements forced upon people by economic rationales or wars. The reasons for emigration always seem to be sought on the realm of need, necessity or obligation, etc."[104] The new political subject, however, is deliberately stateless: "When the subject migrates, doesn't it effect a kind of coup d'etat?"[105] Instead of "manifesting itself as a 'we' that purports to be the people"[106] the refugee, the exile or the swarm withdraws from this politics of the masses. "The 'movement' is reducible to a juxtaposition of individual actions that are performed separately—and therefore can no longer be thought of in terms of a 'fusion'."[107] The community of fugitives is itself fugitive.

Dual Passport
In late July 2016, tens of thousands of European Turks, or Europeans with Turkish migration backgrounds, demonstrated in Cologne against the military coup in Turkey and in favour of the ruling Turkish president Recep Tayyip Erdogan. While contemplating the sea of red flags, Jakob Augstein, a regular commentator for the column "Im Zweifel links" (when in doubt, left) at *Spiegel Online* came to a surprising conclusion: "dual nationality was once thought of as a progressive project. That was a mistake".[108] Under the headline "we were wrong", he invokes the

biologically German national body of the "we" against the "they" who do not want to rally round the German flag.

The German author and entrepreneur Imran Ayata made this reply: "are migrants part of this 'we' or does it only include German Germans, that is, the Augsteins but not the Ayatas?" He reminded his readers that dual citizenship "was not a gift from the then-existing red-green government"[109] but the outcome of decades of protracted political struggles. For him, Augstein's narrow perspective heads in entirely the wrong direction: "today the borders between home and abroad, inside and outside, or 'us' and 'them' are disappearing. This does not only raise the necessity of rising to global challenges like migration and immigration."[110] He concludes by demanding an end to our subjection to nation states, and sees in the phenomenon of multiple citizenship a coming dissolution of enforced national allegiances.

What de Lagasnerie calls "the questioning of allegiances that we often spontaneously subject national structures to"[111] is currently being carried forward by certain clandestine Internet strategies, which include flight, forging national identity papers as well as a "democratic citizenship in the age of globalisation".[112] According to Balibar, the process of illegally crossing the borders of Europe must develop a new kind of practice as a "democratisation of borders"[113] and not be regulated by the authoritarian state. Democratising borders means "putting them at the service of people and subjecting them to their collective control, making them an object of their 'sovereignty'".[114]

However, research by the globalisation expert Saskia Sassen on the transnationalisation of work raises the question of whether a democratic border regime in Europe of the kind proposed by Balibar has not already been obsolete for some time. "What we still narrate in the language of immigration and ethnicity, I would argue, is actually a series of processes having to do with the globalisation of economic activity, of cultural activity, of identity formation. Too often immigration and ethnicity are constituted as otherness."[115] Sassen cannot see how a border could in principle be drawn around the global integration of everything and everyone, or indeed why it should be.

"No One Got Here First"
If then, as Sassen suggests, questions of ethnicity and cross border migration are irrelevant in our cities of the world, there is also no longer any privileged point from which decisions about inclusion and exclusion could be defined, so that, as Balibar puts it, "on the terrain of citizenship, no one 'got here first'".[116] In the negotiation of transnational spaces and structures "everyone, including the 'natives' (must) at least symbolically risk the identity as citizens that they have acquired or inherited from the past and *reconstruct it in the now,* together with others".[117] In a multi-focal world, diverse perspectives must simultaneously be taken into account. According to Balibar, we cannot "define a standpoint on the situation of the world and the tendencies of globalisation without considering ourselves from a global standpoint, which means: from the standpoint of a real universality, that is not (or is no longer) defined by that standpoint".[118]

"Manning and Assange have raised the question of what could be described as the black box of nation states [...] the problem of the relationships between secrecy, the right to know and democratic transparency."[119] The secret state shuts itself off from its citizens, while at the same time confining them as in a penal institution. "Being incarcerated within a state"[120] is how Lagasnerie describes a situation where "we as citizens are subject to a state that has arrogated the right to forbid us from leaving its territory".[121] He quotes John Kerry, then the US Secretary of State, who in reference to Snowden said that "patriots don't go to Russia".

And yet, "why should Snowden owe the United States anything?"[122] The whistleblower had his passport cancelled by the United States. Thus the duty of disobeying one's own state, to which one seems destined by birth, consists in "emancipating yourself from the order of the law [...] leaving the space of its 'jurisdiction' and thereby rejecting it, determining that as far as you are concerned [...] it is not longer *your* law".[123]

Can I free myself from the crime of one nation state by setting off for the sovereign territory of another? When a state denies its citizens their rights, the disenfranchised exercise their right to declare that they couldn't give a damn about the state. "The fact of flight, of immigration, of the explicit refusal to appear before the body that purports to administer justice in 'their' country (is it still their country?)"[124] distances people from the power of the state.

Both Snowden and Assange have become fugitives, but in contrast to gangsters this is part of their political agenda. "Becoming a fugitive means [...] freeing oneself from this sense of belonging, refusing it—and thereby questioning the legal mechanisms of membership of a national community, even questioning the mechanisms of belonging to other types of group that we are caught up in."[125]

Post-Babylon
"When politics was challenged in the name of the social, of social movements or of sociology, it still manifested itself in a variety of different ways and a variety of different places, from the street to the factory

to the university. Today the restoration of politics is expressed in the silence of these forms or in the absence of these places."[126] Jacques Rancière's alter-politics, which can here only be briefly outlined, is in no sense an anti-politics, but it does situate itself in an antagonistic and refracted relationship to a politics that formed the basis of the status quo of western societies. These conditions—representative democracy, liberalism, a constitutional and welfare state, etc.—are today passing away.

A post-Babylonian politics that is now emerging on the horizon "is made from global conditions".[127] In the cities of the world there are no longer any privileged points from which decisions can be defined regarding inclusion and exclusion. Everyone has to "integrate" into this new post-Babylon. With its standardised greeting, "Hello, citizens of the world, we are Anonymous",[128] Anonymous demonstratively leaves the "we" or the "people" behind. It remains to be seen how new, alter-political movements can be developed from the swarm of fugitive worlds, and how digital solidarity can be generated without physical contact. However, without some kind of rupture, without a politics after politics, things will not change: "for I have come to the conclusion that the political body [...] must at least stop regularly risking its own death or collapse by breaking with the consensus and invoking right against right".[129]

---

1   Urban citizenship is opposed to the conservative concept of a new bourgeois culture. It is primarily concerned not with values, morals and customs and the entrenchment of class differences, nor the frantic promotion of particular interests (such as the way homeowners in Hamburg's neighbourhood of Harvestehude opposed the establishment of a refugee hostel in the Sophienterassen). Rather it is about social openness, equal rights and the primacy of urban action. And it is also not to be confused with the new phenomenon of *Bürger-Arbeit* (citizens' work), a form of unpaid leisure activity that is carried out to compensate for the loss of welfare services.

2   "The ambience and attractiveness of a city, for example, is a collective product of its citizens, but it is the tourist trade that commercially capitalises upon that common [...] While this culturally created common cannot be destroyed through use, it can be degraded and banalised through excessive abuse." David Harvey, *Rebel Cities: From the Right to the City to the Urban Revolution,* London, Verso 2013, p. 74.
3   ibid., p. 107.
4   https://kottiundco.net
5   Étienne Balibar: *We, the People of Europe? Reflections on Transnational Citizenship,* Princeton, Princeton University Press 2004 / *Sind wir Bürger Europas? Politische Integration, soziale Ausgrenzung und die Zukunft des Nationalen,* Hamburg, Hamburger Edition 2003, p. 2.
6   For more on this, see Jochen Becker, "Place Internationale. Verwebungen städtischen Handelns: urban citizenship, conricerca, bizim şehir, Refugiés-Stadt", in Arno Brandlhuber, Florian Hertweck, Thomas Mayfried (eds.), *The Dialogic City,* Cologne, Verlag der Buchhandlung Walther König 2015.
7   www.planbude.de
8   Gesa Ziemer, "Stadt gemeinsam entwickeln. Neue Formen der Zusammenarbeit am Beispiel der Hamburger PlanBude" in Andrea Baier, Tom Hansing, Christa Müller, Karin Werner (eds.), *Die Welt reparieren. Open source und Selbermachen als postkapitalistische Praxis,* Bielefeld, Transcript-Verlag 2016.
9   www.myrightisyourright.de
10 Étienne Balibar, *Equaliberty: Political Essays,* Durham/London, Duke University Press 2014 / *Gleichfreiheit. Politische Essays,* Berlin, Suhrkamp 2012, p. 71 of German edition (italics in original).
11 Regarding these, Harvey himself suggests the following: "the organisation of informal labourers along traditional union lines, the pulling together of the Federation of neighbourhood associations, the politicisation of urban-rural relations, the creation of nested hierarchies and of leadership structures alongside egalitarian assemblies, the mobilisation of the forces of culture and of collective memories [...]" (Harvey 2013, p. 150).
12 Harvey 2013, p. 81.
13 Ibd., pp. 69–70.
14 Ibid., p. 135.
15 Ibid., p. 140.
16 Felix Stalder, *Digital Solidarity,* Lüneburg/London, PML Books 2013, p. 51.
17 Ibid., p. 54 f.
18 Ibid., p. 14.
19 Manuel Castells, *Communication Power,* Oxford, Oxford University Press 2009, quoted in Stalder 2013, p. 52.
20 Ibid., p. 57.
21 Manuel Castells, *The Rise of the Network Society: The Information Age: Economy, Society and Culture, Society and Culture, Vol. I,* Maiden/Oxford, Blackwell 1996 (second edition 2009), quoted in Felix Stalder, *Kultur der Digitalität,* Berlin, Suhrkamp 2016, p. 34.
22 Ibid., p. 95.
23 Anna Roth, "Wer nach der Technik fragt, fragt, wie diese Gesellschaft eigentlich funktioniert" Von Digitalisierung bis Big Data—Interview with Anna Roth (...umsGanze!) on the meaning and the purpose of the reproduce(future) con-

24 Ibid.
25 "There are new techniques of surveillance and control in politics. On the other hand, there is the potential for new forms of collectives, for non-representational forms of political organisation and for forms of planning and (self-)governance beyond the state and the market. In the eld of work there has been a partial liberation from drudgery, new skills are being developed, while on the other hand there is a general pressure towards creativity and comprehensive self-optimisation, existing qualifications are constantly being devalued, and in the (former) industrial centres there has even been a revival of piece-work. The distinguishing feature of the current constellation of human and machine is their increasing interconnection, which could be said to be culminating in a cybernetic control loop: the machine is supervised by a human, who is supervised by a machine, which is in turn supervised by a human, and so on ad infinitum" (Roth 2016).
26 www.gnu.org/music/free-software-song.html
27 The platform and project "Pirate Bay", which distributes free music, films and software, is based on the same ideas and also came out of the hacker movement. Eric Raymond, *The Cathedral and the Bazaar: Musings on Linux and Open Source by an Accidental Revolutionary,* Cambridge, O'Reilly 1999, http://www.unterstein.net/su/docs/CathBaz.pdf
28 Raymond 1999.
29 Janet Hope, Biobazaar: *the Open Source Revolution and Biotechnology,* Cambridge, Harvard University Press, 2008, p. 18.
30 Raymond 1999.
31 Known in a commodified world as "prosumers".
32 Raymond 1999.
33 "Your nascent developer community needs something runnable and testable to play with. When you start community building, what you need to be able to present is a plausible promise. Your programme doesn't have to work particularly well. It can be crude, buggy, incomplete and poorly documented. What it must not fail to do is (a) run, and (b) convinced potential co-developers that it can be evolved into something really neat in the foreseeable future." (Raymond 1999).
34 Ibid.
35 Hope 2008, p. 14.
36 Ibid., p. 112.
37 Ibid., p. 108.
38 Ibid., p. 109.
39 Ibid., p. 115.
40 Ibid., p. 137.
41 Ibid., p. 120.
42 Ibid., p. 115.
43 Raymond 1999.
44 "Linux was the first project to make a conscious and successful effort to use the entire world as its talent pool. […] Linus was the first person who learned to play by the new rules that pervasive Internet access makes possible." (Raymond 1999).

45 The basis of a Linux core is therefore free software that has been developed as an open source. According to Wikipedia, in September 2013 there were more than a billion active Android devices worldwide.
46 John Howkins, *The Creative Economy: How People Make Money from Ideas,* London: Penguin 2001.
47 Richard Florida, *The Rise of the Creative Class: How it's Transforming Work, Leisure and Everyday Life,* Basic Books 2002.
48 Raymond 1999.
49 Hope 2008, p. 25.
50 Ibid., p. 107.
51 Ibid., p. 108.
52 Ibid., p. 124.
53 Andrea Bonaccorsi, Cristian Rossi, "Warum Open Source Software", *Research Policy* 32 (7), 2003, p. 1248.
54 Stalder 2016. p. 162.
55 Ibid., p. 81.
56 Doodle, the online calendar for synchronising appointments, has suddenly made a protracted back and forth with each individual person unnecessary.
57 Raymond 1999.
58 Stalder 2013, p. 86.
59 On Wikipedia, for example, only every tenth entry is written by a woman.
60 "Algorithmicity […] is characterised by automated decision-making processes that reduce and shape excessive quantities of information. It turns the volumes of data produced by machines into information that can be accessed by human beings, thereby allowing it to become the basis of individual and collective activity." (Stalder 2016, p. 13)
61 Stalder 2013, p. 54.
62 Ibid., p. 88.
63 Ibid., p. 270.
64 Ibid., p. 36.
65 Ibid., p. 43.
66 Ibid., p. 45.
67 Ibid., p. 46.
68 Ibid., p. 55.
69 Geoffroy De Lagasnerie, *Die Kunst der Revolte. Snowden, Assange, Manning,* Berlin, Suhrkamp 2016, p. 135.
70 Ibid., p. 154.
71 Ibid., p. 154.
72 Ibid., p. 15. Often, however, reality proves to be something different, such as when hackers become employees as a way of optimising the system. Socialising in network and communicative structures means introducing yourself, selling yourself and making yourself known This is based on something called "spontaneousness", but can also assume a compulsive character when faced with the danger of being socially excluded. Current forms of social expression have spread from contributions to special interest groups to the whole spectrum of network society: "in social mass media, everyone must produce (themselves)" (Stalder 2016, p. 93), which can also result in trolls, spam, selfies or other forms of excess.

73 De Lagasnerie 2016, p. 84.
74 Ibid., p. 89.
75 Ibid., p. 95.
76 Ibid., p. 74.
77 Jacques Rancière writes that, "every subjectivation is a de-identification, a tearing away from one's natural place, an opening up of the subject space." Jacques Rancière, *Das Unvernehmen,* Frankfurt am Main, Suhrkamp 2002, p. 48.
78 De Lagasnerie 2016, p. 12.
79 Ibid., p. 19.
80 Ibid., p. 10.
81 Ibid., p. 9.
82 Ibid., p. 57.
83 Ibid., p. 67.
84 Ibid., p. 73.
85 Ibid., p. 73.
86 Ibid., p. 94.
87 Ibid., p. 98.
88 Ibid., p. 19.
89 Ibid., p. 63 f.
90 Ibid., p. 60, italics in the original.
91 Ibid., p. 74.
92 Ibid., p. 74.
93 Ibid., p. 90.
94 Ibid., p. 82.
95 Ibid., p. 79.
96 Ibid., p. 74.
97 Ibid., p. 80.
98 Ibid., p. 101.
99 Ibid., p. 11.
100 Ibid., p. 57.
101 Ibid., p. 160.
102 Ibid., p. 76.
103 Ibid., p. 75.
104 Ibid., p. 135.
105 Ibid., p. 135.
106 Ibid., p. 88.
107 Ibid., p. 90.
108 Jakob Augstein, "Wir haben uns geirrt. Doppelpass für Deutschtürken", *Spiegel Online,* 4 August 2016, www.spiegel.de/politik/deutschland/doppelpass-fuer-deutschtuerken-war-ein-fehler-kolumne-augstein-a-1106072.html
109 Imran Agata, "Der Doppelpass ist kein Geschenk. Antwort auf Augstein", *Spiegel Online,* 8 August 2016, www.spiegel.de/kultur/gesellschaft/doppelte-staatsbuergerschaft-doppelpass-ist-nur-ein-zwischenschritt-a-1106370.html The reference is to the German Social Democrat-Green Party coalition of 1998 to 2005, led by Gerhard Schröder and Joschka Fischer.
110 Ibid.
111 De Lagasnerie 2016, p. 112.
112 Ayata 2016.

113 Balibar 2003, p. 98 of German edition.
114 Ibid., p. 155.
115 Saskia Sassen, "Whose City Is It? Globalisation and the Formation of New Claims", in James Holston (ed.), *Cities and Citizenship,* Durham/London, Duke University Press 1999, p. 190.
116 Balibar 2003, p. 197 of German edition.
117 Ibid., p. 196.
118 Ibid., p. 11.
119 De Lagasnerie 2016, p. 29.
120 Ibid., p. 140.
121 Ibid., p. 134.
122 Ibid., p. 128.
123 Ibid., p. 125 f., italics in the original.
124 Ibid., p. 121.
125 Ibid., p. 123.
126 Rancière 2002, p. 7.
127 Ibid., p. 54.
128 www.youtube.com/watch?v=10ivNtRleSc
129 Balibar 2012, p. 244.

Jochen Becker

Flüchtige Gemeinschaften
Maßstabsarbeit, digitale Solidarität und eine kosmopolitane
Politik nach der Politik

Nach einem langen Protestmarsch quer durch Deutschland und Protest-Hungerstreiks am Brandenburger Tor etablierten Refugees auf dem Kreuzberger Oranienplatz 2012 ein Protestcamp. Die Forderungen und Aktionen der Refugees sind als Teil einer breiten Bewegung des städtischen Handelns zu verstehen. Ihr Kampf um das „Recht auf Stadt" (Henri Lefebvre) produzierte politische Resonanzräume sowie neue Praxen für eine künftige Stadtgesellschaft – und darüber hinaus.

Das Handeln der Refugees mit ihren wandernden Proteststationen ist zu verstehen als ein Aspekt der Produktion einer kosmopolitischen Stadt, als die sich Berlin immer wieder behauptet. Die widerständigen Aneignungen öffentlicher Räume durch die Refugees sowie neuartige Politisierungs- und Mobilisierungsformen haben für die ganze Stadt, für alle Berliner*innen Bedeutung. Sie erproben beispielhaft die notwendigen Strategien für eine Stadtgesellschaft, die aktiv für eine *urban citizenship* im Sinne eines gleichen Rechts aller einsteht.[1]

Diejenigen, welche die Stadt und ihre Atmosphäre[2] bislang maßgeblich geprägt haben, erkennen, dass sie immer weniger an ihrer gemeinsam produzierten Stadt teilhaben können. Sie werden durch die in Wert setzende Gentrifizierung aus ihren Quartieren vertrieben: „Die türkischstämmigen Einwohner […] mussten etliche Demütigungen erleiden und wurden bereits größtenteils aus dem Stadtzentrum vertrieben. Ihr Beitrag zur Stadt Berlin wird ignoriert", so der Stadtforscher David Harvey (2013, S. 192). Unter dem Motto „Wir bleiben Innenstadt" kämpfte die Initiative Kotti&Co[3] mit Erfolg um ihr Recht auf Stadt, Wohnraum und Arbeitsumfeld. Ihr Ort ist verknüpftes (Re-)Produktionsumfeld von Existenz und Einkommen, Wohnen und Arbeiten. Das Recht auf Stadt umfasst somit alle Aspekte städtischen Lebens.

Diese Kämpfe haben Effekte weit über die Stadtgrenzen hinaus, ohne den nationalen oder gar globalen Raum zu überbeanspruchen. Der städtische Rahmen ist strategisch begrenztes Testfeld, längst schon durchzogen von transnationalen Bewegungen, Strömen, Interessen und Sorgen. Metropolen sind Testfelder und bieten Resonanzräume. Was in Berlin als „Hauptstadt der mächtigsten unter den europäischen Führungsnationen" (Balibar 2003, S. 19) oder auch im vergleichbaren Stadtstaat Hamburg besprochen und entschieden wird, mag Gewicht haben weit jenseits der Stadtgrenzen. Der „Sommer der Migration" – also die Autonomie der Migration über die sogenannte Balkan-Route 2015 – fußt auf einer Entscheidung aus dem regierenden Berlin, das eigentlich verbindliche Dublin-Verfahren der EU vorrübergehend außer Kraft zu setzen, hat aber seine rhizomatischen Verbindungen im städtischen Handeln jenseits der Regierung dort.

Verwebungen

In Berlin lässt sich zur Zeit verfolgen, dass vernetzte städtische Initiativen bei Bürgerentscheiden obsiegen, dabei Gesetze umschreiben, Bebauungspläne kippen, handgeschriebene Vereinbarungen mit Politiker*innen aushandeln und insgesamt den administrativen Trott der Dinge ändern können. Das städtische Handeln der vielen Initiativen, die schon alleine für die Erlangung der notwendigen Referendums-Stimmen, aber einfach auch aus tiefer Verzweiflung über das administrative Handeln sich zu breiten und interkulturellen Bündnissen zusammenschließen, verweben sich zu einer neuen *urban citizenship:* Eine Bürgerschaft der Bevölkerung Berlins mit dem langen Atem der Einarbeitung in komplizierte Themen und dem hartnäckigen Willen, die notwendigen Schritte politisch wie auch auf der Straße durchzusetzen.[4] Hier lohnt es sich, die Erfahrungen der Hamburger *PlanBude*[5] hinzuzuziehen, welche ein Planungsverfahren im Stadtteil St. Pauli quasi an sich gezogen hatte, neue Wege der „Wunschproduktion" ausprobierte und die Planungsbehörden wie auch den Eigentümer vor sich hertreiben konnte.[6]

Längst stehen nicht mehr partikulare Interessen der Flüchtlinge, der Senior*innen oder der von Gentrifizierung betroffenen Mieter*innen im Vordergrund, sondern es geht um das kollektiv erfochtene Recht auf Stadt: „My right is your right"[7] statt „Not in my backyard". Durch soziale und strukturelle Verwebungen bildet sich ein städtisches Netzwerk heraus, dass sich gleichermaßen sozial wie medial ausweitet, um – wie der französische Philosoph Étienne Balibar schreibt – „einen hybriden politisch Handelnden zu erzeugen, der sich an einem bestimmten Ort befindet, an dem die Konflikte der Welt auf singuläre Weise, nach transnationalem (und in diesem Sinne immer schon ‚kosmopolitischem') Maßstab aber potentiell wirksam aufeinandertreffen." (Balibar 2012, S. 71, Herv. i. Orig.)

Der Beitrag wird im Folgenden den digital gestützten Verwebungen und flüchtigen Gemeinschaften nachgehen. Wie lässt sich städtisches Handeln jenseits der beschaulichen Dimension des Lokalen im Sinne eines „kosmopolitischen Maßstabs" denken und praktizieren? Können soziale Medien, Codes und Programmierungen die Skalen zwischen lokal und global übersetzen und überbrücken helfen? Hierbei soll den Verschiebungen der Hacker-Kulturen nachgegangen werden, welche nach anfänglichen Euphorien zum festen Bestandteil eines kognitiven Kapitalismus wurden. Neue Akteure allerdings, wie sie der französische Philosoph Geoffroy de Lagasnerie beschreibt, reichen über die Enge systemoptimierender Hacker-Kulturen hinaus. Und eröffnen möglicherweise einen neuen, digital eingebetteten und sich stets neu konstituierenden Raum flüchtiger Gemeinschaften.

Maßstabsarbeit

Die „Frage einer europäischen Öffentlichkeit" wird vor allem auf lokaler Ebene gestellt: Wie lassen sich Politiken von Kleingruppen, Initiativen oder Stadtteilversammlungen vor Ort organisieren, aber zugleich als Teil eines beispielsweise europäischen Projekts denken und auf größerer Ebene demokratisch realisieren? Zumindest auf nationaler Ebene boten in Spanien die spanischen Stadtteil-Assemblas im Zusammenspiel mit der als Partei auftretenden Podemos eine Praxis an, die von Berlin bis Athen aufmerksam verfolgt wurde. Hierbei muss die Rolle der kommunalen und staatlich verfassten Verwaltung stets neu überdacht werden: „Kommunen sind mehr als nur Anbieter von Dienstleistungen. Sie sind demokratische Mechanismen, mithilfe deren ortsgebundene Gemeinschaften von Menschen sich auf lokaler Ebene selbst verwalten", zitiert David Harvey den Stadttheoretiker Andrew Sancton.[8]

Wer oder was also tritt als Mittler auf, ohne zugleich in die Falle repräsentativer und stellvertretender Politiken zu tappen? Wie sollen die Erfahrungen und Praxen der Straße auf der Ebene von Gesamtstadt, Staat oder gar einem europäisch gedachten Kontinent hin in ein Handeln übersetzt werden? Es ist nun einmal „viel einfacher […], kollektives und kooperatives Handeln unter starker Beteiligung der lokalen Bewohner in kleineren Zuständigkeitsbereichen zu organisieren und durchzusetzen" stellt David Harvey fest (2013, S. 151). Harvey wirft damit die zentrale Frage der Skalierung auf, also in welchen gesellschaftlichen Größenordnungen wir operieren: „Wenn wir den Maßstab vergrößern, verändert sich der Charakter der Gemeingüterproblematik grundlegend. […] Was in einem Maßstab nach einer guten Lösung aussieht, gilt in einem anderen Maßstab nicht mehr. […] offenkundig gute Lösungen in einem Maßstab (sagen wir auf lokaler Ebene) lassen sich nicht zwangsläufig zu guten Lösungen in einem anderen Maßstab (etwa auf globaler Ebene) hoch- oder auch herunterrechnen." (ebd., S. 131)

Schon die Verhandlung des „Rechts auf Stadt" ist nur schwer vorstellbar: Wie beispielsweise wollen die 3,5 Millionen Bewohner*innen Berlins dieses Recht untereinander aushandeln? Wie also „organisiert man denn nun eine Stadt? Dies scheint mir eine der Schlüsselfragen zu sein, die die Linke beantworten muss, wenn dem antikapitalistischen Kampf in den nächsten Jahren neues Leben eingehaucht werden soll", schreibt Harvey (ebd., S. 235), und kommt zum offenen Schluss: „Die ehrliche Antwort auf die Frage [...] lautet: Wir wissen es einfach nicht." (ebd., S. 242)

Digitale Solidarität

Möglicherweise zeichnet sich mit Hilfe der Algorythmisierung des Politischen, in der Etablierung von technologie-gestützten Netzwerken und der Einbettung von Protokollen eine Perspektive zur Lösung des Skalenproblems ab. In seiner 2013 veröffentlichten Broschüre *Digital Solidarity* betrachtet der Zürcher Medientheoretiker Felix Stalder neue Formen digital gestützter Solidaritätsformen, die auch in Hinblick auf gesellschaftliche Maßstäblichkeiten neue Wege gehen: „es entsteht so etwas wie eine gemeinsame Kultur: eine Kultur der Autonomie und Solidarität." (Stalder 2013, S. 51) Er arbeitet heraus, dass die neuen Formen der digitalen Solidarität sich durch Teilhabe auszeichnen, und weniger durch die Repräsentationsstrukturen parlamentarischer Politik oder einer Parteizugehörigkeit. „Dies bedeutet nicht, dass es überhaupt keine Führung gäbe, aber diese ergibt sich aus der Fähigkeit, Anhänger, Teilnehmer, Referenten zu gewinnen, und löst sich auf, sobald diese Fähigkeit schwindet." (ebd., S. 54 f.)

Die neuen, in zunehmend komplexere Technologien eingebetteten Formen des Solidarischen fasst Stalder in vier Grundtypen: *„commons,* Versammlungen, Schwärme und schwache Netze" (ebd., S. 14). Diese autonome Kultur des Solidarischen wächst parallel zur Verbreitung und Komplexität des Netzes und seiner rechnergestützten Leistung, ist zwar technologiebasiert, baut aber andererseits auf soziale Kompetenzen auch jenseits des Netzes auf. „Manuel Castells fasst diese Werte als ‚Vertrauen, Toleranz und Miteinander' zusammen. Es könnte sinnvoll sein, sie etwas weiter zu fassen: als Teilen, Zusammenarbeit, Individualität, Partizipation und Vielfalt." (Manuel Castells, Communication Power, Oxford: Oxford University Press, 2009, zit. n. Stalder 2013, S. 52). Solidarisches Handeln ist dabei nicht per se gut, ist sozial recht eng gefasst und steht noch am Anfang: „Die neuen Institutionen [...] stecken noch in den Kinderschuhen. Und sie werden immer noch durch einen relativ kleinen Teil der Bevölkerung getragen, vor allem durch globalisierte junge Menschen." (ebd., S. 57).

Arbeit und Alltag treten verstärkt in sozialeren, kommunikativeren, komplexeren und vernetzten Strukturen auf. Der Markt erobert das Soziale, so wie das Soziale den Markt einnimmt. „Schon Mitte der neunziger Jahre konnte der Soziologe Manuel Castells reüssieren, dass die eigentliche produktive Einheit nicht mehr das Unternehmen sei, sondern das Netzwerk, bestehend aus Firmen oder Firmenteilen unterschiedlicher Größe." (Manuel Castells, Der Aufstieg der Netzwerkgesellschaft, Bd. 1, Opladen, zit. n. Stalder 2016, S. 34) Das Internet als

Kommunikations-, Kontroll- und Koordinationsmedium erscheint allgegenwärtig. Hieraus entwickelt sich eine „neue, spezifische kulturelle Umwelt", welche vormals „unverbundenes Nebeneinander teilweise marginalisierter Praktiken" (ebd., S. 95) verstärkt, verschränkt und integriert.

Auch Anna Roth verweist auf die gesellschaftliche und individuelle Gemachtheit des technologischen Komplexes „[e]ine Herrschafts- und Machtkritik, die annimmt, dass die Technik ‚uns': die Menschen, das Kreative, die Subjektivität, die Kommunikation, das Gesellschaftliche, oder schlicht das ‚Leben' aneignet und verwertet – oder in diesem Falle: auswertet und bewirtschaftet – läuft ins Leere, weil sie übergeht, dass die Technik allererst konstituieren und generieren muss, was sie aneignet und verwertet" (Roth 2016). Als Mitglied der kommunistischen Gruppe ...umsGanze! ist sie an der Organisation des Hamburger Kongresses *reproduce(future). Digitaler Kapitalismus und kommunistische Wette* im November 2016 beteiligt. „Sollen wir die Logik der neuen Techniken unterbrechen, die Schnittstellen trennen, die Technik sabotieren und uns entziehen? Oder sollen wir das Gemeinsame, das in der Technik versammelt ist, aneignen, müssen wir es erobern und allererst einlösen?" (Roth 2016). Der Januskopf jeder neuen Technologie zeigt sich darin, dass Befreiung und Versklavung kaum voneinander zu trennen sind.[9]

You'll be free
„Join us now and share the software / You'll be free, hackers, you'll be free / Hoarders can get piles of money / That is true, hackers, that is true / But they cannot help their neighbors / That's not good, hackers, that's not good."[10]

Hacker-Pionier Richard Stallman hat diesen „Free Software Song" als eine Art „Moral-Code" der Open-Source-Szene verfasst und 1991 auch brüchig im $7/8$-Takt eines bulgarischen Volksliedes eingesungen. Die Selbstbefreiung läge danach nicht im Horten von Geld, sondern in der Hilfe für den Nachbarn, was in Zeiten des Internets nicht alleine räumlich gedacht war. Bis in die frühen 1980er Jahre hinein arbeitete die überschaubare und zugleich verstreute Software-Gemeinde selbstverständlich zusammen und teilte sich über große Distanz hinweg die Quellcodes. Zugang zu Daten – seien es Codes, Informationen oder digitale Objekte – sollten frei sein und billig, veränderbar, sich entwickelnd, unbelastet.[11] Mit der Produktion proprietärer Software durch Unternehmen wie Microsoft wurden diese Commons zur Ware eingehegt, lizensiert, monopolisiert und unveränderbar verkauft.

Dank Stallmans GNU-Software 1984, der Popularisierung des neuen Betriebssystems Linux durch Linus Torvalds 1991 sowie der allgemeinen Zugänglichkeit des Internets etwa zur gleichen Zeit breitete sich schwarmhaft die „Open Source" genannte konzernfreie Software aus, um Daten und Codes weiterhin frei zirkulieren zu lassen. Von Linux wurden in wöchentlichen, manchmal täglichen Abständen immer neue Versionen veröffentlicht und von hunderten Nutzer*innen und Programmierer*innen getestet und verbessert. 2008 gab es schon über 150.000 Software-Projekte mit über 1,5 Millionen Entwickler*innen und Hundertmillionen Nutzer*innen.

Der Hacker, Programmierer und Hobby-Anthropologe Eric Raymond führt in *The Cathedral and the Bazaar* die Unterschiede zwischen proprietärer und freier Software als einen Produktions- und auch Gesellschaftsentwurf aus. „Linux ist subversiv, [...] geschaffen von Tausenden über den ganzen Planeten verstreuten Nebenerwerbs-Hackern, die durch die eng verwobenen Stränge des Internets verbunden sind". (Raymond 1999) Sein vielbeachteter Text, geschrieben aus der Perspektive seiner Profession, ist „vielleicht sogar die Wiege einer neuen Gesellschaftsordnung", wie die Autorin und Rechtsexpertin Janet Hope schreibt (Hope 2008, S. 18). In den erstmals 1997 veröffentlichten Überlegungen skizziert Raymond die Unterschiede: „Das eine Modell ist das der ‚Kathedrale', das in der kommerziell orientierten Software-Welt überwiegt. Das andere ist im Gegensatz dazu das des ‚Basars' und der Linux-Welt. Ich werde hier zeigen, dass diese Modelle auf jeweils entgegengesetzten Annahmen über die Natur des Debuggings von Software beruhen." (Raymond 1999)

Debugging ist die oft mühsame Fehlerbehebung von Programmcodes, die nun von einem verstreut wirkenden Schwarm aus User*innen/Programmierer*innen[12] getätigt wird. Diese, von ihm auch „Mit-Entwickler" genannten Anwender*innen werden „mit ein bisschen Ermunterung [...] Probleme diagnostizieren, entsprechende Änderungen vorschlagen und bei der Verbesserung des Codes in einer Weise mitwirken, die sie alleine nie zustande bringen könnten." (ebd.) Raymond sieht als Linus Torwalds' Pionierleistung weniger das Schreiben des Linux-Kernel als Programmkern als viel mehr die Erfindung des Linux-Modells: „Linus behandelte Anwender als Mit-Entwickler, und das in der effektivsten nur möglichen Weise." (ebd.) Erst die freigesetzten (oder instrumentalisierten) sozialen Dynamiken[13] und meist unbezahlte Selbst-Verpflichtungen der „Mit-Entwickler" schuf ein kollektives Software-Gefüge. Der Basar der User/Entwickler teilt die Arbeit unter sich auf. Im Unterschied zu den (alten) Firmenhierarchien und der Ausrichtung an Profitabilität erscheint die Linux-Gemeinde ein „großer, wild durcheinander plappernder Basar von verschiedenen Zielsetzungen und Ansätzen zu sein" (ebd.).

Laut Janet Hope zeichnet sich die Open Source-Produktion durch „Transparenz, Auswertung von Peer-Review und Feedback-Schleifen, geringe Kosten und Einfachheit der Verwaltung aus und ist eine Mischung aus formalen und informellen

Regierungs-Mechanismen, gruppiert um ein gemeinsames Set von technischen Zielen" (Hope 2008, S. 14 f.). Open Source basiere auf Freiwilligkeit und der Spontaneität des Marktes. Es sei ein zwischen den Peers lose koordiniertes Puzzlespiel. Da es keine formalen Schwellen des Ein- und Austritts gäbe, existiere ein Kommen und Gehen. Man findet seinen eigenen Platz nach seinen Fähigkeiten und Vorlieben. Die Schwäche des Basar-Prinzips markiere letztlich dessen Stärke (ebd., S. 112) und zwar durch „langfristige Beziehungen", „reziproke Fairness" und „offene Bücher" (ebd., S. 108) sowie die horizontale Ausrichtung und das „Kollektive" (ebd., S. 109). Die „beglückende Innovation" (ebd., S. 115) sei schneller, robuster, verlässlicher, günstiger (ebd., S. 137) und könne mit der „Nützlichkeit" (ebd., S. 120) von Open Source Gebrauchswerte statt Tauschwerte schaffen. Zudem produziere das Basar-Prinzip ein neues Miteinander: „Im Open-Source-Software-Kontext zeigen empirische Forschungen, dass dies Spaß, Lernen […], und das Gefühl der Zugehörigkeit zu einer Gemeinschaft umfasst" (ebd., S. 115).

In der bildhaften Gegenüberstellung von Kathedrale und Basar koppelt Raymond Fragen der Software-Produktion mit einem künftigen Gesellschafts- und Ökonomiemodell: „die Entwicklung eines Führungsstils und eines Repertoires von Sitten bei der Zusammenarbeit, die es den Entwicklern gestatteten, Mit-Entwickler anzuziehen und das Maximum aus dem Medium herauszuholen". (Raymond 1999) Raymonds schwärmerischem wie zugleich erhellendem[14] Text folgten ernüchternde Analysen, die diese „Open-Source-Welt" inzwischen als „kognitiven Kapitalismus" (Maurizio Lazzarato) beschreiben. Denn selbst das von Google für Mobilgeräte 2008 eingeführte Android-Betriebssystem basiert – wenn auch mit Einschränkungen – auf Open-Source-Codes.[15] Der „neue Geist des Kapitalismus" (Luc Boltanski/Ève Chiapello) einer „Creative Industry" (John Howkins Begriff von Kreativwirtschaft umfasst neben Programmierungen auch Werbung, Architektur, Kunst, Handwerk, Design, Mode, Film, Musik, darstellende Kunst, Verlagswesen, R & D, Spielzeug und Spiele, TV, Radio und Videospiele) hat eine durchaus heterogene „Creative Class" (Richard Florida) hervorgebracht. Die schroffen Ungleichheiten und oftmals frühkapitalistisch anmutenden Arbeitsverhältnisse führen nun zu Kämpfen innerhalb der „Creative Class" selbst. Verwiesen werden soll hier nur auf die erfolgreiche Kampagne *Mediaspree versenken,* die nicht nur ein breites Gebäude-Cluster von sogenannten „creative industry"-Ansiedlungen entlang der Spree in Berlin zu verhindern wusste, sondern dabei auch den Konflikt zwischen weg-gentrifizierten Daten-Jobbern und dem Milieu der kapitalbewehrten Kreativ-Industriellen spürbar machte. Der daraus formulierte Bürgerentscheid „Spreeufer für alle" erreichte 2008 eine Zustimmung von 87 Prozent.

„Bazaar Gouvernance"

„Sogar auf höheren Ebenen des Entwurfs kann es sehr wertvoll sein, das Denken vieler Mit-Entwickler in den Design-Raum eines Produkts ausschwärmen zu lassen. Stellen Sie sich dazu vor, wie eine Wasserpfütze einen Abfluss findet, oder noch besser, wie Ameisen Essen finden: Erforschung durch Einsickern, gefolgt von einer Diskussion, die über skalierbare Kommunikationsmittel geführt wird." (Raymond 1999)

Janet Hope leitet aus Raymonds Entwurf eine „bazaar gouvernance" ab, „eine Regierungskunst mit Anreizen und Kontrollmechanismen, die sich von denen von Märkten, festen Hierarchien und Netzwerken unterscheidet" (Hope 2008, S. 25). Überlegungen zur Software-Optimierung werden als Techniken der „Basar-Regierungskunst" gelesen, um Staaten oder Unternehmen anders zu leiten. Diese „nicht-marktwirtschaftliche Gouvernance" (ebd., S. 107) errichte keine hierarchischen Kathedralen, die „durch die Maßgabe von Managern oder Führern zentral koordiniert wird" (ebd., S. 108). Janet Hope möchte mit dem Modell der „Bazaar Gouvernance" das Basar-Prinzip eines relativ geschlossenen Hacker-Milieus auf Ebenen des Alltags und des Regierens skalieren. Und nimmt – entgegen ihrer Annahme einer „nicht-marktwirtschaftlichen Gouvernance" – zumindest die Kommodifizierung intellektueller Arbeit hin zu aktuellen Wertschöpfungen im Sinne des Regimes eines „kognitiven Kapitalismus" vorweg. Aber trifft diese Annahme auch für politisches Handeln zu?

Protokolle bilden Standards der Programmierung wie auch der Politik. „Ein Basar-Stil oder der Open-Source-Ansatz für Technologie-Entwicklungen fördert die Annahme von nützlichen Standards, da die Transparenz der Open Source-Tools es klar macht, welche Technologie ist die beste ist für jede Plattform-Funktion." (ebd., S. 124). Wie Andrea Bonaccorsi und Cristian Rossi feststellen, ist „Software selbst eine Konvention oder eine gemeinsame Sprache, in der Fehler durch den Kompilierungsmechanismus identifiziert und korrigiert werden."[16] Die den offenen Codes inneliegende Transparenz macht die Übertragung auf politische Systeme so verführerisch. Die technologischen Standards unterstützen und prägen ja auch das nicht-virtuelle Miteinander: „Protokolle sind also keineswegs nur auf technischer Ebene vorhanden, sondern strukturieren als interpretativer Rahmen auch Sichtweisen, Regeln und Handlungsmuster auf allen Ebenen. Damit sorgen sie für eine gewisse kulturelle Homogenität, ein Set an Gemeinsamkeiten, welche diesen Formationen überhaupt erst ihren gemeinschaftlichen Charakter verleihen." (Stalder 2016, S. 162) Es herrscht zumeist ein Konsens, sich der Protokolle (und meist auch der englischen Sprache) zu bedienen. Das Simple Mail Transfer Protocol (SMTP) zum Beispiel wird als offenes E-Mail-Protokoll seit seiner Entwicklung 1982 bis heute von Milliarden Menschen verbindlich genutzt.

Traditionelle soziale Netzwerke mit rein physischen oder unilateralen Kontaktmöglichkeiten waren auf eine überschaubare Teilhabe von Einzelpersonen beschränkt. Ab einer bestimmten Teilnehmerzahl war eine Konsensfindung jedoch praktisch unmöglich. „Aufgrund dieser Erfahrungen entstand ein Weltbild, das ‚Kleinheit' als zentralen Wert propagierte *(small is beautiful)*." (Stalder 2013, S. 81) Mit Hilfe der Datenprozession durch Computer sind Konsensfindungen auch in großer Teilnehmerzahl spürbar einfacher geworden.[17] „Tatsächlich ist es so, dass so gut wie alle von uns in der Open Source-Welt drastisch unterschätzt haben, wie gut diese Kraft mit der Anzahl der Anwender und gegen die Systemkomplexität skaliert" (Raymond 1999) Zudem bildete eine zunehmend ins Digitale eingebettete soziale Realität und gesellschaftliche Praxis ein Laboratorium für soziale Experimente und das Entdecken neuer sozialer Verknüpfungen heraus. Hinzu kommt ein gerade in technikaffinen Gemeinschaften ausgeprägter Pragmatismus. „Was wir ablehnen: Könige, Präsidenten und Wahlen. An was wir glauben: grober Konsens und *running codes*" (Stalder 2013, S. 86), formuliert der Computerwissenschaftler David D. Clark das Grundverständnis einer pragmatischen wie technikaffinen (Gegen-)Kultur der horizontalen und freiwilligen Kooperation, der vielfältigen sozialen Beziehungen und einer allgemeinen Vertrautheit. Einzelne können Entscheidungen nicht völlig blockieren, eine konkrete Lösung wird allgemein angestrebt, und eine sozial, ethnisch wie auch geschlechtlich homogene Gruppe[18], innerhalb derer man sich zusammenrauft, wird vorausgesetzt.

Die Debatten greifen dabei auf Mailing-Listen, Newsgroups und Chat-Systeme zurück, bei der Viele mit Vielen flexibel und auch zeitversetzt kommunizieren konnten. „Digitale Technologien und soziales Handeln einzelner Nutzer wurden so in einem noch nie dagewesenen Maße miteinander verzahnt." (ebd., S. 88) Mit der Durchsetzung des Smartphones stehen Minicomputer stets zur Verfügung. Der Zugang zum Internet und mehr noch die Einhüllung durch die digitalen Clouds werden im Westen so selbstverständlich angesehen wie die Strom- oder Wasserversorgung.

Mit der Erfindung von *Open Source* wurde die Programmierung als Gemeinschaftsaufgabe verstreuter Akteur*innen eingeführt und Programmcodes als Gemeingut *(commons)* verstanden. Mit Archiven, Filtern und Suchfunktionen ausgestattet, konnten nun auch große Datenmengen organisiert sowie Software über das Internet ausgetauscht und weitergeschrieben werden. Zudem wurde durch die Automatisierung, Filterung, Aggregation, Gewichtung und Übersetzung durch die Algorithmen[19] viel Arbeit abgenommen, um auch als Einzelne*r immer größere Netzwerke bewerkstelligen zu können. Dies geht nur durch die „Fähigkeit, zu suchen, zu filtern und zu extrahieren […] und den Rest zu ignorieren, ohne ihren Ausdruck zu unterdrücken und es für eine mögliche zukünftige Betrachtung zur Verfügung zu halten" (Stalder 2013, S. 54). Mit Blockchain-Technologien wie etwa bei der Währung Bitcoin lassen sich kollaborative Vertrauens-Protokolle aufbauen, die anonym von denen bestimmt werden können, die sie nutzen und somit weder Staat noch Unternehmen zwischenschalten müssen. Google wiederum hilft, in Milliarden für Menschen nicht mehr überschaubaren Websites noch einen Überblick zu bewahren.

Es ließe sich aber – so merken die Herausgeber*innen dieser Publikation zu Recht an – ebenso feststellen: Die Suchmaschine der Firma Google selektiert auf der Grundlage eines intransparenten Algorithmus Ergebnisse einer Schlagwortsuche.

Die Schattenseiten des Systems sind den meisten bewusst, da Datenunternehmen wie Google „ihre" Codes und vorprozessierte Informationen in ge- bzw. verschlossenen Systemen bevorraten und kommerziell ausnutzen. Geteilte Datensysteme wie Wikipedia, DuckDuckGo oder Open Street Map haben sich hingegen nur in engem Rahmen durchsetzen können. „Offene Daten sind eine wichtige Voraussetzung, um die Macht der Algorithmen demokratisch einsetzen zu können. Sie sind eine Voraussetzung für die effektive Vielfalt an Algorithmen, denn jeder kann seinen eigenen Algorithmus schreiben oder jemanden damit beauftragen, um Daten auf unterschiedliche Art und im Hinblick auf verschiedene Erkenntnis- oder Handlungsinteressen hin zu prozessieren." (Stalder 2016, S. 270)

Masche zu Masche
Durch die Digitalisierung aller Bereiche des Lebens *(social networks)* und bald auch der singulären Objekte *(internet of things)* kommen immer mehr *Big Data* hinzu, die immer verstreuter und durch keine Bibliothek oder Redaktion geordnet vorliegen. Durch Feedback-Systeme lernen die Konzern-Systeme im Verlauf ihrer Nutzung hinzu und können inzwischen – z. B. als Apples digitale Sprachassistentin „Siri" – mit uns umgangssprachlich kommunizieren. Zugleich haben diese digitalen, auf Algorithmen basierenden Realitäten ihre Übersetzung in soziale Praxen gefunden. So werden Methoden der digitalen Organisation und Strukturierung von Kommunikation auf physische Kontakte hin übertragen. Insofern sind die körperlichen und die digitalen Welten ineinander integriert und beeinflussen sich gegenseitig. Im Effekt hat man heutzutage viel mehr Freunde, Follower oder solidarisch Mitkämpfende, die in kürzester Zeit mobilisierbar sind, rascher Informationen erhalten, und sich über weite Skaleneffekte hinweg im Großen wie im Kleinen abstimmen können.

Skalen und Zeithorizonte können mit Hilfe digitaler Techniken zu Beginn einer Bewegung oder Initiative erst einmal offen gelassen werden: „Es ist immer schwierig, langfristige institutionelle Strukturen aufzubauen. Aber oft ist dies nicht erforderlich, zumindest nicht am Anfang." (Stalder 2013, S. 36) Kurzfristig anberaumte Stadtteilversammlungen und Platzbesetzungen im realen Raum teilen mit Anderen gemeinsame Beratungen und Erfahrungen, welche durch das Digitale verbreitet, vorbereitet und auch verlängert wird.

Hierbei sind selbst „schwache Netzwerke" wie zum Beispiel Facebook dienlich: „Sie werden oft ‚soziales Internet' oder ‚web 2.0' genannt. Diese Etiketten sind unglücklich, weil die wichtigen Teile nicht die Technologien sind, sondern die sozialen Formationen und Kulturen, die im Gebrauch mit ihnen errichtet werden. Aufgrund ihrer immensen Popularität sind ‚schwache Netzwerke' eine neue Basis dessen, was (inter)persönliche Kommunikation heute bedeutet […]. Sie sind die neue Normalität." (ebd., S. 43) Diese „schwachen Netze" verweben auf einfache zu erlernende Weise diverse Gruppen miteinander, sodass Informationen rasch von Masche zu Masche weiterwandern können. „Sie schaffen ‚kleine Welten', da sie strukturelle Voraussetzungen schaffen, Informationen effizient über große soziale Distanzen zu teilen." (ebd., S. 45) Zugleich besteht hierbei die Gefahr, dass man sich durch vorgeschaltete, personalisierte Filter in eben diesen geschlossenen und automatisierten „kleinen Welten" verfängt.

Blieb die Verwaltung großer Netzwerke früher den Eliten vorbehalten, mit ihren internationalen Konferenzen, Clubs und Zuarbeiter*innen, wurde dieses Privileg „quantitativ gesehen, demokratisiert. Man braucht nicht mehr eine persönliche Sekretärin, die an Geburtstage von 500 Menschen erinnert." (Stalder 2013, S. 46) Durch neue Formen der Operabilität wie auch ihrer Visualisierung kann Politik sich zwischen den einzelnen Menschen und der vor Displays oder auf Plätzen versammelten Masse leichter ein- und auszoomen. „Die Größenordnung kann für einen bestimmten Zweck eingestellt werden, und zwar nicht nur auf Karten." (ebd., S. 55)

Not in Our Name
„Snowden und Assange könnten die Ausgangspunkte der Neubegründung einer radikalen politischen Philosophie sein, der es darum gehen würde, so viele Wirklichkeiten wie möglich der freien Erwägung zu unterziehen" (de Lagasnerie 2016, S. 135), formuliert der französische Philosoph Geoffroy de Lagasnerie und schreibt ähnlich wie schon Felix Stalder dem Internet hierbei eine gewichtige Rolle in der Neuformierung gesellschaftlicher Verhältnisse zu. So fragt er, „ob das Internet nicht in der Lage ist, einen Bruch im Hinblick auf den Einfluss zu vollziehen,

den die Rahmenbedingungen der Sozialisation, die zugleich selbstverständlich und aufgezwungen ist, auf uns ausüben." (ebd., S. 154) Das Internet böte also einen „alternativen Raum der Sozialisation" (ebd., S. 154) und die Option auf eine „*gewählte* Sozialisation" (ebd., S. 155).[20]

Gegenüber Stalders Hoffnung auf eine neue, technologisch gestützte Politik der Straße, Plätze und Foren, welche gesellschaftlich etablierte Formen der Politik zu größerer Maßstäblichkeit verhelfen, erkennt Geoffroy de Lagasnerie allerdings in den Taten von Edward Snowden, Julian Assange und Chelsea Manning eine Form singulärer Politiken, die einen Bruch mit vorherigen Formen des Öffentlichen provozieren. Die drei *whistleblower*, welche sich der Verbreitungskraft des Internets bedient hatten, brechen mit vielen Standards bisheriger (Netz-)Politiken.

Etablierte Politiken bringen sich körperlich, als Stimme und Gesicht ein. „Sich als politisches Subjekt zu subjektivieren bedeutet, sich zu engagieren und sich öffentlich ins Spiel einzubringen; es bedeutet den öffentlichen Raum zu betreten und *für alle sichtbar* ein Bekenntnis, einen Protest, eine Besorgnis zum Ausdruck zu bringen." (de Lagasnerie 2016, S. 84) Indem sich Körper verketten und als Formation wie bei Streiks, Blockaden oder Demonstrationen an die Öffentlichkeit treten, wird dies als politische Artikulation verstanden: „Die politische Bühne ist diejenige, auf der sich die Körper versammeln und einen Ort einnehmen. Indem sie sich zusammenschließen, machen die Körper sich selbst sichtbar und dadurch auch die Bildung eines ‚politischen Körpers'." (ebd., S. 89)

Das Engagement gilt als Eingehen von Risiko, was dem Einzelnen Kosten abverlangt. So „begründet man eine Form von Pathos der Politik: Der Protest würde erfordern, dass man seinen Körper zeigt, seine Identität preisgibt." (ebd., S. 95) Der angedrohte Sprung vom Dach der von Refugees im Sommer 2014 besetzten Kreuzberger Gerhart-Hauptmann-Schule als letztes Mittel des Protests zeigt sich in der extremen Aufopferung des Körpers und des „nackten Lebens" (Giorgio Agamben) in aller Öffentlichkeit: Nur als Opfer wird der Demonstrierende in der Arena des normativ Politischen wirklich ernst genommen.

Bruch mit der Bühne
Snowden, Assange und Manning hingegen wollen sich nicht für ihre Sache *opfern*, sondern suchen sich im Schutz der Anonymität oder des Asyls den drohenden Gerichtsverfahren und nationalstaatlichen Anrufungen zu entziehen. Es geht also darum, „der Problematik des Auftretens im öffentlichen Raum" zu entgehen und „den Kampf durch die Forderung nach einer Praxis der Anonymität und des Nicht-Erscheinens zu entfalten." (ebd., S. 74) Geoffroy de Lagasnerie erkennt

hierbei politische Subjekte, die neue Weisen der Subjektivierung[21] artikulieren: *„Sie stellen die politische Bühne selbst in Frage"* und entwickeln dabei eine „Radikalität der Destabilisierung" (ebd., S. 12).

Die Bühne des öffentlichen Raums – sei es Platz, Parlament, Gericht oder ein Medium – gilt als der klassische Ort des Protests. „Welche implizite Vorstellung von Politik und Widerstand übernehmen wir, wenn wir spontan den großen Mobilisierungen auf einem öffentlichen Platz mehr ‚Wert' zugestehen als einer einsamen Handlung eines Hackers" (ebd., S. 19), fragt Geoffroy de Lagasnerie, und möchte uns dafür sensibilisieren, „dass eine singuläre Bewegung höchstwahrscheinlich nicht als solche erkannt wird", es sei denn sie bedient sich „mit Hilfe einer bereits existierenden Sprache". (ebd., S. 10) Nur wenn eine politische Handlung sich in einen bereits existierenden Rahmen des Protests einfüge, wird sie als solche allgemein erkannt. „Politik zu machen bedeutet, präexistierende Formen aufzunehmen, sich in sedimentierte Rahmen einzufügen, mit ihnen zu handeln, um zu einem bestimmten Zeitpunkt ein konkretes Ziel zu erreichen". (ebd., S. 9) Dies führe entweder dazu, dass neue Formen nicht erkannt, oder ein bekanntes Raster auf diese angewendet würden.

Ziviler Ungehorsam als klassische Form politischen Handelns trennt Geoffroy de Lagasnerie von einer „Kritik der Operationen des Rechts und der politischen Ordnung". (ebd., S. 57) Der öffentliche Dissident alter Schule bleibt Subjekt des Staates, statt dass er eine neue Politik erfindet. „Trotz seines anscheinend einzigartigen und radikalen Charakters reiht sich der zivile Ungehorsam in die Kontinuität der traditionellsten demokratischen Formen ein. Seine erste Eigenschaft ist es, öffentlich zu sein. Das ungehorsame Subjekt oder Kollektiv muss öffentlich, vor aller Augen und ganz bewusst ungehorsam sein" (ebd., S. 67). Chelsea Manning jedoch wurde wider eigenen Willen und nur nach einer Denunziation überhaupt zur öffentlichen Person. Sie/Er hätte es liebend gerne vorgezogen, die geleakten Informationen zum brutalen us-amerikanischen Irak-Krieg wären ohne ihren/seinen Namen in der Welt (ebd., S. 73).

Anonymität vs. Solidarität
Solidarität – verstanden als Haltung der Verbundenheit mit und Unterstützung von Ideen, Aktivitäten und Zielen anderer – setzt Sichtbarkeit, Identifizierbarkeit, eine öffentliche Figur voraus. Der „Zusammenhalt zwischen gleichgesinnten oder gleichgestellten Individuen und Gruppen und den Einsatz für gemeinsame Werte", wie Wikipedia „Solidarität" definiert, erreicht seine Gemeinsamkeit nur durch das öffentliche Moment der – durchaus weit gefassten – Zusammengehörigkeit. Die „internationale Solidarität" hat einen hohen Abstraktionsgrad, aber basiert nicht

auf Anonymität, sondern auf Symbolen, Benennungen und Verkörperungen. Angesichts zunehmend komplexer und globaler Zusammenhänge wird dem solidarisch Einzelnen die Fähigkeit zu Bindung und Engagement über weite Distanzen hinweg abverlangt.

Chelsea Manning hingegen wäre gut und gerne ohne die „Zärtlichkeit der Völker" (Che Guevara) solidarischer Grußadressen ins Militärgefängnis hinein ausgekommen. Ohne die Enthüllung der Identität hätte sie/er vielleicht bis heute im militärischen Apparat weiter gewirkt: „Manning hat *politisch, aber ohne öffentliche Forderung* gehandelt." (ebd., S. 73) Sie/Er definiert sich also nicht als *outsider:* „Die Funktion der Anonymität ist es, den *Insidern* die Mittel zu geben, Informationen aus der Institution an die Öffentlichkeit gelangen zu lassen." (ebd., S. 94) Erst die Anonymität ermöglichte es also Manning, sich wie „protestierende politische Subjekte zu konstituieren" (ebd., S. 98). Mit einer*m Unbekannten wäre Solidarisierung nicht möglich gewesen.

Unverantwortlich
„Diese Personen waren und sind verstreut. Sie handeln nicht konzentriert, sondern isoliert. Dennoch stellt das virtuelle Kollektiv, das sie verkörpern, einen der wesentlichen Orte für die Reformulierung der zeitgenössischen Politik und für die Neufassung der Forderung nach Demokratie dar." (ebd., S. 19) Geoffroy de Lagasnerie sieht in den Handlungen von Snowden, Assange und Manning „die Bruchlinie, die die Neuheit dessen enthält, was sich durch sie vollzieht, und diese Neuheit zugleich auch ermöglicht." (ebd., S. 63 f.) Appelliert die*der Ungehorsame an das rechte Recht, nimmt die Normen als gegeben an und geht hierfür auch vor Gericht, entziehen sich und flüchten die neuen Protagonist*innen vor solchem Einvernehmen: „Snowden, Assange und Manning […] *verkörpern eine Herausforderung gegenüber dem Gesetz selbst.*" (ebd., S. 60, Herv. i. Orig.)

Das Gericht ist hier also nicht mehr das öffentliche, gesuchte Forum, um sich öffentlich und demonstrativ den Streit zu suchen. Während Dissident*innen sich üblicherweise gesetzestreuer verstehen als der Staat und sich dabei selbst als ein strafbares Subjekt für den Schau-Prozess anbieten, konstituiert der systemische Bruch durch Entzug eine neue Politik: „Sie stellen den Begriff des verantwortlichen Subjekts in Frage." (ebd., S. 74) Im Unterschied zu Manning treten Snowden und Assange zwar bewusst in die öffentliche Arena, laufen jedoch in die „einzelgängerische Praxis des Exils" über. „Sie haben sich nicht friedlich und passiv verhaften lassen […] Manning übrigens auch nicht. Ihre Politik bestand in der Flucht." (ebd., S. 74) Sie stellen so den Begriff des „verantwortlichen Subjekts" in Frage.

„es" hackt

Noch verborgener agieren die Personen von Anonymous, deren Protest sich zwar kollektiv artikuliert, dabei jedoch „keine Versammlung einer Gruppe" (de Lagasnerie 2016, S. 90) verzeichnet wird. Ähnlich wie bei Assanges Projekt WikiLeaks – das sich zum Ziel gesetzt hat, *„die Vervielfachung der politischen Subjekte zu ermöglichen, die anonym handeln"* (ebd., S. 82) – werden verborgene oder verschlüsselte Räume eröffnet. Es sollen Orte geschaffen werden, die „die Nicht-Nachverfolgbarkeit der mitwirkenden Personen garantiert" als „Möglichkeit des verdeckten Handelns". (ebd., S. 79) Vor der Enttarnung definierte sich Manning eben nicht als *outsider*: Die garantierte Anonymität gibt gerade den Insidern die Mittel an die Hand, Informationen aus dem Inneren der Institution an die Öffentlichkeit zu bringen. Die „Praxis der Anonymität" (ebd., S. 74) erkennt das Gesetz bzw. die Zugehörigkeit zur Ordnung des Gesetzes nicht an und bietet hierfür auch Anderen verschleiernde, verschlüsselte und anonymisierende Räume des Handelns (z. B. *whistleblowing*) an.

Gruppierungen – oder Labels – wie Anonymous sind als „vielgestaltige, strukturlose Bewegung" nicht um eine politische Linie herum organisiert, sondern „um diese neue Art und Weise des anonymen Handelns." (ebd., S. 80) Sie üben Macht aus, sind aber nicht identifizierbar, löschen Spuren aus, operieren weder mit klassischen Bekenntnissen, Wortführern noch mit Repräsentanten: „es" hackt, blockiert, zerrt ans Licht der Medienöffentlichkeit. Ihr „Prozess der Umverteilung und der Verstreuung der Orte des Protests" (ebd., S. 101) unterscheidet sich dabei von der Unterwelt, welche ja ebenfalls das Licht des Staates scheut. Und hat umgekehrt mit den angestellten Systemoptimierern nichts gemein, die ihr Wissen als Hacker nun Regierungen, Diensten oder Unternehmen zur Verfügung stellen.

Flüchtige Gemeinschaften

In Anlehnung an Foucault regt de Lagasnerie an, „im Sinne der Singularität, der Besonderheit und daher auch der Zäsur zu denken". (de Lagasnerie 2016, S. 11) Der Bruch, den die drei zentralen Figuren seines Buches vollzogen haben, untergräbt die Verabredungen des Nationalstaats, des Souveräns und seiner Grenzziehungen. In den gezielt verstreuten Handlungen von Snowden, Assange und Manning sowie von weiteren Hackern und *whistleblowern* werden Gesetz sowie Nation und Staatsbürgerschaft in Frage gestellt. „Es ginge darum, nicht die Staatenlosigkeit als Gegenstand zu nehmen, sondern die Staatsbürgerschaft. Nicht den Ausnahmezustand, sondern die Regel und das normale Funktionieren des Rechtsstaats." (ebd., S. 57) Geoffroy de Lagasnerie schlägt also vor, „sich neue, plurale, heterogene und flüchtige Gemeinschaften vorzustellen – und folglich auch zu realisieren." (ebd., S. 160) Indem er also existenziell aufgeladene Vokabeln wie

Staatenlosigkeit, Exil, „Abwanderungspraxis" (ebd., S. 76) oder Flucht verwendet, bringt er diverse Projekte in eine gemeinsame und politisierte Arena zusammen, um so die „Kunst der Revolte mit der Praxis des Exils, der Flucht zu verbinden". (ebd., S. 75)

Die Handlungen „klassischer" Flüchtlinge etwa durch die Sahara oder auf der „Balkan-Route" wird durch De Lagasnerie mit der politischen Praxis der drei Aufklärer ins Verhältnis gesetzt: „Die Interpretation von Abwanderungsbewegungen ist häufig entpolitisierend. Sie werden weitgehend als erzwungene Fortbewegungen dargestellt, die von ökonomischen Logiken, Kriegen usw. erzwungen werden. Der Grund für die Emigration scheint immer auf der Seite des Bedürfnisses, der Notwendigkeit, der Pflicht usw. gesucht zu werden." (ebd., S. 135) Das neue politische Subjekt ist jedoch bewusst staatenlos: „Wenn es abwandert, vollzieht das Subjekt dann nicht eine Art von Staatsstreich?" (ebd., S. 135) Statt der „Manifestation eines ‚wir', das [...] als Volk auftritt" (ebd., S. 88) verschließt sich der Flüchtige, der Exilant oder der Schwarm vor dieser Politik der Massen. „Die ‚Bewegung' lässt sich auf ein Nebeneinander individueller Handlungen zurückführen, die getrennt durchgeführt werden – und steht daher nicht mehr im Zeichen der ‚Verschmelzung'". (ebd., S. 90) Die Gemeinschaft der Flüchtigen ist somit ihrerseits flüchtig.

Doppelpass
Ende Juli 2016 demonstrieren in Köln zehntausende europäische Türk*innen bzw Europäer*innen mit türkischem Migrationshintergrund für eine Türkei ohne Militärputsch und zugleich für den herrschenden türkischen Staatspräsidenten Recep Tayyip Erdogan. Jakob Augstein, regelmäßiger Kommentator der Rubrik „Im Zweifel links" auf *Spiegel Online*, kommt in Anbetracht des roten Fahnenmeers zu einem überraschenden Schluss: „Die doppelte Staatsangehörigkeit war einmal als progressives Projekt gedacht. Sie war ein Irrtum." (Augstein 2016) Unter der Überschrift „Wir haben uns geirrt" wird der biodeutsche Volkskörper des „Wir" gegen „Die" aufgerufen, die nicht zur deutschen Fahne eilen wollen.

„Sind Migranten Teil dieses ‚Wir' oder inkludiert es ausschließlich die Deutsch-Deutschen, also die Augsteins schon, aber die Ayatas nicht?", entgegnet der deutsche Autor und Unternehmer Imran Ayata, und erinnert, dass die doppelte Staatsbürgerschaft „kein Geschenk der damaligen rot-grünen Regierung" (Ayata 2016) war, sondern Ergebnis Jahrzehnte langer politischer Kämpfe. Für ihn geht Augsteins verengende Perspektive in eine völlig falsche Richtung: „Heute verschwinden Grenzen von In- und Ausland, drinnen und draußen oder ‚Wir' und ‚Sie'. Daraus erwächst nicht nur die Notwendigkeit, sich globalen Herausforderungen wie Migration und Einwanderung zu stellen". (Ayata 2016) Er fordert also ein Ende nationalstaatlicher Unterwerfungen und sieht in der multiplizierten Staatszugehörigkeit eine Auflösung von erzwungenen Gefolgschaften.

Die „Infragestellung der Zugehörigkeit, die wir den nationalen Strukturen oft spontan zugestehen" (de Lagasnerie 2016, S. 112), wie es Geoffroy de Lagasnerie formuliert, wird gerade durch die verschleiernden Strategien im Internet, die der Flucht oder einer Vervielfältigung nationaler Identitätspapiere bis hin zu einer „demokratischen Staatsbürgerschaft in Zeiten der Globalisierung" (Ayata 2016) vorangetrieben. Die Überschreitung der Grenzen Europas muss laut Étienne Balibar als „Demokratisierung der Grenzen" (Balibar 2003, S. 98) eine neuartige Praxis entwickeln und nicht obrigkeitsstaatlich verordnet werden. Die Demokratisierung der Grenze heißt, „sie in den Dienst der Menschen zu stellen und ihrer kollektiven Kontrolle zu unterwerfen, sie zum Gegenstand ihrer ‚Souveränität' zu machen." (ebd., S. 155)

Die Untersuchungen der Globalisierungsforscherin Saskia Sassen zur Transnationalisierung der Arbeit provozieren allerdings die Frage, ob ein demokratisiertes Grenzkonstrukt Europa im Sinne Balibars nicht längst überholt sei: „Was wir immer noch in der Sprache der Einwanderung und Ethnizität erzählen, ist – so würde ich argumentieren – eigentlich eine Reihe von Prozessen, die mit der Globalisierung ökonomischer und kultureller Aktivitäten sowie mit Identitätsbildungen zu tun hat. Zu oft wird Einwanderung und Ethnizität als das Andere konstituiert." (Sassen 1999, S. 190) Sassen kann nicht erkennen, wie der globalen Integration aller und von allem überhaupt eine Grenze gezogen werden kann oder gar sollte.

„Keine zuerst Gekommenen"
Wenn also, wie Sassen anregt, Fragen von Ethnizität und grenzüberschreitenden Zuwanderungen hinfällig seien in unseren Städten von Welt, gibt es auch keinen privilegierten Punkt mehr, von dem aus Entscheidungen zur In- und Exklusion definiert werden könnten, sodass es also nach Balibar „auf dem Boden des Staatsbürgerlichen keine ‚zuerst Gekommenen' gibt". (Balibar 2003, S. 197) In der Aushandlung transnationaler Räume und Strukturen müssen „alle, auch die ‚Einheimischen', […] zumindest symbolisch ihre erworbene, aus der Vergangenheit ererbte bürgerliche Identität aufs Spiel setzen und sie *im Jetzt rekonstruieren: zusammen mit Anderen*". (ebd., S. 196) In einer multi-fokalen Welt müssen diverse Perspektiven zugleich eingenommen werden. Man kann laut Balibar „keinen Standpunkt zur Lage der Welt und zu den Tendenzen der Globalisierung definieren, ohne sich selbst von einem globalen Standpunkt zu betrachten, das heißt:

vom Standpunkt einer realen Universalität, die nicht (oder nicht mehr) von ihm definiert wird". (ebd. S. 11)

„Manning und Assange haben die Frage nach dem gestellt, was man als die Blackbox der Staaten bezeichnen könnte. […] Problem der Beziehungen zwischen Geheimnis, Recht auf Wissen und demokratischer Transparenz". (de Lagasnerie 2016, S. 29) Der geheime Staat verschließt sich gegenüber den Staatsbürger*innen und umschließt als strafende Einrichtung diese zugleich. „In einem Staat eingeschlossen zu sein" (ebd., S. 140) nennt Geoffroy de Lagasnerie eine Situation, wenn „wir als Staatsbürger einem Staat unterworfen sind, der über das sich angemaßte Recht verfügt, uns zu verbieten, sein Territorium zu verlassen." (ebd., S. 134) Und zitiert den damaligen US-Außenminister John Kerry, der an Snowden gerichtet meinte, dass „Patrioten nicht nach Russland" gingen. Doch „warum sollte Snowden den Vereinigten Staaten etwas schuldig sein?" (ebd., S. 128) Dem Aufklärer wurde der US-Pass für ungültig erklärt. Die Pflicht zum Ungehorsam gegenüber dem Staat, an den man per Geburt gebunden zu sein scheint, besteht also darin, sich „von der Ordnung des Gesetzes zu emanzipieren, […] den Raum seiner ‚Durchsetzung' zu verlassen und es so abzulehnen, sich im Bezug auf es zu bestimmen […]). Es ist nicht mehr *sein* Gesetz". (ebd., S. 125 f., Herv. i. Orig.)

Kann ich mich von Verbrechen des Nationalstaates lösen, indem ich mich in die Hoheitsgebiete eines anderen begebe? Wenn der Staat entrechtet, nehmen sich die Rechtlosen ihr Recht, auf den Staat zu pfeifen. „Die Tatsache der Flucht, der Abwanderung, der ausdrücklichen Weigerung, vor dem zu erscheinen, was sich als Justiz ‚ihres' Landes ausgibt (ist es noch ihr Land?)" (ebd., S. 121) macht die Distanz zur Staatsgewalt auf.

Snowden wie Assange befinden sich auf der Flucht, aber im Unterschied zu Gangstern ist dies Teil ihrer politischen Agenda. „Flüchten bedeutet […], sich von dieser Zugehörigkeit zu lösen, sie abzulehnen – und dadurch die rechtlichen Dispositive der Zugehörigkeit zu einer nationalen Gemeinschaft und sogar in einem allgemeineren Sinne die Dispositive der Zugehörigkeit zu anderen Arten von Gruppen, in die wir verstrickt sind, in Frage zu stellen." (ebd., S. 123)

Post-Babylon
„Als die Politik im Namen des Sozialen, der Sozialbewegung oder der Sozialwissenschaft in Frage gestellt wurde, offenbarte sie sich dennoch in einer Vielfalt von Arten und Orten, von der Straße zur Fabrik oder zur Universität. Die Wiederherstellung der Politik äußert sich heute in der Schweigsamkeit dieser Formen oder in der Abwesenheit dieser Orte." (Rancière 2002, S. 7) Jacques Rancières

Alter-Politik, die hier nur angedeutet werden kann, ist keineswegs Anti-Politik, setzt sich aber in ein widerstreitendes und gebrochenes Verhältnis zu einer Politik, welche fundamental war für die Verhältnisse eines nun vergehenden Westens: Repräsentative Demokratie, Liberalismus, Rechts- und Wohlfahrtsstaat, etc.

Eine am Horizont sich abzeichnende post-babylonische Politik „ist aus Weltverhältnissen gemacht". (ebd., S. 54) In einer Stadt von Welt gibt es keinen privilegierten Punkt mehr, von dem aus Entscheidungen zur In- und Exklusion definiert werden könnten. Alle müssen sich in dieses neue Post-Babylon „integrieren". Anonymous lässt mit ihrem standardisierten Gruß „Hallo, Bürger der Welt, wir sind Anonymous"[22] das „Wir" oder „Volk" demonstrativ hinter sich. Wie sich hierbei neue, alter-politisch zu bezeichnende Bewegungen aus dem Schwarm der flüchtigen Welten entwickeln können, und wie sich digitale Solidarität ohne körperliche Kontakte herstellen lässt, muss sich noch beweisen. Ohne Bruch jedoch, ohne eine Politik nach der Politik, wird es nicht weiter gehen: „Denn ich bin zu der Feststellung gelangt, dass sich die politische Körperschaft [...] zumindest in regelmäßigen Abständen dem Risiko ihres eigenen Todes aussetzen muss bzw. ihres Zerfalls durch das Aufbrechen des Konsenses und die Berufung auf das Recht gegen das Recht." (Balibar 2012, S. 244)

Bibliografie

Augstein, Jakob (2016): Wir haben uns geirrt. Doppelpass für Deutschtürken, *Spiegel Online*, 04. August 2016, www.spiegel.de/politik/deutschland/doppelpass-fuer-deutschtuerken-war-ein-fehler-kolumne-augstein-a-1106072.html

Ayata, Imran (2016): Der Doppelpass ist kein Geschenk. Antwort auf Augstein, *Spiegel Online*, 08. August 2016, www.spiegel.de/kultur/gesellschaft/doppelte-staatsbuergerschaft-doppelpass-ist-nur-ein-zwischenschritt-a-1106370.html

Baier, Andrea, Tom Hansing, Christa Müller, Karin Werner (Hg.) (2016): *Die Welt reparieren. Open Source und Selbermachen als postkapitalistische Praxis,* Bielefeld: Transcript-Verlag.

Balibar, Étienne (2003): *Sind wir Bürger Europas? Politische Integration, soziale Ausgrenzung und die Zukunft des Nationalen,* Hamburg: Hamburger Edition.

Balibar, Étienne (2012): *Gleichfreiheit. Politische Essays,* Berlin: Suhrkamp.

Becker, Jochen (2015): Place Internationale. Verwebungen städtischen Handelns: urban citizenship, conricerca, bizim Đehir, Refugiés-Stadt, in Brandlhuber/Hertweck/Mayfried (Hg.): *The Dialogic City,* Köln: Verlag der Buchhandlung Walther König.

Bonaccorsi, Andrea, Cristina Rossi (2003): Why Open Source software can succeed, in: *Research Policy* 32/7, S. 1243–1258.

De Lagasnerie, Geoffroy (2016): *Die Kunst der Revolte. Snowden, Assange, Manning,* Berlin: Suhrkamp.

Florida, Richard (2002): The Rise of the Creative Class. And How It's Transforming Work, Leisure and Everyday Life, New York: Basic Books.

Harvey, David (2013): *Rebellische Städte: Vom Recht auf Stadt zur urbanen Revolution*, Berlin: Suhrkamp.

Hope, Janet (2008): *Biobazaar – The Open Source Revolution and Biotechnology*, Cambridge: Harvard, University Press.

Howkins, John (2001): *The Creative Economy: How People Make Money From Ideas*, London: Penguin.

Rancière, Jacques (2002): *Das Unvernehmen*, Frankfurt/M: Suhrkamp.

Raymond, Eric (1999): Die Kathedrale und der Basar, www.selflinux.org/selflinux/pdf/die_kathedrale_und_der_basar.pdf

Roth, Anna (2016): Wer nach der Technik fragt, fragt, wie diese Gesellschaft eigentlich funktioniert Von Digitalisierung bis Big Data – Interview mit Anna Roth (…ums Ganze!) zu Sinn und Zweck des reproduce(future)-Kongresses, lowerclassmag, 28. September 2016, http://lowerclassmag.com/2016/09/wer-nach-der-technik-fragt-fragt-wie-diese-gesellschaft-eigentlich-funktioniert/

Sassen, Saskia (1999): Who's City Is It? Globalisation and the Formation of New Claims, in: James Holston (ed.): *Cities and Citizenship*, Durham/London: Duke University Press, 1999.

Stalder, Felix (2013): *Digital Solidarity*, Lüneburg/London: PML Books.

Stalder, Felix (2016): *Kultur der Digitalität*, Berlin: Suhrkamp.

1   *Urban citizenship* steht einem konservativen Begriff neuer Bürgerlichkeit entgegen, weil hier nicht Werte, Moral und Sitten sowie die Verfestigung der Klassenunterschiede im Vordergrund stehen, und auch nicht die wutbürgerliche Durchsetzung von Partikularinteressen (wie z. B. die Eigentümer in Hamburg-Harvestehude gegen ein Flüchtlingsheim an den Sophienterrassen), sondern es geht viel mehr um soziale Durchlässigkeit, gleiche Rechte oder das Primat des städtischen Handelns. Und es ist auch nicht zu verwechseln mit der neuen Bürger-Arbeit als unbezahlte Freizeitaktivität zur Kompensation für den Wegfall wohlfahrtsstaatlicher Leistungen.

2   „Beispielsweise ist die Atmosphäre und Attraktivität einer Stadt ein kollektives Produkt ihrer Bewohner, doch es ist die Tourismusbranche, die kommerziell von diesem Gemeingut profitiert […] Zwar kann dieses kulturell schöpferische Gemeingut nicht durch Gebrauch zerstört werden, aber es kann durch exzessiven Missbrauch seinen Wert verlieren und banalisiert werden." (Harvey 2013, S. 139).

3   https://kottiundco.net

4   Mehr hierzu in Becker 2015.

5   www.planbude.de

6   Gesa Ziemer „Stadt gemeinsam entwickeln. Neue Formen der Zusammenarbeit am Beispiel der Hamburger PlanBude" in: Baier et al. 2016.

7   www.myrightisyourright.de

8   Selbst schlägt Harvey hierzu vor: „Die Organisation informell Beschäftigter nach dem Muster der traditionellen Gewerkschaften, das Zusammenwirken der Föderation der Nachbarschaftsverbände, die Politisierung der Beziehungen zwischen Stadt und Land, das Einrichten verschachtelter Hierarchien und Führungsstrukturen neben Versammlungen von Gleichen, die Mobilisierung der Kräfte von Kultur und kollektivem Gedächtnis […]" (2013, S. 259).

9   „In der Politik gibt es neue Techniken der Lenkung und der Überwachung, andererseits gibt es Potentiale für neue Formen des Kollektiven, für nicht-repräsentative Formen des

Politischen, für Formen der Planung und (Selbst-)Steuerung jenseits von Staat und Markt. Im Bereich der Arbeit gibt es zum Teil Befreiung von stupider Arbeit, neue Fähigkeiten entwickeln sich, andererseits herrscht ein Zwang zur Kreativität und zur umfassenden Selbstoptimierung, eine ständige Entwertung bestehender Qualifikationen und sogar die erneute Verbreitung des Stücklohns auch in den (ehemaligen) industriellen Zentren. Das Merkmal der derzeitigen Konstellation von Mensch und Maschine ist ihre fortgesetzte Verschränkung, die sich zugespitzt in einem kybernetischen Regelkreis darstellen lässt: Die Maschine wird vom Menschen überwacht, der von einer Maschine überwacht wird, die von einem Menschen, ad infinitum." (Roth 2016)

10 www.gnu.org/music/free-software-song.html

11 Die Plattform und das Projekt Pirate Bay als Distribution von kostenfreier Musik, Filmen oder Programmen basiert auf dem gleichen Gedanken und entstammt ebenfalls dem Hacker-Milieu.

12 In einer kommodifizierten Welt nennt man sie *prosumer*.

13 „Ihre keimende Entwicklergemeinde muss etwas Lauffähiges und Testbares haben, um damit spielen zu können. Wenn man mit dem Aufbau der Gemeinde beginnt, benötigt man ein herzeigbares, überzeugendes Versprechen. Ihr Programm braucht nicht besonders gut zu funktionieren. Es kann sehr ungeschliffen, von Bugs geplagt, unvollständig und spärlich dokumentiert sein. Was es aber nicht verfehlen darf, ist, (a) zu laufen, und (b) potentielle Mit-Entwickler davon zu überzeugen, dass es sich in absehbarer Zukunft zu etwas wirklich ordentlichem entwickeln lässt." (Raymond 1999)

14 „Linux war das erste Projekt, das eine bewusste und erfolgreiche Anstrengung unternahm, die ganze Welt als seinen Pool von Talenten zu verwenden. […] Linus war der erste, der lernte, wie man nach den neuen Regeln spielt, die das alles durchdringende Internet ermöglichte." (Raymond 1999)

15 Auf Basis eines Linux-Kernel handelt es sich somit um freie Software, die quelloffen entwickelt wird. Im September 2013 waren laut Wikipedia weltweit mehr als eine Milliarde Android-Geräte aktiviert.

16 Bonaccorsi, Rossi 2003, S. 1248.

17 Doodle, der Online-Kalender zur Synchronisierung von Terminen, hat ein vormals langwieriges Hin und Her mit jeder einzelnen Person schlagartig überflüssig gemacht.

18 So ist bei Wikipedia nur jeder zehnte Beitrag von einer Frau verfasst.

19 „Algorithmizität […] ist geprägt durch automatisierte Entscheidungsverfahren, die den Informationsüberfluss reduzieren und formen. So dass sich aus den von Maschinen produzierten Datenmengen Informationen gewinnen lassen, die der menschlichen Wahrnehmung zugänglich sind und zu Grundlagen des singulären und gemeinschaftlichen Handelns werden können." (Stalder 2016, S. 13)

20 Oft jedoch stellt sich die Realität anders dar, etwa wenn Hacker sich zu Systemoptimierern in Anstellung wandeln. Geselligkeit in netzwerkartigen und kommunikativen Strukturen bedeutet, sich selbst zu präsentieren, zu vermarkten, sich sichtbar zu machen. Dies basiert auf dem, was als *Freiwilligkeit* benannt wird, kann aber um die Gefahr des sozialen Ausschlusses zugleich zwanghafte Züge annehmen. Die aktuellen Formen sozialer Expressivität haben sich von Beiträgen in special-interest-Zirkeln auf die ganze Spannbreite der Netzgesellschaft ausgeweitet: „In den sozialen Massenmedien muss jeder (sich) produzieren" (Stalder 2016, S. 93), was auch Trolle, Spam, Selfies oder andere Überschüsse zur Folge haben kann.

21 „Jede Subjektivierung ist eine Ent-Identifizierung, das Losreißen vom natürlichen Platz, die Eröffnung eines Subjektraums", schreibt Jacques Rancière (S. 48).

22 www.youtube.com/watch?v=10ivNtRleSc

ARKADIUSZ PÓŁTORAK
Hands-On Utopi
Comp
Relational Aesthet
Organized

PAUL BUCKERMANN

and Rampant

xity

, Solidarity and

t Worlds

Hands-On Utopias and Rampant Complexity
Relational Aesthetics, Solidarity and Organized Art Worlds

Human interaction, public participation and mutual collaboration all seem to be deeply connected to solidarity. At the same time, these qualities also play a central role in relational aesthetics. The term was coined by Nicolas Bourriaud and describes a trend in artistic production that has since come to be closely examined. Paul Buckermann talks to the art critic, curator, and specialist in Polish literature Arkadiusz Półtorak about relational aesthetics, its development as a discourse, structural pitfalls in the art worlds, and art as "folk politics".

Paul Buckermann: Is the term "solidarity" or its various concepts related to what Nicolas Bourriaud has described as relational aesthetics? Can you briefly sketch out Bourriaud's central ideas and how notions of solidarity might appear in it?

Arkadiusz Półtorak: Bourriaud's book *Relational Aesthetics* came out in 1998 and dealt with some of the most important phenomena in European art of the 1990s—from today's perspective there seems no doubt about this. It is worth noting, however, that Bourriaud's perspective was that of a successful curator, so that even as a writer he remained concerned mostly with artists that he himself had been associated with (such as Pierre Huyghe, Philippe Parreno or Rikrit Tiravanija). This may be seen both as a strength and a weakness on his part. It is a strength because *Relational Aesthetics* is not only a theoretical treatise but also a document of a particular phenomenon in the Western European art scene, provided by an insider. At the same time it is a weakness, for a multitude of reasons that have already been pointed out by such critics as Claire Bishop. For some commentators, Bourriaud came to embody the figure of an arbitrary, powerful curator, a "superartist" whose activities became more important than artistic practices themselves, and whose influence was generally for the worse than for the better. Moreover, many critics have pointed out that Bourriaud's tendency to overestimate viewers' involvement in participatory forms of art—and his assumption of its political significance—came from a lack of critical insight into the European art scene's institutional frameworks, or indeed into current politics. Last but not least, as a work of theory *Relational Aesthetics* lacks conceptual consistency. Nevertheless, it is very easy to identify some assumptions that recur in Bourriaud's collection of essays (one should note that the book contains articles previously published in a variety of exhibition catalogues or professional magazines). Its *leitmotif* is the concept of art as the invention of new and immediate forms of sociability. The mediation that relational art was meant to oppose was, most importantly, the commodification of human contact: its reduction to the experience of the "user" or "consumer". Thus, in a rather syllogistic manner, one could state that relational aesthetics was proposed as an alternative to a functionalist rationale which prevents the emergence of an organic solidarity based on shared values. This syllogism partly holds true, since for Bourriaud "consumer experience" (like shopping or procrastinating in front of a computer or a TV screen) remains essentially individualistic, while relational art is aimed at instituting new models of togetherness—or, in other words, at "provoking encounters". In a sense, relational art was meant to operate the way alternative economies do: by creating "social interstices" free from the law of profit. It is only in such "convivial" environments, we are told, that one can freely negotiate common values. No wonder, then, that Bourriaud is pretty outspoken about the importance of the spontaneous conversations that relational art used to provoke at exhibition openings and during the participatory events that were part of them. Can one, however, view these as potential moments or "vehicles" of solidarity? I am not sure. Bourriaud took the art world's infrastructure and audiences for granted. They may have generated a lot of spontaneous encounters, but could they actually enrich the scope of modern ways of living? The infrastructure was too narrow and symbolically charged, while the audience was too homogenous. It also seems to me that to speak of solidarity one has to speak of situated experience, and by situatedness I do not mean based in the gallery or museum space. We mostly speak of solidarity in the context of economic or cultural exclusion, and if one seeks inspiration for rethinking these issues in Bourriaud's book one may find oneself disappointed. We are probably better off looking for it in particular works by so-called relational artists, most notably Felix Gonzalez-Torres. His candy pieces may be said to be calling for solidarity with victims of the HIV crisis (if that is not too simplistic a way of putting it).

PB: The theory of relational aesthetics seems deeply embedded in its historical origins. What are the roots that can be traced here? Should it be understood as an internal discourse of the art world, or do you see strong references to other topics of the nineteen nineties, like emerging internet technologies, neoliberal globalization or the "end of history"?

AP: At some point in the book Bourriaud insists that relational aesthetics should be treated as a "theory of form". If we follow this line of argument, we may treat its logic as an expansion of minimalist theatricality—the artwork is there, in a gallery or a town square, to attract the viewer and call for immediate, engaged response, either affective or "interactive"; in other words, it is not there to absorb her in moments of disinterested aesthetic experience. Such a "post-minimalist" understanding of relational art I must credit to the Polish art historian Wojciech Szymański, an unrivalled interpreter of Gonzalez-Torres' oeuvre, who rightly stresses that the gay Mexican artist's strategy relied upon detournement of the cold minimalist form developed a few decades earlier by a group of American white men. I myself, though, am not that interested in relational aesthetics as a "theory of form"—at least not in this particular context. When Bourriaud quotes Serge Daney that "all form is a face looking at us", for a while he assumes a transhistorical perspective that reveals how superficially his own writing is grounded in social history (as if Tiravanija's curry-cooking pieces could be indiscriminately juxtaposed with any historical art form, including, say, Caravaggio's painterly craftsmanship). Nevertheless, this ground is very clear. Bourriaud makes it most explicit when he quotes Louis Althusser or Guy Debord. Many a time he seems to conceive of a post-capitalist art that would offer a certain potential for deceleration, however modest; for an art of micro-scale "hands-on utopias". What seems most interesting to me in this context is that Bourriaud appears very troubled with the media ecologies that were emerging at the end of the twentieth century. On the one hand, when he does situate his "theory of form" in a historical context, he notes that relational art is parasitic upon on the "collective new areas of conviviality" and "new types of transaction with regard to the cultural object" brought about by the Internet and "multimedia systems" (note that such observations find their lengthy extension in Bourriaud's following book, *Post-production*). On the other hand, he is consistently skeptical about these devices. "We feel meagre and helpless when faced with the electronic media", he states in the foreword to *Relational Aesthetics*. The concern for the collective mental well-being that he expresses in many similar passages is that of an anthropologist, one very much reminiscent of the uneasiness that Marc Augé airs in his 1997 book *The War of Dreams:* "The question to be asked [...] is whether all the connections which are set up through the different media, whatever their likely originality, are not from the outset a matter of a symbolic deficit, a problem in creating any social bond *in situ.*"[1] Bourriaud suggests that relational artworks are meant to compensate for this presumed symbolic deficit when they are introduced onto the stage of social interactions as "partial" or "transitory" objects. Of course, whether as such they cease to be objects of disinterested contemplation—as well as signs of social status—remains highly debatable.

PB: Are these major claims still influential in artistic production today? Which broader aesthetic styles, concepts, and motivations make reference to relational art in our decade?

AP: I think that the motivations—or, rather, anxieties—one finds behind relational aesthetics still broadly persist in today's art world. To use a recent example—how are we to conceive of Alexa Karolinski and Ingo Niermann's *Army of Love* exhibited at this year's *Berlin Biennale* if not as a (not-that-) fictional excursion into possible modes of togetherness? It is a rather controversial cinematic fantasy about a society equipped with services providing "sensual love" to combat social injustice and ensure people's emotional welfare. If you look at this year's Biennale, you can find many other works that will make you think of Bourriaud's obsessions: individualism, reification, monstrous computer screens etc.

Unfortunately, the works that remind us most immediately of Bourriaud's proposals for "states of encounter" and "relational form" are the least successful ones, at least at the Berlin festival. This is undoubtedly because the political imagination of today's artists has changed, mostly thanks to the brave people who have chosen to work at the intersection of art and various forms of activism. To these people relational art must seem like a playground for the contemporary salon, and there are good reasons for their reservations. Still, the same artists often adopt strategies reminiscent of those used by people associated with Bourriaud. A certain dramatisation of collective experience—as observed, for instance, in heavily political works by Aernout Mik—will always appear to me reminiscent of such pieces by Pierre Huyghe as *Streamside Day Follies*. Although the stakes—and the context—of Mik's projects are completely different, they achieve their efficacy by parallel means. Just like Huyghe's *Follies*, they are, in a rather scientific sense, simulations; they are aimed at the production of new relations. Here we come to the point when the term "relational aesthetics" may be understood in a deeper, more philosophical sense than it is in Bourriaud's 1998 book.

PB: Which major influences do you trace for these shifts and developments? Is it just a trend towards a deeper intersection between contemporary art and politics?

AP: The way you posed the second question is very symptomatic. Why has the phrase "just a trend towards a deeper intersection between contemporary art and politics" come to sound so vague? People who speak with much ease of such intersections are readily suspected of conceptual ineptitude or cynicism. Take Claire Bishop's arguments against relational aesthetics ("although the works claim to defer to their context, they do not question their imbrication within it"[2]); or take Julian Stallabrass's pungent critique of "biennale politics". In the nineties contemporary art biennales started to mushroom, with their ostensibly political themes "stretched to include just everything" and thus meaning "very nearly nothing"[3], with their flocks of wealthy sponsors and of those very important guests from the blue-chip art world—the international guests invariably more important than the local communities (despite the omnipresent talk of the significance of the latter's cultural or political background for virtually every biennale organized so far). In the "art world order" that Stallabrass writes about in *Art Incorporated*, cultural difference is easily marketable—with the result that no reference to Homi Bhabha or Stuart Hall can rescue a curator or an artist who declares a certain political engagement from accusations of cynicism or hypocrisy. Of course, one may argue that there are more art worlds, more orders, and some of them may actually accommodate genuine political thinking and action. Then the way their participants define "art" may well differ from the ready-made formulations we use in the realm of "art incorporated". But such differences, if they matter, are not tokens of marketable cultural diversity. Instead they indicate very particular positions. They testify to the fact that understanding art and politics as two separate domains that can intersect at times (while otherwise being confined to their usual discursive and operational frameworks)—always acts in support of the status quo: of the "trendy", the white and the middle-class; of cynical reason.

PB: Are these shifts instead connected to a general trajectory of changing conceptions of society, nature and technology in large parts of academia and the intellectual world?

AP: There's no doubt our conception of art demands revision, along with our notions of society or nature. Though it is not just our dictionary that has become obsolete; it is also our infrastructure. Mind you, if one says that "representation" no longer provides a valid conceptual framework for democracy, one does not so much call for a better word as criticize existing legal systems and political institutions. If the word "art" seems devoid of meaning, maybe we can perfectly well do without it and without the infrastructure that promotes its consistent usage? I have heard Maria Hlavajova, one of the most inspiring European curators working today, say, "I would rather see contemporary art museums closing down than more of them being built if we are going to retain our formulaic understanding of art". In her public talks Hlavajova emphasizes that both this formulaic understanding and the existing infrastructure of the art world alike belong to the legacy of "enlightened western modernity", with its insistence on progress, its visions of the future as the privilege of those who are already privileged, and with its unending spiral of critique.

PB: You mentioned the notion of post-capitalist and somehow decelerated "hands-on-utopias" in Bourriaud's work. In political activism, such practices as cooperative production, general assemblies, occupations or temporary autonomous zones have become quite common features of radical politics. Are there any direct intellectual, aesthetic or personal links between the two, or are both just symptoms of broader conceptions of proper critical thinking?

AP: I don't think I can give a straightforward answer to this question, partly because I'm not competent to do so and partly because of the reservations I have about relational aesthetics. First, I am not sure that the activist practices you mentioned really have much in common with Bourriaud's "states of encounter", except perhaps for the creation of temporary autonomous zones (assuming both aim at altering ways of everyday life). I have already remarked on the absence of solidarity in relational aesthetics; it could be a measure of what all the practices we've mentioned have in common.

Second, remember that in the nineties Bourriaud's interest lay, to quote him, not in "broadening the boundaries of art, but in experiencing art's capacities of resistance within the overall social field". From today's perspective we may conclude that this presupposition was the main trap of relational aesthetics. As it turns out, there wasn't that much resistance within the existing institutional network, or at least, Bourriaud was looking in the wrong places. Such collectives as Wochenklausur—known for thinking artistic practice "not as a formal act but as an intervention into society"[4]—were already active in the nineties, but I am not sure whether most of their practice can be termed "relational" if we stick to Bourriaud's understanding of the word (let us recall that relational aesthetics was conceived as a "theory of form", and not a theory of "intervention").

Then, of course, there are many intellectual inspirations that Bourriaud shares with the radical left, with Althusser and Debord at the top of the list. I believe, though, that the decisive philosophical reference in *Relational Aesthetics* is Gilles Deleuze and Felix Guattari. I think it is the Deleuzian presupposition that art aims at creating "percepts" and "affects" (or, to put it simply, at producing "sensations") that allows Bourriaud to insist that "it would be absurd to judge the social and political content of a relational 'work' by purely and simply shedding its aesthetic value". It is important to remember in this context what Alain Badiou says about Deleuzian politics. He points out that there is no room for politics in the philosopher's general classification of human thought, its tripartite division into science, art and philosophy;[5] which means that if art does have a political component, it must linger somewhere "between", "in" and "over" the percepts and affects involved in creative activities. On the one hand, for people like Wochenklausur such a Deleuzian understanding of art and politics can only amount to something rather trivial (as is criticizing the society of the spectacle without direct references to the class struggle or Europe's colonial past, something we also find in *Relational Aesthetics*). On the other hand, if Badiou is right to add that the gist of Deleuze's "lingering politics" may be summed up as the call to create "novelties little and great", such a vocation may be attributed both to the practices of relational artists and to activists, and we cannot dismiss this fact easily. I believe that contemporary academia has not yet fully recognized the creative potential of activisms and politically engaged art. Their examples are usually discussed within debates on representation and identity in the field of cultural studies, and I do not think most of these debates do justice to operational logics of activism and its poetic quality. There is usually more to it than, say, "raising the visibility of subalterns" (while raising it as such is not enough to make an art biennale politically significant, to add to my response to the previous question).

PB: Recently, the aforementioned political tactics have been criticised for ignoring the sheer complexity, extension and speed of contemporary capitalism. Leftist authors like Nick Srnicek and Alex Williams[6] doubt whether decelerating practices can adequately confront the epistemic and technological infrastructures of economic and political power-circuits. Are these remarks also applicable to artistic practices which refer to relational aesthetics?

AP: Definitely. Any practices (artistic or outright political) that fetishise the notion of immediacy are bound to fall victim to the criticism you mention. The speculative realist philosopher Timothy Morton wrote in his *Hyperobjects*[7] that we live in an age of asymmetry. What he means is that the scale of all the most troubling issues in today's social debates—like the environmental crisis Morton himself problematizes—exceed by far the creative, transformative or "interventionist" potential of any local action. Thus any activist, artist or engaged citizen might face accusations of hypocrisy and of acting in their own interest. No wonder, then, that more and more political thinkers are declaring their trust in "big science" and not in art, which puts the latter in a rather difficult position. One might say that the prospects for a politically inclined avant-garde have disappeared, unless we are ready to accept that art's agency cannot go beyond aesthetically reflecting the experience of human helplessness against "hyperissues", or that artists have to team up with scientists. Forms of art that deal with the everyday, "go back to the human scale", ones that privilege immediacy—which include relational aesthetics—may be of little value here. They represent what the accelerationist thinkers Alex Williams and Nick Srnicek have called "folk politics".

PB: This makes me think of Fredric Jameson's attempt to theorise cognitive mapping[8] from the nineteen eighties, which has been brought up recently by accelerationists like Srnicek[9] and Williams, and by speculative realists. Here, aesthetic forms would combine with science and theory to make complex structures like global capitalism graspable and build the ground for sophisticated political strategies. Are Bourriaud's ideas the total opposite of this strong emphasis on the future in accelerationist politics, which has an affinity with cognitive mapping?

AP: Do you remember which of the thinkers we've already mentioned is one of Jameson's greatest inspirations in the paper on cognitive mapping? It is Althusser, the self-proclaimed post-Marxist, the guiding influence for many thinkers involved with "micropolitics", the one whose reflections on "aleatory materialism" and "states of encounter"[10] Bourriaud grounds his aesthetics in! Still, it is precisely *versus* Althusser and his acolytes that Jameson emphasizes: "I do want to argue that without a conception of the social totality (and the possibility of transforming a whole social system), no properly socialist politics is possible". No wonder that, with such a clear view on doing politics, Jameson seems to be appealing to Srnicek and Williams, the inventors of a systemically automated future—of "luxury post-capitalism"—as a point of reference. They oppose all attempts "to make global capitalism small enough to be thinkable", and the author of *Archaeologies of the Future*[11] does the same when he coins the idea of cognitive mapping.

But we should be wary: contrary to Srnicek and Williams, Jameson himself does not get away from the concept of immediacy either completely or easily. While the accelerationists pungently criticize the left for sticking to temporal, spatial and conceptual immediacy (i.e., reactionary fetishisation of immediate results, locality and "valorizing personal experience over systematic thinking"), Jameson leaves enough room in his theory of the (social) totality to accommodate the notion of art as the representation of individual experience. When Nancy Fraser asks him why cognitive mapping is actually a task of the aesthetic, he states: "I think that you can teach people how this or that view of the world is to be thought or conceptualized, but the real problem is that it is increasingly hard for people to put that together with their own experience as individual psychological subjects, in daily life". The aesthetic is understood here as a vehicle of experience in its utmost immediacy. Jameson also remarks that the fact that postmodernism gives "hints and examples of [...] cognitive mapping on the level of content" is clearly demonstrable. Here, I believe, he points to postmodernism's emphasis on cultural difference – as is visible in many post-colonial enterprises, both artistic and theoretical: in making subalterns' experience *more* accessible to the colonisers as "individual psychological subjects" etc. For postmodernists it is as important to bridge the gap between both sides as it was, say, for critical theory and cultural studies to do justice to the experience of working class people back in the seventies (take Stuart Hall or, most notably, Oskar Negt and Alexander Kluge). Still, postmodernism's "hints and examples" are said to be effective only at the level of content. The suitable manners of representation—the suitable *forms*—remain unimaginable for Jameson. I think that relational aesthetics may actually fit the formula as long as it deals with subjectivation within everyday rituals and encounters; but then again I am just speaking of content. Is the Althusserian "materialism of encounter" as appropriated in relational aesthetics especially suited to the needs of cognitive mapping; is it a *relational form?* Perhaps any contemporary art form may come in handy if used in the right way and in the right context. The latter matters a lot: in the wrong context everything that was meant, say, to *reveal* the workings of capitalism may fall victim to those very same mechanisms. Capitalism thrives on parasitism. It is extensively parasitical even upon its own critique—suffice it to recall the reception of politically engaged art biennales, or rather, biennales that are *meant* to be politically engaged and subversive. Art is a system, a complex field; every formal or thematic novelty has to be positioned in a dense web of curatorial proceedings, institutional networks, career ladders etc. Don't get me wrong, though. I am not saying that convincing examples of cognitive mapping or any other procedure that would expand our knowledge about our social setting in the globalized world are absent from today's art world. On the contrary, I think that artists and curators have done a lot to secure our understanding of art as knowledge production, and to ensure that art may be treated as an intermediary between academic knowledge and immediate, daily experience (as I said when you asked me if the motivations behind relational aesthetics persist, alienation and reification are just two themes among many that remain popular for good reasons, and contemporary artists deal with them in revealing and touching ways). I do not share Jameson's hope that one day we shall welcome an astounding innovation that would finally make art perfectly fit for the needs of cognitive mapping. I imagine this kind of mapping as a long-durational, distributed process. I do not believe that "achieved cognitive mapping will be a matter of form"[12], at least not of a very particular one. This sentence just makes me think of what Peter Osborne wrote in his groundbreaking book on postconceptual art, *Anywhere Or Not At All:* he remarks that "delegation of functional goals to individual artistic decisions" is an expression of the belief in art's autonomy: a belief that remains largely ignorant of art's sociological context.[13] We have already discussed how this faith betrayed Nicholas Bourriaud. It is important to add that his subsequent books, *Postproduction*[14] and *The Radicant*[15], mark his partial recognition of that betrayal. Partial, I say, because he is always reluctant to examine the institutional set-up of the art world, and he never gives up on seeing contemporary art as "a bearer of a coherent political project".[16] On the other hand, is not a healthy dose of utopianism necessary for our well-being? I would rather leave that as an open question and an open ending to our dialogue.

1 Marc Augé, *The War of Dreams: Studies in Ethno Fiction,* London, Pluto Press 1999 [1997], p. 116.
2 Claire Bishop, "Relational aesthetics and antagonism", *October* 110, 2004, p. 65.
3 Julian Stallabras, *Art Incorporated,* Oxford, Oxford University Press 2004, p. 31.
4 http://www.wochenklausur.at/index1.php?lang=en
5 Alain Badiou, "Existe-t-il quelque chose comme une politique deleuzienne?", in *Cités* 40, 2015. www.cairn.info/revue-cites-2009-4-page-15.htm
6 Nick Srnicek, Alex Williams, *Inventing the Future: Postcapitalism and a World Without Work,* London, Verso 2015; #ACCELERATE MANIFESTO for an Accelerationist Politics, 2013. http://criticallegalthinking.com/2013/05/14/accelerate-manifesto-for-an-accelerationist-politics/
7 Timothy Morton, *Hyperobjects. Philosophy and Ecology after the End of the World,* Minneapolis, Minnesota University Press 2013.
8 Fredric Jameson, "Cognitive Mapping" in *Marxism and the Interpretation of Culture,* Cary Nelson, Lawrence Grossberg eds., University of Illinois Press 1988.
9 Nick Srnicek, "Navigating Neoliberalism: Political Aesthetics in an Age of Crisis", *after us* 1 2015.
10 Louis Althusser, *Materialismus der Begegnung. Späte Schriften,* Berlin/Zürich, Diaphanes 2010.
11 Fredric Jameson, *Archaeologies of the Future: The Desire Called Utopia and Other Science Fictions,* London, Verso 2005.
12 Jameson, op. cit., p. 356.
13 Peter Osborne, *Anywhere Or Not At All: Philosophy of Contemporary Art,* London, Verso 2013, p. 161.
14 Nicolas Bourriaud, *Postproduction. Culture as Screenplay: How Art Reprograms the World,* Berlin/New York, Sternberg Press 2005.
15 Nicolas Bourriaud, *The Radicant,* Berlin/New York, Sternberg Press 2009.
16 Nicolas Bourriaud, *Altermodern,* London, Tate Publishing 2009, p. 99.

Konkrete Utopien und ungeheure Komplexität
Über relationale Ästhetik, Solidarität und organisierte Kunstwelten

Zwischenmenschliche Interaktion, öffentliche Partizipation und gegenseitige Kooperation, all das scheint eng verknüpft zu sein mit Solidarität. Zugleich spielen diese Aspekte auch eine zentrale Rolle in der relationalen Ästhetik. Dieser Begriff, von Nicolas Bourriaud geprägt, beschreibt einen Trend im künstlerischen Schaffen, der seither genau unter die Lupe genommen wurde. Paul Buckermann spricht mit dem Kunstkritiker, Kurator und Literaturwissenschaftler Arkadiusz Półtorak über die relationale Ästhetik, ihre Entwicklung als Diskurs, über strukturelle Fallstricke in den Kunstwelten und über Kunst als *Folk Politics*.

Paul Buckermann: Haben der Begriff „Solidarität" bzw. die verschiedenen Solidaritätskonzepte einen Bezug zu dem, was Nicolas Bourriaud als relationale Ästhetik beschrieben hat? Könntest du Bourriauds zentrale Gedanken kurz skizzieren und umreißen, wie und wo darin Vorstellungen von Solidarität auftauchen?

Arkadiusz Półtorak: Bourriauds Buch *Esthétique relationnelle* erschien 1998 und setzte sich mit einigen der wichtigsten Erscheinungen in der europäischen Kunst der Neunzigerjahre auseinander – aus heutiger Perspektive scheint daran kein Zweifel zu bestehen. Man muss aber sagen, dass Bourriauds Blickwinkel der eines erfolgreichen Kurators war und er sich auch als Autor vor allem mit Künstler*innen befasste, mit denen er selbst in Verbindung stand (wie etwa Pierre Huyghe, Philippe Parreno und Rirkrit Tiravanija). Darin mag man eine Stärke und eine Schwäche Bourriauds erkennen: Eine Stärke, weil die *Esthétique relationnelle* nicht nur eine theoretische Abhandlung ist, sondern auch Dokument eines bestimmten Phänomens in der westeuropäischen Kunstszene, das uns ein Insider lieferte. Zugleich ist es eine Schwäche, und zwar aus vielerlei Gründen, auf die bereits Kritiker*innen wie Claire Bishop hingewiesen haben. Für einige Kommentator*innen verkörperte Bourriaud letztlich die Gestalt eines willkürlichen und mächtigen Kurators: eines „Superkünstlers", dessen Tätigkeit wichtiger wurde als die künstlerischen Praktiken selbst und dessen Einflussnahme die Sachen im Allgemeinen nicht verbesserte, sondern verschlechterte. Zudem haben viele Kritiker*innen betont, dass Bourriauds Tendenz, die Beteiligung des Publikums an den partizipatorischen Kunstformen zu überschätzen, – und seine Annahme, diese Beteiligung sei von politischer Bedeutung – rühre von einem Mangel her: einer mangelnden kritischen Einsicht in die institutionellen Rahmenbedingungen der europäischen Kunstszene bzw. auch in die aktuelle Politik. Nicht zuletzt mangelt es der *Esthétique relationnelle* als theoretischem Werk an konzeptueller Konsistenz. Dennoch ist es sehr einfach, einige Grundannahmen auszumachen, die in Bourriauds Aufsatzsammlung immer wiederkehren (denn das Buch besteht ja aus Artikeln, die zuvor bereits in verschiedenen Ausstellungskatalogen oder Fachzeitschriften erschienen waren). Das Leitmotiv ist ein Begriff der Kunst als die Erfindung neuer und unmittelbarer Formen der Geselligkeit. Die Vermittlung, der sich die relationale Kunst in erster Linie entgegenstellen wollte, war die Kommodifizierung des menschlichen Kontakts: dessen Reduktion auf die Erfahrung des „Users" oder „Konsumenten". Ganz syllogistisch ließe sich also sagen, die relationale Ästhetik ist eingeführt worden als Alternative zu einer funktionalistischen Logik, die das Aufkommen einer organischen, auf gemeinsamen Werten gegründeten Solidarität verhindert. Das stimmt zum Teil, da die „Konsument*innenerfahrung" (wie das Shoppen oder das Prokrastinieren vor einem Computer- oder Fernsehbildschirm) für Bourriaud wesentlich individualistisch bleibt, wohingegen die relationale Kunst darauf abzielt, neue Modelle des Zusammenseins anzuregen – oder anders gesagt: „Begegnungen zu provozieren". Gewissermaßen sollte die relationale Kunst so funktionieren wie Alternativökonomien: nämlich „soziale Zwischenräume" zu schaffen, die frei vom Profitgesetz sind. Nur in solchen „geselligen" Umgebungen, heißt es, kann man gemeinsame Werte frei verhandeln. Es verwundert also nicht, dass Bourriaud ganz klar die Bedeutung der spontanen Gespräche betont, die die relationale Kunst für gewöhnlich bei Vernissagen und den dort stattfindenden partizipatorischen Ereignissen provozierte. Aber kann man diese als potenzielle Momente oder „Vehikel" von Solidarität ansehen? Da bin ich mir nicht sicher. Bourriaud setzte die Infrastruktur und das Publikum der Kunstwelt als selbstverständlich voraus. Beide haben sicherlich eine Menge spontane Begegnungen hervorgebracht, aber konnten sie wirklich die Bandbreite moderner Lebensweisen bereichern? Die Infrastruktur war zu eng und symbolisch zu sehr aufgeladen, während das Publikum zu homogen war. Mir scheint auch, wenn man von Solidarität spricht, muss man von situierter Erfahrung sprechen – und mit Situiertheit meine ich nicht die Verankerung im Galerie- oder Museumsraum. Von Solidarität sprechen wir meistens im Zusammenhang mit einem wirtschaftlichen oder kulturellen Ausschluss; aber wenn man in Bourriauds Buch nach Anregungen sucht, diese Themen neu zu denken, wird man wohl enttäuscht werden. Wahrscheinlich sind wir da besser beraten, danach in den einzelnen Werken der sogenannten relationalen Künstler*innen zu suchen, insbesondere bei Felix Gonzalez-Torres. Von seinen Bonbonhaufen lässt sich sagen, sie fordern Solidarität mit den Opfern der AIDS-Krise (wenn das nicht zu vereinfacht formuliert ist).

PB: Die Theorie der relationalen Ästhetik scheint eng verbunden zu sein in ihren historischen Ursprüngen. Welche Wurzeln lassen sich bei ihr ausmachen? Ist sie zu verstehen als interner Diskurs der Kunstwelt, oder erkennst du starke Bezüge zu anderen Themen der Neunziger, wie etwa der aufkommenden Internet-Technologie, der neoliberalen Globalisierung oder dem „Ende der Geschichte"?

AP: Irgendwo in dem Buch beharrt Bourriaud darauf, die relationale Ästhetik solle als eine „Theorie der Form" behandelt werden. Wenn wir uns dieser Argumentation anschließen, können wir ihre Logik als eine Erweiterung der minimalistischen Theatralik auffassen: Das Kunstwerk ist da – in einer Galerie oder auf einem öffentlichen Platz – um den*die Betrachter*in anzuziehen und eine unmittelbare, engagierte Reaktion, eine affektive oder „interaktive" Reaktion einzufordern. Anders gesagt, es ist nicht da, um sie in Momente einer neutralen ästhetischen Erfahrung einzubetten. Ein solches „postminimalistisches" Verständnis der relationalen Kunst habe ich dem polnischen Kunsthistoriker Wojciech

Szymański zu verdanken, einem unangefochtenen Interpreten des Œuvres von Gonzalez-Torres, der zurecht unterstreicht, dass die Strategie dieses homosexuellen mexikanischen Künstlers auf der Umfunktionierung *(détournement)* jener kalten minimalistischen Form beruhe, die einige Jahrzehnte zuvor von einer Gruppe weißer amerikanischer Männer entwickelt worden war. Ich selbst hingegen interessierte mich nicht für die relationale Ästhetik als eine „Theorie der Form" – zumindest nicht in diesem spezifischen Zusammenhang. Wenn Bourriaud mit „jede Form ist ein Gesicht, das uns ansieht" Serge Daney zitiert, nimmt er für eine Weile einen transhistorischen Blickwinkel ein, der offenbart, wie oberflächlich sein eigenes Schreiben in der Gesellschaftsgeschichte verwurzelt ist (als könnten Tiravanijas Curry-Koch-Stücke ganz unterschiedslos neben jede andere historische Kunstform gestellt werden, sagen wir: Caravaggios malerische Kunstfertigkeit). Nichtsdestotrotz ist dieser Boden, auf dem er steht, klar und deutlich: Bourriaud macht das ganz explizit, wenn er Louis Althusser oder Guy Debord zitiert. Oftmals scheint er sich eine postkapitalistische Kunst vorzustellen, die ein gewisses, wenn auch geringes Entschleunigungspotenzial bieten würde – das Potenzial einer Kunst als konkrete Utopie im Miniaturformat. Was mir in diesem Zusammenhang am interessantesten erscheint, ist, dass Bourriaud große Probleme zu haben scheint mit den Medienökologien, wie sie am Ende des zwanzigsten Jahrhunderts aufkamen. Wenn er seine „Theorie der Form" in einem geschichtlichen Kontext situiert, sagt er einerseits, dass die relationale Kunst ein Parasit der „neuen kollektiven Bereiche der Geselligkeit" und der „neuen Transaktionstypen hinsichtlich des kulturellen Objektes" ist, welche das Internet und die „Multimediasysteme" mit sich gebracht haben (solche Beobachtungen finden ihre ausführliche Fortsetzung in Bourriauds folgendem Buch: *Post-production*). Andererseits ist er diesen Instrumenten gegenüber durchweg skeptisch: „Wir fühlen uns schwach und hilflos gegenüber den elektronischen Medien", schreibt er im Vorwort zur *Esthétique relationnelle.* Die Sorge um das kollektive geistige Wohlbefinden, das er in vielen ähnlichen Passagen äußert, ist die Sorge eines Anthropologen – die sehr stark an das Unbehagen erinnert, dem Marc Augé in seinem 1997 erschienenen Buch *La guerre des rêves* Luft macht: „Letztlich kann sich die Frage danach stellen, ob nicht alle Beziehungen, die mittels der Medien – ungeachtet ihrer möglichen Originalität – entstehen, zunächst in einem symbolischen Defizit, nämlich der Schwierigkeit gründen, eine soziale Verbindung *in situ* herzustellen."[1] Bourriaud behauptet, dass relationale Kunstwerke dieses mutmaßliche symbolische Defizit ausgleichen wollen, indem sie als „Teil"- oder „Übergangs"-Objekte auf die Bühne sozialer Interaktionen gebracht werden. Ob sie als solche aufhören, Objekte der neutralen, unbeteiligten Kontemplation – und Zeichen des sozialen Status – zu sein, bleibt freilich äußerst fraglich.

PB: Sind das wichtige Positionen, die heute noch Einfluss haben auf die künstlerische Produktion? Welche sonstigen ästhetischen Stile, Konzepte und Beweggründe nehmen in unserem Jahrzehnt Bezug auf die relationale Kunst?

AP: Ich denke, dass die Beweggründe – oder vielmehr Ängste –, die hinter der relationalen Ästhetik stehen, in der Kunstwelt von heute immer noch weithin fortbestehen. Um ein jüngeres Beispiel aufzugreifen: Wie sollen wir *Army of Love* von Alexa Karolinski und Ingo Niermann – ausgestellt auf der *Berlin Biennale* [2016] – begreifen, wenn nicht als (nicht ganz so) fiktionalen Ausflug in mögliche Modi des Zusammenseins? Dabei handelt es sich um eine recht umstrittene filmische Fantasie einer Gesellschaft, in der mit Dienstleistungen der „sinnlichen Liebe" gesellschaftliche Ungerechtigkeit bekämpft und das emotionale Wohlergehen der Menschen sichergestellt werden soll. Sieht man sich die diesjährige Biennale an, findet man viele andere Arbeiten, die einen an Bourriauds Obsessionen erinnern: Individualismus, Verdinglichung, monströse Computerbildschirme, etc. Unglücklicherweise sind jene Arbeiten die am wenigsten erfolgreichen (zumindest auf der Berliner Biennale), die uns am unmittelbarsten an Bourriauds Ansätze des „Zustands der Begegnung" *(état de rencontre)* und der „relationalen Form" erinnern. Das liegt zweifelsohne daran, dass sich die politische Imagination der heutigen Künstler*innen verändert hat – und zwar zumeist dank der mutigen Menschen, die sich entschieden haben, am Schnittpunkt der Kunst und der verschiedenen Formen von Aktivismus zu arbeiten. Diesen Menschen muss relationale Kunst wie ein Spielplatz für den zeitgenössischen Salon vorkommen, und für ihre Vorbehalte gibt es gute Gründe. Dennoch, dieselben Künstler*innen setzen oftmals auch auf Strategien, die an Leute erinnern, die mit Bourriaud in Verbindung stehen. Eine gewisse Dramatisierung kollektiver Erfahrung – wie sie etwa in den sehr politischen Arbeiten von Aernout Mik zu beobachten ist – wird mich immer an Stücke von Pierre Huyghe erinnern, an *Streamside Day Follies* zum Beispiel. Obwohl die Aussage – und der Kontext – von Miks Projekten vollkommen anders ist, erreichen sie ihre Wirkung mit gleichen Mitteln. Ganz genau wie Huyghes *Follies,* sind sie im wissenschaftlichen Sinne Simulationen: sie zielen auf die Herstellung neuer Beziehungen, neuer Relationen. Hier kommen wir an den Punkt, wo der Begriff „relationale Ästhetik" in einem tiefgreifenderen, philosophischeren Sinne als in Bourriauds Buch von 1998 verstanden werden kann.

PB: Was sind für dich die Hauptfaktoren dieser Verschiebungen und Entwicklungen? Ist das nur ein Trend in Richtung einer tiefgreifenderen Überschneidung zwischen zeitgenössischer Kunst und Politik?

AP: Wie du die zweite Frage gestellt hast, das ist sehr symptomatisch. Wieso klingt der Satz „nur ein Trend in Richtung einer tiefgreifenderen Überschneidung zwischen zeitgenössischer Kunst und Politik" so vage? Leute, die sehr unbefangen von solchen Überschneidungen sprechen, werden schnell der begrifflichen Stümperhaftigkeit oder des Zynismus verdächtigt. Nehmen wir Claire Bishops Argumentation gegen die relationale Ästhetik („obwohl die Arbeiten behaupten, sich ihrem Kontext zu fügen, stellen sie ihre Verflechtung mit ihm nicht infrage")[2]; oder auch Julian Stallabrass scharfe Kritik an der „Biennale-Politik": In den Neunzigern seien Biennalen der Gegenwartskunst wie Pilze aus dem Boden geschossen, mit ihren angeblich politischen Themen – so „gedehnt, dass sie einfach alles umfassen" und also „fast gar nichts" bedeuten[3] – und ihren Scharen an wohlhabenden Sponsor*innen und sehr wichtigen Gästen aus der gehobenen Kunstwelt, wo die internationalen Gäste stets wichtiger sind als die örtliche Community (ungeachtet des allgegenwärtigen Geredes über die Bedeutung des kulturellen oder politischen Hintergrunds dieser Community für quasi jede Biennale, die bisher organisiert wurde). Kulturelle Differenz lässt sich in der „Kunstweltordnung", über die Stallabrass in *Art Incorporated* schreibt, leicht vermarkten – mit dem Ergebnis, dass sich ein*e Kurator*in bzw. Künstler*in, der*die sich für politisch engagiert erklärt, auch nicht mit Verweisen auf Homi Bhabha oder Stuart Hall vor Anschuldigungen retten kann, zynisch oder scheinheilig zu sein. Freilich lässt sich argumentieren, dass es mehrere Kunstwelten, mehrere Ordnungen gibt, und dass einige von ihnen tatsächlich echtes politisches Denken und Handeln in sich bergen. Dann aber wird sich die Definition der Beteiligten von „Kunst" wohl stark unterscheiden von den vorgefertigten Formulierungen, die wir im Bereich der *art incorporated* verwenden. Aber solche Unterschiede sind, wenn sie denn eine Rolle spielen, nicht Zeichen einer vermarktungsfähigen kulturellen „Diversity". Stattdessen zeigen sie ganz spezielle Positionen an. Sie belegen die Tatsache, dass das Verständnis von Kunst und Politik als zwei getrennte Bereiche – Bereiche, die sich bisweilen überschneiden können, während sie ansonsten auf ihre üblichen diskursiven und funktionalen Rahmensetzungen beschränkt sind – immer zugunsten des Bestehenden, des Status quo, wirkt: zugunsten des „Trendigen", des Weißen und der Mittelklasse, zugunsten der zynischen Vernunft.

PB: Stehen diese Verschiebungen stattdessen in Verbindung mit einer allgemeinen Entwicklung der Vorstellungen von Gesellschaft, Natur und Technologie, die sich in weiten Teilen der universitären und intellektuellen Welt verändern?

AP: Es besteht kein Zweifel, dass unsere Kunstkonzeption eine Revision erfordert, wie auch unsere Vorstellungen von Gesellschaft und Natur. Es ist aber nicht nur unser Vokabular, das inzwischen obsolet ist, sondern auch unsere Infrastruktur. Denn wenn man sagt, dass „Repräsentation" keinen stichhaltigen begrifflichen Rahmen für die Demokratie mehr bietet, dann fordert man weniger ein besseres Wort, sondern kritisiert vielmehr die bestehenden Rechtssysteme und politischen Institutionen. Wenn dem Wort „Kunst" jeglicher Sinn abzugehen scheint, vielleicht können wir dann sehr gut ohne dieses Wort auskommen, und ohne die Infrastruktur, die seine beständige Verwendung befördert? Ich habe Maria Hlavajova – eine der anregendsten der heute tätigen europäischen Kurator*innen – sagen hören: „Wenn wir unser formelhaftes Kunstverständnis beibehalten, dann sollten die Museen für zeitgenössische Kunst lieber dichtmachen, als dass man noch neue baut". Bei ihren öffentlichen Auftritten unterstreicht Hlavajova immer wieder, dass dieses formelhafte Kunstverständnis und gleichermaßen auch die bestehende Infrastruktur der Kunstwelt zum Vermächtnis der „aufgeklärten westlichen Moderne" gehören: mit ihrem Beharren auf dem Fortschritt, mit ihren Visionen der Zukunft als Privileg der ohnehin Privilegierten und mit ihrer endlosen Kritikspirale.

PB: Du erwähntest die Vorstellung von postkapitalistischen, irgendwie entschleunigten „konkreten Utopien" in Bourriads Werk. Im politischen Aktivismus sind solche Praktiken – wie kooperatives Produzieren,

Vollversammlungen, Besetzungen und temporäre autonome Zonen – inzwischen relativ übliche Kennzeichen radikaler Politik. Gibt es direkte intellektuelle, künstlerische oder persönliche Verbindungen zwischen beiden; oder sind sie beide nur Symptome für weitere Konzeptionen angebrachten, kritischen Denkens?

AP: Ich glaube, darauf keine klare Antwort geben zu können; teils, weil ich die Kompetenz dazu nicht habe, und teils wegen meiner Vorbehalte gegenüber der relationalen Ästhetik. Erstens bin ich mir nicht sicher, dass die von dir erwähnten aktivistischen Praktiken wirklich viele Gemeinsamkeiten haben mit Bourriauds „Begegnungszuständen" – ausgenommen hiervon vielleicht die Schaffung temporärer autonomer Zonen (wenn man annimmt, dass beide darauf abzielen, die Lebensweisen im Alltag zu verändern). Über die Abwesenheit von Solidarität in der relationalen Ästhetik habe ich schon gesprochen: diese Abwesenheit könnte ein Maßstab für die Gemeinsamkeiten all der erwähnten Praktiken sein.

Erinnern wir uns zweitens, dass Bourriauds Interesse in den Neunzigern – um ihn zu zitieren – nicht in der „Ausdehnung der Grenzen der Kunst [bestand], sondern im Erfahren der Widerstandspotentiale der Kunst im gesamtgesellschaftlichen Feld". Aus heutiger Perspektive können wir schlussfolgern, dass diese Annahme der Hauptfallstrick der relationalen Ästhetik war. Es stellte sich heraus, dass es so viel Widerstand gegen das institutionelle Netzwerk nicht gab – oder zumindest suchte Bourriaud an den falschen Orten danach. Solche Kollektive wie Wochenklausur – das bekannt ist für seinen Begriff von künstlerischer Praxis: „nicht mehr als formaler Akt sondern als Eingriff in unsere Gesellschaft"[4] – waren schon in den Neunzigern aktiv. Ich bin mir aber nicht sicher, ob man den Großteil dieser Praxis als „relational" bezeichnen kann, wenn wir bei Bourriauds Begriffsverständnis bleiben (wir erinnern uns: die relationale Ästhetik als eine „Theorie der Form", und nicht als Theorie der „Intervention").

Selbstverständlich gibt es viele intellektuelle Inspirationen, die Bourriaud mit der radikalen Linken teilt – und ganz oben auf der Liste stehen Althusser und Debord. Ich glaube aber, die entscheidende philosophische Referenz von *Esthétique rélationnelle* sind Gilles Deleuze und Félix Guattari. Ich denke, die Deleuze'sche Grundannahme – Kunst ziele auf die Schaffung von „Perzepten" und „Affekten" (oder einfach formuliert: auf die Herstellung von „Empfindungen") – macht Bourriauds Beharren möglich, mit dem er meint, „es wäre absurd, den sozialen und politischen Inhalt eines relationalen ‚Werks' zu beurteilen, indem man seinen ästhetischen Wert schlicht und einfach beiseitelässt". Es ist in diesem Zusammenhang wichtig, sich zu erinnern, was Alain Badiou über Deleuze'sche Politik sagt: Badiou betont, dass es in der allgemeinen Klassifikation menschlichen Denkens Deleuzes – für diesen Philosophen, der das menschliche Denken dreiteilte in Wissenschaft, Kunst und Philosophie – keinen Raum für Politik gibt.[5] Das bedeutet, wenn die Kunst eine politische Komponente hat, dann muss die irgendwo „zwischen", „in" und „über" den Perzepten und Affekten der schöpferischen Tätigkeiten verweilen. Einerseits kann so ein Deleuze'sches Kunst- und Politikverständnis für Menschen wie Wochenklausur nur auf etwas ziemlich Triviales hinauslaufen (wie etwa das Kritisieren der

Gesellschaft des Spektakels ohne direkten Verweis auf den Klassenkampf oder auf die koloniale Vergangenheit Europas – was wir auch in *Esthétique relationnelle* finden). Wenn, andererseits, Badiou mit seinem Zusatz recht hat, dass sich das Wesentliche von Deleuzes „Politik des Verweilens" zusammenfassen ließe als der Aufruf zur „Schöpfung von etwas Neuem – etwas Kleines oder Großes", dann kann eine solche Berufung sowohl den Praktiken relationaler Künstler*innen als auch Aktivist*innen zugeschrieben werden; und wir können diese Tatsache nicht einfach abtun. Ich glaube, dass die zeitgenössische akademische Welt das schöpferische Potenzial der Aktivismen und der politisch engagierten Kunst noch nicht völlig erkannt hat. Beispiele für letztere erörtert man für gewöhnlich im Feld der Kulturstudien in den Debatten über Repräsentation und Identität – und ich denke nicht, dass die meisten dieser Debatten der Funktionslogik des Aktivismus und seiner poetischen Qualität gerecht werden. Es geht dem Aktivismus gemeinhin um mehr als nur, sagen wir, „die Sichtbarkeit der Subalternen zu steigern" (wobei – ein Nachsatz zu meiner Antwort auf die vorherige Frage – dieses Steigern an sich nicht ausreicht, eine Kunstbiennale politisch bedeutsam zu machen).

PB: Unlängst sind die erwähnten politischen Taktiken dafür kritisiert worden, dass sie die schiere Komplexität, Ausdehnung und Geschwindigkeit des gegenwärtigen Kapitalismus ignorieren würden. Linke Autor*innen wie Nick Srnicek und Alex Williams bezweifeln,[6] dass entschleunigende Praktiken gegen die epistemische und technologische Infrastruktur der wirtschaftlichen und politischen Machtkreisläufe antreten können. Lassen sich diese Bemerkungen auch auf jene künstlerischen Praktiken anwenden, die sich auf die relationale Ästhetik beziehen?

AP: Definitiv. Jede Praxis (ob künstlerisch oder explizit politisch), die die Vorstellung der Unmittelbarkeit fetischisiert, muss unweigerlich der von dir erwähnten Kritik zum Opfer fallen. Der spekulativ-realistische Philosoph Timothy Morton schrieb in seinem Buch *Hyperobjects*,[7] dass wir in einem Zeitalter der Asymmetrie leben. Er meint damit, dass das Ausmaß der problematischsten Themen der heutigen gesellschaftlichen Debatten – wie die Umweltkrise, die Morton selbst anspricht – das kreative, transformative bzw. „interventionistische" Potenzial jedes örtlich begrenzten Handelns weit übersteigt. Folglich kann sich jede*r Aktivist*in, Künstler*in oder engagierte*r Bürger*in Anschuldigungen ausgesetzt sehen, scheinheilig zu sein und aus Eigeninteresse zu handeln. Da ist es kein Wunder, dass immer mehr politische Denker*innen ihr Vertrauen öffentlich in die „harten Wissenschaften" *(big science)* setzen, und nicht in die Kunst – was die Kunst in eine ziemlich schwierige Lage versetzt. Man kann sagen, dass die Perspektiven für eine politisch gesonnene Avantgarde verschwunden sind, solange wir nicht zu akzeptieren bereit sind, dass die Wirkungsmacht der Kunst nicht darüber hinausgehen kann, die Erfahrung der menschlichen Hilflosigkeit angesichts der „Hyperthemen" ästhetisch zu reflektieren, und dass Künstler*innen sich mit Wissenschaftler*innen zusammentun müssen. Kunstformen, die sich mit dem Alltag befassen, die „zurück zum menschlichen Maß" wollen, die der Unmittelbarkeit den Vorzug geben – und dazu gehört die relationale Ästhetik –, sind hier wohl von geringem Nutzen. Sie stehen für das, was die akzelerationistischen Theoretiker Alex Williams und Nick Srnicek *Folk Politics* genannt haben.

PB: Das erinnert mich an Fredric Jamesons Versuch aus den Achtzigerjahren, das *cognitive mapping* zu theoretisieren,[8] das unlängst von Akzelerationist*innen wie Srnicek[9] und Williams sowie von spekulativen Realist*innen wieder aufgegriffen wurde. Darin könnten ästhetische Formen eine Verbindung mit der Wissenschaft eingehen, um komplexe Strukturen wie den globalen Kapitalismus greifbar zu machen und die Grundlage für elaborierte, politische Strategien zu schaffen. Sind die Ideen Bourriauds das genaue Gegenteil dieses starken Fokus' auf die Zukunft in der akzelerationistischen Politik, die eine Affinität zum *cognitive mapping* hat?

AP: Erinnerst du dich, welcher der von uns schon erwähnten Theoretiker*innen eine der größten Inspirationsquellen für Jamesons Aufsatz über *cognitive mapping* ist? Es ist Althusser: der selbsterklärte Postmarxist; der führende Einfluss auf viele Theoretiker*innen der „Mikropolitik"; derjenige, auf dessen Überlegungen zum „aleatorischen Materialismus" und zu den „Zuständen der Begegnung"[10] Nicolas Bourriaud seine Ästhetik gründet! Jameson richtet sich indes eben *gegen* Althusser und dessen Gefolgsleute, wenn er betont: „Ich will ausführen, dass ohne eine Vorstellung von der gesellschaftlichen Totalität (und von der Möglichkeit, ein ganzes Gesellschaftssystem zu transformieren,) eine eigentlich sozialistische Politik nicht möglich ist". Kein Wunder, dass Jameson – mit solch einem klaren Blick auf das Politikmachen – als Bezugspunkt attraktiv zu sein scheint für Srnicek und Williams, für die Erfinder einer systematisch automatisierten Zukunft: des „Luxus-Postkapitalismus". Sie widersetzen sich allen Versuchen, „den globalisierten Kapitalismus klein zu reden, um ihn denken zu können" – und Jameson, der Verfasser von *Archaeologies of the Future,*[11] tat dasselbe als er die Idee des *cognitive mapping* prägte.

Wir sollten jedoch auf der Hut sein: Im Gegensatz zu Srnicek und Williams, kommt Jameson vom Begriff der Unmittelbarkeit nicht vollständig bzw. nicht so einfach los. Während die Akzelerationist*innen die Linke scharf dafür kritisieren, dass sie an der zeitlichen, räumlichen und begrifflichen Unmittelbarkeit festhält (das heißt reaktionäre Fetischisierung unmittelbarer Ergebnisse und Örtlichkeit, „persönliche Erfahrung über systematisches Denken stellen"), lässt Jameson in seiner Theorie der (gesellschaftlichen) Totalität genügend Raum für die Vorstellung der Kunst als Repräsentation individueller Erfahrung. Als Nancy Fraser ihn fragt, warum *cognitive mapping* in Wirklichkeit eine Aufgabe der Ästhetik sei, sagt er: „Nun, ich denke, dass man Menschen beibringen kann, wie diese oder jene Sicht auf die Welt zu denken oder vorzustellen ist; das wirkliche Problem besteht aber darin, dass es den Menschen zunehmend schwerfällt, das mit ihrer eigenen Erfahrung als einzelne psychologische Subjekte im Alltagsleben zusammenzubringen." Das Ästhetische wird hier als ein Hilfsmittel der Erfahrung in ihrer äußersten Unmittelbarkeit verstanden. Jameson bemerkt auch, dass sich die folgende Tatsache klar demonstrieren lässt: der Postmodernismus gibt „Hinweise und Beispiele von […] *cognitive mapping* auf der Inhaltsebene". Hier, glaube ich, verweist er auf den postmodernen Fokus auf die kulturelle Differenz – wie er sichtbar ist in vielen postkolonialen Unternehmungen sowohl künstlerischer als auch theoretischer Art: darin, die Erfahrung der Subalternen *zunehmend* zugänglich zu machen für die Kolonisator*innen als „individuelle psychologische Subjekte", etc. Die Lücke zwischen den beiden Seiten zu überbrücken, ist für die Postmodernen genauso wichtig wie es das in den Siebzigerjahren, sagen wir, für die Kritische Theorie und die Cultural Studies war, der Erfahrung der Menschen der Arbeiter*innenklasse Gerechtigkeit widerfahren zu lassen (nehmen wir Stuart Hall, oder ganz besonders Oskar Negt und Alexander Kluge). Indes, so heißt es, die postmodernen „Hinweise und Beispiele" sind nur auf der Ebene des Inhalts wirksam. Die passenden Repräsentationsweisen – die passenden *Formen* – bleiben für Jameson unvorstellbar. Ich denke, das gilt tatsächlich auch für die relationale Ästhetik, solange sie sich mit der Subjektivierung in Alltagsritualen und -begegnungen befasst; hier aber spreche ich nur vom Inhalt. Ist der Althusser'sche „Materialismus der Begegnung", wie er in der relationalen Ästhetik angeeignet ist, besonders zugeschnitten für die Bedürfnisse des *cognitive mapping* – ist er eine „relationale Form"? Vielleicht kann sich jede Form zeitgenössischer Kunst als nützlich erweisen, wenn sie in der richtigen Weise und im richtigen Kontext verwendet wird. Letzterer spielt eine große Rolle: Im falschen Kontext kann alles, was – sagen wir – die Funktionsweise des Kapitalismus *aufdecken* sollte, eben genau diesen Mechanismen zum Opfer fallen. Der Kapitalismus gedeiht aufgrund von Parasitentum. Er ist äußerst parasitär, selbst gegenüber der Kritik an ihm – man denke nur an die Rezeption von politisch engagierten Kunstbiennalen, oder vielmehr von Biennalen, die politisch engagiert und subversiv sein *wollen*. Die Kunst ist ein System, ein komplexes Feld; alles formale oder thematische Neue muss positioniert werden in einem dichten Netz von kuratorischen Vorgängen, institutionellen Netzwerken, Karriereleitern, etc. Versteh mich nicht falsch: Ich sage nicht, dass überzeugende Beispiele für *cognitive mapping* oder andere Verfahren – die unser Wissen über unser gesellschaftliches Gefüge in der globalisierten Welt erweitern – in der heutigen Kunstwelt abwesend wären. Im Gegenteil, ich denke, dass Künstler*innen und Kurator*innen viel getan haben, um unser Verständnis von Kunst als Erkenntnisproduktion zu garantieren und sicherzustellen, dass man Kunst behandelt als einen Mittler zwischen den akademischen Erkenntnissen und der unmittelbaren, täglichen Erfahrung (das sagte ich schon als du mich fragtest, ob die Beweggründe hinter der relationalen Ästhetik noch fortbestehen: Entfremdung und Verdinglichung sind nur zwei Themen von vielen, die aus guten Gründen populär bleiben; und zeitgenössische Künstler*innen setzen sich mit ihnen auf aufschlussreiche und ergreifende Weise auseinander). Ich teile Jamesons Hoffnung nicht, dass wir eines Tages eine erstaunliche Innovation werden begrüßen können, die schließlich die Kunst vollkommen in die Bedürfnisse des *cognitive mapping* einpasst. Ich stelle mir diese Art der Kartierung *(mapping)* als einen langwierigen, dezentralen Prozess vor. „Vollendetes *cognitive mapping* wird eine Formfrage sein"[12] – das allerdings glaube ich nicht, zumindest nicht einer sehr spezifischen Form. Dieser Satz Jamesons erinnert mich gerade daran, was Peter Osborne in seinem bahnbrechenden Buch über postkonzeptionelle Kunst *Anywhere Or Not At All* schrieb: Die „Delegierung funktionaler Ziele an individuelle künstlerische Entscheidungen", schreibt er, ist ein Ausdruck des Glaubens an die Autonomie der Kunst: eines Glaubens, der des soziologischen Kontextes der Kunst sich weitgehend unbewusst ist und bleibt.[13] Wir haben schon darüber gesprochen, wie Nicolas Bourriaud von diesem Bekenntnis verraten wurde. Wichtig ist der Zusatz, dass seine folgenden Bücher – *Postproduction*[14] und *Radikant*[15] – seinerseits teilweise eine Anerkennung dieses Verrats markieren. Ich sage „teilweise", weil er sich immer sträubt, die institutionelle Struktur der Kunstwelt unter die Lupe zu nehmen – und weil er es nie aufgibt, die zeitgenössische Kunst als „Träger eines kohärenten politischen Projekts" zu betrachten.[16] Andererseits: Braucht es nicht, für unser Wohlbefinden, eine gehörige Prise Utopismus? Lassen wir dies als offene Frage stehen, als *open end* unseres Gesprächs.

1 Marc Augé, *The War of Dreams: Studies in Ethno Fiction*, Pluto Press 1999, übers. v. Liz Heron, S. 116. Hier übersetzt nach dem Original: *La guerre des rêves. Exercices d'ethno-fiction*, Éditions du Seuil 1997, S. 175.
2 Claire Bishop, Relational aesthetics and antagonism, in: *October* 110, 2004, S. 65.
3 Julian Stallabrass, *Art Incorporated: the story of contemporary art*, Oxford University Press 2004, S. 31.
4 http://www.wochenklausur.at/index1.php?lang=de
5 Alain Badiou, Existe-t-il quelque chose comme une politique deleuzienne?, in: *Cités* 40, 2009. www.cairn.info/revue-cites-2009-4-page-15.htm
6 Nick Srnicek & Alex Williams, *Inventing the Future: Postcapitalism and a World Without Work*, Verso 2015 (*Die Zukunft erfinden. Postkapitalismus und eine Welt ohne Arbeit*, Edition Tiamat 2016, übers. v. Thomas Atzert); Dies., #ACCELERATE MANIFESTO for an Accelerationist Politics, 2013. http://criticallegalthinking.com/2013/05/14/accelerate-manifesto-for-an-accelerationist-politics/ (#BESCHLEUNIGUNGSMANIFEST für eine akzelerationistische Politik, übers. v. Samir Sellami & Frederik Tidén. http://akzelerationismus.de/beschleunigungsmanifest.pdf; bzw. in: Armen Avanessian et al. [Hrsg.], *#Akzeleration*, Merve 2013, S. 21–39)
7 Timothy Morton, *Hyperobjects. Philosophy and Ecology after the End of the World*, Minnesota University Press 2013.
8 Fredric Jameson, Cognitive Mapping, in: Cary Nelson & Lawrence Grossberg (Hrsg.), *Marxism and the Interpretation of Culture*, University of Illinois Press 1988.
9 Nick Srnicek, Navigating Neoliberalism: Political Aesthetics in an Age of Crisis, in: *after us* 1, 2015. (Erschienen auf Deutsch in: Paul Buckermann & Anne Koppenburger & Simon Schaupp (Hrsg.), *Kybernetik, Kapitalismus, Revolutionen. Emanzipatorische Perspektiven im technologischen Wandel*, Unrast 2017, übers. v. Andreas Förster.)
10 Siehe Louis Althusser, *Materialismus der Begegnung. Späte Schriften*, Diaphanes 2010, übers. v. Franziska Schottmann.
11 Fredric Jameson, *Archaeologies of the Future: The Desire Called Utopia and Other Science Fictions*, Verso 2005.
12 Jameson, a.a.O., S. 356.
13 Peter Osborne, *Anywhere Or Not At All: philosophy of contemporary art*, Verso 2013, S. 161.
14 Nicolas Bourriaud, *Postproduction. Culture as screenplay: how art reprograms the world*, Sternberg Press 2005 (2002), übers. v. Jeanine Herman.
15 Nicolas Bourriaud, *The Radicant*, Sternberg Press 2009. (*Radikant*, Merve 2009, übers. v. Katarina Grän & Ronald Voullié.)
16 Nicolas Bourriaud, *Altermodern*, Tate Publishing 2009, S. 99.

MARCUS STEINWEG

NINE REMA[RKS]
ART, ATTEN[TION]
CONTING[ENCY]
SOLIDARI[TY]
LIGHTHEAR[TED]

RKS ON
IVENESS,
ENCY,
Y AND
EDNESS

Marcus Steinweg

Nine Remarks on Art, Attentiveness, Contingency, Solidarity and Lightheartedness

The following remarks address the relationship of artistic and philosophical production to questions of their place in the world, their relationship with each other and what collective subjectivity might be. I will limit myself to nine points:

1. Attentiveness
In a 1978 interview with *Rolling Stone* magazine, Susan Sontag makes this remark: "What I want to be is fully present in my life—to be really where you are, contemporary with yourself *in* your life, giving full attention to the world, which *includes* you. You are not the world, the world is not identical to you, but you're in it and you're paying attention to it. That's what a writer does—a writer pays attention to the world. Because I'm very against this solipsistic notion that you find it all in your head. You don't, there really is a world that's there whether you're in it or not."[1] Sontag knows that there is no such thing as complete self-presence and closed self-transparency, or rather that they exist only as philosophically ideal illusions. What she calls *attentiveness* and *presence* does not mean abandoning oneself to a metaphysical illusion of presence. Rather the contrary: the subject is conjoined with the external world. It can never hope to retreat into a position of solipsism. It is itself already outside, both in the world and a part of it, interwoven into it and determined by it. At issue is how the human subject is interwoven into the world and how this is linked to artistic practice, which can only ever relate to existing realities, whether they be social, economic, political

or cultural in nature. As part of the world, the subject confronts it with its attentiveness. To do this is one of life's most basic dynamics. At the same time, this attentiveness can develop to become a sensibility that demands formulation in art or philosophy. However much there may be a "*rivalry* between the world and the work",[2] as writers such as Roland Barthes have noted in relation to Kafka, so too is every work interwoven into the world—which it becomes part of by directing its attention upon it, while refusing to let itself be assimilated into it. Every work of art bears witness to the world from which it comes. Yet it also always does this by its resistance to the dictates of that world. The work's relationship to the world is complex. It cannot be reduced to a simple formula. But it always comes out of the subject's heightened attentiveness towards his own situation.

2. Situation

The subject is a situated subject. It does not act in a vacuum. Rather it is part of a zone of facts that is determined by a variety of factors and which the subject itself acts upon as a determinant. Social, cultural, economic, political, institutional and other parameters structure its world. The subject's reality includes its real dependency. It is never free of the codings that determine its objective being in the world. As a result, it has no alternative other than to relate to its world as attentively as possible, which includes a certain criticality, the readiness to question the world order it is part of, in order to better understand it. This questioning demands a high degree of critical sensibility, in that it requires both engagement with the situation and a certain distance from it. Only it is a distance that operates within a given state of affairs. It involves an active distancing from the accepted parameters of established reality while fully confronting its existence as fact. Part of taking a critical attitude towards one's own situation is to constantly examine it. The subject is also situated in the sense that its situation is continuously changing. It follows that its thinking and analysis of this situation must change when the situation changes. This process never arrives at a final, definitively determined outcome. Moreover, part of properly engaging in a situation involves gaining a certain distance on it. The subject intensifies its contact with its reality by introducing a contradiction into it. What Gilles Deleuze calls the "basic affinity between a work of art and an act or resistance"[3] articulates the fissure between the subject and its world.

3. Fissure

Reality is fissured. It has no absolute consistency. There are spaces in it in which it is possible to act freely. Every artistic undertaking is an expression of the factuality of such spaces. It reveals them in the creative act. There is no reason to abandon the category of the creative as obsolete. Art still involves creation, even when the creative act is divided among a large number of protagonists and actors. It is still about keeping open the fissures in the fabric of reality instead of nervously closing them up, for these fissures are indices of the openness of our world. It is an openness that converges with its incompleteness, with its status as an indefinite reality. The actors in the artistic process can at the very least agree on this: that the reality of the world constitutes a transformable texture, which art can inspire us to actively continue weaving. On this view, *art* is an act of weaving and shaping that inscribes new patterns into this texture by provoking new configurations of its elements. The world's fissured nature marks its ontological inconsistency, its incommensurability and explosive heterogeneity. Only (collective) engagement with the inconsistency, incommensurability and heterogeneity of the world can lead to artistic outcomes that adequately reflect it.

4. Thinking in the Collective

There is no thinking that does not in itself constitute a collective practice. Thinking is by definition thinking in the collective. The myth of solitary thinking ignores the thinking subject's connectedness to the world. The latter is always acting within forms of life and language games, as Wittgenstein puts it, that it shares with other subjects. It is only on the basis of shared evidence that it is possible to question these forms of life, and gain insight into their arbitrariness and inconsistency. This is as true of scientific thinking as it is of artistic and philosophical reflection. They never take place inside a vacuum. The thinking subject (and when I say thinking, that also includes artistic practice) always thinks in contact and from contact with others. It thinks within the same world that it shares with other subjects, some of whom are closer to it than others. It is from this state of belonging that it gains the substance or material of its critical positioning within the world. For what is thinking, other than the attempt to orientate oneself within the world—that is, to orientate oneself in the world and to change it, in so far as any real thinking constitutes an intervention into the texture of reality? There is no innocent thinking, since every act of thinking is an intervention into the state of the world. To think means already to act; it means stirring up the coordinates of a situation in order to reconfigure them. This can be done through models of artistic participation as well as philosophical alliances, scientific teamwork and political groupings. Transformations in the fabric of reality are the products of imperceptible processes. The first task of progressive thinking would be to direct one's attention upon them, in order, if necessary, to accelerate and intensify them.

5. The Other

It is well known that the category of the Other is central to Levinas and Derrida. Žižek has reminded us that the only way we can take the

Other seriously is not to overhastily assimilate his own ideas about himself. The Other, he writes, is toxic. An analysis of the Otherness of the Other cannot be carried out along pre-defined "humanist" lines. If it were, we would lose sight of Otherness and with it the problem that it always also represents. Psychoanalysis shows that Otherness runs through the subject itself. It is already in itself an Other. It is never wholly identical with itself. It stands in an originary conflict with itself. Derrida's last interview bears the title "Je suis en guerre contre moi-même". It is about his illness. At the same time, the title names deconstruction's essential statement on the category of the subject and the self. Subject and self find themselves originally shot through by Otherness, strangeness, indeed by monstrousness. The subject's self-mediation is routed through the conflict with the Otherness, strangeness and monstrousness that is immanent to it. In this sense it can be said that there is no subject that is not already several within itself, as Deleuze and Guattari at one point suggest. The subject is an originary hybrid, a bastard entity.

6. Solidarity

Thinking is in solidarity with Otherness because Otherness, to put it in Lacanian terms, is part of the Real of reality. The alliance with the Real is the opening up of that part of reality's construction that cannot be internalised. The Real is what cannot be neutralised within the tissue of reality. Confronting this insistent Otherness has nothing to do with pathos or heroism. It marks nothing other than the subject's opening onto the world, which Sontag describes as heightened attentiveness. Being sensitive to the world around one means being interested in its complexity, its contradictoriness and its diversity. Before it focuses on any individual subjects, the true act of solidarity is with the character of the world as the world. The heightened realism of both philosophical and artistic thinking consists in allying and cooperating with the diverse ways this act relates to the world.[4] In it, subjects operate as in a situation of reduced clarity. Part of thinking and acting in the collective involves blindness as well as communication. Even misunderstandings and breakdowns in the communicative process can become resources for improving understanding. Because thinking can only ever be experimental—can only ever be an experience with an open outcome—it must include a readiness to come to conclusions that are not acceptable. The thinking subject is always looking for new openings and solutions—openings that will lead it not away from reality, but towards it. This requires, however, that it resist all established models of reality. Interpretations of the world are world views, are ideology. Any dynamic of thinking that is critical of ideology still has to break with existing notions of ideology critique. It must question everything, including the cult of question and critique.

7. Connections

Looking for new connections means looking for them in places where they are invisible. Forming unlikely alliances is the minimal requirement of any thinking that aims to do more than merely repeat what exists. Collectives are fragile communities of solidarity that accept the irreducible Otherness of the Other, instead of violently neutralising it. Both artistic and philosophical practice is in part about bringing together what has been kept apart. They are always concerned with collaging together a new reality. To do this they must first churn reality up, dissolving its hardened crusts and destabilising its fixed forms of existence. It is only this way that new connections—another image of actuality, an altered reality—become possible. That is why an openness to the unknown is part of every experimental thinking. This has nothing to do with utopianism. Utopianism always knows where it is heading. Experimental thinking doesn't know where it is going. All it knows is that it wants to go somewhere else to where it already is. It refuses to stagnate within the realm of what is familiar, safe or approved. This makes it an anti-conservative practice. Deleuze writes that "The strength of an artist is his capacity to renew".[5] Art aims at change because the existing world always demands its own stabilisation, in other words, a dogma of the Now. But artistic thinking means boring holes in all dogmas to reveal their hollow and repressive nature. The New resists the world as it exists by showing what has been repressed from it: other ways of being and forms of life, undreamt-of possibilities of social and political organisation.

8. Openness to Contingency

One could speak of artistic practices having an openness to contingency. Attentiveness to the world is attentiveness to its contingency: it is the way it is, but need not be so. The contingent marks the non-necessary. Thinking's heightened realism requires the recognition of this non-necessity. It implies engaging with existing economic, political, cultural, military, social and other realities through a certain degree of dissidence. That does not mean it ignores these realities. It simply denies them their authority over itself. In so far as there is dissidence and deviation from the dominant mechanisms and imperatives of power, it engages in an intensive analysis of their fragility. One word for this fragility is contingency. Another would be inconsistency. There are connections—some explicit, some implicit—among all intellectually and artistically active subjects through this common, though often separately practiced, openness to contingency, which amounts to work on transforming the world as it exists. It is therefore not simply negative. It does not exhaust itself in setting limits to or dismissing actual reality. Its motor is the affirmation of the indeterminate. It affirms the image of a faceless future, without regressing into idealistic projections or utopian reveries.

9. Lightheartedness

In his essay "Is Art Lighthearted?", Adorno writes: "What is lighthearted in art is, if you like, the opposite of what one might easily assume it to be: not its content but its demeanour, the abstract fact that it is art at all, that it opens out over the reality to whose violence it bears witness at the same time."[6] To put it bluntly: lightheartedness is not stupidity. It has nothing to do with opportunistically assimilating oneself into the world as it exists. Rather it uses the power of imagination to move above the field of constituent realities. There is no art without the power of imagination. It is from this that it draws its dynamic and its necessity. Art's realism is one that risks dreaming without falling into daydreaming. This partly involves a determination to imagine reality other than it is. That is the lightheartedness above the terrain of violence of which Adorno speaks. It intensifies its contact with the territory it crosses by gaining distance on it. From this distance it tests its plausibility and relevance. It is part of art's immanent political nature that it avoids throwing itself into the present without maintaining some distance upon it. The very fact that there is art at all already means that it has used a rudimentary fantasy to withdraw, and actually free itself a little, from the dictates of dominant realities. If art were to drown itself in ahistorical pessimism and narcissistic defeatism, then it would lose its reason to exist. As Heiner Müller once put it, it operates beyond hope and despair. Its lightheartedness is an indication of its openness to contingency, the awareness of an indefinite tomorrow of which no one can say what form it will take.

1 Jonathan Cott, *Susan Sontag: The Complete Rolling Stone Interview,* New Haven, Yale University Press 2013, p. 4.
2 Roland Barthes, *The Preparation of the Novel: Lecture Courses and Seminars at the Collège de France (1978–1979 and 1979–1980),* New York, Columbia University Press 2011, p. 200.
3 Gilles Deleuze, "Was ist der Schöpfungsakt?", in *Schizophrenie und Gesellschaft. Texte und Gespräche von 1975–1995,* Frankfurt am Main, Suhrkamp 2005, p. 307.
4 I call this kind of realism "heightened" because it questions the consistency of existing realities while fully confronting them, instead of unquestioningly accepting them.
5 Gilles Deleuze, "Manfred: eine außergewöhnliche Erneuerung", in *Schizophrenie und Gesellschaft. Texte und Gespräche von 1975–1995,* Frankfurt am Main, Suhrkamp 2005, p. 179.
6 Theodor W. Adorno, "Is Art Lighthearted?", in *Notes to Literature, Volume 2,* New York, Columbia University Press 1992, p. 348.

Marcus Steinweg

Neun Bemerkungen zu Kunst, Aufmerksamkeit, Kontingenz, Solidarität und Heiterkeit

Die folgenden Bemerkungen gelten dem Verhältnis künstlerischer wie philosophischer Produktion zu Fragen ihrer Welteinbettung, ihres Verhältnisses untereinander und dem, was kollektive Subjektivität sein kann. Ich beschränke mich auf neun Punkte:

1. Aufmerksamkeit

Im *Rolling Stone*-Interview von 1978 konstatiert Susan Sontag: „Ich möchte in meinem Leben vollkommen präsent sein – genau dort sein, wo ich gerade bin, ganz bei mir selbst sein, meine volle Aufmerksamkeit auf die Welt richten, die auch mich einschließt. Du bist nicht die Welt, die Welt ist nicht mit dir identisch, aber du bist in ihr und schenkst ihr deine Aufmerksamkeit. Das ist die Tätigkeit des Schriftstellers – der Schriftsteller schenkt der Welt seine Aufmerksamkeit. Ich bin entschieden gegen die solipsistische Auffassung, dass alles in unseren Köpfen stattfindet. Das stimmt nicht, es gibt eine äußere Welt, ob man sich in ihr bewegt oder nicht."[1] Sontag weiß, dass es volles Beisichsein und geschlossene Selbsttransparenz nicht gibt, oder nur als philosophisch-idealistisches Phantasma. Was sie *Aufmerksamkeit* nennt und *Präsentsein,* heißt nicht, sich einem metaphysischen Präsenzphantasma hinzugeben. Im Gegenteil: Das Subjekt ist mit der Außenwelt verklammert. Ihm wird es nicht gelingen, sich in einem Solipsismus einzuschließen. Es selbst ist bereits draußen, in der Welt als ein Teil von ihr, mit ihr verwoben, durch sie bestimmt. Es geht um die Frage der Weltverwobenheit des menschlichen Subjekts und wie sie sich mit der künstlerischen Praxis verbindet, die nicht anders kann als sich zu den bestehenden Realitäten zu verhalten, seien sie sozialer, ökonomischer, politischer oder kultureller Natur. Als Teil der Welt bringt das Subjekt ihr Aufmerksamkeit entgegen. Es gehört zur einfachsten Lebensdynamik dies zu tun. Zugleich lässt sich diese Aufmerksamkeit zu einer Sensibilität steigern, die nach künstlerischer oder philosophischer Formulierung verlangt. So sehr es auch eine „*Rivalität* zwischen der Welt und dem Werk"[2] geben mag, wie Roland Barthes unter anderem in Bezug auf Kafka feststellt, so sehr ist jedes Werk von der Welt – der es angehört, indem es ihr höchste Aufmerksamkeit entgegenbringt, ohne sich ihr widerstandslos zu assimilieren – durchschossen. Jedes künstlerische Werk zeugt von der Welt, in der es entsteht. Doch tut es dies immer auch durch Resistenz ihren Diktaten gegenüber. Das Weltverhältnis des Werks ist komplex.

Es lässt sich nicht auf eine einfache Formel bringen. Immer aber verdankt es sich der gesteigerten Aufmerksamkeit des Subjekts gegenüber seiner Situation.

2. Situation

Das Subjekt ist situatives Subjekt. Es bewegt sich nicht im luftleeren Raum. Vielmehr gehört es einer Tatsachenzone an, die vielfältig determiniert ist und selbst als Determinante auf es einwirkt. Gesellschaftliche, kulturelle, ökonomische, politische, institutionelle u. a. Parameter strukturieren seine Welt. Zur Realität des Subjekts gehört reale Dependenz. Nie ist es frei von Kodierungen, die sein objektives Sein in der Welt bestimmen. Folglich bleibt ihm nichts anderes übrig, als sich so aufmerksam wie möglich zu seiner Welt zu verhalten, was eine gewisse Kritizität einschließt, die Bereitschaft den Weltzusammenhang, dem es angehört, in Frage zu stellen, um ihn besser zu verstehen. Infragestellung, die ein Höchstmaß an kritischer Sensibilität verlangt, insofern sie ein Sicheinlassen auf die Situation ebenso verlangt, wie Abstandnahme, eine gewisse Distanz. Nur handelt es sich um eine Distanz, die inmitten der gegebenen Lage operiert. Eine aktive Distanzierung von den geltenden Parametern der etablierten Realität bei voller Konfrontation ihrer faktischen Existenz. Zur kritischen Einstellung gegenüber der eigenen Situation gehört die fortlaufende Auseinandersetzung mit ihr. Situativ ist das Subjekt auch in dem Sinn, als dass sich seine Situation kontinuierlich ändert. Folglich müssen das Denken und die Analyse dieser Situation sich mit ihrer Veränderung verändern. Es kommt zu keinem finalen Ergebnis mit letzter Gültigkeit. Zum Sicheinlassen auf seine Situation gehört weiterhin das Markieren eines gewissen Abstands zu ihr. Das Subjekt intensiviert den Kontakt zu seiner Realität, indem es ihr einen Widerstand einträgt. Was Gilles Deleuze die „grundlegende Affinität zwischen einem Kunstwerk und einem Widerstandsakt"[3] nennt, artikuliert den Riss zwischen dem Subjekt und seiner Welt.

3. Riss

Die Realität ist rissig. Sie entbehrt absoluter Konsistenz. Es gibt Spielräume der Freiheit in ihr. Jedes künstlerische Vorhaben drückt die Faktizität solcher Spielräume aus. Es eröffnet sie im schöpferischen Akt. Es gibt keinen Grund, die Kategorie des Schöpferischen als obsolet abzutun. Immer noch geht es in der Kunst um Schöpfung, auch dort, wo der Schöpfungsakt sich auf eine Mehrzahl von Protagonist*innen und Akteur*innen verteilt. Immer geht es darum, die Risse im Realitätsgefüge, statt furchtsam zu verschließen, offen zu halten, denn sie indizieren die Offenheit unserer Welt. Offenheit, die mit ihrer Unabgeschlossenheit konvergiert, mit ihrem Status als indefinite Realität. Das ist das Mindeste, worauf sich die Akteur*innen im künstlerischen Prozess einigen: dass die Weltrealität eine transformable Textur bildet, an der aktiv weiter zu weben *Kunst* heißen kann. Kunst als Akt des Webens und Gestaltens, der ihr neue Muster einträgt, indem er neue Konfigurationen ihrer Elemente provoziert. Die Rissigkeit der Welt markiert ihre ontologische Inkonsistenz, ihre Inkommensurabilität und explosive Heterogenität. Nur das (kollektive) Sicheinlassen auf den Inkonsistenz-, Inkommensurabilitäts- und Heterogenitätswert der Welt kann zu künstlerischen Ergebnissen führen, die welthaltig sind.

4. Denken im Kollektiv

Es gibt kein Denken, dass nicht per se eine kollektive Praxis darstellte. Denken ist per definitionem Denken im Kollektiv. Der Mythos vom einsamen Denken ignoriert die Weltangebundenheit des denkenden Subjekts. Immer bewegt es sich in, wie Wittgenstein es nennt, Lebensformen und Sprachspielen, die es mit anderen Subjekten teilt. Erst auf der Grundlage geteilter Evidenzen wird ihre Infragestellung möglich, die Einsicht in ihre Arbitrarität und Inkonsistenz. Das gilt für das wissenschaftliche Denken wie für die künstlerische und philosophische Reflexion. Nie geschehen sie im luftleeren Raum. Immer denkt das denkende Subjekt (und wenn ich Denken sage, impliziert das auch die künstlerische Praxis) in Kontakt und aus dem Kontakt mit Anderen. Es denkt innerhalb dieser einen Welt, der es mit anderen Subjekten, von denen einige ihm näher stehen als andere, angehört. Es ist diese Zugehörigkeit aus der es die Substanz oder das Material seiner kritischen Weltverortung gewinnt. Denn was ist Denken anderes, als der Versuch einer gewissen Weltorientierung? Weltorientierung und Weltveränderung, insofern jedes echte Denken eine Intervention in die Realitätstextur darstellt. Es gibt kein unschuldiges Denken, da jedes Denken in den Weltzusammenhang interveniert. Denken bedeutet bereits zu handeln; innerhalb einer Situation ihre Koordinaten durcheinanderzuwirbeln, sie zu rekonfigurieren. Das kann durch künstlerische Partizipationsmodelle wie durch philosophische Allianzen, wissenschaftliches Teamwork und politische Gruppierungen geschehen. Die Transformationen im Realitätsgewebe sind das Produkt oft unmerklicher Prozesse. Erste Aufgabe progressiven Denkens wäre, ihnen Aufmerksamkeit zu schenken, um sie, wenn nötig, zu beschleunigen und zu intensivieren.

5. Der Andere

Es ist bekannt, dass die Kategorie des Anderen bei Levinas und Derrida zentral ist. Žižek hat daran erinnert, dass der Andere nur dann ernstgenommen wird, wenn man ihn nicht überhastet seinen Vorstellungen von ihm assimiliert. Der Andere ist toxisch, schreibt er. Die Auseinandersetzung mit der Andersheit des Anderen kann nicht in vordefinierten, „humanistischen" Bahnen laufen. Wäre es so, fiele die

Andersheit unter den Tisch und damit das Problem, das sie immer auch darstellt. Die Psychoanalyse zeigt, dass die Andersheit durch das Subjekt selbst hindurchläuft. Es ist in sich bereits selbst ein Anderer. Niemals fällt es mit sich in eins. Es steht in einem originären Konflikt mit sich selbst. Derridas letztes Interview trägt den Titel „Je suis en guerre contre moi-même". Es geht um seine Krankheit. Zugleich benennt der Titel die wesentliche Aussage der Dekonstruktion zur Kategorie des Subjekts und des Selbst. Subjekt und Selbst finden sich originär von Andersheit, Fremdheit, ja, Monstrosität durchzogen. Die Selbstvermittlung des Subjekts läuft über die Auseinandersetzung mit der ihm immanenten Andersheit, Fremdheit, Monstrosität. Insofern ließe sich sagen, dass es kein Subjekt gibt, das nicht bereits mit sich selbst zu mehreren ist, wie Deleuze und Guattari einmal nahelegen. Das Subjekt ist ein originärer Hybride, eine Bastard-Entität.

6. Solidarität

Denken solidarisiert sich mit Andersheit, weil Andersheit zur Realität als ihr Reales, um es mit Lacan zu formulieren, gehört. Die Allianz mit dem Realen ist Öffnung auf den nicht internalisierbaren Anteil der Realitätskonstruktion. Real ist, was sich nicht in Realitätsgespinsten neutralisieren lässt. Die Konfrontation dieser insistenten Andersheit hat nichts mit Pathos oder Heroismus zu tun. Sie markiert nichts anderes als die Weltöffnung des Subjekts, die Susan Sontag als gesteigerte Aufmerksamkeit beschreibt. Sensibel für seine Welt zu sein, bedeutet sich für ihre Komplexität zu interessieren, für ihre Kontradiktorik und Mannigfaltigkeit. Der eigentliche Akt der Solidarität betrifft, bevor er einzelne Subjekte fokussiert, den Weltcharakter der Welt. Der gesteigerte Realismus philosophischen wie künstlerischen Denkens liegt in der Allianz und Kooperation mit der Diversität seines Weltzusammenhangs.[4] In ihm agieren die Subjekte wie in einer Situation reduzierter Übersichtlichkeit. Zum Denken und Handeln im Kollektiv gehören Kommunikation wie Blindheit. Auch Missverständnisse, Brüche im kommunikativen Ablauf, können Ressourcen von Verständigung sein. Weil es Denken nur als Experiment gibt – als Erfahrung mit offenem Ausgang – gehört zu ihm die Bereitschaft, zu Ergebnissen zu gelangen, die nicht antizipierbar sind. Immer sucht das denkende Subjekt nach neuen Wegen und Auswegen. Nicht aus der Realität heraus, sondern in sie hinein. Das aber verlangt Resistenz gegenüber allen etablierten Realitätsmodellen. Weltinterpretationen sind Weltanschauungen, sind Ideologie. Die ideologiekritische Dynamik des Denkens bricht mit den bestehenden Vorstellungen noch von Ideologiekritik. Sie muss alles in Frage stellen: den Kult der Frage und Kritik eingeschlossen.

7. Anschlüsse

Nach neuen Anschlüssen zu suchen, heißt, sie dort zu suchen, wo sie unsichtbar sind. Unwahrscheinliche Allianzen einzugehen ist die Minimalanforderung an jedes Denken, das mehr sein will als Repetition des Bestehenden. Kollektive sind brüchige Solidargemeinschaften, die der irreduziblen Andersheit des Anderen Rechnung tragen, statt sie gewaltsam zu neutralisieren. Zur künstlerischen wie zur philosophischen Praxis gehört das Zusammenführen des Auseinandergehaltenen. Immer geht es darum, die Wirklichkeit neu zu collagieren. Dafür muss es sie durcheinander wirbeln, ihre Verkrustungen auflösen, ihre fixen Bestände destabilisieren. Nur so sind neue Anschlüsse möglich, ein anderes Bild des Wirklichen, eine veränderte Realität. Daher gehört zu jedem experimentellen Denken, die Öffnung auf das Unbekannte. Das hat nichts mit Utopismus zu tun. Der Utopismus kennt das Ziel, zu dem er hindrängt. Das experimentelle Denken weiß nicht, wohin es geht. Was es weiß, ist, dass es woanders hin will, als wo es ist. Es weigert sich, im Bekannten, Abgesicherten, Offizialisierten zu stagnieren. Das macht aus ihm eine antikonservatorische Praxis. „Die Stärke eines Künstlers ist die Erneuerung"[5], schreibt Deleuze. Kunst zielt auf Veränderung, weil das Bestehende zu seiner Stabilisierung aufruft, das heißt zum Dogma des Jetzt. Künstlerisches Denken aber bedeutet, Löcher in sämtliche Dogmen zu bohren, ihre Hohlheit und Autorität zu demonstrieren. Das Neue widersteht dem Bestehenden, indem es auf das von ihm Verdrängte zeigt: auf andere Seinsweisen und Lebensformen, auf ungeahnte Möglichkeiten gesellschaftlicher wie politischer Organisation.

8. Kontingenzoffenheit

Man könnte von der Kontingenzoffenheit künstlerischer Praxen sprechen. Aufmerksamkeit auf die Welt ist Aufmerksamkeit auf ihre Kontingenz: Sie ist wie sie ist, aber sie muss nicht so sein. Das Kontingente markiert das Nicht-Notwendige. Der gesteigerte Realismus des Denkens verlangt die Anerkennung dieser Nicht-Notwendigkeit. Er impliziert Auseinandersetzung mit den bestehenden ökonomischen, politischen, kulturellen, militärischen, sozialen etc. Realitäten durch ein gewisses Maß an Dissidenz. Das heißt nicht, dass er von diesen Realitäten absieht. Er verweigert ihnen schlicht ihre Autorität über sich. Wenn es so etwas wie Dissidenz und Abweichung von den dominanten Dispositiven und Imperativen gibt, dann in der intensivierten Auseinandersetzung mit ihrer Brüchigkeit. Ein Wort für diese Brüchigkeit ist Kontingenz. Ein anderes wäre Inkonsistenz. Es gibt Verbindungen – mal explizite, mal implizite – unter allen denkenden wie künstlerisch aktiven Subjekten durch diese gemeinsame, wenn auch oft getrennt vollzogene, Kontingenzoffenheit, die Arbeit an der Transformation des Bestehenden ist. Sie ist deshalb nicht einfach negativ. Sie erschöpft sich nicht in der Angrenzung oder Absetzung von der aktualen Realität. Ihr Motor ist die Affirmation des

Unbestimmten. Sie bejaht das Bild einer gesichtslosen Zukunft, ohne in idealistische Projektionen oder utopistische Träumereien zu regredieren.

9. Heiterkeit

In „Ist die Kunst heiter?" schreibt Adorno: „Das Heitere an der Kunst ist, wenn man so will, das Gegenteil dessen, als was man es leicht vermutet, nicht ihr Gehalt sondern ihr Verhalten, das Abstrakte, daß sie überhaupt Kunst ist, aufgeht über dem, von dessen Gewalt sie zugleich zeugt."[6] Um es unverblümt auszusprechen: Heiterkeit ist nicht Dummheit. Sie hat nichts mit opportunistischer Assimilation ans Bestehende zu tun. Eher überfliegt sie das Feld der konstituierten Realitäten mit der Kraft der Imagination. Keine Kunst ohne Einbildungskraft. Aus ihr bezieht sie ihre Dynamik und Notwendigkeit. Der Realismus der Kunst ist einer, der zu träumen riskiert, ohne in Träumerei zu verfallen. Dazu gehört der Wille, Realität anders als sie ist zu imaginieren. Das ist die Heiterkeit über dem Boden der Gewalt, von der Adorno spricht. Sie intensiviert ihren Kontakt zum überflogenen Territorium, indem sie einen Abstand zu ihm installiert. Aus dem Abstand prüft sie seine Plausibilität und Relevanz. Es gehört zu ihrer immanenten Politizität, sich nicht abstandslos ins Gegenwärtige zu werfen. Dass es Kunst gibt, heißt bereits, dass sie sich durch eine elementare Phantasie von den Diktaten der dominanten Realitäten abhebt und ein Stück weit tatsächlich von ihnen befreit. Es gäbe keinen Grund für Kunst, ertränke sie sich in geschichtslosem Pessimismus und in narzisstischer Schwarzseherei. Sie bewegt sich, wie man mit Heiner Müller sagen könnte, jenseits von Hoffnung und Verzweiflung. Ihre Heiterkeit indiziert ihre Kontingenzoffenheit, das Wissen um ein indefinites Morgen, von dem niemand sagen kann, welche Gestalt es annimmt.

---

1 Susan Sontag & Jonathan Cott, *The Doors und Dostojewski. Das Rolling-Stone-Interview,* Hamburg 2016, S. 26.
2 Roland Barthes, *Die Vorbereitung des Romans. Vorlesung am Collège de France 1978–1979 und 1979–1980,* Frankfurt a. M. 2008, S. 309.
3 Gilles Deleuze, Was ist der Schöpfungsakt?, in ders., *Schizophrenie und Gesellschaft. Texte und Gespräche von 1975–1995,* Frankfurt a. M. 2005, S. 307.
4 Gesteigert, nenne ich diesen Realismus, weil er in voller Konfrontation der bestehenden Realitäten ihre Konsistenz befragt, statt sie fraglos anzunehmen.
5 Gilles Deleuze, Manfred: eine außergewöhnliche Erneuerung, in ders., *Schizophrenie und Gesellschaft,* Frankfurt a. M. 2005, S. 179.
6 Theodor W. Adorno, Ist Kunst heiter?, in ders., *Noten zur Literatur IV,* Frankfurt a. M. 1974, S. 149.

Alexander Koch

Mobilising S[...]
Art, Vocabul[...]
and Resolida[...]
after Richar[...]

idarity
y Politics
sation
Rorty

Alexander Koch

Mobilising Solidarity
Art, Vocabulary Politics and Resolidarisation after Richard Rorty

Richard Rorty's book *Contingency, Irony and Solidarity,* published in 1989, has significantly influenced the way I think about the social function of art for almost twenty years. And for almost twenty years I have been wondering why so few people in the art world have read this book.[1] It makes an important contribution towards helping us understand why and how art has a part in shaping social reality. I find myself repeatedly resorting to Rorty in discussions about the political nature of art, its social relevance and its social role. And I do so often shaking my head, because I cannot see why these discussions still revolve around problems that, since Rorty, we no longer need to have and should no longer have. In what follows, I shall recapitulate Rorty's position in order to suggest that, after him, talking about art means talking about solidarity.

The Contingency of Community
Rorty describes three different kinds of contingency: the contingency of language, the contingency of the self and the contingency of community. Contingency means that there is nothing more to be said about these three dimensions of the social other than that they became what they are not by necessity but for particular historical reasons, and at the end of the day are a product of a historical period that could have turned out differently to the way it did. Rorty presents western culture as a long series of attempts to outwit this contingency by eminent thinkers, who assure each other that, as long as they think and debate enough, they can arrive at true and definitive statements about the world, existence and human beings—at ultimate reasons or conclusive propositions on

the nature of things, in short, at a "final vocabulary".[2] In Rorty's view it was Plato who infected all his descendants with the fascinating thought that a few especially talented thinkers could manage to talk and write enough sense for their words to provide not merely a description of reality, but a description of reality as it *really* is.[3] This double concept of reality based on a privileged access to truth and objectivity has seduced western intellectuals—from the metaphysicians of the ancient world to analytical philosophers of language—into seeing more in their discussions than just the repetition and renewal of symbols and metaphors that generations preceding them have invented in order to communicatively get along with each other.

Rorty shares the fascination for Plato's idea. But informed by Wittgenstein's philosophy and Dewey's pragmatism, he thinks we should ditch Plato's thinking and curb our metaphysical enthusiasm. He believes that we[4] would be better off if we swapped the concept of linguistic representation for the more modest notion that we use language to solve problems. Rorty sees nothing more in a person's or community's final vocabulary than their ability to formulate statements from a contingent reservoir of new and inherited propositions, with which they can for the time being identify and which they will use just as long as they function relatively smoothly. If the experiences, challenges and aims of a community or individual change, so too does their final vocabulary. They distance themselves from statements and convictions that they have grown out of, and start describing themselves and the circumstances of their lives differently to how they have up until then. Rorty's anti-essentialism aims at freeing our understanding of our own language from the illusion that it is the product of higher instances than our own needs and purposes. He makes the case that we develop vocabularies suited to these needs and intentions, without behaving as if they represented anything fundamental.

What is true of language is also true of the self. For Rorty the self is a shifting network of idiosyncratic convictions and hopes with no objective foundations, most of which we have simply picked up somewhere. It is an assemblage of experiences and remembered images and phrases, some of which we are conscious of, some not, that we call our self. He understands subjectivity not as some inner human essence that can be unearthed, assuming one knew where to look for it. "There is nothing deep down inside us except what we ourselves [and others—A.K.] have put there".[5] Rorty sees the subject's striving for personal autonomy as a desire to appropriate the narratives in which it figures—narratives which mark the limits of its own self-understanding—in order to give them new readings. We do not emancipate ourselves from the descriptions others have made of us by uncovering some supposed inner essence of our being, but rather by reinterpreting those descriptions, modifying them and adding unexpected passages to them. The self's redescription of itself is not the birth of the subject's autonomous narration of itself, but rather a critique of the themes and styles of all those who have had a part in writing our story.

The same is true of community—albeit with consequences that are harder to accept than the narcissistic affront to our sense of self that contemplation of our own contingency brings. According to Rorty, communities are also founded on nothing more than changing narratives about at which point they draw the line between those people whom we call *we,* and others whom we call *the others.* For an anti-essentialist, one particular form of community cannot be privileged over another on the grounds that it can be better justified rationally or because the line it draws more closely conforms to human nature. The same is also true of democracy. Ideas of equality, justice and self-determination are not expressions of a form of reason that has managed to discover the principles of true humanity and attain the heights of a just way of life.

These ideas are cultural assets that owe their emergence to a long series of social struggles and political processes, books and artworks, disputes and agreements—and not to compelling philosophical arguments that democracies embody the right form of collective organisation, arguments which non-democracies simply refuse to accept.

In this regard, Rorty's disagreement with Jürgen Habermas over the universality of human rights is well-known. While Habermas assumes that any group of people in an ideal communicative situation would necessarily come to the shared view that every human being is possessed of inalienable rights, Rorty sees in these rights nothing more nor less than a relatively large group of people's normative decision to want to live in a world where such rights are guaranteed by the appropriate institutions. What is universal about them is not that they exist beyond space and time and independently of legal discourses, but that at some point a majority of people got behind the idea of unconditionally attributing them to all human beings. Rorty thinks that telling those holding contrary views that they are mistaken, and would sooner or later come round to our way of thinking if only they thought about the matter for long enough, is pointless. He replaces the distinction between right and wrong notions of how we should treat each other with the distinction between those kinds of treatment that accord with a community's ideas of a world worth living in, and other kinds of treatment that contradict these ideas.

Many critics take the view that, in doing so, Rorty forgoes the chance of taking a firm moral standpoint from which—for example—democratic values could be defended from forms of totalitarianism independently of any historical context. What could ground our solidarity with people who are being treated cruelly by other people, when there is no firm basis from which such cruelties could be opposed? The fact is that

Rorty doesn't only believe that there are no identifiable ahistorical principles in which our words, self-image or collective bonds could be definitively grounded; he also thinks that we have no need of such principles—indeed, that to support them is to attack democracy. It is not the case that questions of who we are, what we should think and how we can act are unanswerable without recourse to ultimate certainties—rather the contrary. If we free ourselves of the desire for such certainties, then an open discussion can begin which might allow us to answer the crucial questions for ourselves, and in so doing come to the conclusion that a community based on solidarity is something we want badly enough to fight for. Why, though, should we come to this conclusion in the first place? Why should we come to the position of wanting to be in solidarity with each other, and of incorporating metaphors of solidarity into our vocabulary, if not because we are certain this position is true?[6]

First: Rorty describes what he sees as the most promising intellectual position for a democratic and post-metaphysical culture by introducing the figure of the "liberal ironist".[7] In Rorty's vocabulary, ironists are people who see nothing more in their deepest convictions than contingent artefacts, and who are nevertheless willing to courageously defend these convictions. Ironists do not believe that they will find a book somewhere containing definitive and eternally valid propositions on how they should behave towards themselves and others. This doesn't stop them from supporting particular forms of behaviour and rejecting others. According to Rorty, *liberal* ironists stand for the idea that a community of people in which freedom, power and wealth are as equally distributed as possible would be the best community imaginable, and that this community should include as many people as it possibly can. Liberal ironists set themselves the task of extending the number of people that they feel connected to as far as they can. The fact that this task is *just an idea* does not detract from their conviction that this idea is good enough to be declared a basic premise.

Second: Rorty suggests that in order for this to succeed we should distinguish between our own private need for autonomy and certainty—our hope for a final vocabulary that could give an unshakeable foundation to our selves and to our own feelings of belonging—and the public project of a social world in which solidarity and equality are the highest goods. He thinks it is neither possible nor desirable to bring our idiosyncratic desires, preferences and fundamental beliefs into harmony with the desires, preferences and fundamental beliefs of everyone else. He envisages a quintessentially secular culture whose members would be capable of regarding their most intimate fantasies and metaphysical longings as a private matter, and refrain from troubling others with them. Instead they would regard it as the community's urgent task to view suffering of any and every kind as the worst thing that people can do to each other, and to work to create a form of society that minimises this suffering.

Third: there seem at present to be hardly any societies that are actually pursuing this task. Rorty had few illusions regarding the United States. In 1996 he wrote: "If I had to bet which country would go fascist next, my bet might be on the United States."[8] For our purposes, though, the crucial point is that, according to Rorty, we will not overcome social cruelty by finding objective, rational grounds for why it is false, but by developing a passion for the idea of living in a world where cruelty does not occur. This passion would not be sparked by other people trying to kid us into thinking they've found evidence for why some beliefs and ways of life are better than others. Rather, it would be sparked by a heightened sensitivity to the violence and degradation that we and others experience. This sensitivity would make it more difficult for us to think of people we don't know as individuals who have different feelings to us and whose happiness counts for less than the happiness of our friends or neighbours.

Fourth and last: it is for this reason that Rorty thinks philosophy will have little to contribute to a project of a community based on solidarity as long as it conceives of itself as a discipline of rational justification, rather than a genre of inspirational literature. Philosophy should think of itself as just one kind of text among others, texts whose relevance does not consist in the fact that one of them comes closer to the truth than another, but rather that some of them inspire a passion for social change and some do not. Rorty gives more credit to novels like Vladimir Nabokov's *Lolita* and George Orwell's *1984* for making more people sensitive to the life, passions and sufferings of others than he does to works of epistemology. This is why philosophers should stop searching in these works for clues to something that lies beyond our own ideas and actions. Instead they should dedicate their work to what Rorty calls cultural politics: to debates over which vocabulary seems more suited to implementing common social ambitions, over which forces influence these vocabularies, and how these forces can be supported or opposed. In addition, Rorty sees in "strong poets"[9] (his examples include Freud and Marx) the creators of new vocabularies, many of whom initially met with rejection, and some of whom have over time become part of our common cultural heritage. Having made this brief outline of Rorty's position, I will now proceed to develop some of the implications of his arguments.

Vocabulary Politics

Rorty's philosophical and political anti-essentialism goes hand in hand with an anti-representational conception of language and texts that we can easily transpose onto an anti-representational conception of practices and objects, including (and especially) that of the aesthetic.[10] This conception amounts to seeing art as nothing more nor less than a section of the contingent vocabulary that we use to picture to ourselves who we are and what we do, how we relate to the ideas, people and things that we encounter or produce, including those things we don't understand. From an anti-representational perspective, I have no problem with the fact that artistic practices and objects do this in a specific way, but I cannot see why this way should lay claim to a special depth and truth—to something that is supposedly more than just a product of ourselves, a product of time and chance. Nor do I have any use for the distinction between aesthetic acts or objects that *merely describe* reality and others that *describe it as it really is*—not to mention others that critique, transcend, question, produce or deconstruct it, or whatever else it is that gets said about art. On the other hand, I can see a big difference between those aesthetic acts and objects that force us to confront our own and others' cruelty, or can mobilise an imaginative capacity that is in solidarity with others, and other acts and objects that cannot or will not do this.

In other words: from an anti-representational point of view, the thing about art is that it co-authors the vocabularies we identify with, and by which we describe ourselves and our communities. These are the vocabularies that help orientate our perceptions, thoughts and actions, and they are the things that artists pick up, change, and occasionally reject in order to propose new ones. Whenever these vocabularies and the way they are used change, then the way we see ourselves and others—and ultimately how we live—also changes. That's why I consider interventions into the network of metaphors that communities use to better understand themselves to be interventions into their reality. From the point of view of an anti-representational concept of art, the question is therefore not whether or not art participates in social processes and influences their development, but whether it does so in such a way that brings us closer to the idea of a social formation that we would sooner have than the existing one. In general, a community will be prepared to move in directions that it can already picture itself following.[11] Without an imaginative horizon, a different future, a different self or a different community is barely conceivable, and very difficult to achieve. Aesthetic practices, objects and discourses have it within their power to sketch out such horizons.

So the point of the conception of art I'm proposing with Rorty is to see in aesthetic objects and practices an instance of what I call vocabulary politics.[12] Vocabulary politics refers to the social conflict over contingent and contested versions of society's self-descriptions, which ultimately come down to alternative ways of living together. I believe that this view sufficiently answers the question of art's social function and the possible ways it can be politicised. I don't need a deeper foundation or a better theoretical grounding for art's political nature, or for its *criticality*. I am quite content to regard the art world as one of the arenas in which our reality is contested and our future is negotiated. And I think it is extremely useful to think of these negotiations in terms of a contest between different vocabularies of subjective and social imagination—which are, among other things, apparent in the aesthetic form of works, in how they are presented and in how they are discussed. Not one of these vocabularies can be said to be more valid than another, but some we will find to be helpful and useful, others unhelpful, and still others just irritating.

What *can* be debated is what we should consider helpful and what irritating. It would be great to see an (art) world in which this debate is played out and in which no one thinks any longer that it is about anything other than comparisons, revisions and additions to existing vocabularies and their respective potentials to further our social ambitions and visions. Rorty does not think it would be either helpful or possible to try to settle conflicts between competing and mutually incompatible vocabularies by reducing them to the common denominator of such supposedly objective principles as historical development, rational consensus or human reason. For him, the antagonism between the proponents of different social imaginations and aims is irreconcilable. This is also how Chantal Mouffe sees it,[13] who like Rorty has described it as the merit of democratic cultures to be able to accept antagonisms and institutionally legitimise them. For Mouffe, democratic dissent turns opposing sides into opponents rather than enemies by enabling them to fight out their conflict without violence in a commonly recognised arena, instead of beating the hell out of each other somewhere.

As a liberal ironist and anti-essentialist, Mouffe agrees with Rorty that an emancipative vocabulary politics cannot consist of much more than the attempt to foster strong feelings and passions for the ideals of solidarity, and of making one's own liberal, pluralistic vocabulary attractive enough to have the chance of being accepted by others. It is here that the concept of vocabulary politics finds its true purpose. What will determine whether metaphors and visions based around solidarity prevail in our negotiations over our future prospects is whether a sufficiently large number of people can mobilise their imagination and passion for such visions, and whether we use metaphors capable of encouraging this mobilisation. Rorty's view is that we get along together better when we describe a more just world using words and images that are moving, engaging and plausible to so many people that they no longer want to—and perhaps no longer can—imagine a world that is any less just. And that they think, act and organise accordingly. At the same time, we need to find a language to describe both our own cruelties and those of others that will put us off them for ever. Those working in and observing the art world should regard the mobilisation and dissemination of such visions of solidarity as an urgent task, one that comes before all others else.

Resolidarisation

Those who suspect that my case for mobilising solidarity puts the horse of aesthetic practices before the cart of communitarian propaganda need not worry. I hope to use Rorty to remove precisely this kind of misapprehension. Though art may be a tool of vocabulary politics, I have no intention of instrumentalising it, nor should it spell out to us how we ought to live. And nor do I think that we will get anywhere by distinguishing between works that promote solidarity as such and those that do not—any more than I believe that we could or should do so. Nevertheless, members of a post-metaphysical culture who regard their own vocabularies and social forms as contingent should be able to decide what kind of art they consider to be good and proper, useful and meaningful, and what kind they don't. For anti-essentialists, this decision can only be based on their own needs, convictions and purposes. Anti-essentialists who are also ironists refrain from giving conclusive reasons for this decision, and do their very best to reach it by themselves. (Anti-essentialists who have read authors such as Freud or Foucault would add that this capacity for self-determination has its limits). Liberal ironists will make a case for an art that brings them and others closer to the aim of being more fair-minded, more considerate, and less sadistic; they will consider good and meaningful those artistic forms and modes of expression that concur with their ambitions for solidarity, and will regard others as unnecessary or irritating.

That is why I said at the beginning that to speak about art after Rorty means, for me, to speak about solidarity. Not because art and solidarity automatically go together, but because I believe that they *ought* to. For if our reality depends on our imaginative capacities, if our imaginative capacities depend on the vocabulary available to it, and if it is we who make vocabularies, in part by means of art, then the same must be true of our reality—and then every expression of solidarity in the reservoir of social imagination is a step towards a world without cruelty. And in my view, that is what emancipation aims at. I feel that Rorty's anti-essentialism entirely accords with the way that increasing numbers of people see things today. Few people now would seriously deny the contingency of language, the self and the community. And I would suggest to those who do that they spare the public their longing for universal certainty, and treat it instead as a private matter. However, not everyone will agree on what the consequences of Rorty's position are. They mean a change in perspective in how we relate to art. Much of the discourses and products of art, along with the texts and discussions that address them, have been shaped by the essentialist tradition. According to Rorty, questions such as what is the true essence of art and its realitionship to reality, what constitutes a work's real political meaning or its genuine quality—what a work is about, or what its maker had in mind—can be understood as attempts to obscure what it is our arguments and relations are really about, to stifle discussion of them by demanding objective statements, definitive answers and conclusive vocabularies.

Anyone interested in art and its relationship to politics should have nothing to do with this. The art world would be utterly different if it threw overboard the heritage of a discourse of rational justification, as Rorty has done for philosophy, and base itself on anti-essentialist and anti-representational premises. Then its members would simply change the discussion every time something came up that we would normally consider to be profound, fundamental or basic. Questions such as "what are the limits to painting?", "how realistic is a documentary film?" or "is Jeff Koons really a good artist?" would then become hollow. I don't think we miss out on anything crucial by leaving them *essentially* unanswered. This doesn't mean that we won't be able to think of any differences between what is and what is not painting, between documentary films and reality or between good and bad artists. I just think that—for the reasons given above—we shouldn't rack our brains about whether these differences are of a fundamental nature. If we find ourselves losing sleep over these kinds of questions, then we should discuss them with our friends.

By contrast, our public discussions could and should be about how, for example, we are able to distinguish between the conceptual coherence of a sculpture by Jeff Koons and the social aims it pursues, and whether we agree with those aims. I think that arguing with each other this way about what kind of art we think is good and what kind we don't is a brilliant idea. It could be useful to have a social history of art—or even a history of its solidarity—for this kind of thing; something that might help us understand how particular forms and styles, and ways of seeing things and behaving came into the world, what form of society they supported, why they prevailed and why we eventually got used to them. And how, should we ever think it advisable, we could get rid of them. The way we should approach artistic works and practices, how we relate to them and discuss them, should be like this: which forms of social organisation do they promote? Do they bring together people and things that would generally have nothing to do with each other, appear strange to each other, are hostile to each other or supposedly belong to different groups—do they leave them where they are, or do they drive them apart?

I still hope to see an art world whose members passionately discuss what forms of expression make a world they want imaginable, instead of a world they don't want. This seems not only desirable to me but also urgent. For it is clear we are currently living through a crisis of solidarity, which is putting many people at risk, and which demands new ways of seeing and acting, new vocabularies and metaphors that expand, rather than contract, the radius of people who see each other as a community. It is apparent that the existing models of social representation and practices and feelings of solidarity are no longer adequate to the changes of the last decades, of which the most important seems to me to be the establishment of a global finance feudalism that both destroys social cohesion while at the same time having to reconstruct it through an ever more oppressively powerful bureaucracy. There are many reasons why we are passing through a historic period in which our sense of community is outgrowing and abandoning historic mechanisms and institutions of control. Family, faith community, class consciousness, national identity: all these centres of gravity for common feelings of belonging and practical support are losing their power of attraction. I think we would do better not to mourn this process as one of desolidarisation, but rather to welcome it as an epochal upheaval, and work to move it towards an era of resolidarisation.

By resolidarisation I do not mean repairing broken social bonds and their old organisational forms, but rather transforming them. Solidarity, empathy, the need for belonging, a readiness to cooperate and sense of community are not disappearing. They are resettling in temporary environments, in new communicative practices, projects and technologies, in a variety of new private and public ways of relating to others, and are finding all kinds of new reasons for doing so. They are changing their horizon and their focus, their criteria and their form of organisation, their locations and their temporality. At present all these things seem to be in transformation. The contingency of community is an experience that is being shared globally by increasing numbers of people (some of whom are inclined to join backlash movements for precisely this reason); these people are looking for, and finding, other points of reference and narratives as a way to reorientate their desires and capacities for solidarity. Such phenomena as the Internet, the Occupy movement or current migration movements offer occasions for long digressions on how the social fabric of the planet is to be reconstructed. What will emerge from this remains uncertain.

Mobilisation
In this situation, (the) art (world)[14] is in a position to bring new definitions of different alternatives for living together into the arena of vocabulary politics, which could accelerate, rather than retard, a mobilisation of solidarity. Rorty's reminder of "strong poets" of the past makes a useful contribution towards this. He reads authors such as Nietzsche or Proust as people whose desire for personal autonomy enabled them to study books and events of the past not ever more closely and "philosophically", but rather ever more imaginatively. And they did so to the extent that they were able to redefine these books and events in a language that served their own purposes, and which had ever less to do with the past and ever more with the demands of a new era that was searching for its own language—a language that was first assembled in texts like those by Nietzsche and Proust before being taken up elsewhere. If we were to find an equivalent to this notion of strong poetry in the visual arts, then we might think of the work of such artists as Paul Cezanne or Vladimir Malevich: both attempted to get rid of old vocabularies of representation by changing them and adapting them to new challenges, until each finally found himself in possession of a new vocabulary, a new tool, that was better suited to the contemporary situation than the old tools, and

which therefore caught on. Rorty borrowed from Thomas S. Kuhn's *Structure of Scientific Revolutions*[15] the idea that, in this process, new tools not only served existing purposes better, but also brought new purposes into being, because things could be done with them that would have been unimaginable before.

Such "revolutions" or "poetic moments"[16] that we would today probably describe as performative, and which would formerly have been termed avant-gardism, change the way some people, and later perhaps many people, see and describe each other. According to Rorty, such moments arise primarily in situations when things no longer function properly, when what has been the common language up until then ceases to be effective, and everything is suddenly up for grabs at once, including language itself.[17] In these crisis situations—and we find ourselves in one today—"people begin to toss around old words in new senses, to throw in the occasional neologism, and thus to hammer out a new idiom".[18] Initially no one can say what the idiom is for, until it comes to seem plausible and useful enough to increasing numbers of contemporaries who adopt it as their own, and at some point it becomes common sense. Rorty's idea of strong poetry may reproduce an outmoded concept of the author, and makes no attempt to hide its Romantic origins. Nevertheless, it can be useful in the context of the current ongoing processes of resolidarisation. And it gains momentum if we relate it to the few passages from Rorty's work where he mentions philosophy, art and aesthetics in almost a single breath.

Rorty rejects the humanist idea that our sense of community could ever actually extend to include the whole of humanity, let alone anything beyond it. According to him, it is unlikely that we would ever come to stop distinguishing between people we share particular views with and whom we consider to be part of our own community, and other people whom, try as we might, we simply cannot understand and who in our eyes are not one of *us*.[19] Reconciling ourselves with this fact and making every effort to strive within existing conditions for "an ever better reorganisation of existing human relations and institutions, that is, one based on a human life worth living"[20] is what Rorty calls the (political and moral) beautiful. On this view, the beautiful in art would be the most harmonious organisation possible of aesthetic things and moments, one that makes these relations and institutions more comprehensible, and criticises, improves or reshapes them in a manner that lies within the scope of what is possible (and sayable) for us. Another word for this notion of the beautiful is reformism.

In contrast to this, Rorty sees in the sublime something similar to the radicality of revolutionary events: "the search for people and institutions of a kind we cannot describe in any detail, because they are not subject to the conditions that we still cannot imagine life without".[21] This means that the distinction between reformism and radicalism, between the beautiful and the sublime, "more or less coincides with the dividing line between […] participation in forms of social behaviour whose norms one understands, and invitations to turn one's back on these forms of behaviour."[22] That is, invitations to performative moments of which Kuhn would say that they bring new aims and purposes, new passions and forms of organisation into the world. This is why, for the mobilization of solidarity I envisage, it is precisely the sublime in art that holds out the promise of aesthetic acts which evoke a universal *We,* an ineffable community of equals, an ungroundable solidarity somewhere beyond existing norms and forms of behaviour. A solidarity whose practices, objects and metaphors would appeal to nothing more basic than the longing many of us feel to find ourselves repelled by the kinds of cruelty and segregation that we still cannot imagine life without today, and which too many of us accept as normal.

1 That I have so far come across so few people in the art world who share my fondness for Rorty has perhaps to do with the fact that the American intellectual declared himself a liberal, which in the European context would be equivalent to a social democrat, and today people understandably expect little that is good from a political affiliation of this kind. Perhaps another thing that puts people off him is that he barely wrote a single word about visual art; his point of reference was literature. But perhaps also the other reason why the proponent of neo-pragmatism has so few followers in the art world is that barely anyone has read him. To this day his name is as rarely to be found in the relevant art and theory bookshops as it is in the footnotes to the writings on sale there. This is remarkable, given that in the United States he is considered one of the most influential and controversial thinkers of the second half of the twentieth century, on a par with Habermas, Derrida and Foucault.

2 Richard Rorty, *Contingency, Irony and Solidarity*, Cambridge, Cambridge University Press 1989, p. 73 ff.

3 Richard Rorty, "Trotsky and the Wild Orchids", in *Philosophy and Social Hope*, New York, Penguin Books 1999, p. 9 ff.

4 The editors of this text have repeatedly asked me who exactly I mean when I use the word *we*. I think my answer would run as follows: I offer a point of view that I would like to be able to make attractive to as many readers as possible, and I use *we* normatively to stand for a group of people whom I hope would see things in a similar way to me. Since my argument closely follows Rorty's, it is natural to represent this group of people as the anti-essentialists and liberal ironists whom we both imagine as the inhabitants of post-metaphysical cultures.

5 Richard Rorty, *Consequences of Pragmatism: Essays 1972–1980,* Minneapolis, University of Minnesota Press 1982, p. xlii.

6 Here I am leaving out the major subject of empathy and its evolutionary and neuronal background. No doubt there are reasons why we feel solidarity with others. And the same reasons also contain arguments for why it is easier to feel solidarity for smaller, closer groups of individuals than for larger and more distant groups of individuals. However, recourse to the biological or psychological basis for solidarity would change nothing about the general thrust of my argument, and at worst it could be read as an attempt to bring essentialist justifications into it.

7 Richard Rorty, *Contingency, Irony, Solidarity*, Cambridge, Cambridge University Press 1989, p. 93 ff.

8 "Emancipating our Culture" in *Debating the State of Philosophy: Habermas, Rorty and Kolakowski,* in Jozef Niznik and John T. Sanders eds., Editors Institute of Philosophy and Sociology of the Polish Academy of Sciences Westport, CT, Praeger 1996, p. 29.

9 Rorty 1989, p. 28 ff.

10 Rorty himself does not complete—or barely completes—this step. This has always seemed to me a shortcoming, since the real relevance of his position for art only becomes clear when his arguments are transferred from the field of philosophy and literature to the field of art. This has its own dangers, which is why I would rather have had that Rorty himself had worked on them.

11 See Cornelius Castoriadis, *Gesellschaft als imaginäre Institution, Entwurf einer politischen Philosophie,* Frankfurt am Main, Suhrkamp 1990.

12 See Alexander Koch, "Kunstfeld 4. Die Privatisierung der Subjektivation und die taktische Öffnung des Feldes" in Beatice von Bismarck and Alexander Koch eds., *Beyond Education. Kunst, Ausbildung, Arbeit und Ökonomie,* Frankfurt am Main, Revolver 2005, pp. 145–164.
13 See Chantal Mouffe, "Deconstruction, Pragmatism and the Politics of Democracy" in Chantal Mouffe ed., *Deconstruction and Pragmatism,* London, Routledge 1996, p. 1 ff.
14 I find it increasingly difficult to distinguish between art and the art world (or the field of art). For all kinds of reasons I am finding it increasingly hard to distinguish between aesthetic objects and the social use that is made of them.
15 Thomas S. Kuhn, *The Structure of Scientific Revolutions,* Chicago, University of Chicago Press 1962.
16 See Richard Rorty, "Deconstruction and Circumvention" in his *Essays on Heidegger and Others: Philosophical Papers,* vol 2, Cambridge, Cambridge University Press 2010, p. 88.
17 Ibid.
18 Ibid.
19 Rorty has rightly been criticised for declaring the values and aims of his own community of liberal United States Democrats to be the social fantasy that has done more for emancipation than other fantasies, and should therefore become the model for all others. Obviously we should promote those metaphors and convictions that we consider to be great achievements, such as equal rights or freedom of expression, in order to convince others of their importance. But it is not enough to declare oneself the member of a community whose ideas one feels closest to, no matter how great one may consider it to be, and make these ideas palatable to others.
20 Richard Rorty, *Die Schönheit, die Erhabenheit und die Gemeinschaft der Philosophen,* Frankfurt am Main, Fischer 2000, p. 33.
21 Ibid., p. 33.
22 Ibid., p. 16 f. Invitations of this kind have been made by writers such as Bruno Latour, who has suggested that we should reconceive the distinction between subject and object such that we come to think of objects—buildings and cities, technologies and algorithms, the increase in sea levels, the hole in the ozone layer and much more besides—as social actors and subjects with whom we interact and to whom we relate. If we combine this invitation with the idea that we are living in a period of resolidarisation, the result is an unfamiliar but promising horizon for the question of how broadly we draw the circle of those we refer to as *we,* for example, how wide the radius is of all those things and events of which we are part.

Alexander Koch

Solidarische Mobilmachung
Kunst, Vokabularpolitik und Resolidarisierung *nach* Richard Rorty

Kontingenz, Ironie und Solidarität, dieses Buch von Richard Rorty, erschienen 1989, ist seit fast 20 Jahren die wichtigste Quelle für mein Denken über die soziale Funktion der Kunst. Und seit fast 20 Jahren wundere ich mich, wieso dieses Buch in der Kunstwelt so wenig gelesen wird.[1] Denn es hilft uns ein großes Stück weiter, die Frage in ein sinnvolles Licht zu rücken, warum und wie die Kunst an der Gestaltung sozialer Wirklichkeit beteiligt ist. In Diskussionen über das Politische der Kunst, über ihre gesellschaftliche Relevanz und ihren gesellschaftlichen Auftrag falle ich immer wieder auf Rorty zurück. Oft kopfschüttelnd, weil mir nicht einleuchtet, warum diese Diskussionen noch einmal um Probleme kreisen, die man nach Rorty nicht mehr haben muss und nicht mehr haben sollte. Ich werde Rortys Position rekapitulieren, um vorzuschlagen, dass *nach* ihm über Kunst zu sprechen bedeutet, über Solidarität zu sprechen.

Die Kontingenz des Gemeinwesens

Rorty beschreibt eine dreifache Kontingenz: die Kontingenz der Sprache, die Kontingenz des Selbst und die Kontingenz des Gemeinwesens. Kontingenz meint, dass sich über diese drei Dimensionen des Sozialen nicht mehr sagen lässt, als dass sie aus bestimmten historischen Gründen wurden, was sie sind, ohne Notwendigkeit; letztlich ein Produkt der Zeit, das auch anders hätte ausfallen können. Rorty schildert die abendländische Kultur als eine lange Reihe von Versuchen, dieser Kontingenz ein Schnippchen zu schlagen, indem sich kluge Köpfe gegenseitig versichern, sie könnten, da sie rationale Wesen seien, durch ausreichendes Nachdenken und Debattieren zu wahren und endgültigen Aussagen über die Welt, das Sein und den Menschen gelangen: zu letzten Gründen, zu finalen Sätzen über das Wesen der Dinge, zu einem „abschließenden Vokabular".[2] In Rortys Augen war es Platon, der alle seine Nachkommen mit dem faszinierenden Gedanken ansteckte, einigen besonders begabten Denkern könnte es gelingen, so vernünftig zu sprechen und zu schreiben, dass ihre Worte nicht nur eine Beschreibung der Wirklichkeit lieferten, sondern eine Beschreibung der Wirklichkeit, wie sie *wirklich* ist.[3] Dieser verdoppelte Wirklichkeitsbegriff eines privilegierten Zugangs zu Wahrheit und Objektivität hat von der klassischen Metaphysik bis zur Analytischen Sprachphilosophie abendländische Intellektuelle dazu verleitet, in ihren Gesprächen mehr sehen zu wollen als nur die Wiederholung und Erneuerung von Symbolen und Metaphern, die sich vorangegangene Generationen ausgedacht haben, um kommunikativ miteinander klar zu kommen.

Rorty teilt die Faszination für Platons Idee. Geschult an Wittgenstein und an Deweys Pragmatismus meint er aber, wir sollten Platons Gedanken fallen lassen und unsere metaphysische Begeisterung bändigen. Er findet, wir[4] wären besser dran, wenn wir das Konzept sprachlicher Repräsentation eintauschten gegen die schlichtere Vorstellung, dass wir Worte gebrauchen, um Probleme zu lösen. Rorty sieht in dem abschließenden Vokabular einer Person oder einer Gemeinschaft nicht mehr als deren aktuelle Fähigkeit, aus einem kontingenten Reservoir ererbter und neu hinzugefügter Sätze Aussagen zu bilden, mit denen sie sich bis auf weiteres identifizieren können und die so lange Verwendung finden, wie sie relativ reibungslos funktionieren. Ändern sich die Erfahrungen, die Herausforderungen und die Ziele einer Gemeinschaft oder eines Individuums, ändert sich deren abschließendes Vokabular. Sie nehmen Abstand von Aussagen und Überzeugungen, die sich überlebt haben und beginnen, sich selbst und ihre Lebensumstände anders zu beschreiben als bislang. Rortys Antiessentialismus läuft darauf hinaus, das Verständnis unserer eigenen Sprache von dem Phantasma zu befreien, sie verdanke sich höheren Instanzen als unseren eigenen Bedürfnissen und Absichten. Er votiert dafür, dass wir an Vokabularen arbeiten sollten, die diesen Bedürfnissen und Absichten gerecht werden, ohne so zu tun, als ginge es dabei um etwas Grundsätzliches.

Was für die Sprache gilt, gilt auch für das Selbst. Für Rorty ist das Selbst ein variables Netz aus idiosynkratischen Überzeugungen und Hoffnungen, die nirgends objektive Wurzeln besitzen und die wir größtenteils irgendwo aufgeschnappt haben. Eine Ansammlung von Erlebnissen und von erinnerten Bildern und Sätzen, die uns teils bewusst sind, teils nicht, und die wir unser Ich nennen. Subjektivität versteht er nicht als des Menschen inneren Kern, der sich ausgraben ließe, vorausgesetzt man kenne die Stelle, an der man zu graben hätte. „Tief unten in uns ist nicht mehr als das, was wir selbst [und andere, Anm. d. A.] dorthin gelegt haben."[5] In dem Streben nach persönlicher Autonomie sieht Rorty den Wunsch eines Subjekts, sich die Erzählungen anzueignen, in denen es vorkommt und die die Grenzen seines Selbstverständnisses markieren, und diesen Erzählungen neue Wendungen zu geben. Wir emanzipieren uns nicht von den Beschreibungen, die andere von uns verfasst haben, indem wir auf die vermeintliche Essenz unseres Daseins stoßen, sondern indem wir diese Beschreibungen umdeuten, variieren, und unvorhergesehene Passagen hinzufügen. Die Neubeschreibung des Selbst ist nicht die Geburt einer autonomen Subjekterzählung, sondern Kritik an den Motiven und Stilen all jener, die an unserer Geschichte mitgeschrieben haben.

Gleiches gilt für das Gemeinwesen – jedoch mit Konsequenzen, die schwieriger zu akzeptieren sind als die narzisstische Kränkung eines Selbstbewusstseins in Anbetracht seiner eigenen Kontingenz. Auch Gemeinschaften stehen Rorty zufolge auf nicht mehr als den Schultern beweglicher Erzählungen darüber, an welcher Stelle sie die Grenzen zwischen solchen Menschen ziehen, zu denen sie *Wir* sagen, und anderen Menschen, die sie *die Anderen* nennen. Aus antiessentialistischer Sicht gibt es keine Handhabe, bestimmte Formen von Gemeinschaft deshalb zu privilegieren, weil sie rational besser begründbar seien als andere und beim ziehen ihrer Grenzen dem Wesen des Menschen gerechter werden. Das gilt auch für die Demokratie. Vorstellungen von Gleichheit, Gerechtigkeit und Selbstbestimmung sind nicht Ausdruck einer Vernunft, der es gelungen ist, die Prinzipien wahrer Humanität zu erkennen und auf der Höhe des richtigen Lebens anzukommen. Diese Vorstellungen sind Kulturgüter, die ihre Entstehung einer langen Reihe von sozialen Kämpfen und politischen Prozessen, Büchern und Kunstwerken sowie Disputen und Übereinkünften verdanken – und nicht etwa philosophischen Belegen dafür, dass Demokratien die richtige Art und Weise kollektiver Organisation verkörpern, während Nichtdemokraten diese Belege nicht wahrhaben wollen.

Berühmt ist in diesem Zusammenhang Rortys Dissens mit Jürgen Habermas über die Universalität der Menschenrechte. Während Habermas annimmt, in einer vernünftigen Kommunikationssituation würde jedwede Gruppe von Gesprächsteilnehmer*innen zwangsläufig zu der geteilten Einsicht gelangen, dass jeder Mensch über unveräußerliche Rechte verfüge, sieht Rorty in solchen Rechten nicht mehr und nicht weniger als die normative Entscheidung einer relativ großen Gruppe von Leuten, in einer Welt leben zu wollen, in der solche Rechte von geeigneten Institutionen garantiert werden. Universell an ihnen ist nicht, dass sie jenseits von Raum und Zeit und unabhängig von juristischen Diskursen existieren, sondern dass sich irgendwann eine Mehrheit hinter die Idee stellte, sie voraussetzungslos allen Menschen zuzuschreiben. Vertreter*innen anders lautender Überzeugungen entgegenzuhalten, sie lägen falsch und würden uns früher oder später beipflichten, wenn sie nur unbehelligt und lange genug grübelten, hält Rorty für aussichtslos. Er ersetzt die Unterscheidung zwischen richtigen und unrichtigen Auffassungen darüber, wie wir miteinander umgehen sollten, durch die Unterscheidung zwischen solchen Arten des Umgangs miteinander, die in den Augen einer Gemeinschaft in Einklang mit ihren Vorstellungen von einer lebenswerten Welt stehen, und anderen Arten des Umgangs, die diesen Vorstellungen widersprechen.

In den Augen mancher Kritiker*innen gibt Rorty damit die Chance auf, einen verbindlichen moralischen Standpunkt einzunehmen, mit dem sich etwa demokratische Werte unabhängig vom jeweiligen historischen Kontext gegen Totalitarismen verteidigen ließen. Worauf könnte Solidarität mit Menschen fußen, die von anderen Menschen grausam behandelt werden, wenn es keine verbindliche Basis gibt, von der aus sich solcher Grausamkeit entgegentreten ließe? Tatsächlich glaubt Rorty nicht nur daran, dass sich keine ahistorischen Prinzipien ausmachen lassen, in denen wir unsere Worte, unser Selbstbild und unseren kollektiven Zusammenhalt ein für alle mal verankern können; er findet auch, dass wir solche Prinzipien nicht benötigen, ja, dass es ein Angriff auf die Demokratie sei, sie zu fordern. Die Beantwortung der Frage, wer wir sind, was wir denken sollen und wie wir handeln können, wird ohne den Rückgriff auf letzte Gewissheiten nicht etwa aussichtslos. Im Gegenteil. Wenn wir uns die Sehnsucht nach solchen Gewissheiten abgewöhnen, beginnt das offene Gespräch, in dessen Verlauf wir die für uns entscheidenden Fragen selbst beantworten und dabei zu dem Schluss kommen können, ein solidarisches Gemeinwesen für so wünschenswert zu halten, dass wir bereit sind, leidenschaftlich dafür zu streiten. Warum aber sollten wir überhaupt zu diesem Schluss kommen? Wenn nicht durch Gewissheit, wie sonst sollten wir zu der Auffassung gelangen, solidarisch sein zu wollen und Metaphern der Solidarität in unseren Wortschatz aufzunehmen?[6]

Erstens: Rorty beschreibt die intellektuelle Position, die ihm für eine demokratische und postmetaphysische Kultur vielversprechend scheint, indem er die Figur der „Liberalen Ironikerin"[7] einführt. Ironikerinnen sind in Rortys Vokabular Menschen, die in ihren tiefsten Überzeugungen nicht mehr sehen als kontingente Artefakte und die dennoch Willens sind, unerschrocken für diese Überzeugungen einzustehen. Ironikerinnen glauben nicht daran, dass sie irgendwo ein Buch finden werden, in dem sich finale, ewig gültige Sätze darüber nachlesen lassen, wie sie mit sich und anderen umzugehen haben. Das hindert sie nicht daran, bestimmte Formen des Umgangs zu fordern und andere abzulehnen. *Liberale* Ironikerinnen treten laut Rorty für die Idee ein, dass die Vorstellung einer Gemeinschaft von Menschen, in der Freiheit, Macht und Vermögen so gleich verteilt sind wie irgendwie möglich, die beste Gemeinschaft wäre, die sich vorstellen lässt, und dass diese Gemeinschaft so viele Menschen umfassen sollte, wie irgend möglich. Liberale Ironikerinnen verschreiben sich dem Ziel, die Anzahl der Menschen, denen sie sich verbunden fühlen, so weit zu fassen, wie sie können. Dass dieses Ziel *nur eine Idee* ist, tut der Überzeugung keinen Abbruch, diese Idee so gut zu finden, dass man sie zur Prämisse erklärt.

Zweitens: Damit das gelingt, schlägt Rorty vor, sollten wir unser privates Bedürfnis nach Autonomie und Gewissheit – die Hoffnung auf ein abschließendes Vokabular, das der eigenen Sprache, dem eigenen Selbst und den eigenen Zugehörigkeitsempfindungen eine unverrückbare Grundlage gibt – von dem öffentlichen Projekt einer sozialen Welt unterscheiden, in der Solidarität und Gleichheit die höchsten Güter sind. Er sieht weder eine Chance noch eine Notwendigkeit dafür, unsere idiosynkratischen Begehren, Vorlieben und Glaubensgrundsätze in Einklang zu bringen mit den Begehren, Vorlieben und Glaubensgrundsätzen aller anderen. Die Mitglieder der durch und durch säkularen Kultur, die ihm vorschwebt, würden in der Lage sein, ihre intimen Fantasien und metaphysischen Sehnsüchte als Privatsache zu betrachten und darauf verzichten, andere damit zu behelligen. Stattdessen würden sie es als vordringliches Ziel eines Gemeinwesens betrachten, Leiden jedweder Form und zu jedweder Zeit als das Schlimmste anzusehen, das Menschen einander antun können, und an einer Gesellschaftsformation zu arbeiten, die dieses Leiden minimiert.

Drittens: Derzeit scheint kaum eine Gesellschaft dieses Ziel de facto anzusteuern. Was die USA betrifft, machte sich Rorty wenig Illusionen. 1996 schrieb er: „Wenn ich zu wetten hätte, welches Land als nächstes faschistisch wird, würde ich wohl auf die Vereinigten Staaten wetten."[8] Der entscheidende Punkt für unser Thema ist aber, dass wir, Rortys Ansicht nach, soziale Grausamkeit nicht dadurch überwinden, dass wir objektive, rationale Gründe dafür finden, warum sie falsch ist, sondern dass wir eine Leidenschaft für die Vorstellung entwickeln, in einer Welt zu leben, in der Grausamkeit nicht vorkommt. Eine solche Leidenschaft werde nicht dadurch entfacht, dass einige Leute anderen Leuten weismachen wollen, sie hätten Beweise dafür gefunden, warum bestimmte Überzeugungen und Lebensweisen besser sind als andere. Entfacht werde sie vielmehr durch eine gesteigerte Sensibilität für die Gewalt und Entwürdigung, die uns und anderen widerfährt. Diese Empfindlichkeit mache es schwerer, fremde Menschen als Personen zu betrachten, die anders fühlen als man selbst und deren Glück weniger schwer wiegt als das Glück von Freund*innen und Nachbar*innen.

Viertens und letztens: Aus diesem Grund kann Rorty zufolge die Philosophie wenig zum Projekt eines solidarischen Gemeinwesens beitragen, solange sie sich als rationale Begründungsdisziplin begreift anstatt als ein Genre inspirierender Literatur: Als eine Sorte von Texten zwischen anderen Sorten von Texten, deren Relevanz nicht darin liegt, dass die einen der Wahrheit näherkommen als andere, sondern dass manche von ihnen eine Passion für soziale Veränderung entfachen und andere nicht. Rorty traut Romanen wie Vladimir Nabokovs *Lolita* und George Orwells *1984* zu, mehr Menschen empfindsam für das Leben, die Leidenschaften und die Qualen anderer Menschen zu machen als erkenntnistheoretische Schriften. Deshalb sollten Philosophen damit aufhören, in solchen Schriften nach Anhaltspunkten für etwas zu suchen, das unseren Ideen und Taten übergeordnet ist. Sie sollten ihre Arbeit stattdessen dem widmen, was Rorty Kulturpolitik nennt: Debatten darüber, welche Vokabulare ihnen brauchbar erscheinen für die Umsetzung gemeinsamer sozialer Ambitionen, welche Kräfte auf diese Vokabulare Einfluss nehmen, und wie sich diesen Kräften beispringen oder entgegentreten lässt. Zusätzlich sieht Rorty in „starken Dichtern"[9] (Beispiele sind für ihn u. a. Freud und Marx) die Urheber*innen neuer Vokabulare, von denen viele anfangs auf Ablehnung stießen und manche im historischen Prozess zum Allgemeingut wurden. Damit ist in diesem Text die gedankliche Absprunghöhe erreicht, auf die ich es abgesehen habe.

Vokabularpolitik
Rortys philosophischer und politischer Antiessentialismus geht einher mit einer antirepräsentationalen Auffassung von Sprache und Texten, die wir getrost auf eine antirepräsentationale Auffassung von Praxen und Objekten übertragen können, auch (und gerade) von ästhetischen.[10] Diese Auffassung läuft darauf hinaus, in der Kunst nicht mehr und nicht weniger zu sehen als einen Ausschnitt des kontingenten Vokabulars, mit dessen Hilfe wir uns ein Bild davon machen, wer wir sind und was wir tun, und welcher Art unsere Beziehungen sind zu den Ideen, den Menschen und den Dingen, die uns begegnen oder die wir hervorbringen, einschließlich der Dinge, die wir nicht verstehen. Aus antirepräsentationaler Perspektive habe ich keine Mühe mit dem Umstand, dass künstlerische Praxen und Objekte dies auf spezifische Weise tun, kann aber nicht erkennen, warum dieser Weise etwas von besonderer Tiefe und Wahrheit zu eigen sein soll, etwas, das mehr wäre als nur unser eigenes Produkt – ein Produkt von Zeit und Zufall. Aus dieser Perspektive kann ich auch nichts mit der Unterscheidung zwischen solchen ästhetischen Verfahren oder Gegenständen anfangen, die die Wirklichkeit *nur beschreiben,* anderen, die sie *beschreiben, wie sie wirklich ist* und wieder anderen, die sie kritisieren, transzendieren, hinterfragen, herstellen, dekonstruieren und was sonst der Kunst noch so nachgesagt wird. Ich kann hingegen einen großen Unterschied erkennen zwischen solchen ästhetischen Verfahren und Gegenständen, die uns gegen unsere eigene Grausamkeit und die anderer Leute aufbringen und ein solidarisches Vorstellungsvermögen mobilisieren können, und anderen, die das nicht können oder nicht wollen.

Mit anderen Worten: Der Witz an der Kunst ist aus antirepräsentationaler Sicht, dass sie die Vokabulare mitverfasst, mit denen wir uns identifizieren und in denen wir uns und unser Gemeinwesen beschreiben. Vokabulare, die unserer Wahrnehmung, unserem Denken und unserem Tun eine Richtung geben, und die Künstler*innen aufgreifen, variieren und manchmal verwerfen, um neue vorzuschlagen. Was immer sich an diesen Vokabularen und an ihrem Gebrauch verändert, ändert die Art und Weise, wie wir uns und andere sehen und wie wir letztlich leben. Deshalb betrachte ich Interventionen in das Metaphernwerk, mit dessen Hilfe sich ein Gemeinwesen ein Bild von sich macht, als Interventionen in dessen Realität. Aus der Sicht eines antirepräsentationalen Kunstbegriffs ist die Frage folglich nicht, ob die Kunst am gesellschaftlichen Prozess teilnimmt und dessen Verlauf beeinflusst, sondern ob sie das auf eine Weise tut, die uns der Vorstellung einer Gesellschaftsformation näher bringt, die uns lieber ist als die aktuelle. Meist geht ein Gemeinwesen Wege, die zu gehen es sich bereits ausmalen kann.[11] Ohne einen imaginativen Horizont sind eine andere Zukunft, ein anderes Selbst, eine andere Gemeinschaft kaum denkbar und schwer machbar. Der Entwurf solcher Horizonte liegt innerhalb des Möglichen ästhetischer Praxen, Objekte und Diskurse.

Die Pointe des von mir mit Rorty vorgeschlagenen Kunstverständnisses liegt also darin, in ästhetischen Gegenständen und Handlungen Mitspieler dessen zu sehen, was ich Vokabularpolitik nenne:[12] die soziale Auseinandersetzung um kontingente und widerstreitende Varianten gesellschaftlicher Selbstbeschreibung, die auf verschiedene Möglichkeiten des Zusammenlebens hinauslaufen. In dieser Sichtweise ist für mich die Frage nach der gesellschaftlichen Funktion der Kunst und nach ihrer möglichen Politisierung hinreichend beantwortet. Eine tiefere Ebene – oder eine bessere theoretische Fundierung – des Politischen der Kunst, oder ihrer *Kritikalität,* brauche ich nicht. Ich bin vollauf zufrieden damit, die Kunstwelt als eine der Arenen zu betrachten, in denen unsere Wirklichkeit umkämpft und unsere Zukunft ausgehandelt wird. Und ich finde die Vorstellung überaus hilfreich, dass in diesen Verhandlungen unterschiedliche Vokabulare subjektiver und gesellschaftlicher Imaginationskraft im Spiel sind – unter anderem in Form von Werken, deren Präsentationen und der Kommunikationen über sie – von denen keines behaupten kann, mehr rechtens zu sein als ein anderes, und von denen wir dennoch manche hilfreich und nützlich, andere unnütz, und einige ärgerlich finden werden.

Was wir hilfreich und was wir ärgerlich finden sollten, darüber lässt sich streiten. Ich stelle mir mit Begeisterung eine (Kunst-)Welt vor, in der dieser Streit geführt wird und in der niemand mehr meint, es ginge dabei um etwas anderes als um Vergleiche, Revisionen und Ergänzungen bestehender Vokabulare und deren Fähigkeiten, unseren sozialen Ambitionen und Visionen auf die Sprünge zu helfen. Rorty hat nicht den Eindruck, dass es dabei möglich oder hilfreich sei, Konflikte zwischen konkurrierenden und sich einander widersprechenden Vokabularen auszuräumen, indem man sie an vermeintlich objektive Instanzen wie den Lauf der Geschichte, den rationalen Konsens oder die menschliche Vernunft erinnert und so auf einen gemeinsamen Nenner zu bringen meint. Der Antagonismus zwischen den Anhänger*innen verschiedener sozialer Vorstellungswelten und Ziele ist in seinen Augen unauflösbar. So sieht es auch Chantal Mouffe,[13] die wie Rorty den Vorzug demokratischer Kulturen als deren Fähigkeit beschrieben hat, Antagonismen zu akzeptieren und institutionell zu legitimieren. Im demokratischen Dissens werden Mouffe zufolge Kontrahent*innen dadurch zu Gegner*innen statt zu Feind*innen, dass sie ihren Konflikt in einer gemeinsam anerkannten Arena gewaltfrei austragen können, anstatt sich irgendwo die Köpfe einzuschlagen.

Als liberale Ironikerin und Antiessentialistin pflichtet Mouffe Rorty bei, dass eine emanzipative Vokabularpolitik in nicht viel mehr bestehen könne als dem Versuch, starke Gefühle und Leidenschaften für solidarische Ideale zu entfachen und das eigene liberale, pluralistische Vokabular so attraktiv zu machen, dass es Aussicht auf Verbreitung hat. Damit bekommt der Begriff der Vokabularpolitik sein eigentliches Profil. Ob bei der Aushandlung unserer Zukunftsaussichten Metaphern und Visionen die Oberhand gewinnen, in denen Solidarität eine zentrale Rolle spielt, entscheidet sich daran, ob eine ausreichend große Zahl von Menschen ihre Vorstellungskraft und Passion für solche Visionen mobilisieren kann, und ob wir Metaphern verwenden, die diese Mobilisierung voranbringen. Rorty ist der Meinung, dass wir dabei weiterkommen, wenn wir eine gerechtere Welt in Worten und Bildern beschreiben, die für möglichst viele Menschen so ergreifend, anziehend und plausibel sind, dass diese sich eine weniger gerechte Welt nicht mehr vorstellen mögen und vielleicht nicht mehr vorstellen können. Und entsprechend denken, handeln und sich organisieren. Zugleich sollten wir eine Sprache für unsere eigenen und anderer Leute Grausamkeiten finden, die uns diese ein für alle mal verleidet. Produzierende und Beobachtende der Kunstwelt sollten sich nicht zu schade sein, die Mobilisierung und Verbreitung solidarischer Phantasien als ihr vordringliches Ziel zu betrachten und sollten ihm alle anderen Ziele unterordnen.

Resolidarisierung

Wer nun argwöhnt, mein Plädoyer für eine Solidarische Mobilmachung wolle ästhetische Praxen vor den Karren kommunitaristischer Propaganda spannen, kann unbesorgt sein. Genau solche Fehlschlüsse hoffe ich dank Rorty aus dem Weg schaffen zu können. Auch wenn die Kunst ein vokabularpolitisches Werkzeug ist, liegt mir fern, sie zu instrumentalisieren, noch sollte uns die Kunst vorbuchstabieren, wie wir zu leben haben. Ich denke auch nicht, dass wir weiterkommen, indem wir solidarische Werke und Kunstformen von nicht-solidarischen per se unterscheiden. Auch glaube ich nicht, dass wir das können oder sollten. Allerdings sollten sich Mitglieder einer postmetaphysischen Kultur, die ihre Vokabulare und Gemeinschaftsformen als kontingent betrachten, normativ entscheiden, welche Kunst sie für gut und richtig, sinnvoll und bedeutsam halten, und welche nicht. Für Antiessentialist*innen kann diese Entscheidung auf nichts anderem beruhen als auf ihren eigenen Bedürfnissen, Überzeugungen und Absichten. Antiessentialist*innen, die zugleich Ironikerinnen sind, verzichten darauf, abschließende Gründe für diese Entscheidung anzugeben und raffen sich dazu auf, sie selbstbestimmt zu treffen. (Antiessentialist*innen, die z. B. Freud oder Foucault gelesen haben, fügen hinzu, dass diese Selbstbestimmung Grenzen hat). Liberale Ironikerinnen werden für eine Kunst plädieren, die sie und andere dem Ziel näher bringt, fairer, aufmerksamer, und weniger sadistisch zu sein; und sie werden diejenigen künstlerischen Formen und Ausdrucksweisen gut und bedeutsam finden, die mit ihren solidarischen Ambitionen in Einklang stehen, und alle anderen als verzichtbar oder als ärgerlich betrachten.

Deshalb sagte ich eingangs, dass *nach* Richard Rorty über Kunst zu sprechen, für mich darauf hinausläuft, über Solidarität zu sprechen. Nicht, weil Kunst und Solidarität automatisch auf dem gleichen Blatt stehen, sondern weil ich finde, dass sie es *sollten*. Denn wenn unsere Wirklichkeit abhängt von unserem Vorstellungsvermögen, wenn unser Vorstellungsvermögen abhängt von dem Vokabular, das ihm zur Verfügung steht, und wenn Vokabulare von uns gemacht werden, auch mittels Kunst, dann trifft das Gleiche auf unsere Wirklichkeit zu – und dann ist jede solidarische Wendung im Reservoir gesellschaftlicher Vorstellungskraft ein Schritt in eine Welt, die sich von Grausamkeiten distanziert. Und darauf will Emanzipation meines Erachtens hinaus. Rortys Antiessentialismus steht meinem Gefühl nach völlig im Einklang mit der Art, wie immer mehr Menschen heute die Dinge sehen. Der Kontingenz der Sprache, des Selbst und des Gemeinwesens werden nur wenige ernstlich widersprechen. Und denen, die es tun schlage ich vor, die Öffentlichkeit mit ihrer Sehnsucht nach universeller Gewissheit zu verschonen und sie als Privatsache zu behandeln. Aber den Konsequenzen aus Rortys Position werden nicht alle gleich zustimmen. Für unseren Umgang mit Kunst bedeuten sie einen Perspektivwechsel. Ein großer Teil der künstlerischen Diskurse und Produktionen sowie der Texte und Gespräche, die sich mit ihnen befassen, trägt immer noch essentialistisches Erbgut. Was denn nun wirklich das Wesen der Kunst und ihr Verhältnis zur Wirklichkeit sei, was die eigentliche politische Bedeutung oder die wahre Qualität eines Werkes ausmache, worum es *in* einer Arbeit *geht* oder was ihr*e Autor*in wohl *im Kopf hatte,* all das sollten wir nach Rorty als Versuche auffassen, die Zwecke und Ziele unserer Argumente und Beziehungen zu verdunkeln und das Gespräch über sie mit dem Verlangen nach objektiven Aussagen, letzten Antworten und abschließenden Vokabularen abzuwürgen.

Wer nach dem Politischen der Kunst fragt, sollte dabei nicht mitmachen. Die Kunstwelt wäre eine gänzlich andere, würde sie das Erbe rationaler Begründungsdiskurse über Bord werfen, so wie es Rorty für die Philosophie tut, und auf antiessentialistischen und antirepräsentationalen Prämissen aufbauen. Dann würden ihre Mitglieder jedes Mal das Gespräch wechseln, wenn etwas von dem ins Spiel kommt, was wir üblicherweise tiefschürfend, elementar oder grundsätzlich finden. Fragen wie „Was sind die Grenzen der Malerei?", „Wie realistisch ist ein Dokumentarfilm?", oder „Ist Jeff Koons wirklich ein guter Künstler?" würden dann hohl. Ich habe nicht den Eindruck, dass uns irgendetwas Entscheidendes entgeht, wenn wir sie *im Wesentlichen* unbeantwortet lassen. Nicht, dass uns keine Unterschiede zwischen Malerei und Nicht-Malerei, Dokumentarfilm und Realität, oder zwischen guten und schlechten Künstler*innen einfallen würden. Ich denke nur, dass wir uns aus oben genannten Gründen nicht gemeinsam darüber die Köpfe zerbrechen sollten, ob diese Unterschiede grundsätzlicher Natur sind. Können wir deshalb schlecht schlafen, sollten wir Fragen dieser Art im Kreis von Freunden nachgehen.

Öffentlich hingegen können und sollten wir beispielsweise darüber sprechen, wie wir zwischen der konzeptuellen Plausibilität einer Skulptur von Jeff Koons und den sozialen Zielen, die sie verfolgt, unterscheiden können, und ob wir diesen Zielen zustimmen. Ich halte es für eine hervorragende Idee, uns auf solche oder ähnliche Weise darüber zu streiten, welche Kunst wir gut finden und welche nicht. Dabei könnte eine Sozial- oder gar eine Solidargeschichte der Kunst hilfreich sein, die uns zu verstehen hilft, auf welchem Wege bestimmte Formen und Stile, Verhaltens- und Sichtweisen in die Welt kamen, für welche Gesellschaftsformation sie einstanden, warum sie sich durchsetzten und warum wir uns schließlich an sie gewöhnt haben. Und wie wir sie wieder loswerden können, falls uns das ratsam scheint. Wir sollten künstlerische Werke und Praxen, unseren Umgang mit ihnen und unsere Gespräche über sie von diesem Ende her denken: An welchen sozialen Anordnungen wirken sie mit? Bringen sie Leute und Dinge, die sich fern liegen, gegenseitig komisch vorkommen, antagonistisch gegenüberstehen oder zu vermeintlich verschiedenen Ordnungen gehören, zusammen, belassen sie sie dort, wo sie sind, oder treiben sie sie weiter auseinander?

Ich sehe mit Freude einer Kunstwelt entgegen, deren Mitglieder leidenschaftlich darüber diskutieren, welche Ausdrucksweisen eine Welt vorstellbar machen, die sie wollen, anstatt einer, die sie nicht wollen. Das erscheint mir nicht nur wünschenswert sondern auch dringlich. Denn augenscheinlich erleben wir derzeit eine Krise der Solidarität, deren Verlauf für viele brenzlig wird und die nach neuen Sichtweisen und Verhaltensweisen, nach neuen Vokabularen und Metaphern verlangt, die den Radius der Leute, die sich gegenseitig als Ihresgleichen betrachten, erweitert statt verengt. Die aktuellen Muster sozialer Repräsentation und solidarischer Praxen und Empfindungen passen offensichtlich nicht mehr zu den Veränderungen während der letzten Jahrzehnte, von denen mir die Errichtung eines globalen Finanzfeudalismus, der gesellschaftlichen Zusammenhalt zerstört und zugleich immer gewaltsamer bürokratisch konstruieren muss, die wichtigste scheint. Es gibt viele Gründe dafür, warum wir eine historische Phase der Emanzipation unseres Gemeinsinns durchlaufen, der sich aus historischen Dispositiven und Institutionen verabschiedet. Familie, Glaubensgemeinschaft, Klassenbewusstsein,

Staatsbürgerschaft, all diese Gravitationszentren für empfundene Mitgliedschaft und praktizierten Beistand verlieren ihre Anziehungskraft. Ich bin der Meinung wir kommen weiter damit, wenn wir diesen Prozess nicht als Entsolidarisierung beklagen, sondern ihn als einen Epochenumbruch begrüßen und vorantreiben: als eine Ära der Resolidarisierung.

Mit Resolidarisierung meine ich nicht die Reparatur zerrissener sozialer Bande und ihrer alten Ordnungen, sondern deren Wandel. Solidarität, Einfühlungsvermögen und Zugehörigkeitsbedürfnisse, Kooperationssinn und Kollektivität verschwinden nicht. Sie siedeln um in vorübergehende Milieus, in neue kommunikative Praxen, Projekte und Technologien, in eine Vielzahl neuer privater und öffentlicher Weisen, miteinander in Beziehung zu stehen, und in diverse neue Gründe, das zu tun. Sie ändern ihren Horizont und ihren Fokus, ihre Kriterien und Organisationsweisen, ihre Orte und ihre Temporalität. All das scheint zurzeit in Transformation. Die Kontingenz des Gemeinwesens ist eine global geteilte Erfahrung von immer mehr Menschen (von denen manche gerade deshalb zu Backlash-Bewegungen neigen), die andere Bezugspunkte und Narrative für die Neuausrichtung ihrer solidarischen Begehren und Kapazitäten suchen und finden. Allein das Internet, die Occupy-Bewegung oder aktuelle Migrationsbewegungen würden lange Exkurse darüber erlauben, wie sich das planetare soziale Gewebe restrukturiert. Was dabei herauskommt, ist offen.

Mobilmachung
In dieser Situation ist die Kunst(-welt)[14] in der Lage, Neubeschreibungen verschiedener Möglichkeiten des Zusammenlebens in die vokabularpolitische Arena zu tragen, die eine solidarische Mobilmachung beschleunigen statt bremsen. Dafür ist Rortys Erinnerung an die „starken Dichter" der Vergangenheit kein schlechter Beitrag. Er liest Autoren wie Nietzsche und Proust als Menschen, deren Wunsch nach persönlicher Autonomie sie dazu veranlasst hatte, Bücher und Ereignisse der Vergangenheit nicht immer genauer und *philosophischer* zu studieren, sondern immer phantasievoller. So lange, bis sie diese Bücher und Ereignisse in einer Sprache neu beschreiben konnten, die ihrem eigenen Willen entsprach und die immer weniger mit der Vergangenheit zu tun hatte und immer mehr mit den Erfordernissen einer neuen Zeit, die nach ihrer Sprache suchte. Einer Sprache, die sich in Texten wie denen von Nietzsche und Proust erstmals zusammensetzte, ehe sie dann um sich griff. Auf ein Beispiel aus der bildenden Kunst übertragen, besteht diese Vorstellung von starker Dichtung darin, etwa die Werke von Paul Cezanne oder Kasimir Malewitsch als Versuche beider Künstler zu betrachten, alte Vokabulare der Repräsentation loszuwerden, indem sie diese so lange variierten und an veränderte Herausforderungen anpassten, bis beide schließlich ein jeweils

neues Vokabular in Händen hielten, ein neues Werkzeug, das der aktuellen Situation besser gerecht wurde als die alten Werkzeuge, und das daher Schule machte. Von Thomas S. Kuhns „Struktur wissenschaftlicher Revolutionen"[15] lieh sich Rorty die Idee, dass neue Werkzeuge dabei nicht nur bestehenden Zwecken besser dienen, sondern auch neue Zwecke hervorbringen, weil sich mit ihnen Dinge anstellen lassen, auf die man vorher gar nicht gekommen war.

Solche „Revolutionen" oder „poetischen Augenblicke",[16] die wir heute wohl als performativ bezeichnen würden und die man früher auch Avantgardismus genannt hätte, machen einen Unterschied in der Weise, wie manche, und dann vielleicht viele, sich und andere sehen und beschreiben. Zu solchen Augenblicken, so Rorty, komme es vor allem in Situationen, in denen die Dinge nicht mehr richtig funktionieren, eine bisher gebräuchliche Sprache nicht mehr weiter hilft und plötzlich alles gleichzeitig zur Debatte steht, einschließlich der eigenen Sprache selbst.[17] In diesen krisenhaften Situationen, und in einer solchen befinden wir uns, „beginnen die Leute, alte Wörter in neuer Bedeutung auszuprobieren, hin und wieder einen Neologismus einzustreuen und auf diese Weise eine neue Sprechweise zusammenzuzimmern",[18] von der Anfangs niemand wirklich sagen kann, wozu sie taugt, bis sie immer mehr Zeitgenoss*innen so plausibel und hilfreich erscheint, dass sie sich diese Sprechweise zu eigen machen und sie irgendwann zum Common Sense wird. Rortys Idee von starker Dichtung mag einen altmodischen Autorenbegriff wiedergeben und kann und will ihre romantischen Wurzeln nicht verbergen. Trotzdem kann sie uns weiterhelfen hinsichtlich der offenen Resolidarisierungsprozesse unserer Zeit. Und sie nimmt Fahrt auf, wenn wir sie in Zusammenhang bringen mit den wenigen Seiten, auf denen Rorty über Philosophie, Kunst und Ästhetik mehr oder weniger in einem Atemzug schreibt.

Rorty weist die humanistische Idee zurück, unser Gemeinsinn könne sich faktisch auf die ganze Menschheit erstrecken oder gar auf alles darüber hinaus. Es sei unwahrscheinlich, dass wir an irgendeinem Punkt damit aufhören würden zwischen Leuten zu unterscheiden, mit denen wir bestimmte Ansichten teilen und die wir als Teil unserer eigenen Wir-Gemeinschaft betrachten, und anderen Leuten, deren Ansichten wir beim besten Willen nicht nachvollziehen können und die in unseren Augen nicht zu *Uns* gehören.[19] Sich mit dieser Tatsache im Grunde abzufinden und unsere Anstrengungen darauf zu verwenden, innerhalb gegebener Verhältnisse „eine immer bessere, also auf ein menschenfreundlicheres Leben zielende Umordnung jetzt bestehender menschlicher Beziehungen und Institutionen anzustreben", das nennt Rorty das (politisch und moralisch) Schöne. Das Kunstschöne wäre demnach eine möglichst harmonische Anordnung ästhetischer Dinge und Momente, die diese Beziehungen und Institutionen in ein verständliches Licht rücken und sie auf eine Weise kritisieren, verbessern und umgestalten, die im Rahmen unserer Möglichkeiten (und unserer Sagbarkeit) liegt. Ein anderes Wort für dieses Schöne ist Reformismus.

Dem gegenüber sieht Rorty in dem Erhabenen etwas, das der Radikalität des revolutionären Ereignisses gleicht: „Die Suche nach Menschen und Institutionen von einer Art, über die wir keinerlei Einzelheiten angeben können, weil sie frei von Bedingungen sind, die wir uns noch nicht wegdenken können."[20] Die Unterscheidung zwischen Reformismus und Radikalismus, zwischen Schönem und Erhabenem, fällt dabei „ungefähr zusammen mit der Grenzlinie zwischen [...] der Beteiligung an sozialen Verhaltensweisen, deren Normen man begreift, und Einladungen, diesen Verhaltensweisen den Rücken zu kehren."[21] Einladungen also zu performativen Momenten, von denen sich mit Kuhn sagen lässt, dass sie neue Zwecke und Ziele, neue Leidenschaften und Ordnungen in die Welt setzen. Für die solidarische Mobilmachung, die mir vorschwebt, birgt das Erhabene der Kunst demzufolge das Versprechen auf ästhetische Ereignisse eines universellen *Wir*, eines nicht sagbaren Unseresgleichen, einer unbegründbaren Solidarität irgendwo jenseits bestehender Normen und Verhaltensweisen. Einer Solidarität, deren Praxen, Objekte und Metaphern sich auf nichts berufen, das grundsätzlicher wäre als die Sehnsucht, selbst die Sorten von Grausamkeit und Trennung befremdlich zu finden, die wir uns heute noch nicht wegdenken können und die daher zu viele normal finden.

1 Dass meine Vorliebe für Rorty in der Kunstwelt bislang nur begrenzt auf Gegenliebe traf, liegt vielleicht daran, dass sich der*die US-Intellektuelle zu Hause zum Liberalismus bekannte, im europäischen Kontext also zur Sozialdemokratie, und mit Grund erhofft man sich von dieser politischen Lagerzuschreibung heute wenig Gutes. Vielleicht steht seiner Rezeption auch im Wege, dass er kaum je ein Wort über die bildende Kunst geschrieben hat, sein Bezugspunkt war die Literatur. Vielleicht hat der Vertreter des Neo-Pragmatismus aber auch deshalb in der Kunstwelt nicht viele Anhänger, weil ihn kaum jemand gelesen hat. In den einschlägigen Kunst- und Theoriebuchhandlungen findet man ihn bis heute genauso selten wie in den Fußnoten der dort gehandelten Schriften. Bemerkenswert, denn in den Vereinigten Staaten gilt er als einer der einflussreichsten und kontroversesten Denker der zweiten Hälfte des 20. Jahrhunderts, auf Augenhöhe mit Habermas, Derrida und Foucault.
2 Rorty, Richard. *Contingency, Irony, and Solidarity.* Cambridge: Cambridge University Press, 1989, S. 73 ff.
3 Rorty, Richard. Trotsky and the Wild Orchids, in *Philosophy and Social Hope.* New York: Penguin Books, 1999, S. 9 ff.
4 Die Lektor*innen dieses Textes haben mich wiederholt gefragt, wen genau ich meine, wenn ich *Wir* schreibe. Ich denke meine Antwort läuft auf das gleiche hinaus wie dieser Text: Ich biete einen Standpunkt an, den ich einer möglichst großen Zahl von Leser*innen attraktiv machen möchte und setze *Wir* normativ als eine Gruppe von Menschen, von der ich mir erhoffen würde, sie sähen die Dinge ähnlich wie ich. Da ich nahe an Rorty argumentiere, liegt es nahe, sich diese Gruppe von Menschen als die Antiessentialisten und Liberalen Ironiker*innen vorzustellen, die wir beide als Bewohner*innen postmetaphysischer Kulturen

im Sinn haben.

5   Rorty, Richard. *Consequences of Pragmatism: Essays: 1972–1980.* Minneapolis: University of Minnesota Press, 1982, S. xlii.

6   Das große Thema der Empathie und ihrer evolutionären und neuronalen Hintergründe lasse ich hier aus. Ohne Zweifel gibt es Gründe dafür, warum wir Solidarität empfinden. Und die gleichen Gründe enthalten auch Argumente dafür, warum Solidarität zu kleineren, näheren Gruppen von Individuen selbstverständlicher ist als zu größeren, ferneren Gruppen von Individuen. Der Rekurs auf biologische oder psychologische Grundlagen von Solidarität würde an der Stoßrichtung meines Textes aber nichts ändern und schlimmsten Falls als Versuch gelesen, essentialistische Gründe für diese Stoßrichtung anzuführen.

7   Rorty, Richard. *Contingency, Irony, and Solidarity.* Cambridge: Cambridge University Press, 1989, S. 93 ff.

8   Emancipating our Culture, in: *Debating the State of Philosophy: Habermas, Rorty and Kolakowski;* Jozef Niznik, John T. Sanders (Hrsg.), Editors Institute of Philosophy and Sociology of the Polish Academy of Sciences Westport, CT: Praeger, 1996, S. 29

9   Rorty, Richard. *Contingency, Irony, and Solidarity.* Cambridge: Cambridge University Press, 1989, S. 28 ff.

10 Rorty selbst vollzieht diesen Schritt nicht oder kaum. Das erschien mir immer als Mangel, weil die eigentliche Relevanz seiner Position für die Kunst erst dann Gestalt annimmt, wenn man seine Argumente vom Gegenstandsbereich der Philosophie und Literatur auf den Gegenstandsbereich der Kunst transponiert. Und das hat seine Tücken, von denen es mir lieber wäre, Rorty selbst hätte sich mit ihnen beschäftigt.

11 Vgl. Castoriadis, Cornelius. *Gesellschaft als imaginäre Institution, Entwurf einer politischen Philosophie.* Suhrkamp, Frankfurt am Main, 1990.

12 Vgl. Koch, Alexander. Kunstfeld 4. Die Privatisierung der Subjektivation und die taktische Öffnung des Feldes, in: Beatrice von Bismarck, Alexander Koch (Hg.): *Beyond Education. Kunst, Ausbildung, Arbeit und Ökonomie,* Revolver, Frankfurt am Main 2005, S. 145–164.

13 Vgl. Mouffe, Chantal: „Dekonstruktion, Pragmatismus und die Politik der Demokratie", in: Mouffe, Chantal (Hg.). *Dekonstruktion und Pragmatismus.* Passagen Verlag, Wien, 1999, S. 26 ff.

14 Es fällt mir immer schwerer, zwischen Kunst und Kunstwelt (oder Kunstfeld) zu unterscheiden. Ich kann ästhetische Objekte und den gesellschaftlichen Gebrauch, in dem sie stehen, aus vielerlei Gründen immer erfolgloser als zwei verschiedene Dinge betrachten.

15 Kuhn, Thomas S.: *Die Struktur wissenschaftlicher Revolutionen.* Suhrkamp, Frankfurt am Main, 1973.

16 Vgl. Rorty, Richard. „Deconstruction and circumvention" in: ders., *Essays on Heidegger and Others. Philosophical Papers,* Bd. 2. Cambridge, S. 88.

17 Ebd.

18 Ebd.

19 Man hat Rorty zu Recht dafür kritisiert, dass er die Werte und Ziele seiner eigenen Wir-Gemeinschaft der liberalen US-Demokrat*innen zu derjenigen sozialen Phantasie erklärt, die es emanzipatorisch weiter gebracht hat als andere Phantasien und daher Schule machen sollte. Zwar leuchtet es ein, dass wir für diejenigen Metaphern und Überzeugungen, die wir für großartige Errungenschaften halten, wie zum Beispiel Gleichberechtigung oder Gesinnungsfreiheit, werben sollten, um andere dazu zu bewegen, sie ebenso großartig zu finden. Aber es reicht nicht aus, sich zu der Gemeinschaft zu bekennen, deren Ideen einem am nächsten stehen, gleich wie großartig man sie findet, und diese Ideen anderen schmackhaft zu machen.

20 Rorty, Richard. *Die Schönheit, die Erhabenheit und die Gemeinschaft der Philosophen.* Suhrkamp, Frankfurt am Main, 2000, S. 33.

21 Ebd., S. 16 f. Eine solche Einladung kommt zum Beispiel von Autor*innen wie Bruno Latour, die vorgeschlagen haben, wir sollten die Unterscheidung zwischen Objekt und Subjekt dahingehend überdenken, dass wir Gegenstände, Gebäude und Städte, Technologien und Algorithmen, den Anstieg des Meeresspiegels, das Ozonloch, und vieles mehr

als soziale Akteure und als Subjekte begreifen können, mit denen wir interagieren und in Beziehung stehen. Bringen wir diese Einladung mit der Vorstellung zusammen, dass wir in einer Zeit der Resolidarisierung leben, ergibt sich ein ungewohnter, aber vielversprechender Horizont für die Frage, wie weit der Kreis all derer und all dessen reicht, zu denen und zu dem wir *Wir* sagen, bzw. wie groß der Radius all jener Dinge und Geschehnisse ist, in denen wir vorkommen.

Ana Teix[...]
Peter He[...]
SOLIDARITY AND [...]
NEGATING THE RH[...]
OF SUBMISSION AS [...]

ira Pinto
mans

SHIONISM
TORIC
ESTINY

Solidarity and Fashionism
Negating the Rhetoric of Submission as Destiny

Peter Hermans: To discuss solidarity in the current political and cultural climate puts one in a strange place. The understanding of solidarity as "a fundamentally political gesture of identifying with a political task, even if [...] it doesn't correspond exactly with what one thinks and feels",[1] has shifted in different ways. On the one hand, postcolonial discourses critique solidarity as a gesture of charitable superiority; they see the language of emancipation as a coercive intrusion, and refuse to talk to and through the means of a "dead" interlocutor—the white "West" and the modernist rhetoric and philosophical canon associated with it. On the other hand, the call for solidarity with the downtrodden and underprivileged has also increasingly been adopted by the victim rhetoric of populist movements. Given this change in context and use, where do you think this uneasy position leaves the discussion of solidarity?

Ana Teixeira Pinto: Where to begin? At present it seems that the greatest obstacle to a broad left coalition is the divide between two competing discourses, namely Marxism and identity politics. The problem, I believe, hinges on the tension between industrial production and the forms of social reproduction it engenders: for the coal miner, coal-mining, however hazardous, is the only guarantee of a livelihood; for workers earning less than the living wage, fast food is simply what you can afford, no matter how many acres of rainforest are cleared away to make room for cattle. These are only ethical questions from the perspective of the western middle class, for everyone else these are simply the conditions you live under, not consumer choices you might ponder. Protecting workers' rights and jobs is likely to mean, under these circumstances and in the absence of a supranational approach, protecting a mode of production, which—though life-sustaining in a limited sense—is ultimately life-destroying. The same dilemma can be felt when it comes to the question of wage labour and its hidden gender and racial dimension. Both the sexual division of labour and the international division of labour perpetuate patriarchal and racial hierarchies, and, as Silvia Federici has argued, the western working class as been complicit in this process by devaluing women and Third World labourers. The whole discussion about the "white" working class, for instance, is symptomatic in the way it fictionalises these racist tropes.[2] If you look at different traditions, such as anarcho-syndicalism, you'll find a different take. Instead of proposing to take control of the state apparatus through revolution, and then implementing a "communist" economic model (nationalisation, centralisation, etc.), the idea is to bring into being a different economic model through *communisation,* that is, the establishment of non-capitalist social relations and modalities of exchange, which in turn would effect a social revolution, albeit slowly—here one could also question the fetishisation of speed, but that's another issue.

This is in a nutshell the idea embodied in movements such as Occupy, and it's interesting to see how they come under criticism for "lacking a political programme"…

PH: Such criticisms also articulate the problem of how to think across different scales, without invoking the sense of an abyss, of not knowing what to do in the face of a global scale. Which scale(s) are you immediately confronted with? Now that the historical phase of an overlap between capitalism and western hegemony appears to be fading, the realisation that globalisation is not intrinsically a guarantee of western superiority and privileges is provoking violent reactions, given that those whose lives are being impacted are *here*.[3]

ATP: Right, Yuk Hui for instance referred to the neo-reactionary theory that is emerging out of cyber-libertarianism as an anxiety about globalisation, i.e. an anxiety about how to manage globalisation without loss of hegemony.[4] I think you are right to point to the question of "scale", but "scale" is also a rhetorical operation: the depiction of capitalism as an overwhelming totality generates a feeling of despondency, people feel nothing can be done and devalue all the local struggles, and all the battles that were fought and won …

PH: Or they go looking for new models for retaining or regaining that hegemony in "sovereign democracy",[5] as projected onto states such as Russia, China, Singapore or by reanimating historical forms of governance, as the case with "neocameralism".[6]

However, models focusing on sovereign states overlook so-called globalisation from below, which Hui also refers to, and which has a much more immediate impact on the lives of people and complicates any binary distinction between centre and periphery, or between here and there.

ATP: Right, I agree and perhaps the only way to counter these forms of vertical sovereignty (and vertical warfare) is through horizontal movements, however headless they may appear.

PH: In relation to art, *solidarity* serves to point at the trope of art as having a supposedly unique vantage point, as probing or forecasting wider societal development or as an avant-garde notion of being at the forefront for the "disruptive" creation of new models of expression and organization. The underlying current is that the sociality of art, when it is a space for political discussion, critical thinking and theoretical production, is often seen as one that is intrinsically subversive or emancipatory rather than the product of a hegemonic discourse. This myth continues to be reproduced, but is becoming all the more absurd now that the artist embodies the ideal precarious worker who owns nothing but their creativity, happily recoded in cultural branding strategies and gentrification. Against the backdrop of growing inequality, this shift (again) places the artist socially in some kind of—polemically speaking—court jester role. Beyond the explicit or implicit politics of artworks themselves, what do you think of this development, or what do you think of the argument? Could there be anything productive in this "jester" role, in this proximity to power and capital?

ATP: I think your comment needs unpacking: the question of the aesthetic is not necessarily connected to contemporary art's modalities of production and distribution and art can (and does) operate politically in ways that bypass aesthetics altogether. To try to narrow it down: contemporary art can operate in ways that contradict the social and political aspirations of most artists, for instance by promoting financial speculation, by providing a liberal mask to repressive regimes, by promoting gentrification, etc. A common response to this problem is to abandon art-making altogether (there is a popular sticker that says: "leave the gallery, start a soup kitchen!"). I personally find it rather more interesting to reconceptualise the meaning and scope of what one calls "contemporary art." The recent collaboration between the NSU tribunal and Forensic Architecture (shown at *documenta 14*) is a good example of this, though I am a bit wary of mentioning it because I don't mean for it to be taken as a prescription. At any rate, the figure of the "jester" belongs to an older paradigm (Paul McCarthy, Maurizio Cattelan, Jordan Wolfson) whose conventions of plasticity are in my view exhausted—to be perfectly honest I think the whole "pop" routine of celebration-as-critique is exhausted—as is the "creative class" shtick.

PH: Even though we hope it can play a role in sculpting a future imaginary, I can also understand this wariness, this desire not to reduce art to an aesthetic instrument, as such turning it into propaganda, or forcing it into the narrow confines of a professionalised "contemporary art". With regard to the re-codification of food trucks, education, archive work, DJ sets, novels, small businesses (and one could add human rights work, as in your example) into things called artworks, Chris Kraus observed that "these activities have become so degraded and negligible within the culture that the only chance for them to *appear* is within contemporary art's coded yet infinitely malleable discourse."[7]

The proliferation of artistic work as a range of world-making practices often leaves one wondering about the political in the aesthetics. Regardless of their ingenuity, sincerity or doubtful character, these practices, whether intentionally or not, do underline—simply by leaving it unclear whether they are art or something else—that politics is not just about ideas, aesthetics, symbols and establishing rituals, as you are faced with the questions of who do you connect with, who is involved and who decides what and how and who gets paid.[8] To paraphrase Deleuze and Guattari; there can be passwords hidden under slogans.[9] Do you think there cannot be any productive dimension to working with illapses, camouflage, satire, with the symbols, language and styles of the hegemonic culture?

ATP: I tend to agree that social space and social practices are so degraded that "art" functions as a form of valuation. As to the question of *détournement*, misappropriation, yes absolutely, the problem however is that nowadays there seems to be a certain confusion between *détournement* and recuperation, in which a fantasy of transgression is used to mask a matter-of-fact complicity and a jaded cynicism.

PH: *Complicity* I find difficult, because on an economic and political level, our lives are intrinsically based on exploitation of some sort and therefore on complicity as part of the "silent majority". Capitalism is realised onto and through the actions and decisions of people …

ATP: Or maybe you can ask yourself a different question. I mean, rather than asking: "what is the truth of capitalism?" which is the question these *unveiling* or *disclosure* based practices pose, one can ask "how can capitalism be negated?"

PH: With regard to technology, there is a tendency in many classical left-wing circles to formulate a position towards technology that solely identifies it with the Silicon Valley model of governance via platforms, or as a tool for surveillance. This view often appears reactionary, since it can border on a vague technophobia, an unwillingness to engage with technological tools masked by a generalised, undifferentiated disavowal and a sense of alarmist despair and misunderstanding in the face of the current situation, to which the only alternative, according to this logic, can be some kind of local exit strategy. This is troubling in the sense that it contributes to the mystification of technology as a great "unknown", analogous to conceptions of technology as "second nature".

ATP: I think it would be a mistake to see "technology" as a politically neutral force. It has been pointed that one of the mistakes the Soviets made in the aftermath of the October revolution was to adopt Taylorism; since Taylorism has a hierarchical bias and promotes deskilling, they ended up with state monopoly capitalism instead of socialism.[10] This might be an over-simplification, but technological development is always accumulated as capital of one sort or the other. I think it's fine to go off-grid, but that is not the only available avenue (nor one I would undertake). There are other, simpler, options on the table, such as repoliticising the debate over the digital commons. The great socialist utopia that was actually built, to quote McKenzie Wark, is service infrastructure.[11] Having private companies as the sole providers of essential public services implies a fundamental social division between a digital plutocracy that owns all the assets and a vast underclass of users who pay for access. The defining struggle of our age will be the struggle over who owns "the internet," most importantly artificial intelligence.

PH: Yes. This underlines the importance of a technological literacy in coming to understand the (realistic) possibilities, and addressing issues such as the ownership of data and infrastructure. The "silent majority" returns here as the tacit agreement of the user agreement, masking the managerial obfuscation and outsourcing of choice and responsibility to individual "users" and their behaviour. What position are you placed in, what do you have access to, and on which conditions? I agree that discussions around cyber legislation and net neutrality will be defining for the future of the internet as a common infrastructure. Here, discussions of surveillance, datamining and tracking cannot be reduced to a middle class iDevice conception of privacy and security. To paraphrase the Occupy slogan, what do the global 85 percent, the Android phones, do? Are they left in the proverbial Stone Age as surplus? It should be clear that technology will not solve governance. A good example here would be blockchain technologies. You can use technologies "to enhance the processes of governance (transparency, online deliberation, e-voting), but in the end you see that they face the same governance issues as conventional third-party enforcers."[12]

ATP: Well, one could describe this in terms of a paradigm shift: whereas modernity and the modern forms of social organisation were predicated on a separation of church and state—downgrading the status of the church—it seems we are now witnessing a further decoupling, this time round between the political and the technological, and, as a result, witnessing the downgrading of the political as it is pushed to the margins of the decision-making process. Another way to describe the problem would be to say that whereas all forms of social organisation predicated on the privatisation of property give rise to a class relation, private property itself is not synonymous with capitalism, and the class relations that emerge out of financialisation are not necessarily relations between capital owners and wage labour.[13] Financialisation changes the social process by which capital itself is created, and whatever we choose to call it—digital feudalism, klepto-fascism, post-democracy—the coming convergence of financialisation and digital technology is at odds with our current models and modes of social (re)production. Remember Leonard Cohen? "I've seen the *future*, brother. It *is murder*." It is, or rather it is low intensity genocide, which will take the form of negligent homicide, via withdrawal of care.

PH: Even in the technologically more versed circles and associated events and discourses, such as the latest *Transmediale,* there seems to be a pervasive sense of despair and anxiety, explicit and implicit, about the technological agency of progressive forces. For all the analyses that are being put forward here, there doesn't seem to be much overlap with the more practical technology-versed crypto-anarchist hacker scenes. Part of this may have to do with the fact that the foundations of cyber-libertarianism are partially sourced from the crypto-anarchist foundations of hacker culture.[14]

ATP: When it comes to questions like technophilia versus technophobia, I think there is an ideological dimension which needs to be examined. The political content of cyber-libertarianism is Ayn Rand.[15] But let me try to answer this in a different way: Marx did not call the form of social organization that sprung up around Victorian steel mills "coal culture". He called it capitalism. The term "digital culture" obscures the processes of social formation and capital accumulation that digital technology enables. The other issue is that one uses the word "technology" to refer to entities whose technological coefficient is minimal, like apps or social media. The narrative that the "left" is technophobic does not amount to more than the (warranted) opposition to Silicon Valley "disruption"[16] by a handful of left-wing coalitions. On the other hand, there is a hidden racial dimension that ties technology to an imaginary temporality, and which is seldom addressed: technology is codified as progress, i.e. the future, and associated to the "west", allegedly the engine of history. Silicon Valley is now the cipher for this techno-futurism, which traffics on narratives of speed, wealth, globalization and efficiency. By contrast, black and brown nations are always depicted as stuck in the past: tribal, underdeveloped, chaotic, superstitious. In other words, there is an alignment of technology, whiteness and futurity. Afro-futurism challenged this alignment, because, as Kodwo Eshun put it, to be poor is to be condemned to live in the past.[17] To me, one cannot address the question of technology without challenging these narratives and this whiteness that is constantly tied to all things digital …

PH: I find the question of technology in the context of solidarity and art interesting mainly because it is a discussion about the tools and the means for communication and production and the ideologies embedded into them. Even if the all-encompassing ideas about "Big Data" and "singularity" (as the exit from human agency, from democracy, and eventually, from planet Earth) can be derided as a reactionary and colonial, white fantasy, these ideologies have real consequences, not least in terms of a practical focus on the means—such as infrastructures—and strategies of communication and mobilisation. If solidarity is basically the practice of working with and through vocabularies and (visual) languages, the question is how to relate to existing paradigms and tactics. With regard to alt-right meme culture, you have elsewhere[18] criticised the adoption or appropriation of its strategies, tactics and languages as a means of fighting it, as in "trolling the trolls" or finding better memes.[19] Why do you think that using the same tactics is a mistake, an affirmation of existing conditions?

ATP: The concept of singularity is very good example: by displacing political struggles onto the site of some chimeric antagonism between man and machine, this narrative obscures the question of ownership and (in)equality. The weaponisation of artificial intelligence, personified as a distilled form of *white-maleness-with-*

out-white-men, also stymies political theory, electing as sole concerns questions of survival and extinction. In my view, this is a "male fantasy" which traffics in chauvinist epistemes: "deep-learning" algorithms may be intelligent but are not necessarily conscious, while the putative potential of the "cyborg" as a man-machine hybrid has become reality in the form of the fully responsive environment of the smart city, not in the over-explicit phallicism of a Terminator-like figure.

In this vein, I would add that affirmational strategies tend to add "to the power of the thing critiqued" rather than subtracting from it. The concept of the meme represents a cultural analogue to the concept of the gene in evolutionary biology, hence to employ this term means that we are buying into the naturalisation of culture, and again, dramatising competition and selective pressures. It is important to note that these are not simply theories that might reflect some chauvinistic, conservative or racial bias; these are the theories that produce these biases; these are the theories that legitimise the matrix of supremacy and suppression via the rhetoric of merit and survival of the fittest. "Memetic theory" reflects this at a very fundamental level: by understanding communication from the vantage point of advertising, it reduces argument to sloganeering.

PH: Whether with regard to the "Overton window"[20] or "metapolitics",[21] these (contested) ideas of language politics build on the strategy of inserting a certain terminology or vocabulary in order to expand the normative frame of what kind of language is considered plausible and acceptable.[22] Whether in the form of the legends currently unfolding under the banner of "fake news" or cryptic branding (such as "alt-woke"),[23] both are piggybacking on the attention economy of social media. I do find the aspect of fashions and styles interesting here, the generational perception of what is desirable or "pop", because it actually asks questions about what is supposed to be common sense, without reducing politics to just a form of online shopping.[24]

ATP: When it comes to the alt-right, I keep hearing comparisons with the "Streisand effect"—that is, the more you thematise it, the more it grows. I find this argument wholly inadequate: the material economy does not follow the same logic as the attention economy. To suggest that it does betrays a bourgeois prejudice. Then there is the question of the psychology of meme culture and whether the detached cynicism it promotes is conducive to political engagement, or instead fosters mistrust and nihilism. When people talk about these new far-right strains they tend to deny how close they are to fascism (I mean historical fascism) because they tend to see fascism as some sort of motivational or aspirational endeavour. But the (Italian) fascist's motto was *me ne frego* (I don't give a damn) and the Futurists slogan was *Fiat ars – pereat mundus* (Let art be created, though the world perish) and their whole psychological landscape hinges on nihilism. Needless to say, fascism does not hold a monopoly on nihilism, you will find it at the intersection of accelerationism and cyber libertarianism, such as NRx[25], and you will find it in Silicon Valley's "disruptive innovation" mantra, and in most contemporary pop culture, or in the style known as post-internet art.

Instead of focusing on memes, I think we should pay attention to language. I say this because I think images never mean much by themselves, the meaning is not in the image, it's in the narrative, in the chain of associations, that the image activates. The alt-right claims that the Frankfurt school (a code word for Jews) created cultural Marxism (another code word for Jews) to destroy white civilization. The neo-reactionaries replace cultural Marxism with the Calvinist left but they retain the idea of the "left" as a phantasmal antagonist, some sort of chimeric hate-object. Then you have left-accelerationism speaking of a "reactive left" or "folk politics", and again the same signifying chain is activated, and again the "left" appears as an undifferentiated bad-object, which stands for failure and impotency. I think these narratives, which align Prometheanism—the belief in the power of humans to defeat nature with the help of technology-, potency and power, tend to produce an aesthetic effect but do not provide us with any theoretical tool with which to make sense of our situation.

PH: The psychology (and nihilistic celebration) of the "end of the world as we know it" narrative I find very striking here. One could argue that the very real catastrophes of biological extinction and climate change should be of much greater concern than the danger that humanity may be rendered redundant by artificial intelligence. Perhaps still more importantly, in any discussion of solidarity the historical determinism of Marxist and accelerationist creative destruction leaves unanswered the question of who will accelerate or *disrupt* things for whom.[26] In this sense, accelerationism seems to have a purchase on how "we" in the West are living, acknowledging we are going through a transition phase without going too much into the "ring of fire", the troubled phase of transition where acceleration is manifested by (tactical) escalation, a succession of crises.[27] And while I do think that a focus on strategy and tactics is more fruitful than designing "pure" utopias, the question remains of whether this hyperbolic conflation of means and ends does not mirror the managerial logic of contemporary governance, protocols and interfaces recoded as smoothing, stabilising protections.[28]

ATP: Yes, as Evan Calder Willliams argues, "to envision the future in a way that is not ultimately complicit with the conditions that constitute the present [...] involves [...] a recognition that nothing clearly marks a passage *into* the future without undoing the forms that bind lives, materials, and systems, in variably punitive ways, to a mode of time designed around the continuity of the present." By *future* "we may well mean just that sensation of coming unstuck in and from the present."[29] We need to depart from the cliché of criticality as something purely reactive (showing contradictions, revealing lies and deconstructing ideologies), and employ negation as a productive principle in order to stop the miserable present from reproducing itself.

PH: I think the sense of getting *unstuck* relates to a number of transitions, not least in respect of agency. If the digital collapses the logic of production with its consumption "without offering a future beyond the technological updating of these drifting repetitions", where does that leave one?[30] But also, why suppose that mere exposure to a "dangerous" idea would win people over? Are you then not dismissing them as stupid? How can we avoid becoming part of the condition of "meta-slavery" where we are either a slave to the zeitgeist or a slave to the meta-discourse that criticizes the zeitgeist?[31] The clichés of the times are the algorithmic identities and predictable roles, the ready-made, scripted, drama between the stock characters of sock puppets, spokespersons, victims, prophets, hacks and celebrities. This corresponds to a totalitarian logic, in which any non-conformist statement is delegitimised by calling into doubt the intention and integrity of the speaker. To put it poetically, where do we start with the work, rather than the magic, of solidarity?

ATP: If I understood correctly, you are asking "who is the collective subject?" in the sense of political agent, as in "who is the revolutionary agent?" I guess the answer is still the same: whoever asks the question of property. Clearly the "west" is not asking the question of property at the moment, beyond the narrow confines of some academic discussions, but there are manifold movements, even within the crevices of the "west," who are.

About your other point, obviously there is a conundrum in the way protocols, as techniques of governance, come into force. According to Felix Stalder, for instance, protocols lie at the heart of the question to which cybernetics became the answer: how can society be governed without recourse to politics?[32] Protocols come into force through voluntary adoption. Enforcement is decentralised and ubiquitous but, once adopted, protocols became conditions upon which economic or social agents are constituted. In other words, protocols are enforced by the matrix of interdependencies they engender, as well as by the interactions they afford. But because protocols have an inherent anti-political bias these transformations also allowed for a restoration of corporate profit and elite power. And though the things afforded by these protocols are initially beneficial (such as Facebook, the EU, the WTO, Airbnb), it soon becomes clear they carry hidden costs. Leaving the space defined by the protocol is seldom an option however, because the financial or social costs would be considerably higher than the costs imposed by the protocol into which one enters—in the case of Facebook for instance, you trade privacy and integrity for loss of relevance and, by extension, loss of revenue. For Stalder this leads us to a psychological paradox: everybody is voluntarily doing what no one truly wants to do.

PH: I asked this question about agency as a way of pointing to the process of negotiation between "where you are placed" and "where you place yourself", of not placing people in a corner from the start, inside a master/slave role. One should be wary of anything that seems to represent the "will" of any (group of) people as something holistic, but agency can only be gained through a negotiation between the individual and collective modes, without fetishising the one or the other.

ATP: Morgan Quaintance just addressed this thirst for *empowerment* in an essay on "cultic cultures", in which he describes the appetite for non-conformist ideologies as a form of "seekership", which seems to foster a cultic milieu, permeated by cyber-obscurantism.[33] I think this pull towards monomania and this esoteric drift is tied to what Jameson described as the tendency to see the world as an extension of one's own paranoid subjectivity. In his view, the digital turn seems to correlate with a crisis in representation: though equipped with a growing variety of optical media, we are increasingly unable to grasp the algorithmic totality which surrounds us. Data's primary mode of existence, as Alexander Galloway argues, is not a visual one,[34] and the twin forces of globalization and digitalistion tend to widen the gap between individual experience and the economic structures that determine it. What happens to art when phenomenological experience—the raw material aesthetics is made of—becomes secondary to information flows? Frederic Jameson proposes that one could counter this condition by means of "cognitive mapping":[35] a cartography of the structural coordinates which underpin the diffuse world of post-Fordist economies. This concept has no status in contemporary art, but a certain number of artists do seem to put it into practice by tying personal biography with collective history—a way of negotiating personal reflection and political agency by mobilising affect and emotion.

1. Milo Rau in: Dominikus Müller, "Get Real: A Conversation with Theatre Director Milo Rau about Responsibility, Empathy and 'Meta-Slavery'", *Friezed/e*, 24, https://frieze.com/article/get-real?language=en
2. Silvia Federici, *Revolution at Point Zero: Housework, Reproduction and Feminist Struggle,* Oakland, PM Press 2012, p. 208.
3. Hamid Dabashi, *Can Non-Europeans Think?*, London, Zed Books 2015, p. 82. In relation to the condition of coloniality, that first produced the "Global South", Dabashi writes:
"So this 'we' is no longer color-coded or continental and includes all those disenfranchised by the global operation of capital whether in the north or south of planet Earth, or deep into cyberspace, or else flown into outer space, and those richly privileged by the selfsame operation. In its originary modernity this globalized capital was made mythically 'European'. It no longer is. It has been de-Europeanized, freed from its overreaching fetishes. Rich Arab, Indian, Russian, Chinese, Latin American, or African entrepreneurs, mafia states, deep states, garrison states, Israeli warlords, and mercenary murderers of Isis are part and parcel of a worldly reality that has for ever dispensed with the myth of 'the West.'" (Online: *Zed Books blog*, Juli 2016, https://www.zedbooks.net/blog/posts/fuck-you-zizek)
4. Yuk Hui, "On the Unhappy Consciousness of Neoreactionaries" *e-flux* 81, April 2017, http://www.e-flux.com/journal/81/125815/on-the-unhappy-consciousness-of-neoreactionaries/

5   The term "sovereign democracy" or "managed democracy", as used in recent years, is attributed to Vladislav Surkov, by that time advisor to President Vladimir Putin, to describe a situation in which "democratic institutions are maintained without any democratic freedoms". Surkov was stylised as the grey cardinal of the Kremlin, seen as the architect of the (dis)information strategy of the regime, especially in relation to the 2013 annexation of the Crimea. This (neo-orientalist) fascination with (East-)Asia has a history, starting with the narrative of the "Asian Tigers" in the 1990s invoking the myth of "Asian values [as] a sort of Confucian version of Weber's glorification of the Protestant work ethic", later repeated onto the United Arab Emirates (esp. Dubai) and Qatar. See Peter Pomerantsev, "Putins Rasputin", *London Review of Books,* Vol. 33, No. 20, 2011, pp. 3–6 and Peter Pomerantsev, "The Hidden Author of Putinism. How Vladislav Surkov invented the new Russia", *The Atlantic,* November 2014, https://www.theatlantic.com/international/archive/2014/11/hidden-author-putinism-russia-vladislav-surkov/382489/; Josephine Armistead, "The Silicon Ideology", 18 May 2016, https://archive.org/details/the-silicon-ideology, p. 12.

6   Originating in 18th century Prussia, cameralism describes the science and technology of administration, focused on standardisation and efficiency. The concept was picked up again in the neo-reactionary blogosphere to depict an (esoteric) efficiency-based conception of a society without politics, ruled by a managerial elite (and AI). Similar ideas are appealed to via concepts such as "gov-corp", states to be governed like a company, or the Seasteading movement, which seeks to establish artificial island communities as outpost of "innovation", seceding from the "hindering" jurisdiction of national states.

7   Chris Kraus, "Lessons: Art School", in *Akademie X. Lessons in Art + Life,* London/New York, Phaidon 2015, pp. 166–173.

8   In this context, see Dena Yago, "On Ketamin and Added Value", *e-flux* 82, May 2017, http://www.e-flux.com/journal/82/133913/on-ketamine-and-added-value/

9   Gilles Deleuze & Félix Guattari, *A Thousand Plateaus. Capitalism and Schizophrenia,* New York, Continuum 2004, p. 110, cited and discussed in Tiqqun, The Cybernetic Hypothesis, 2010, p. 35. https://theanarchistlibrary.org/library/tiqqun-the-cybernetic-hypothesis

10 Published by Frederick Taylor in 1911, Taylorism prescribes a practice of "scientific management" and efficiency of work and follows three main principles: break complex jobs down into simple ones; measure everything that workers do; and link pay to performance, giving bonuses to high-achievers and punishing sluggards. For a discussion of Taylorism in contemporary "digital" economies, see "Digital Taylorism", *The Economist,* 10 September 2015, https://www.economist.com/news/business/21664190-modern-version-scientific-management-threatens-dehumanise-workplace-digital

11 McKenzie Wark, "Renotopia", *Harvard Design Magazine* 4, Fall/Winter 2015, http://www.harvarddesignmagazine.org/issues/41/renotopia

12 Vili Lehdonvirta, "The Blockchain Paradox", *Oxford Internet Institute,* University of Oxford, 21 November 2016, https://www.oii.ox.ac.uk/blog/the-blockchain-paradox-why-distributed-ledger-technologies-may-do-little-to-transform-the-economy

13 McKenzie Wark, "The Sublime Language of My Century", *Public Seminar,* 14 May 2016, http://www.publicseminar.org/2016/05/the-sublime-language-of-my-century/

14 Cyber-libertarianism has its roots equally in the internet's early hacker culture and in American libertarianism. From hacker culture it inherited the general antagonism to any form of regulation or censorship that might stand in the way of "free" (i.e., unhindered) access of the internet. From American libertarianism it inherited the classical libertarian emphasis on personal autonomy and rejection of government interference. This is not unlike the anti-statism of hacker and crypto-anarchist (f.e. cyberphunk, or more recently, Anonymous) thinking, which argues for the right to encrypt and stay anonymous as an inherent expression of freedom. Setting it apart from cyber- and crypto-anarchists emphasis on decentralization and collaborative modes of organisation, this particular conception of libertarianism celebrates the market and private entrepreneurship and embraces meritocratic hierarchies. The term is as such related to the "the Californian Ideology", a mixture of New Left and New Right beliefs based on a shared interest in anti-statism, the counterculture of the 1960s and techno-utopianism and current discussions around "Platform Capitalism". See Armistead, 2016, Gabriella Coleman, *Hacker, Hoaxer, Whistleblower, Spy, The Many Faces of Anonymous,* London, Verso 2015, 476 p.; Richard Barbrook & Andy Cameron, "The Californian Ideology", *Mute* 3, Autumn 1995, http://www.metamute.org/editorial/articles/californian-ideology; Nick Srnicek, *Platform Capitalism,* Cambridge, Polity Press 2017.

15 Ayn Rand was a political philosopher and writer, whose ideas, through her fictional works *The Fountainhead* and *Atlas Shrugged,* found a wide circulation among (economically) conservative and libertarian circles. Rand

propagates rational egoism in a laissez-faire capitalism and rejects altruism. The plot of *Atlas Shrugged* involves a caste of "the most creative industrialists, scientists and artists" respond to the demands of a welfare state by going on strike and retreating to build an independent, free economy.

16 "Disruptive innnovation" is the entrepreneurial mantra of the tech industry, a new-age version of Joseph Schumpeter's "creative destruction."

17 Kodwo Eshun, "Further Considerations on Afrofuturism", *CR: The New Centennial Review,* Vol. 3, 2, Summer 2003, pp. 287–302 (Article) – p. 289.
"In the colonial era of the early to middle twentieth century, avant-gardists […] revolted in the name of the future against a power structure that relied on control and representation of the historical archive. Today, the situation is reversed. The powerful employ futurists and draw power from the futures they endorse, thereby condemning the disempowered to live in the past."

18 Ana Teixeira Pinto, "Artwashing: NRx and the Alt-Right", *Texte zur Kunst* 106, June 2017, pp. 162–170.

19 Another example of this discussion of re-appropriating from a political philosophy perspective is Chantal Mouffe's appeal to develop a left populism in response to right populism. However, the question is how fruitful an approach this can be, seen that the tactics of the Identitarian movement, for example, are often already adoptions of "traditional" left-wing forms of actions (sit-ins, blockades and flashmobs) and these forms themselves were developed in response to 20th century forms of right-wing activity and state policies.
See Chantal Mouffe, "The Populist Moment" in the frame of the symposium *A New Fascism?,* Fridericianum, Kassel, 17 December 2016, Video-documentation: https://www.youtube.com/watch?v=XGEQ6TEYQMI

20 The libertarian concept of the Overton window, describing the frame of "acceptable" policies, regained popularity as an explanatory concept after the Brexit vote and the election of Donald Trump. See Laura Marsh, "The Flaws of the Overton Window Theory", *New Republic,* 27 October 2016, https://newrepublic.com/article/138003/flaws-overton-window-theory

21 Metapolitics does not only describe the dialogue of politics about itself. Metapolitics had also become a key concept in the French *Nouvelle Droite* since the 1960s and has in recent years resurged in discussions about *Neue Rechte* in Germany and elsewhere. Influenced by Gramscis concept of hegemony, metapolitics is here understood as a long-term strategy to modify the dominant political culture and make it more susceptible to a non-democratic mode of politics and attaint cultural dominance. This approach of striving for cultural dominance focuses on the so-called "pre-political" space, on conquering the hearts and the minds, creating culture and discourse (through publishing houses, think tanks, journals, concerts) and influencing public opinion rather than seeking immediate political power. At the same time, the blend of ideas and tactics invokes an ambiguity that also serves as a (tactical) confusion. See Tamir Bar-On, "The French New Right Neither Right, Nor Left?", *Journal for the Study of Radicalism,* Vol. 8, 1, 2014, pp. 1–44, Alain Badiou, *Metapolitics,* London, Verso 2005, Tobias Rapp, "Rechtes Denken: der Dunkle Ritter Götz. Was denken Rechte? Ein Besuch bei dem Autor und Verleger Götz Kubitschek", *Der Spiegel,* 17 December 2016, https://magazin.spiegel.de/SP/2016/51/148565071/index.html

22 Nina Power, "The Language of the New Brutality", *e-flux* 83, Juni 2017, http://www.e-flux.com/journal/83/141286/the-language-of-the-new-brutality/ on Victor Klemperer's *LTI – Lingua Tertii Imperii* (Language of the Third Reich), and Roger Griffin, "Lingua Quarti Imperii: The Euphemistic Tradition of the Extreme Right", in: Matthew Feldman & Paul Jackson (eds.), *Doublespeak. The Rhetoric of the Far Right since 1945,* Stuttgart, Ibidem 2014, S. 39–60. For a discussion of a historical example, see Johannes Fabian, *Language and Colonial Power: The Appropriation of Swahili in the former Belgian Congo,* Cambridge, Cambridge University Press 1986.

23 Alt-Woke (see manifesto here: https://docs.google.com/document/d/1yd_6E2L9zkRddkEZDXUdSKyeV5J2MA4Uu_nSCkcPAic) positions itself as an appropriation of intensity- and irony-based alt-right tactics putting forward progressive positions.

24 See McKenzie Wark "Our Aesthetics", *Verso,* 27 June 2017, https://www.versobooks.com/blogs/3291-our-aesthetics

25 NRx (Neoreaction) is the description of a vague set of (esoteric) reactionary ideas surrounding technological singularity and its political implications. See Armistead, 2016.

26 For an expansive discussion of these different narratives and their implications, see Déborah Danowski, Eduardo Viveiros do Castro, *The Ends of the World,* Cambridge, Polity Press 2016. trans. Rodrigo Guimarães Nunes; Danowski & Viveiros do Castro, *Há mundo por vir? Ensaio sobre os medos e os fins,* Desterro: Cultura e Barbárie 2015.

27 Matthew Taylor, "Seductive Dangers of Speed", Conversation with Nina Power, Benjamin Noys and Andy Beckett, *RSA Radio,* 1 July 2017, https://soundcloud.com/rsaradio/speed

28 Marcel Hénaff, *Violence dans la Raison? Conflit et cruauté,* Paris, Editions de l'Herne 2014, pp. 17–55.
29 Evan Calder Williams, „Volcano, Waiting", in: Defne Ayas & Adam Kleinman (eds.), *WdW Review Vol.1: Arts, Culture, and Journalism in Revolt 2017,* Rotterdam, Witte de With Center for Contemporary Art 2017, p. 650; online: http://wdwreview.org/sediments/future
30 Kerstin Stakemeier, "Prosthetic Productions. The Art of Digital Bodies / On "Speculations on Anonymous Materials" at Fridericianum, Kassel", *Texte zur Kunst* 93, March 2014, pp. 166–181. Also see Kerstin Stakemeier, "Exchangables: Aesthetics against Art", *Texte zur Kunst* 98, June 2015, pp. 124–143.
31 Milo Rau in Müller, 2016.
32 Felix Stalder on "State Technologies:Data", *Now is the Time of Monsters. What comes after nations?,* at Haus der Kulturen der Welt, Berlin, 23 March 2017, https://www.hkw.de/en/app/mediathek/audio/55710
33 Morgan Quaintance, "Cultic Cultures", *Art Monthly* 404, March 2017, pp. 6–11.
34 Alexander Galloway "Are Some Things Unrepresentable?" *Theory Culture Society,* Vol. 28, 2011, p. 85–102, http://raley.english.ucsb.edu/wp-content/Engl800/Galloway-some-things-unrepresentable.pdf
35 Fredric Jameson "Cognitive Mapping" in *Marxism and the Interpretation of Culture,* Cary Nelson & Lawrence Grossberg eds., Urbana/Chicago, University of Illinois Press 1988.

Solidarität und Fashionism
Zur Negation der Schicksalshaftigkeit einer Unterwerfungsrhetorik

Peter Hermans: Es ist schon seltsam, in dem aktuell politischen und gesellschaftlichen Klima über Solidarität nachzudenken. Das Verständnis von Solidarität als einer „grundlegenden politischen Geste", nämlich „sich mit einer politischen Aufgabe zu identifizieren, auch wenn sie [...] nicht bis ins Detail dem entspricht, was man selbst denkt und fühlt",[1] ist stark in Bedrängnis geraten. Einerseits kritisieren postkoloniale Diskurse die Solidarität als eine Geste karitativer Überlegenheit, sie betrachten die Sprache der Emanzipation als gewaltsame Einmischung und weigern sich, mit einem „toten" Gesprächspartner und mit Hilfe seiner Instrumente zu kommunizieren – nämlich mit dem weißen „Westen" und dem damit verbundenen rhetorischen und philosophischen Kanon der Moderne. Andererseits ist der Ruf nach Solidarität mit den Unterdrückten und Unprivilegierten auch zunehmend übernommen worden im Opferdiskurs populistischer Bewegungen. Was bedeutet diese ungute Situation, dieser Wandel in Kontext und Verwendung, deiner Meinung nach für den Solidaritätsbegriff?

Ana Teixeiro Pinto: Wo fange ich am besten an? Das größte Hindernis für ein großes linkes Bündnis scheint heute die Spaltung in zwei konkurrierende Diskurse zu sein: in Marxismus und Identitätspolitik. Der Streit erwächst meiner Meinung nach aus dem Spannungsverhältnis zwischen Industrieproduktion und den Formen gesellschaftlicher Reproduktion, die daraus resultieren. Für den Bergmann ist der Kohleabbau, so risikoreich er auch sein mag, die einzige Einkommensquelle. Und für die *working poor* ist Fastfood einfach das Einzige, was sie sich leisten können – da spielt es keine Rolle, wie viele Hektar Regenwald für die Rinderzucht abgeholzt werden. Um ethische Fragen handelt es sich dabei nur aus Sicht der westlichen Mittelklasse, für alle anderen sind das einfach die eigenen Lebensbedingungen, keine durchdachten Konsumentscheidungen. Unter diesen Umständen und in Ermangelung eines supranationalen Ansatzes, läuft das Engagement für Arbeitnehmer*innenrechte und Arbeitsplätze tendenziell darauf hinaus, eine Produktionsweise zu verteidigen, die im engeren Sinne zwar lebensnotwendig, letzten Endes aber tödlich ist. Vor demselben Dilemma stehen wir in der Frage der Lohnarbeit und deren verborgener Geschlechter- und Rassismusproblematik. Die geschlechtliche Arbeitsteilung und die internationale Arbeitsteilung verstetigen patriarchale sowie rassistische Hierarchien und, wie Silvia Federici argumentiert, die Arbeiterklasse im Westen war an diesem Prozess der Entwertung von Frauen und von Arbeiter*innen der Dritten Welt beteiligt.[2] Die Debatte um die *weiße* Arbeiter*innenklasse ist symptomatisch in der Art, wie sie solche rassistischen Zuschreibungen fiktionalisiert. Wenn man sich andere Traditionslinien wie den Anarchosyndikalismus ansieht, findet man ganz andere Überzeugungen. Es geht dann nicht darum, per Revolution die Kontrolle über den Staatsapparat zu übernehmen und dann ein „kommunistisches" Wirtschaftssystem einzuführen (Verstaatlichung, Zentralisierung usw.); die Idee ist vielmehr, durch *Vergemeinschaftung* ein anderes Wirtschaftssystem zu schaffen, sprich die Begründung nicht-kapitalistischer Gesellschaftsverhältnisse und Tauschformen, die ihrerseits (obgleich langsam) zu einer sozialen Revolution führen würden. An dieser Stelle ließe sich auch der Geschwindigkeitsfetisch kritisieren, aber das ist ein anderes Thema. Kurz gefasst, ist das der Gedanke, den Bewegungen wie *Occupy* verkörpern. Und es ist schon interessant zu sehen, wie sie alle kritisiert werden, weil ihnen „ein politisches Programm fehlt" …

PH: Eine solche Kritik artikuliert aber auch das Problem, wie sich über verschiedene Ebenen hinweg denken lässt, ohne dabei den Eindruck zu vermitteln, vor einem Abgrund und angesichts der globalen Ebene ganz ratlos dazustehen. Mit welchen Ebenen bist du unmittelbar konfrontiert? Aktuell scheint ja die historische Phase einer Überschneidung von Kapitalismus und westlicher Hegemonie an ihr Ende zu gelangen und die Erkenntnis, dass die Globalisierung nicht per se ein Garant für die Überlegenheit und die Privilegien des Westens ist, führt in dem Moment zu gewaltsamen Reaktion, da die Betroffenen nicht anderswo leben, sondern *hier*.[3]

ATP: Genau. Yuk Hui, beispielsweise, schrieb über die neoreaktionäre Theorie, dass sie als Globalisierungsangst aus dem Cyberlibertarismus hervorgeht, genauer von der Frage gewurmt wird, wie man die Globalisierung gestalten kann ohne die Hegemonie einzubüßen.[4] Ich halte deinen Hinweis auf die Frage der „Ebene" für wichtig und richtig; aber die Rede von der „Ebene" ist auch taktische Rhetorik: Die Darstellung des Kapitalismus als überwältigende Totalität erzeugt auch ein Gefühl der Niedergeschlagenheit und die Leute meinen dann, man könne sowieso nichts ausrichten und belächeln all die lokalen Kämpfe, all die Konflikte, die geführt und erfolgreich geführt wurden.

PH: Oder sie begeben sich auf die Suche nach neuen Modellen, um diese Hegemonie zu bewahren oder zurückzuerlangen und stoßen auf die „souveräne Demokratie" wie sie in Russland, China und Singapur durchexerziert wird.[5] Oder sie holen, beispielsweise in Gestalt des „Neokameralismus", historische Regulierungs- und Regierungspraktiken hervor.[6] Solche Ansätze mit dem souveränen Staat als Zentrum aber übersehen die sogenannte Globalisierung von unten (über die Hui ebenfalls schreibt), die auf das Leben der Menschen sehr viel unmittelbarere Auswirkungen hat und jegliche binäre Unterscheidung in Zentrum/Peripherie, in hier/dort erschwert.

ATP: Richtig, dem stimme ich zu. Und vielleicht kann man diesen Formen vertikaler Souveränität (und vertikaler Kriegsführung) nur durch horizontale Bewegungen entgegentreten, so kopflos diese auch wirken mögen.

PH: In der Kunst dient *Solidarität* zum Verweis auf das Selbstbild, man habe einen angeblich einzigartigen Blickwinkel und erforsche oder prognostiziere größere gesellschaftliche Entwicklungen – oder auch als Avantgarde-Begriff: Man stehe als Künstler*in an vorderster Front der „disruptiven" Schöpfung neuer Ausdrucks- und Organisationsmodelle. Grundlegend ist hier, dass die kollektive Dimension der Kunst – sofern sie ein Raum für politische Debatte, kritisches Denken und Theorieproduktion ist – oft als ein Impuls betrachtet wird, der nicht das Ergebnis eines hegemonialen Diskurses ist, sondern an sich subversiv oder emanzipatorisch sei. Dieser Mythos wird immer noch reproduziert, erscheint heutzutage aber umso absurder als die Künstler*innen die ideale prekäre Arbeiter*in verkörpern, die nur ihre

Kreativität hat; und das wird dann fröhlich recodiert in Selbststilisierung *(cultural branding)* und Gentrifizierung. Vor dem Hintergrund wachsender Ungleichheit macht diese Veränderung die Künstler*in gesellschaftlich (abermals) zu einer Art Hofnarr, um es polemisch zu sagen. Was hältst du, jetzt mal unabhängig vom expliziten oder impliziten politischen Gehalt einzelner Kunstwerke, von dieser Entwicklung – oder auch von dieser Überlegung? Lässt sich diese „Narren"-Rolle, diese Nähe zu Macht und Kapital, womöglich produktiv wenden?

ATP: Ich will versuchen, deinen Gedanken ganz zu entfalten: Die Frage der Ästhetik steht nicht notwendigerweise in Zusammenhang mit den Produktions- und Distributionsbedingungen zeitgenössischer Kunst, und Kunst kann in völliger Umgehung der Ästhetik politisch wirken, und das tut sie auch. Um konkreter zu werden: Die zeitgenössische Kunst kann in einer Art und Weise wirken, die zu den gesellschaftlichen und politischen Zielen der meisten Künstler*innen im Widerspruch steht, zum Beispiel indem sie die Finanzspekulation befördert, unterdrückenden Regimes einen liberalen Anstrich verleiht oder die urbane Verdrängung vorantreibt, usw. Eine geläufige Antwort auf dieses Problem ist es, das Kunstschaffen ganz aufzugeben – es gibt da einen bekannten Aufkleber, der lautet: „Raus aus der Galerie, eröffne eine Suppenküche!" Ich persönlich finde es interessanter, den Sinn und die Ebene dessen begrifflich neu zu fassen, was man „zeitgenössische Kunst" nennt. Die jüngste Zusammenarbeit zwischen NSU-Tribunal und *Forensic Architecture,* die auf der *documenta 14* gezeigt wurde, ist ein gutes Beispiel dafür, obwohl ich es eigentlich ungern anbringe, weil ich es nicht als Universalrezept verstanden wissen will. Jedenfalls gehört die Figur des „Narren" zu einem älteren Paradigma (Paul McCarthy, Maurizio Cattelan, Jordan Wolfson), dessen Plastizitätskonventionen in meinen Augen inzwischen ebenso kraftlos sind wie das ganze Theater mit der „kreativen Klasse" – und um ganz ehrlich zu sein, ich denke, das ganze „Pop"-Spiel der affirmativen Kritik hat sich erschöpft.

PH: Auch wenn wir hoffen, die Kunst könne eine künftige Vorstellungswelt mitgestalten, kann ich die Abneigung dagegen doch verstehen, Kunst auf ein ästhetisches Mittel zu reduzieren und sie somit in Propaganda zu verwandeln bzw. sie in die engen Schranken einer professionalisierten „Contemporary Art" zu zwängen. In Bezug auf die Rekodifizierung von Imbisswagen, Bildung, Archivarbeit, DJing, Romanen und Kleingewerbeeinheiten (sowie, das war dein Beispiel, von Menschenrechtsarbeit) als sogenannte Kunstwerke bemerkte Chris Kraus unlängst: „diese Tätigkeiten sind in der Gesellschaft nun so abgewertet und unbedeutend, dass sie nicht anders in Erscheinung treten können als im kodierten, aber unendlich geschmeidigen Diskurs der zeitgenössischen Kunst."[7]

Die Zunahme künstlerischer Arbeit als eine Sparte weltschaffender Praktiken wirft oftmals Fragen über das Politische in der Ästhetik auf. Ungeachtet ihres Einfallsreichtums, ihrer Aufrichtigkeit oder auch ihres zweifelhaften Charakters unterstreichen diese Praktiken (un-)absichtlich – einfach indem sie im Unklaren belassen, ob sie Kunst oder etwas Anderes sind –, dass es bei Politik nicht bloß um Ideen, Ästhetik, Symbole und Ritualisierungen geht. Denn immer kommen

Fragen auf wie: Mit wem tritt man in Verbindung? Wer ist beteiligt? Wer entscheidet was und wie? Wer wird bezahlt?[8] Um Deleuze und Guattari zu paraphrasieren: Unter den Parolen und Befehlen verbergen sich Passwörter.[9] Denkst du wirklich, dass es völlig unproduktiv ist, mit *illapsus,* Tarnung und Satire, mit den Symbolen, der Sprache, den Stilfiguren der hegemonialen Gesellschaft zu arbeiten?

ATP: Ich sehe das tendenziell genauso, dass der soziale Raum und soziale Praktiken derart abgewertet sind, dass „Kunst" als eine Form der Aufwertung fungiert. In der Frage des *détournement,* der Zweckentfremdung und des Umfunktionierens, stimme ich absolut zu. Problematisch ist nur, dass es heute offenbar ein gewisses Durcheinander gibt zwischen *détournement* und Vereinnahmung *(recuperation)* gibt, mit dem man die faktische Komplizenschaft und einen müden Zynismus durch Transgressionsfantasien verschleiert.

PH: *Komplizenschaft* finde ich hier problematisch, denn unser aller Leben gründen ja auf ökonomischer und politischer Ebene wesentlich auf irgendeiner Art von Ausbeutung – also auf der Komplizenschaft als Teil einer „schweigenden Mehrheit". Der Kapitalismus verwirklicht sich vor dem Hintergrund und mittels der Handlungen und Entscheidungen konkreter Menschen …

ATP: Vielleicht kann man die Frage anders stellen, also nicht: „Worin besteht die Wahrheit des Kapitalismus?", wie jene Ansätze fragen, die auf *Entschleierung* oder *Enthüllung* fußen, sondern: „Wie gelingt die Negation des Kapitalismus?"

PH: Gegenüber Technologie neigen viele klassisch linke Kreise zu einer Haltung, die die Technologie ausschließlich mit dem plattformbasierten Regulierungssystem aus Silicon Valley gleichsetzt und/oder als Überwachungsinstrument betrachtet. Das wirkt oftmals reaktionär, denn es grenzt bisweilen an eine unklare Technophobie, an die Verweigerung einer Auseinandersetzung mit den technologischen Instrumenten. Diese Verweigerung führt zu einem allgemeinen, undifferenzierten Unverständnis der aktuellen Lage und einer Art alarmistischer Verzweiflung. In dieser Logik gäbe es nur einen Ausweg: eine Art örtlich begrenzte Exit-Strategie. Das ist insofern beunruhigend, als dass diese Logik zur Mystifizierung der Technologie als große „Unbekannte" ganz genauso beiträgt wie das Gerede von Technologie als „zweiter Natur".

ATP: Es wäre in meinen Augen ein Fehler, „Technologie" als politisch neutrale Kraft zu betrachten. Beispielsweise spricht man berechtigterweise davon, dass die Übernahme des Taylorismus einer der kapitalen Fehler der Sowjets nach der Oktoberrevolution war: Da der Taylorismus Hierarchien privilegiert und die Dequalifizierung begünstigt, endeten die Sowjets nicht im Sozialismus, sondern im Staatsmonopolkapitalismus.[10] Es ist vielleicht stark vereinfacht gesagt, aber der technologische Fortschritt wird – in der einen oder anderen Form – immer als Kapital akkumuliert. Ich denke, es ist völlig okay, sich dem Zwang zur Online-Sichtbarkeit zu entziehen, aber für mich wäre das ist nichts. Und es gibt ja andere, einfachere Wege, wie etwa die Repolitisierung der Debatte über die digitalen Gemeingüter *(digital commons)*. Um McKenzie Wark zu zitieren: Die große sozialistische Utopie, die tatsächlich errichtet wurde, ist die Dienstleistungsinfrastruktur.[11] Aber wenn Privatunternehmen die einzigen Anbieter zentraler öffentlicher Dienste sind, bedeutet das eine grundlegende gesellschaftliche Spaltung zwischen einer digitalen plutokratischen Klasse, die alle Vermögenswerte besitzt, und einer riesigen Unterklasse von Nutzer*innen, die für ihren Zugang bezahlen. Der entscheidende Kampf unseres Zeitalters wird der Kampf darum sein, wer „das Internet" und insbesondere die künstliche Intelligenz besitzt.

PH: Genau. Das unterstreicht, wie wichtig Technologiekompetenz ist, um die (realistischen) Möglichkeiten zu verstehen und Probleme wie etwa das Eigentum an Daten und Infrastruktur anzugehen. Die schweigende Mehrheit kehrt hier wieder als stillschweigende Zustimmung zu den Nutzungsbedingungen, so kaschiert man die Verschleierung durch die Chefetagen und lagert Wahl und Verantwortung an die einzelnen „Nutzer*innen" und ihr Verhalten aus. Das berührt Fragen wie: Welche Position weist man dir zu? Wozu hast du Zugang? Und zu welchen Konditionen? Ich denke auch, dass die Debatten um Cyber-Gesetzgebung und Netzneutralität über die Zukunft des Internets als öffentliche Infrastruktur entscheiden werden. Und da können die Debatten um Überwachung, *Datamining* und Ortungsdienste auch nicht reduziert werden auf die Datenschutz- und Sicherheitsanforderungen von iUsern aus der Mittelklasse. In Abwandlung einer *Occupy*-Losung: Was ist mit den globalen 85 Prozent, den Android-Telefonen? Bleiben die einfach in der sprichwörtlichen Steinzeit, als Überschuss? Klar ist, dass die Regulierungsfrage nicht technologisch gelöst wird. Ein gutes Beispiel dafür sind die *Blockchain*-Technologien, die lassen sich zwar „verwenden, um die Regelsetzungsprozesse zu verbessern (durch Transparenz, Online-Entscheidungsfindung, elektronische Stimmabgabe)", aber letzten Endes gilt doch: „sie stehen vor denselben Grundfragen der Regelsetzung wie herkömmliche neutrale Exekutiv- und Kontrollinstanzen."[12]

ATP: Nun, man könnte von einem Paradigmenwechsel sprechen: Während die Moderne und die modernen Formen der Gesellschaftsorganisation auf einer Trennung von Kirche und Staat basierten – auf einer Herabstufung der Kirche –, scheinen wir gegenwärtig Zeug*innen einer weiteren Entkopplung zu sein, diesmal des Politischen vom Technologischen. Folglich erleben wir eine Herabstufung des Politischen, das an den Rand des Entscheidungsprozesses gedrängt wird. Das Problem lässt sich auch anders fassen: Zwar bringen alle Formen einer auf Privateigentum gründenden Gesellschaftsorganisation ein Klassenverhältnis hervor, aber Privateigentum ist nicht gleich Kapitalismus und die Klassenverhältnisse, die aus der Finanzialisierung erwachsen, sind nicht notwendigerweise Beziehungen zwischen Kapitaleigner*innen und Arbeit.[13] Die Finanzialisierung verändert den gesellschaftlichen Prozess, in dem das Kapital selbst geschaffen wird – und egal wie wir es nennen (Digitalfeudalismus, Kleptofaschismus, Postdemokratie), das kommende Zusammengehen von Finanzialisierung und digitaler Technologie liegt über Kreuz mit den sozialen (Re-)Produktionssystemen und -weisen, die wir aktuell haben. Erinnere dich an Leonard Cohen: „I've seen the *future*, brother. It is *murder.*" Es geht um Mord, oder vielmehr um niederschwelligen Völkermord, der durch Fürsorgeentzug die Form der fahrlässigen Tötung annehmen wird.

PH: Selbst in technologisch versierteren Kreisen und den dazugehörigen Veranstaltungen und Diskursen, zum Beispiel auf der letzten *Transmediale,* scheinen sich implizit wie explizit eine gewisse Verzweiflung und Sorge hinsichtlich der technologischen Handlungsfähigkeit der fortschrittlichen Kräfte breitzumachen. Trotz all der vorgestellten Analysen scheint es keine große Schnittmenge mit der pragmatischeren technologieversierten krypto-anarchistischen Hackerszene zu geben. Teils erklärt sich das sicher durch die Tatsache, dass die Grundlagen des Cyberlibertarismus oftmals Gemeinsamkeiten mit den Grundlagen der Hackerkultur zeigen.[14]

ATP: Solche Fragen wie Technophilie versus Technophobie haben meiner Meinung nach auch eine ideologische Dimension, die man sich anschauen muss: Der Cyberlibertarismus übernahm seine politischen Werte von Ayn Rand.[15] Doch ich will anders ansetzen: Marx bezeichnete die Gesellschaftsform, die sich im Umfeld der viktorianischen Stahlwerke rasant entwickelte, keineswegs als „Kohlezeitalter". Er nannte sie Kapitalismus. Der Begriff „Digitalzeitalter" kaschiert die Prozesse der Gesellschaftsformierung und Kapitalakkumulation, die durch Digitaltechnologien möglich werden. Ein weiterer Knackpunkt ist folgender: Mit dem Wort „Technologie" bezeichnet man gemeinhin auch Gegenstände mit minimalem technologischen Koeffizienten, also etwa Apps und soziale Medien. Und die Geschichte, „die Linke" sei technophob, erschöpft sich doch darin, dass sich eine Handvoll linker Gruppen (legitimerweise) gegen die „Disruption"[16] à la Silicon Valley

stellt. Andererseits bindet eine verborgene rassistische Dimension die Technologie an eine selten thematisierte Zeitlichkeitsvorstellung: Technologie wird als Fortschritt, d. h. als Zukunft kodiert und mit dem Westen, dem angeblichen Motor der Geschichte, assoziiert. Derzeit symbolisiert das Silicon Valley diesen Technofuturismus, der einen Reibach macht mit Geschichten von Tempo, Wohlstand, Globalisierung und Effizienz. Im Gegensatz dazu werden schwarze und farbige Nationen immer als in der Vergangenheit verhaftet dargestellt: stammesmäßig zersplittert, unterentwickelt, chaotisch, abergläubisch. Anders gesagt, es gibt eine Verknüpfung von Technologie, Weißsein und Zukunft. Der Afrofuturismus stellte diese Verknüpfung radikal infrage, denn – so formulierte Kodwo Eshun – wer arm ist, ist zu einem Leben in der Vergangenheit verdammt.[17] In meinen Augen kann man die Frage der Technologie nicht angehen, ohne diese Geschichten und dieses Weißsein, das immer und immer wieder mit allem Digitalen in Verbindung gebracht wird, radikal infrage zu stellen.

PH: Mich interessiert die Technologiefrage im Kontext von Solidarität und Kunst vor allem deshalb, weil sie eine Diskussion über die Werkzeuge und Mittel der Kommunikation und der Produktion sowie über die darin eingebetteten Ideologien anstößt. Auch wenn man die allumfassenden Ideengebäude um „Big Data" und „technologische Singularität" (als Ende der menschlichen Handlungsmacht, der Demokratie und schließlich des Planeten Erde) als reaktionäres und koloniales, weißes Phantasma verspotten mag, haben diese Ideologien doch reale Folgen, nicht zuletzt in der praktischen Konzentration auf die Kommunikations- und Mobilisierungsmittel (etwa die Infrastrukturen) und die dazugehörigen Strategien. Falls Solidarität grundsätzlich die Praxis der Arbeit mit und in Form von Worten und (Bild-)Sprachen ist, dann stellt sich die Frage nach dem Verhältnis zu den bestehenden Paradigmen und Taktiken. In der Debatte um die Bekämpfung der *Alt-Right*-Mem-Community hast du den Ansatz kritisiert,[18] deren Strategien, Taktiken und Sprachgebrauch zu übernehmen und zu vereinnahmen – also den „Troll zu trollen" oder einfach die besseren Meme zu entwickeln.[19] Warum denkst du, das Einsetzen derselben Taktik wäre ein Fehler, eine Affirmation der bestehenden Verhältnisse?

ATP: Das Singularitätskonzept ist ein sehr gutes Beispiel. Indem es die politischen Kämpfe verschiebt, hin zu einem schemenhaften Antagonismus zwischen Mensch und Maschine, verschleiert die Erzählung der technologischen Singularität die Eigentums- und (Un-)Gleichheitsfrage. Dass die künstliche Intelligenz – Sinnbild einer reinen Form *weißer Männlichkeit ohne Weiße* – als Waffe eingesetzt und die Überlebens- und Vernichtungsfrage zum einzigen Problem erhoben wird, lähmt auch die politische Theorie. In meinen Augen ist das ein „männliches Phantasma", das mit chauvinistischen Grundannahmen arbeitet. Denn „selbständig lernende" *(„deep-learning")* Algorithmen sind womöglich intelligent, haben aber nicht notwendigerweise ein Bewusstsein. Gleichzeitig ist das angebliche Potenzial des *Cyborg* als Hybrid aus Mensch und Maschine bereits Wirklichkeit geworden: in Form der Smart City, einer sensorisch-reaktiven Umwelt, und nicht im übermäßig expliziten Phallizismus einer Terminator-artigen Figur.

Hinzufügen möchte ich, dass nicht-negative Strategien „die Macht des kritisierten Gegenstands" in der Regel steigern, anstatt sie zu schmälern. Der Mem-Begriff ist eine kultursoziologische Analogie zum Gen-Begriff der Evolutionsbiologie – wenn wir diesen Begriff verwenden, akzeptieren wir also die Naturalisierung der Kultur und, ich wiederhole mich, stilisieren den Wettbewerbs- und Selektionsdruck. Man muss sich eines klarmachen: Es handelt sich hier nicht einfach um Theorien, die ein paar chauvinistische, konservative und/oder rassistische Vorurteile reflektieren, sondern diese Theorien produzieren diese Vorurteile – es sind diese Theorien, die die Matrix von Überlegenheit und Ausrottung mit Hilfe einer Rhetorik à la Verdienst und „Überleben des Stärkeren" rechtfertigen. Die „memetische Theorie" spiegelt das auf einer ganz grundsätzlichen Ebene: Sie begreift Kommunikation vom Standpunkt der Werbewirtschaft und argumentiert also nicht, sondern greift zum Schlagwort.

PH: Diese (umstrittenen) Ideen einer Sprachpolitik – ob sie sich nun auf das „Overton-Fenster"[20] oder die „Metapolitik"[21] beziehen – fußen auf der Strategie, mittels der Platzierung bestimmter Begriffe und Worte den normativen Rahmen des Sprachgebrauchs zu erweitern, der als nachvollziehbar und akzeptabel gilt.[22] Egal ob es nun die Gerüchte sind, die derzeit unter dem Label *fake news* Raum greifen, oder die spielerische Ambivalenz *(cryptic branding)* von *Alt-Woke*,[23] beide profitieren von der Aufmerksamkeitsökonomie der sozialen Medien. Interessant finde ich in diesem Zusammenhang den Aspekt der Hypes, der Stilfiguren und der je nach Generation unterschiedlichen Wahrnehmung, was begehrenswert und „pop" ist …

Denn ohne Politik dabei auf eine Form von Onlineshopping zu reduzieren, wirft dieser Aspekt wirklich Fragen darüber auf, was als normal angesehen wird.[24]

ATP: Wenn es um die *Alt-Right* geht, höre ich immer wieder Vergleiche mit dem „Streisand-Effekt", sprich: Je stärker man ein Problem thematisiert, desto größer wird es. Ich finde dieses Argument vollkommen unzutreffend, denn die materielle Ökonomie gehorcht anderen Gesetzen als die Aufmerksamkeitsökonomie. Das Gegenteil zu behaupten zeugt nur von einem bürgerlichen Vorurteil. Es stellt sich auch die Frage nach der Psychologie des Mem-Milieus und ob dessen abgehobener Zynismus nun zu politischem Engagement führt, oder doch eher zu Misstrauen und Nihilismus. Wenn es um diese neuen rechtsextremen Strömungen geht, neigen die Leute dazu, deren Nähe zum Faschismus (ich meine den historischen Faschismus) zu bestreiten, weil sie den Faschismus in der Regel als eine Art bewusstes oder zielgerichtetes Unterfangen auffassen. Dabei lautete das Motto der (italienischen) Faschist*innen *me ne frego* (is' mir scheißegal) und die Losung der Futurist*innen hieß *Fiat ars, pereat mundus* (Es werde Kunst, und gehe die Welt darob zugrunde) – diese ganze Geisteswelt hat also einen Hang zum Nihilismus. Ich muss wohl nicht extra betonen, dass der Faschismus kein Patent auf den Nihilismus hat. Man findet ihn auch an der Schnittstelle von Akzelerationismus und Cyberlibertarismus, bei NRx beispielsweise,[25] man findet ihn im Silicon-Valley-Mantra der „disruptiven Innovation", in einem Großteil der heutigen Popkultur sowie in der Stilrichtung der „Post-Internet-Kunst".

Anstatt uns auf die Meme zu stürzen, sollten wir uns meiner Meinung nach der Sprache zuwenden. Und zwar, weil Bilder an sich nie viel bedeuten können. Die Bedeutung liegt nicht in dem Bild, sondern in der Erzählung, in der Assoziationskette, die das Bild aktiviert. Die *Alt-Right* behauptet, die Frankfurter Schule habe den „Kulturmarxismus" erfunden (beides Codeworte für „die Juden"), um die weiße Zivilisation zu vernichten. An die Stelle des Kulturmarxismus setzen die Neoreaktionäre zwar „die calvinistische Linke", aber sie halten an dem Gedanken „der Linken" als gespenstischem Gegenspieler, einer Art schemenhaftes Hassobjekt, fest. Dann gibt es noch den linken Akzelerationismus, der von einer „passiven Linken" und von „Folk-Politik" spricht – und einmal mehr wird dieselbe Bedeutungskette aktiviert, und einmal mehr erscheint „die Linke" als ein homogenes Schlechtes, das für Scheitern und Ohnmacht steht. Diese Erzählungen verknüpfen *Prometheanism* – die Kraft des Menschen mit Hilfe von Technologie die Natur zu besiegen –, Potenz und Macht; so erzeugen sie in der Regel eine ästhetische Wirkung – aber sie bieten uns nicht ein einziges theoretisches Instrument, mit dem wir unsere Situation verstehen könnten.

PH: Sehr bezeichnend finde ich in diesem Zusammenhang die Psychologie der Geschichte vom „Ende der Welt, wie wir sie kennen" (und die nihilistische Begeisterung dafür). Es ließe sich argumentieren, dass man sich über die höchst realen Bedrohungen der biologischen Ausrottung und des Klimawandels sehr viel mehr Sorgen machen sollte als über das Risiko, die Menschheit könnte von der künstlichen Intelligenz überflüssig gemacht werden. Für das Nachdenken über Solidarität ist vielleicht noch wichtiger, dass der historische Determinismus der schöpferischen Zerstörung, die den Marxist*innen und Akzelerationist*innen so teuer ist, keine Antwort auf die Frage gibt, wer denn für wen den Gang der Dinge beschleunigen oder *aufmischen* wird.[26] In diesem Sinne thematisiert der Akzelerationismus zwar „unsere" westliche Lebensweise und räumt ein, dass wir eine Übergangsphase durchlaufen, allerdings lehnt er sich nicht sehr weit aus dem Fenster in jener schwierigen Übergangsphase, in der die Beschleunigung die Form einer (taktischen) Eskalation, einer Aneinanderreihung von Krisen annimmt.[27] Strategie und Taktik ins Zentrum der Überlegungen zu rücken, wäre nach meiner Überzeugung zwar fruchtbarer als das Entwerfen „reiner" Utopien, dessen ungeachtet stellt sich aber doch eine Frage: Ist diese überzogene Verschmelzung von Mittel und Zweck nicht ein Spiegelbild der Managementlogik in den heutigen Entscheidungsprozessen, Protokollen und Schnittstellen, die man zu stabilisierenden Riten recodiert hat?[28]

ATP: Stimmt, und das sagt auch Evan Calder Williams: „ein Bild der Zukunft zu entwerfen, das auch in letzter Konsequenz keine Verschwörung mit den konstitutiven Bedingungen der Gegenwart darstellt," hat womöglich vor allem eine Voraussetzung, nämlich „die Erkenntnis, dass ein Übergang *in die* Zukunft erst durch die Zerstörung derjenigen Formen eindeutig gekennzeichnet wird, die Lebewesen, Gegenstände und Systeme mittels unterschiedlich schwerer Sanktionen an einen Zeitmodus fesseln, der für die Kontinuität der Gegenwart konzipiert ist. So meinen wir mit *Zukunft* eben das Gefühl, sich in und von der Gegenwart abzulösen."[29] Wenn wir verhindern wollen, dass sich diese elendige Gegenwart reproduziert, müssen wir uns von dem Klischee lösen, Kritik sei etwas rein Passiv-Reaktives (das Widersprüche aufzeigt, Lügen aufdeckt und Ideologien dekonstruiert), und die Negation als produktives Prinzip anwenden.

PH: Ich denke, dieses *Ablösen* meint eine Reihe von Übergängen, nicht zuletzt in Sachen Handlungsmacht. Wo stehen wir, wenn das Digitale die Logiken von Produktion und Konsumtion in einen Topf wirft, „ohne dabei eine Zukunft jenseits der technischen Aktualisierung dieser driftenden Wiederholungen anzubieten"?[30] Es stellt sich aber auch die Frage, warum man annehmen sollte, der bloße Kontakt mit einer „gefährlichen" Idee würde die Menschen für sie einnehmen? Hieße das nicht, sie für dumm zu halten? Wie können wir es vermeiden, Teil der „Meta-Sklaverei" zu werden, in der man entweder Sklav*in des Zeitgeists oder Sklav*in eines Meta-Diskurses ist, der den Zeitgeist kritisiert?[31] Die Klischees unserer Epoche sind die algorithmischen Identitäten und vorhersehbaren Rollen: das *ready-made* Drama zwischen den seriellen Charakteren der Sockenpuppen, Sprecher*innen, Opfer, Prophet*innen, Mitläufer*innen und Prominenten. Dieses Rollenspiel folgt einer totalitären Logik, in der jede nonkonforme Äußerung dadurch delegitimiert wird, dass man die Intention und Integrität der Sprecher*in in Zweifel zieht. Poetisch gesprochen: Wo beginnen wir mit einer Solidarität, die Arbeit ist und keine Zauberei?

ATP: Wenn ich richtig verstanden habe, fragst du nach dem *kollektiven Subjekt* im Sinne des politischen Akteurs, also wie in: „Wer ist das revolutionäre Subjekt?" Ich meine, die Antwort ist immer noch dieselbe: Alle, die die

Eigentumsfrage stellen. Der „Westen" stellt die Eigentumsfrage im Augenblick eindeutig nicht, jedenfalls nicht außerhalb der engen Grenzen einiger akademischer Kreise – aber es gibt vielfältige Bewegungen, die das tun, auch in den Mauerspalten des „Westens".

Zu deinem anderen Punkt: Es ist offensichtlich rätselhaft, wie Protokolle als Regulierungstechniken Wirkungsmacht erlangen. Felix Stalder zufolge, um ein Beispiel zu nennen, sind Protokolle bzw. Regelwerke der Dreh- und Angelpunkt der Frage, deren Antwort inzwischen die Kybernetik ist: Wie regiert man die Gesellschaft ohne den Rückgriff auf Politik?[32] Protokolle erlangen ihre Wirkungsmacht durch die freiwillige Akzeptanz. Die Durchsetzung erfolgte dezentralisiert und allerorts. Als aber die Protokolle erst einmal akzeptiert waren, wurden sie zu den konstitutiven Bedingungen der wirtschaftlichen oder gesellschaftlichen Akteur*innen. Anders gesagt, Protokolle werden durchgesetzt sowohl mittels der Matrix jener gegenseitigen Abhängigkeiten, die sie hervorbringen, als auch mittels der Interaktionen, die sie ermöglichen. Weil Regelwerke an sich aber auch eine antipolitische Voreingenommenheit aufweisen, ermöglichen diese Transformationen auch eine Restauration der Idee von Unternehmensprofit und Eliten-Macht. Obwohl diese Protokolle anfangs nützliche Aspekte aufweisen (wie bei Facebook, der EU, der WTO und Airbnb), wird sehr schnell klar, dass sie versteckte Kosten mit sich bringen. Den Raum zu verlassen, den das Protokoll definiert, ist indes selten eine Option, denn die finanziellen oder sozialen Kosten wären beträchtlich höher als die Kosten, die jenes Regelwerk verlangt, in das man eintritt – im Falle von Facebook, beispielsweise, tauscht man Privatsphäre und Datenschutz gegen Relevanz und im weiteren Sinne auch Einkommen ein. Laut Stalder stehen wir dadurch vor einem psychologischen Paradox: Jede*r tut freiwillig, was niemand wirklich will.

PH: Meine Frage zur Handlungsmacht zielte auf die Vermittlungsprozesse zwischen *welchen Platz weist man dir zu* und *welchen Platz weist du dir zu,* denn man stellt die Menschen ja nicht von Anfang an in eine Ecke, in die Rolle des Herren bzw. des Knechts. Man sollte sich zwar vor Allem hüten, das „den Willen" (einer Gruppe) von Menschen als etwas Ganzheitliches zu repräsentieren scheint, dennoch kann man Handlungsmacht wahrscheinlich nur erlangen durch die Vermittlung zwischen individuellem und kollektivem Modus, ohne einen von beiden zu fetischisieren.

ATP: Genau diesen Hunger nach *Ermächtigung* („empowerment") hat Morgan Quaintance gerade in einem Aufsatz über „hippe Kulturen" thematisiert, in dem er die Lust auf nonkonformistische Ideologien als eine Form der Suche beschreibt, die offenbar ein hippes Milieu begünstigt, das vom Cyberobskurantismus durchdrungen ist.[33] Ich denke, der Sog in Richtung Monomanie und der esoterische Trend stehen in Verbindung mit dem, was Jameson als Neigung beschrieb, die Welt als Erweiterung der eigenen paranoiden Subjektivität zu sehen. In dieser Perspektive scheint die digitale Wende in Beziehung zu stehen zu einer Krise der Repräsentation: Obwohl wir mit einer zunehmenden Vielfalt optischer Medien ausgestattet sind, sind wir immer weniger in der Lage, die algorithmische Totalität zu erfassen, die uns umgibt.

Die primäre Daseinsweise der Daten ist keine visuelle, wie Alexander Galloway erklärt,[34] und die Zwillingskräfte Globalisierung und Digitalisierung erweitern in der Regel die Lücke zwischen der individuellen Erfahrung und den ökonomischen Strukturen, die diese Erfahrung bestimmen. Was passiert mit der Kunst, wenn die phänomenologische Erfahrung – der Rohstoff der Ästhetik – gegenüber Informationsflüssen zweitrangig wird? Fredric Jameson regt an, dem mit „cognitive mapping"[35] entgegenzutreten: mit der Kartierung der strukturellen Koordinaten, die der diffusen Welt post-fordistischer Ökonomien zugrunde liegen. Dieses Konzept hat in der zeitgenössischen Kunst keinen festen Stand, aber einige Künstler*innen setzen es anscheinend praktisch um, indem sie die persönliche Biographie mit der kollektiven Geschichte verbinden – so vermittelt man persönliche Reflexion und politische Handlungsmacht in der Mobilisierung von Affekt und Gefühl.

1   Milo Rau in: Dominikus Müller, „Get Real: Ein Gespräch mit dem Regisseur Milo Rau über Verantwortung, Empathie und ‚Meta-Sklaverei'", online: *Frieze d/e,* Nr. 24, https://frieze.com/article/get-real?language=de
2   Siehe Silvia Federici, *Revolution at Point Zero: Housework, Reproduction and Feminist Struggle,* Oakland: PM Press 2012.
3   Hamid Dabashi, *Can Non-Europeans Think?,* London: Zed Books 2015, S. 82. Dabashi schreibt in Bezug auf die Kolonialität, die den „globalen Süden" hervorbrachte:
   „Dieses ‚wir' ist also nicht mehr farbig codiert oder auf Kontinente bezogen und umfasst alle, die vom globalen Vorgehen des Kapitals entrechtet wurden – ob im Norden oder im Süden unseres Planeten Erde, ob tief im Cyperspace oder sonstwo in luftigen Höhen –, und [auch] diejenigen, die dieses Vorgehen reich privilegiert. Ursprünglich, in der Moderne, war dieses globalisierte Kapital Teil eines ‚europäischen' Mythos. Das ist es nicht mehr. Es ist enteuropäisiert, von seinen überzogenen Fetischen befreit worden. Reiche arabische, indische, russische, chinesische, lateinamerikanische oder afrikanische Unternehmer, mafiöse Staaten, geheime Seilschaften *(deep states),* Kasernenstaaten, israelische Kriegstreiber und die Söldner und Mörder des IS sind untrennbar mit einer profanen Wirklichkeit verbunden, die endgültig auf den Mythos ‚des Westens' verzichtet hat." (Online: *Zed Books blog,* Juli 2016, https://www.zedbooks.net/blog/posts/fuck-you-zizek)
4   Yuk Hui, „On the Unhappy Consciousness of Neoreactionaries", online: *e-flux* 81, April 2017, http://www.e-flux.com/journal/81/125815/on-the-unhappy-consciousness-of-neoreactionaries
5   Der Begriff „souveräne Demokratie" oder „gelenkte Demokratie", wie er in den letzten Jahren Verwendung fand, wird Wladislaw Surkow zugeschrieben. Der damalige Berater von Präsident Wladimir Putin beschrieb damit eine Situation, in der „demokratische Institutionen ohne demokratische Freiheiten aufrechterhalten werden". Surkow wurde hochstilisiert zur grauen Eminenz im Kreml und zum Urheber der (Des-)Informationsstrategie des Regimes, insbesondere im Kontext der Annexion der Krim im Jahr 2013. Die (neo-orientalistische) Faszination für (Ost-)Asien ihrerseits reicht in die 1990er Jahre zurück und beginnt mit der Geschichte von den „Tigerstaaten", mit dem Mythos, „die asiatischen Werte" seien „eine Art konfuzianischer Variante von Webers Verherrlichung der protestantischen Arbeitsethik." Später wiederholte sich diese Zuschreibung für die Vereinigten Arabischen Emirate (hier insbesondere Dubai) und Katar. Siehe Peter Pomerantsev, „Putin's Rasputin", *London Review of Books,* Bd. 33, Nr. 20, 2011, S. 3–6, sowie Peter Pomerantsev, „The Hidden Author of Putinism. How Vladislav Surkov invented the new Russia", *The Atlantic,* November 2014, www.theatlantic.com/international/archive/2014/11/hidden-author-putinism-russia-vladislav-surkov/382489; Josephine Armistead, „The Silicon Ideology", 18. Mai 2016, https://ia800403.us.archive.org/25/items/the-silicon-ideology/the-silicon-ideology.pdf, S. 12.
6   Der Kameralismus entstand im 18. Jahrhundert in Preußen und beschreibt eine Verwaltungswissenschaft und -methode, die sich auf Standardisierung und Effizienz konzentriert. Der Begriff wurde in der neoreaktionären Blogosphäre

aufgegriffen und soll die (esoterische) effizienzbasierte Vorstellung einer Gesellschaft ohne Politik abbilden – einer Gesellschaft, die von einer Manager-Elite (mittels künstlicher Intelligenz) regiert wird. Andere Konzepte rufen ähnliche Ideen auf, etwa der „gov-corp"-Ansatz, wonach Staaten wie Unternehmen geführt werden sollen, oder auch die *Seasteading*-Bewegung, die sich in Gemeinschaften auf künstlichen Inseln als Vorposten der „Innovation" von der „hinderlichen" Gesetzgebung der Nationalstaaten lösen will.

7   Chris Kraus, „Lessons: Art School", in: *Akademie X. Lessons in Art + Life,* London/New York: Phaidon 2015, S. 166–173.

8   In diesem Zusammenhang, siehe Dena Yago, „On Ketamin and Added Value", online: *e-flux* 82, Mai 2017, http://www.e-flux.com/journal/82/133913/on-ketamine-and-added-value

9   Gilles Deleuze & Félix Guattari, *Tausend Plateaus,* Berlin: Merve 1992, übers. v. Gabriele Ricke u. Ronald Voullié, S. 153; zitiert und diskutiert in: Tiqqun, *Kybernetik und Revolte,* Zürich/Berlin: Diaphanes 2007, übers. v. Ronald Voullié, S. 82 f., online: https://translationcollective.files.wordpress.com/2012/06/kybernetik.pdf

10 Der Taylorismus fordert praktisch eine „wissenschaftliche Betriebsführung" und Arbeitseffizienz. Frederick Taylors Veröffentlichung von 1911 stellt drei Hauptprinzipien auf: Herunterbrechen komplexer Arbeiten in einfache; Vermessung aller Tätigkeiten der Arbeiter*innen; und Einführung eines Leistungslohns mit Boni für Tatkräftige und Kündigung für Schlafmützen. Für eine Erörterung der Rolle des Taylorismus in den aktuellen „digitalen" Ökonomien, siehe „Digital Taylorism: A modern version of ‚scientific management' threatens to dehumanise the workplace", in: *The Economist,* 10. September 2015, https://www.economist.com/news/business/21664190-modern-version-scientific-management-threatens-dehumanise-workplace-digital

11 McKenzie Wark, „Renotopia", in: *Harvard Design Magazine,* Nr. 41 (Herbst/Winter 2015), http://www.harvarddesignmagazine.org/issues/41/renotopia

12 Vili Lehdonvirta, „The Blockchain Paradox", am *Oxford Internet Institute,* University of Oxford, 21. November 2016, https://www.oii.ox.ac.uk/blog/the-blockchain-paradox-why-distributed-ledger-technologies-may-do-little-to-transform-the-economy

13 McKenzie Wark, „The Sublime Language of My Century", *Public Seminar,* 14. Mai 2016, http://www.publicseminar.org/2016/05/the-sublime-language-of-my-century/

14 Der Cyberlibertarismus hat seinen Ursprung sowohl in der frühen Hacker-Kultur als auch im amerikanischen Libertarismus. Von der Hacker-Kultur hat es seinen allgemeinen Antagonismus gegenüber jeglicher Regulierung und Zensur, die einem „freien" (ungehinderten) Zugang zum Internet im Weg stehen könnte, geerbt. Aus dem amerikanischen Libertarismus übernahm er den klassischen libertarischen Anspruch auf persönliche Autonomie und die Verweigerung jeglicher staatlichen Einmischung. Dies ist dem anti-staatlichen Impetus von Hacker- und Krypto-Anarchist*innen nicht unähnlich (z. B. *cyberphunk,* oder *Anonymous*), welche im Recht auf Verschlüsselung und Anonymität einen inhärenten Ausdruck von Freiheit sehen. Der Unterschied besteht darin, dass Krypto- und Cyber-Anarchist*innen Dezentralisierung und kollaborativen Organisationsmodellen große Bedeutung beimessen, wohingegen Vertreter*innen des Cyberlibertarismus den Markt und privates Unternehmertum zelebrieren sowie meritokratische Hierarchien befürworten. Der Begriff ist demnach auch mit „der kalifornischen Ideologie" verwandt: einer Mischung inspiriert von anti-staatlichem Denken, der Gegenkultur der 1960er, Techno-Utopismus und derzeitigen Diskussionen um „Platform Capitalism".
Siehe Armistead 2016, in Endnote 5. Gabriella Coleman, *Hacker, Hoaxer, Whistleblower, Spy, The Many Faces of Anonymous,* London: Verso 2015; Richard Barbrook & Andy Cameron, „The Californian Ideology", *Mute* 3, Autumn 1995, http://www.metamute.org/editorial/articles/californian-ideology; Nick Srnicek, *Platform Capitalism,* Cambridge: Polity Press, 2017.

15 Ayn Rand war eine Philosophin und Schriftstellerin, deren Ideen in der Form von fiktionalen Werken wie „The Fountainhead" und „Atlas Shrugged" eine weite Verbreitung in konservativen und libertarischen Kreisen findet. Rand propagiert rationalen Egoismus in einem Laissez faire-Kapitalismus und lehnt Altruismus ab. Die Handlung von „Atlas Shrugged" beschreibt eine Kaste der kreativsten Industriellen, Wissenschaftler*innen und Künstler*innen, die dem Wohlfahrtsstaat mit einem Streik begegnen und sich zurückziehen, um eine unabhängige, freie

Ökonomie einzuführen.

16 „Disruptive Innovation" ist das Firmenmantra der Techy-Branche und ist eigentlich nichts anderes als eine *New Age*-Variante von Joseph Schumpeters „schöpferischer Zerstörung".

17 Kodwo Eshun, „Further Considerations on Afrofuturism", in: *CR: The New Centennial Review,* Bd. 3, Nr. 2 (Sommer 2003), S. 287–302, hier S. 289.
„In der kolonialen Epoche von Anfang bis Mitte des 20. Jahrhunderts erhoben sich die Avantgardisten […] im Namen der Zukunft gegen eine Machtstruktur, die sich auf die Kontrolle und Repräsentation des historischen Gedächtnisses stützte. Heute ist die Lage umgekehrt: Die Mächtigen beschäftigen Futuristen, sie ziehen ihre Macht aus den Formen der Zukunft, die sie gutheißen und zwingen damit die zur Machtlosigkeit Verdammten, in der Vergangenheit zu leben."

18 Ana Teixeira Pinto, „Artwashing: NRx und die sogenannte alternative Rechte", in: *Texte zur Kunst* 106, Juni 2017, übers. v. Bert Rebhandl, S. 162–170, https://www.textezurkunst.de/106/artwashing-de

19 Ein weiteres Beispiel für die politisch-philosophische Debatte um Wiederaneignung ist die Forderung von Chantal Mouffe, in Reaktion auf den Rechtspopulismus einen linken Populismus zu entwickeln. Es stellt sich indes die Frage, wie fruchtbar ein solcher Ansatz sein kann: Denn die Taktiken der identitären Bewegung, beispielsweise, sind oft bloß die Übernahme von „traditionell linken" Aktionsformen (Sit-Ins, Blockaden, Flashmobs), welche ihrerseits im 20. Jahrhundert in Reaktion auf das Vorgehen der Rechten und auf staatliche Politik entwickelt wurden. Siehe Chantal Mouffe, „The Populist Moment", im Rahmen des Symposiums *A New Fascism?,* Kassel, 17. Dezember 2016, Mitschnitt online: https://www.youtube.com/watch?v=XGEQ6TEYQMI

20 Der libertäre Begriff des *Overton*-Fensters (oder Diskurs-Fensters) beschreibt den Rahmen „akzeptabler" Politik und erlangte nach der Brexit-Abstimmung und der Wahl Donald Trumps neue Popularität als Erklärungsmodell. Siehe Laura Marsh, „The Flaws of the Overton Window Theory", online: *New Republic,* 27. Oktober 2016, https://newrepublic.com/article/138003/flaws-overton-window-theory

21 Die Meta-Politik ist nicht nur das Gespräch der Politik über sich selbst. Meta-Politik war in den 1960er Jahren auch zu einem Schlüsselbegriff der französischen *Nouvelle Droite* geworden, der dann in den letzten Jahren im Zusammenhang mit der „Neuen Rechten" in Deutschland und anderswo wieder diskutiert wurde. Die so verstandene Meta-Politik ist angelehnt an Gramscis Hegemonie-Begriff und bezeichnet eine langfristige Strategie mit dem Ziel, die vorherrschende politische Kultur zu verändern (sie für eine nicht-demokratische Art der Politik empfänglicher zu machen) und eine kulturelle Prägekraft zu erlangen. Dieser Ansatz konzentriert sich auf den sogenannten „vorpolitischen" Raum und darauf, die Herzen und Köpfe zu erobern, ein Diskursmilieu zu schaffen (mit Hilfe von Verlagen, „Instituten", Zeitschriften und Konzerten) und die öffentliche Meinung zu beeinflussen, anstatt nach unmittelbarer politischer Macht zu streben. Dabei führt diese Mischung aus Gedankengut und Taktik zu einer Uneindeutigkeit, die auch der (taktischen) Verwirrung dient. Siehe Tamir Bar-On, „The French New Right Neither Right, Nor Left?", in: *Journal for the Study of Radicalism,* Bd. 8, Nr. 1 (2014), S. 1–44; Alain Badiou, *Über Metapolitik,* Zürich/Berlin: Diaphanes 2003, übers. v. Heinz Jatho; sowie Tobias Rapp, „Der dunkle Ritter. Was denken Rechte? Ein Besuch bei dem Autor und Verleger Götz Kubitschek", in: *Der Spiegel* 51/2016, https://magazin.spiegel.de/SP/2016/51/148565071/index.html

22 Siehe Nina Power, „The Language of the New Brutality", online: *e-flux* 83, Juni 2017, http://www.e-flux.com/journal/83/141286/the-language-of-the-new-brutality, über Victor Klemperers LTI (Lingua Tertii Imperii, die Sprache des Dritten Reiches), sowie Roger Griffin, „‚Lingua Quarti Imperii': The euphemistic tradition of the extreme right", in: Matthew Feldman & Paul Jackson (Hgg.), *Doublespeak. The Rhetoric of the Far Right since 1945,* Stuttgart: Ibidem 2014, S. 39–60. Für die Erörterung eines historischen Beispiels, siehe Johannes Fabian, *Language and Colonial Power: The Appropriation of Swahili in the Former Belgian Congo 1880–1938,* Cambridge: Cambridge University Press 1986.

23 Alt-Woke beansprucht für sich die Aneignung der auf Intensität und Ironie basierenden Alt-Right-Taktiken zur Verbreitung fortschrittlicher Positionen. Siehe ANON, „#Alt-Woke: A Manifesto", https://docs.google.com/document/d/1yd_6E2L9zkRddkEZDXUdSKyeV5J2MA4Uu_nSCkcPAic

24 Siehe McKenzie Wark, „Our Aesthetics", online: *Verso blog,* 27. Juni 2017, https://www.versobooks.com/blogs/3291-our-aesthetics

25 NRx („Neoreaktion") bezeichnet ein verschwommenes Ensemble (esoterisch-)reaktionärer Gedanken, deren Gravitationszentrum die technologische Singularität und ihre politischen Konsequenzen ist. Siehe Armistead 2016, in Endnote 5.

26 Für eine ausführliche Besprechung dieser verschiedenen Erzählungen und ihrer Folgen, siehe Déborah Danowski & Eduardo Viveiros do Castro, *The Ends of the World,* Cambridge: Polity Press 2016, übers. v. Rodrigo Guimarães Nunes; bzw. Danowski & Viveiros do Castro, *Há mundo por vir? Ensaio sobre os medos e os fins,* Desterro: Cultura e Barbárie 2015.

27 Matthew Taylor, „Seductive Dangers of Speed" – Im Gespräch mit Nina Power, Benjamin Noys und Andy Beckett, *RSA Radio,* 1. Juni 2017, online: https://soundcloud.com/rsaradio/speed

28 Marcel Hénaff, *Violence dans la Raison? Conflit et cruauté,* Paris: Editions de l'Herne 2014, S. 17–55.

29 Evan Calder Williams, „Volcano, Waiting", in: Defne Ayas & Adam Kleinman (Hgg.), *WdW Review Vol. 1: Arts, Culture, and Journalism in Revolt 2017,* Rotterdam: Witte de With Center for Contemporary Art 2017, S. 650; online: http://wdwreview.org/sediments/future

30 Kerstin Stakemeier, „Prothetische Produktionen. Die Kunst digitaler Körper. Über ‚Speculations on Anonymous Materials' im Fridericianum, Kassel", in: *Texte zur Kunst* 93 (März 2014), S. 166–181, Zitat S. 173. Siehe auch Kerstin Stakemeier, „Austauschbarkeiten: Ästhetik gegen Kunst", *Texte zur Kunst* 98 (Juni 2015), S. 124–143.

31 Nach Milo Rau in Müller 2016, siehe Endnote 1.

32 Felix Stalder über „Staatstechnologien. Daten" im Rahmen von *Die Jetztzeit der Monster. What comes after nations?,* im Haus der Kulturen der Welt, Berlin, 23. März 2017, Mitschnitt auf Englisch: https://www.hkw.de/en/app/mediathek/audio/55710

33 Morgan Quaintance, „Cultic Cultures", in: *Art Monthly* 404 (März 2017), S. 6–11.

34 Alexander Galloway, „Are Some Things Unrepresentable?", in: *Theory Culture Society,* Bd. 28 (2011), S. 85–102, online: http://raley.english.ucsb.edu/wp-content/Engl800/Galloway-some-things-unrepresentable.pdf

35 Fredric Jameson, „Cognitive Mapping", in: Cary Nelson & Lawrence Grossberg (Hrsg.), *Marxism and the Interpretation of Culture,* Urbana/Chicago: University of Illinois Press 1988, S. 347–360.

Contributors / Beitragende

Jochen Becker is an author, curator and lecturer. He is a founding member of metroZones | Center for Urban Affairs and the editor of *BIGNES? – Größe zählt, Image/Politik, Städtisches Handeln* (b_books, 2001) as well as the co-editor of the metroZones book series (b_books Berlin). From 2014 to 2015 he was director of the Art & Architecture programme at the Royal Institute of Art in Stockholm. Since 2014 he has been the co-curator of *station urbaner kulturen* in Berlin-Hellersdorf. His recent curatorial projects include *Global Prayers – Redemption and Liberation in the Cities* (Haus der Kulturen der Welt, Berlin / Neue Gesellschaft für Bildende Kunst, Berlin / Camera Austria, Graz, 2009–2014), *Self Made Urbanism Rome* (Neue Gesellschaft für Bildende Kunst, Berlin, 2013 / Metropoliz Rom, 2015 / Maxxi Museum Rom, 2015) and with metroZones *Mapping along the Refugee Complex* (Berlin Field Recodings Maxim-Gorki-Theater 2015, Connecting Spaces HKW Berlin 2016). Becker is currently working on the project *Chinafrika: Under Construction* (steirischer herbst Graz 2015/16, Gallery for Contemporary Art Leipzig, Kunstfest Weimar 2017).

Paul Buckermann is a research assistant at NFS Eikones – Iconic Criticism at the University of Lucerne. After studying Political Science and Sociology at Bielefeld University he worked as research assistant at the research training group Automatisms at the University of Paderborn and held teaching posts in the sociology of art and sociological theory at Bielefeld University. In his PhD thesis he analyses tendencies towards quantification in the contemporary art world and how this knowledge shapes global art worlds through communication. Recent publications include: "Autonome Kunst und frühe Kunstmuseen in Europa. Spuren von Ausdifferenzierungsprozessen in der Gründungsphase des Alten Museums Berlin" (Autonomous art and early art museums in Europe. Traces of functional differentiation in the foundation of Berlin's Altes Museum), in: *Autonomie der Kunst? Zur Aktualität eines gesellschaftlichen Leitbildes* (Autonomy of the Arts? On the topicality of a social concept), edited by N.T. Zahner and U. Karstein, VS Verlag (2016); "Back from Business: On Commensuration, Construction, and Communication of a Global Art World in the Ranking Kunstkompass", KAPSULA (1/2016). An anthology on the technological conditions of emancipatory politics, edited by Buckermann, Anne Koppenburger and Simon Schaupp, was published by Unrast Verlag in the spring of 2017.

Nanna Heidenreich is a lecturer in Media and Cultural Studies teaching at various universities. In 2016 she was visiting professor for Media Studies at the University of Hildesheim, and before that worked as a research fellow at the University of Arts in Braunschweig. Since 2009 she has also been part of the curatorial team for the Berlinale programme *Forum Expanded,* and since November 2015 has worked as a researcher and curator for the Haus der Kulturen der Welt in Berlin. Her subject areas in this position have included migration, escape and immigration. As curator she developed a series of events entitled *Aufnahme* (2016), and in collaboration with Katrin Klingan and Rana Dasgupta the project *Now is the Time of Monsters* (2017). Recent publications include Birgit Hein: Film as Idea – Birgit Hein's texts on film/visual art, Berlin: Vorwerk 8 2016, edited with Florian Krautkrämer and Heike Klippel; *total. Universalismus und Partikularismus in postkolonialer Medienwissenschaft* (total. Universalism and particularism in postcolonial media studies) Bielefeld: transcript 2015, edited with Ulrike Bergermann; *V/erkennungsdienste, das Kino und die Perspektive der Migration* (Cinema and its perspectives on migration) Bielefeld: transcript 2015.

Peter Hermans is a writer and artist, currently living and working in Leipzig. He studied Political Science and Urban Cultures across Europe, at a.o. the University of Ghent, Manchester Metropolitan University and the Estonian Academy of Arts. From October 2017 on he will be holding the position of lecturer in communication design at Burg Giebichenstein University of Art and Design Halle and is currently finishing a Fine Art degree at the Academy of Fine Arts Leipzig with Prof. Peter Piller. He writes, performs and makes videos. His recent performances and exhibitions include *common room,* IAb, Bielefeld, with Steven Emmanuel (2016), *dunya,* part of *Tricky Tongues,* Maze9, Tel Aviv (2016), *Membrana,* Cankarjev Dom, Ljubljana, (2016), *private access* at *Opaque Infrastructures* (curated by Tekla Aslanishvili and Giorgi Gago Gagoshidze, 2016), the video and lecture-performance *HIPS (Hide In Plain Sight)* at the Kunstverein Nürnberg (2014) and *Kunst im Tunnel,* Düsseldorf (2014). His writings have appeared in both academic and art publications, including *suppose there's right and wrong, it's probably right,* W139, Amsterdam (2017), "perception is material" in *Darkrooms: Räume der Un/Sichtbarkeit,* Neofelis Verlag, Berlin, edited by Sophia Kunze and Marietta Kesting (2017).

Rahel Jaeggi is Professor of Practical Philosophy with emphasis on Social Philosophy and Political Philosophy at the Humboldt University of Berlin. From 2015 to 2016 she was the Theodor Heuss Professor at the New School for Social Research in New York. Jaeggi's research areas include Social Philosophy, Political Philosophy, Ethics, Philosophical Anthropology, Social Ontology, Critical Theory and the enhancement of Critical Theory (in a broad sense). Her publications include *Welt und Person – Zum anthropologischen Hintergrund der Gesellschaftskritik Hannah Arendts* (World and Person – On the Anthropological Background to Hannah Arendt's Social Critique) Berlin 1997; *Entfremdung. Zur Aktualität eines sozialphilosophischen Problems* (Alienation: On the Actuality of a socio-philosophical problem) Frankfurt, New York 2005; *Was ist Kritik?* (What is Critique?) edited by Rahel Jaeggi and Tilo Wesche, Frankfurt 2009; *Nach Marx: Philosophie, Kritik, Praxis* (After Marx: Philosophy, Critique, Practice), edited by Rahel Jaeggi und Daniel Loick, Frankfurt 2013; *Alienation,* New York 2014.

Anna Jehle is as a freelance curator, working on independent exhibition and research projects as well as in an institutional context. Since 2016 she has been lecturer in Prof. Clemens von Wedemeyer's *expanded cinema* class at the Leipzig Academy of Fine Arts. As a member of the board she co-curates the program of KV – Verein für Zeitgenössische Kunst Leipzig. In 2015–16 she was director of the temporary project space IAb in Bielefeld. The IAb was located in a peripheral location of the city, its programme dedicated to experimenting with formats of becoming public for a diverse audience. From 2012 to 2014 she worked for the Bielefelder Kunstverein. Over the last few years she also curated, amongst others, the exhibitions *fremd* (GRASSI Ethnographic Museum Leipzig, 2016, with Anke Dyes, Benjamin Meyer-Krahmer and Clemens von Wedemeyer), *Ahmet Öğüt – Apparatuses of Subversion* (Horst-Janssen-Museum Oldenburg, 2014, with Anja Lückenkemper) and Up Till Now – Reconsidering Historical Performances and Actionist Art from the GDR (Gallery for Contemporary Art Leipzig, 2013, with Julia Kurz). She studied Cultural Science, Urbanism and Political Science at the Universities of Brussels, Leipzig, Manchester and Tallinn, as well as Cultures of the Curatorial at the Academy of Fine Arts Leipzig with Prof. Dr. Beatrice von Bismarck and Prof. Thomas Weski.

Alexander Koch is a gallerist, curator, author and adviser on cultural strategies. He studied Fine Arts in Dresden and Leipzig. From 2000 to 2005 he was a university lecturer in Leipzig at the Academy of Fine Arts. In 2008 he co-founded the KOW Gallery in Berlin, whose programmatic focus lies on the field of socially oriented art, representing international positions such as Renzo Martens, Hito Steyerl, Chto Delat?, Tobias Zielony or Clemens von Wedemeyer. At the same time Koch is the co-founder and director of *Neue Auftraggeber / New Patrons* in Germany. The programme, established in 2008, helps citizens to commission art works themselves. Since 2013 he has been initiating new patrons projects in Nigeria, Cameroon, South Africa, India and other countries. Since 1998 his numerous exhibitions and texts reflect upon the institutional and economic transformations of the recent present and their respective consequences for contemporary art. Koch's theoretical writings include key texts on art's attempts to abandon the category of art and internal differentiation within the field of art.

Ana Teixeira Pinto is a writer and cultural theorist based in Berlin. She is a lecturer at Berlin University of the Arts and a research fellow at Leuphana University, Lüneburg. Her writings have appeared in publications such as e-flux journal, art-agenda, Mousse, Frieze/de, Domus, Inaethetics, Manifesta Journal, or Texte zur Kunst. She is the editor of *The Reluctant Narrator* (Sternberg Press, 2014) and has recently contributed to *Alleys of Your Mind: Augmented Intelligence and its Traumas* (edited by Matteo Pasquinelli, 2015) and *Nervous Systems* (Edited by Anselm Franke, Stephanie Hankey and Marek Tuszynski, 2016).

Arkadiusz Półtorak is a curator, critic and Polonist. He graduated from the Inter-faculty Individual Studies in the Humanities programme at the Jagellonian University in Kraków, and is currently working towards his PhD thesis at the Department of Literary Anthropology and Cultural Studies at the Faculty of Polish Studies at UJ. His academic work focuses on the relationships between creative practices, theory of media and media activism, as well as materialism in contemporary philosophy. He is a recipient of the government-funded "Diamentowy Grant" (research programme, Ministry of Science and Higher Education in Poland, 2015–18). He writes regularly on topics related to contemporary arts for *Szum* magazine; he also curates exhibitions and has collaborated with artists such as Norman Leto, Mateusz Kula or Agata Biskup. He is the co-founder of the Kraków-based project space Elementarz dla mieszkańców miast (Handbook for City-Dwellers).

Marcus Steinweg lives and works in Berlin as philosopher and artist. He teaches at Berlin University of the Arts and edits the journal *Inaesthetics* published by Merve Verlag. He also frequently collaborates with artists such as Thomas Hirschhorn and Rosemarie Trockel on exhibition and publication projects. His practice includes own artistic projects, curating and lecturing across the world. Over the last four years he has delivered a series of talks entitled *Überstürztes Denken* (Precipitous Thinking) at Volksbühne Berlin. His recent publications include *Behauptungsphilosophie* (Philosophy of Predication) Berlin, Merve 2006; *Duras* with Rosemarie Trockel, Berlin, Merve 2008; *Politik des Subjekts* (Politics of the Subject) Zürich/Berlin, Diaphanes 2009; *Aporien der Liebe* (Aporias of Love) Berlin, Merve 2010; *Kunst und Philosophie* (Art and Philosophy) Cologne, Walter König 2012; *Philosophie der Überstürzung* (Philosophy of Precipitancy) Berlin, Merve 2013; *Inkonsistenzen* (Inconsistencies) Berlin, Matthes & Seitz 2015, *Evidenzterror* (Terror of Evidence) Berlin, Matthes & Seitz 2015; *Gramsci Theater,* Berlin, Merve 2014 and *Splitter* (Shiver) Berlin, Matthes & Seitz 2017.

Jochen Becker arbeitet als Autor, Kurator sowie Dozent und ist Mitbegründer von metroZones | Center for Urban Affairs. Er ist Herausgeber von *BIGNES? – Größe zählt, Image/Politik, Städtisches Handeln* (b_books, 2001) sowie Mitherausgeber der metroZones-Buchreihe. 2014 und 2015 leitete Jochen Becker das Programm *art & architecture* am Royal Institute of Art in Stockholm. Seit 2014 ist er Co-Kurator der *station urbaner kulturen* in Berlin-Hellersdorf. Zu seinen jüngsten kuratorischen Projekten zählen *Global Prayers – Redemption and Liberation in the City*, Haus der Kulturen der Welt, Berlin / Neue Gesellschaft für Bildende Kunst, Berlin / Camera Austria, Graz (2009–2014), *Self Made Urbanism Rome,* Neue Gesellschaft für Bildende Kunst, Berlin (2013) / Metropoliz Rom (2015) / Maxxi Museum Rom (2015), und gemeinsam mit metroZones *Mapping along the Refugee Complex* [*Berlin Field Recodings,* Maxim-Gorki-Theater (2015), *Connecting Spaces,* HKW Berlin (2016)]. Derzeit arbeitet Jochen Becker an *Chinafrika. Under Construction,* steirischer herbst Graz (2015/16), Galerie für Zeitgenössische Kunst Leipzig, Kunstfest Weimar (2017).

Paul Buckermann ist wissenschaftlicher Assistent am NFS Eikones – Bildkritik/Iconic Criticism an der Universität Luzern. Nach dem Studium der Politikwissenschaft und Soziologie an der Universität Bielefeld war er wissenschaftlicher Mitarbeiter am Graduiertenkolleg Automatismen an der Universität Paderborn und lehrte Kunstsoziologie und soziologische Theorie an der Universität Bielefeld. In seinem Dissertationsprojekt untersucht er Quantifizierungstendenzen in zeitgenössischen Kunstwelten und wie dieses Wissen globale Kunstwelten kommunikativ herstellt. Aktuelle Texte sind: „Autonome Kunst und frühe Kunstmuseen in Europa. Spuren von Ausdifferenzierungsprozessen in der Gründungsphase des Alten Museums Berlin", in: *Autonomie der Kunst? Zur Aktualität eines gesellschaftlichen Leitbildes,* hg. von N.T. Zahner & U. Karstein, Wiesbaden: VS (2016); „Back from Business. On Commensuration, Construction, and Communication of a Global Art World in the Ranking Kunstkompass", KAPSULA (1/2016); 2017 erschien im Unrast Verlag *Kybernetik, Kapitalismus, Revolutionen,* ein von Paul Buckermann, Anne Koppenburger und Simon Schaupp herausgegebener Sammelband zu Technologieverhältnissen emanzipatorischer Politiken.

Nanna Heidenreich ist Medien- und Kulturwissenschaftlerin und lehrt an verschiedenen Hochschulen, u. a. vertrat sie im Sommer 2016 die Professur für Medienkulturwissenschaften an der Universität Hildesheim. Zuvor war sie wissenschaftliche Mitarbeiterin an der Hochschule für Bildende Künste Braunschweig. Seit 2009 ist sie Teil des kuratorischen Teams des Programms *Forum Expanded* bei der Berlinale und seit November 2015 für das Haus der Kulturen der Welt zum Themenbereich Migration, Flucht und Einwanderung kuratorisch und beratend tätig, u. a. mit der Reihe *Aufnahme* (2016) und dem zusammen mit Katrin Klingan und Rana Dasgupta konzipierten Projekt *Die Jetztzeit der Monster* (2017). Aktuelle (Buch-)Publikationen: *Birgit Hein: Film als Idee – Birgit Heins Texte zu Film/Kunst,* hg. mit Florian Krautkrämer und Heike Klippel, Berlin: Vorwerk 8 (2016); *total. Universalismus und Partikularismus in postkolonialer Medienwissenschaft,* hg. mit Ulrike Bergermann, Bielefeld: transcript (2015); sowie *V/erkennungsdienste, das Kino und die Perspektive der Migration,* Bielefeld: transcript (2015).

Peter Hermans ist Autor und Künstler. Er lebt und arbeitet in Leipzig. Er studierte Politikwissenschaften und Urbanistik in verschiedenen europäischen Städten, u. a. an der University of Ghent, der Manchester Metropolitan University und der Estonian Academy of Arts. Ab Oktober 2017 ist er als künstlerischer Mitarbeiter im Kommunikationsdesign an der Burg Giebichenstein Kunsthochschule Halle tätig und absolviert derzeit seinen Abschluss in Bildender Kunst bei Prof. Peter Piller an der Hochschule für Grafik und Buchkunst Leipzig. Er schreibt, performt und macht Videos. Seine zuletzt gezeigten Performances und Ausstellungen beinhalten *common room,* lAb, Bielefeld, mit Steven Emmanuel (2016), *dunya,* Performance im Rahmen der Ausstellung *Tricky Tongues,* Maze9, Tel Aviv (2016), *Membrana,* Cankarjev Dom, Ljubljana, (2016), *private access,* Performance im Rahmen von *Opaque Infrastructures,* kuratiert von Tekla Aslanishvili and Giorgi Gago Gagoshidze (2016), *HIPS (Hide In Plain Sight),* Video- und Lecture Performance, Kunstverein Nürnberg (2014) und Kunst im Tunnel, Düsseldorf (2014). Seine Schriften werden gleichermaßen in wissenschaftlichen und kunstspezifischen Kontexten veröffentlicht, so beispielsweise „suppose there's right and wrong, it's probably right", W139, Amsterdam (2017) oder „perception is material" in *Darkrooms: Räume der Un/Sichtbarkeit,* hg. von Sophia Kunze und Marietta Kesting, Berlin: Neofelis Verlag (2017).

Rahel Jaeggi ist seit 2009 Professorin für Praktische Philosophie an der Humboldt-Universität zu Berlin. 2015/2016 unterrichtete sie als Theodor Heuss-Professorin an der New School for Social Research in New York. Ihr thematischer Schwerpunkt liegt in den Bereichen der Sozialphilosophie, der philosophischen Ethik, der Sozialontologie und der philosophischen Anthropologie. Gegenstand ihrer Forschung ist die Weiterentwicklung zentraler Motive Kritischer Theorien (im weiten Sinne). Veröffentlichungen sind u. a.: *Welt und Person. Anthropologische Grundlagen der Gesellschaftskritik Hannah Arendts,* Berlin (1997); *Entfremdung. Zur Aktualität eines sozialphilosophischen Problems,* Frankfurt/M., New York (2005); *Was ist Kritik? Philosophische Positionen,* hg. zusammen mit Tilo Wesche, Frankfurt/M. (2009); *Nach Marx,* hg. zusammen mit Daniel Loick, Berlin (2013); *Kritik von Lebensformen,* Berlin (2013), Engl.: *Alienation,* New York (2014).

Anna Jehle ist als Kuratorin in institutionellen und freien Kontexten tätig. Seit 2016 ist sie künstlerische Mitarbeiterin in der Klasse *expanded cinema* von Clemens von Wedemeyer an der Hochschule für Grafik und Buchkunst Leipzig. Als Vorstandsmitglied des KV – Verein für zeitgenössische Kunst Leipzig co-kuratiert sie dort das Programm. 2015/2016 gründete sie den temporären Projektraum lAb in Bielefeld, wo sie das Potential eines Kunstraumes hinsichtlich kollaborativer, unkonventioneller und handlungsaktivierender Möglichkeiten untersuchte. Von 2012 bis 2014 war sie im Bielefelder Kunstverein tätig. Darüber hinaus realisierte sie u. a. die Ausstellungsprojekte *fremd,* GRASSI Museum für Völkerkunde zu Leipzig, mit Anke Dyes, Benjamin Meyer-Krahmer und Clemens von Wedemeyer (2016), *Ahmet Ögüt – Apparatuses of Subversion,* Horst-Janssen-Museum Oldenburg, mit Anja Lückenkemper (2014), *Up Till Now – Wiedervorlagen historischer Performance und Aktionskunst aus der DDR,* Galerie für Zeitgenössische Kunst Leipzig, mit Julia Kurz (2013). Anna Jehle studierte Kulturwissenschaften, Urbanistik und Politikwissenschaft an den Universitäten Brüssel, Leipzig, Manchester und Tallinn. 2013 absolvierte sie den postgradualen Studiengang Kulturen des Kuratorischen bei Prof. Dr. Beatrice von Bismarck und Prof. Thomas Weski an der Hochschule für Grafik und Buchkunst Leipzig.

Alexander Koch ist Galerist, Kurator, Autor und kulturstrategischer Berater. Er studierte Bildende Kunst in Dresden und Leipzig, von 2000 bis 2005 war er Dozent an der Hochschule für Grafik und Buchkunst in Leipzig. Er ist Mitbegründer der Galerie KOW in Berlin und dort seit 2008 aktiv. Das Programm der Galerie steht für eine gesellschaftlich orientierte Kunst mit internationalen Positionen wie Renzo Martens, Hito Steyerl, Chto Delat?, Tobias Zielony oder Clemens von Wedemeyer. Zugleich ist er seit 2008 Co-Initiator und Leiter der *Neuen Auftraggeber / New Patrons* in Deutschland, einem Programm, das Bürger*innen unterstützt, künstlerische Projekte selbst in Auftrag zu geben. Seit 2013 entwickelt Koch New Patrons-Initiativen in Nigeria, Kamerun, Südafrika, Indien und weiteren Ländern. Seine zahlreichen Ausstellungen und Publikationen reflektieren seit 1998 die institutionellen und ökonomischen Transformationen der jüngeren Gegenwart und deren Konsequenzen für die zeitgenössische Kunst. Als Theoretiker schrieb Koch unter anderem Grundlagentexte über den Ausstieg aus der Kunst und die Binnendifferenzierung des Kunstfeldes.

Ana Teixeira Pinto ist Kulturwissenschaftlerin und arbeitet als Autorin in Berlin. Sie unterrichtet an der Universität der Künste, Berlin und als Forschungsbeauftragte an der Leuphana Universität, Lüneburg. Ihre Texte wurden in Publikationen wie dem e-flux journal, art-agenda, Mousse, Frieze/de, Domus, Inaethetics, Manifesta Journal oder Texte zur Kunst veröffentlicht. Sie ist Herausgeberin des Buches *The Reluctant Narrator* (Sternberg Press, 2014) und hat jüngst zu folgenden Publikationen beigetragen: *Alleys of Your Mind: Augmented Intelligence and its Traumas* (herausgegeben von Matteo Pasquinelli, 2015) und *Nervöse Systeme* (herausgegeben von Anselm Franke, Stephanie Hankey und Marek Tuszynski, 2016).

Arkadiusz Półtorak ist Kurator, Kritiker und Wissenschaftler auf dem Gebiet der polnischen Philologie. Er absolvierte einen studiengang- und fachbereichübergreifenden Abschluss in den Geisteswissenschaften an der Jagellonian University in Krakau. Derzeit schreibt er an seinem PhD-Projekt im Fachbereich der Literalen Anthropologie und der Kulturwissenschaften an der Fakultät Polnischer Studien der UJ. In seiner wissenschaftlichen Forschung beschäftigt er sich mit den Beziehungen von kreativen Praxen, der Theorie von Medien und medialem Aktivismus, sowie Materialismus in der zeitgenössischen Philosophie. Er erhält das staatliche Stipendium „Diamentowy Grant" (Forschungsprogramm, Ministerium für Wissenschaft und Hochschulbildung in Polen, 2015–2018). Półtorak schreibt regelmäßig für das Szum Magazin. Zudem kuratiert er Ausstellungen und kollaborierte mit Künstler*innen, wie Norman Leto, Mateusz Kula oder Agata Biskup. Półtorak ist Mitgründer des Projektraumes Elementarz dla mieszkańców miast (The Handbook for City-Dwellers) in Krakau.

Marcus Steinweg lebt und arbeitet als Philosoph und Künstler in Berlin und lehrt dort an der Universität der Künste. Steinweg ist Mitherausgeber der im Merve Verlag erscheinenden Zeitschrift *Inaesthetics*. Zudem arbeitet er regelmäßig zusammen mit den Künstler*innen Thomas Hirschhorn und Rosemarie Trockel an Kunst- und Buchprojekten. Er realisiert eigene künstlerische Arbeiten, kuratiert Ausstellungen, hält weltweit Vorträge und organisiert seit vier Jahren die Vortragsreihe *Überstürztes Denken* an der Berliner Volksbühne. Zu seinen jüngsten Publikationen zählen: *Behauptungsphilosophie,* Berlin: Merve (2006); *Duras,* mit Rosemarie Trockel, Berlin: Merve (2008); *Politik des Subjekts,* Zürich/Berlin: Diaphanes (2009); *Aporien der Liebe,* Berlin: Merve (2010); *Kunst und Philosophie / Art and Philosophy,* Köln: Walter König (2012); *Philosophie der Überstürzung,* Berlin: Merve (2013); *Inkonsistenzen,* Berlin: Matthes & Seitz (2015); *Evidenzterror,* Berlin: Matthes & Seitz (2015) und *Gramsci Theater,* Berlin: Merve (2016). Kürzlich erschien *Splitter,* Berlin: Matthes & Seitz (2017).

Imprint / Impressum

This two-part publication is published in Bielefeld, Germany, to mark the 30th anniversary of the artists and residency initiative Artists Unlimited / Diese zweiteilige Publikation erscheint anlässlich des 30-jährigen Jubiläums der Künstler*innen- und Residency Initiative Artists Unlimited in Bielefeld

Editors / Herausgeber*innen: Artists Unlimited, Anna Jehle, Paul Buckermann

Kinship in Solitude (Part / Teil 1)
Copy editing / Lektorat: Paul Buckermann, Peter Hermans, Anna Jehle, Anne Koppenburger, Lars Rosenbohm, Juliane Schickedanz
Translations / Übersetzungen: Andreas Förster (English – German / Englisch – Deutsch) Nathaniel McBride (German – English / Deutsch – Englisch)
Authors / Autor*innen: Jochen Becker, Paul Buckermann, Nanna Heidenreich, Peter Hermans, Rahel Jaeggi, Anna Jehle, Alexander Koch, Ana Teixeira Pinto, Arkadiusz Półtorak, Marcus Steinweg

Archiv Klaus-Dieter Braun (Part / Teil 2)
Image archive / Bildarchiv: Klaus-Dieter Braun
Concept and editing / Konzept und Bildauswahl: Rebecca Butzlaff, Christine Gensheimer, Angelika Höger, Timo Katz, Lotte Reimann, Lars Rosenbohm, Tim Sürken

Design / Gestaltung: Rebecca Butzlaff, Tim Rehm, Tim Sürken
Printing / Druck: druckhaus köthen
Lithography / Lithografie: Heinrich Holtgreve
Binding / Buchbindung: Stein + Lehmann

© 2017 Authors and artists / Autor*innen und Künstler*innen, Artists Unlimited, adocs publishing

ISBN 978-3-943253-19-1
1st edition / 1. Auflage

adocs publishing
Oliver Gemballa
Annenstraße 16
D-20359 Hamburg
adocspublishing.com

Artists Unlimited
August-Bebel-Straße 94
D-33602 Bielefeld
artists-unlimited.de

We want to express our sincere gratitude to Klaus for the trust in making available his personal archive for this project / Großer Dank gilt Klaus für das Vertrauen uns sein persönliches Archiv für dieses Projekt zur Verfügung zu stellen

This publication has been made possible with the kind support of / Diese Publikation wurde ermöglicht mit der freundlichen Unterstützung von

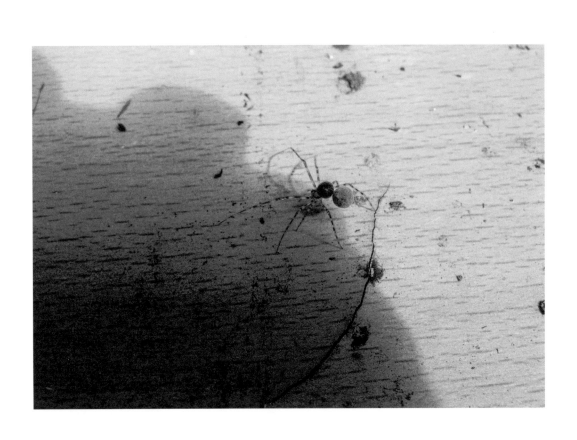

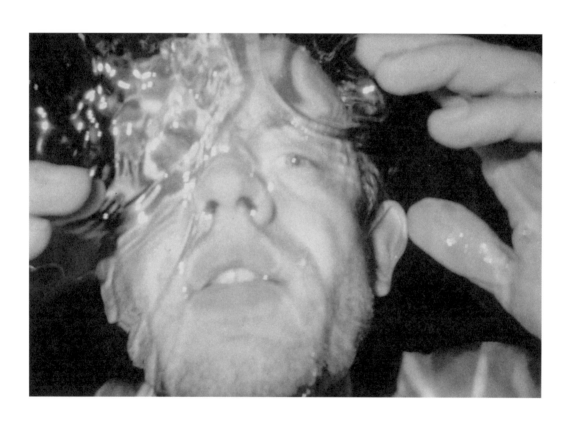

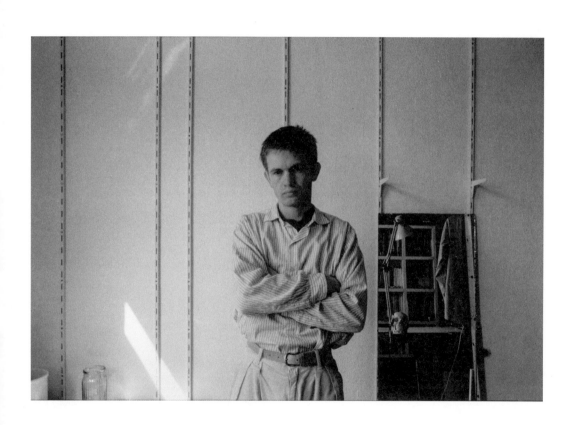

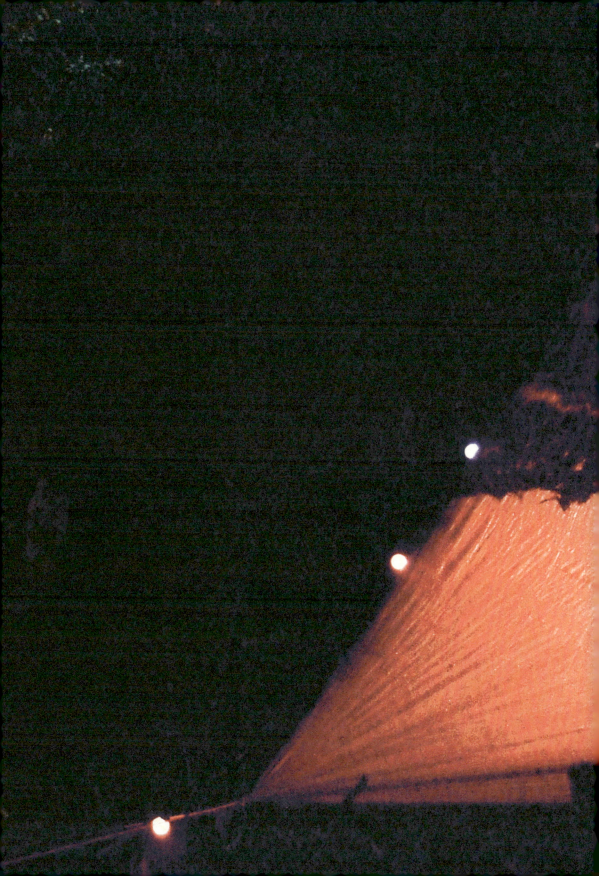

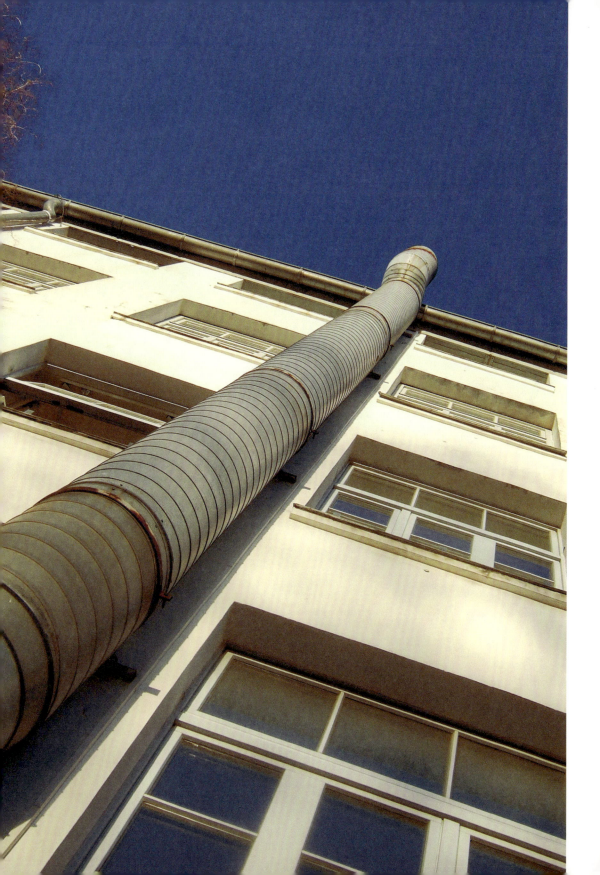

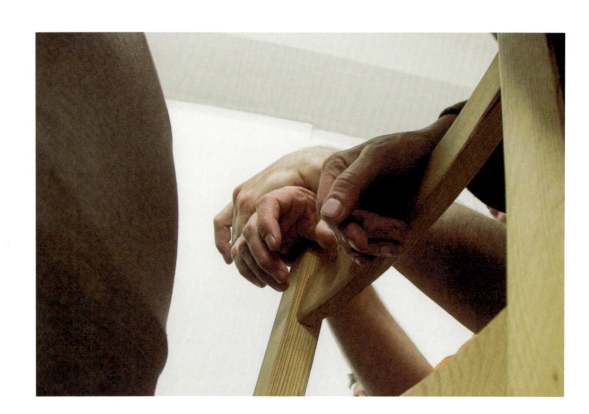

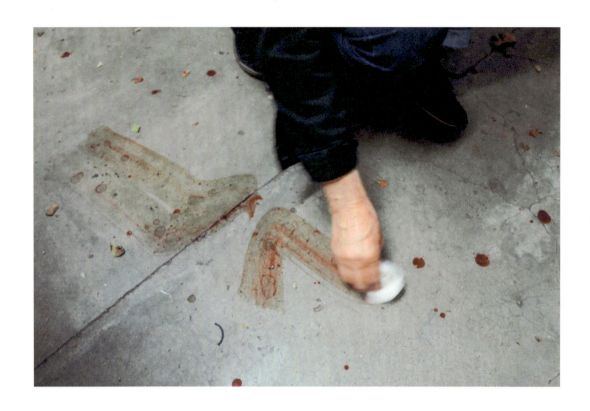

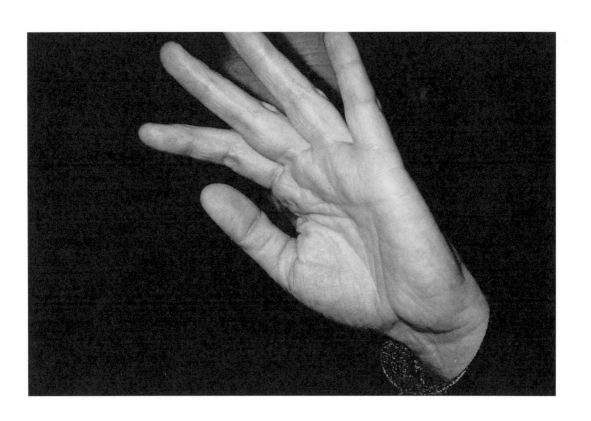

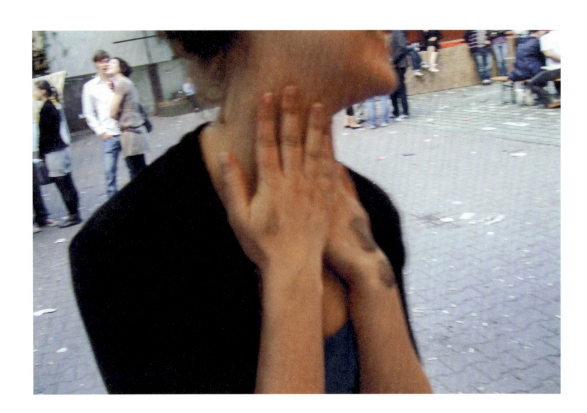

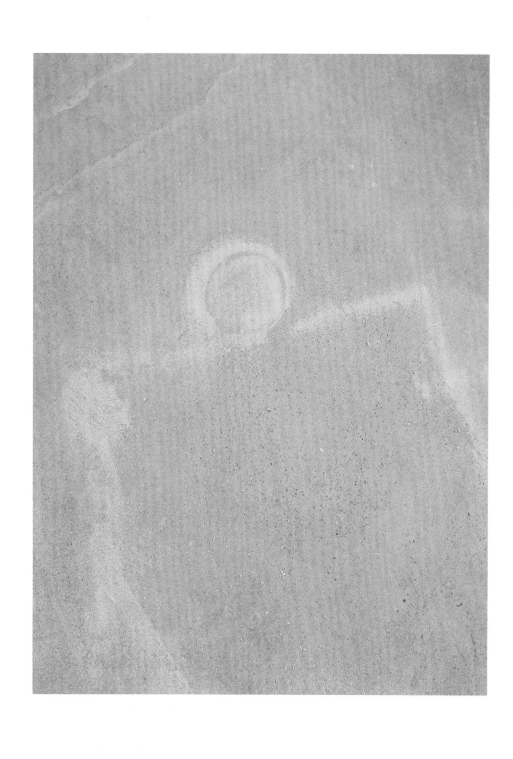

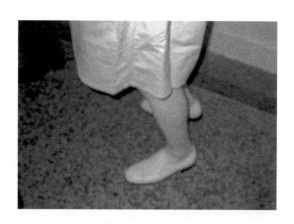

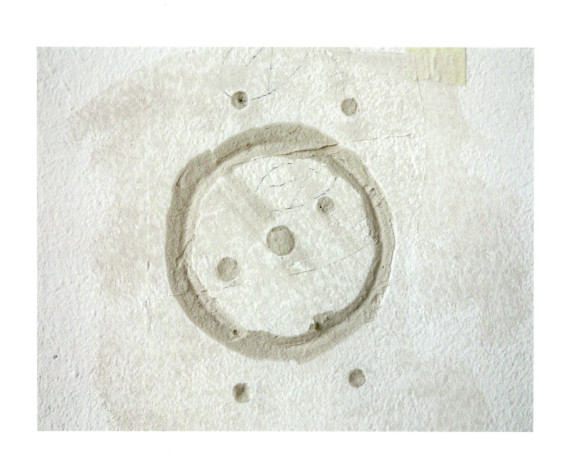

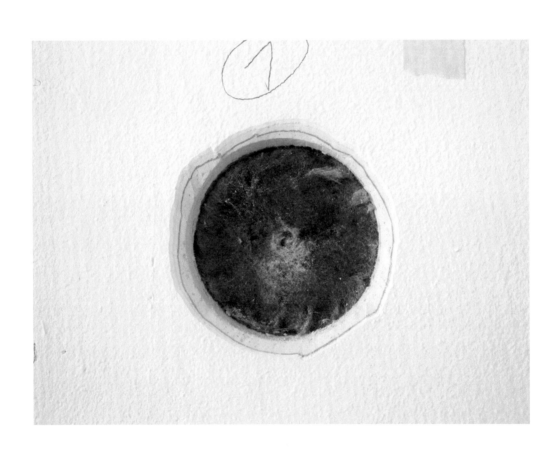

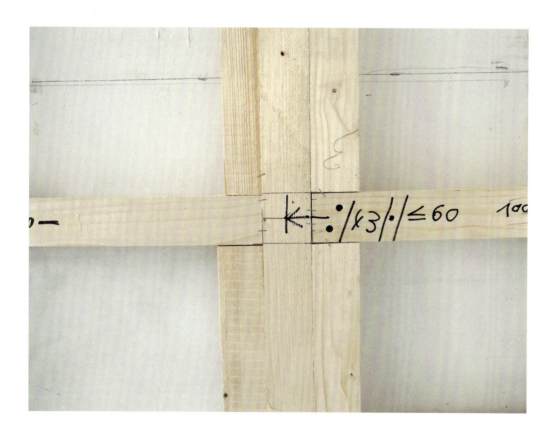

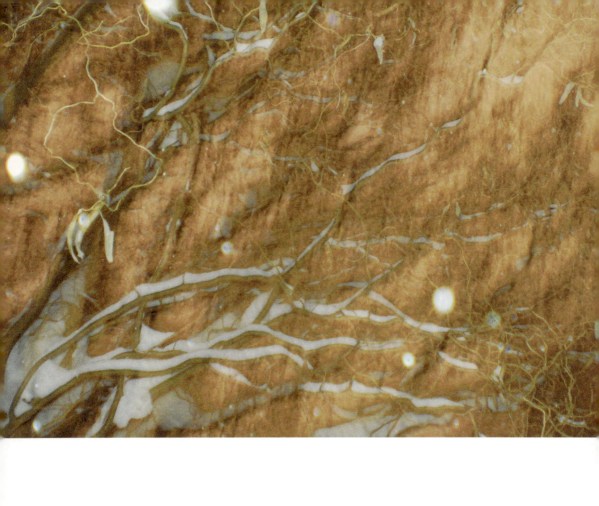

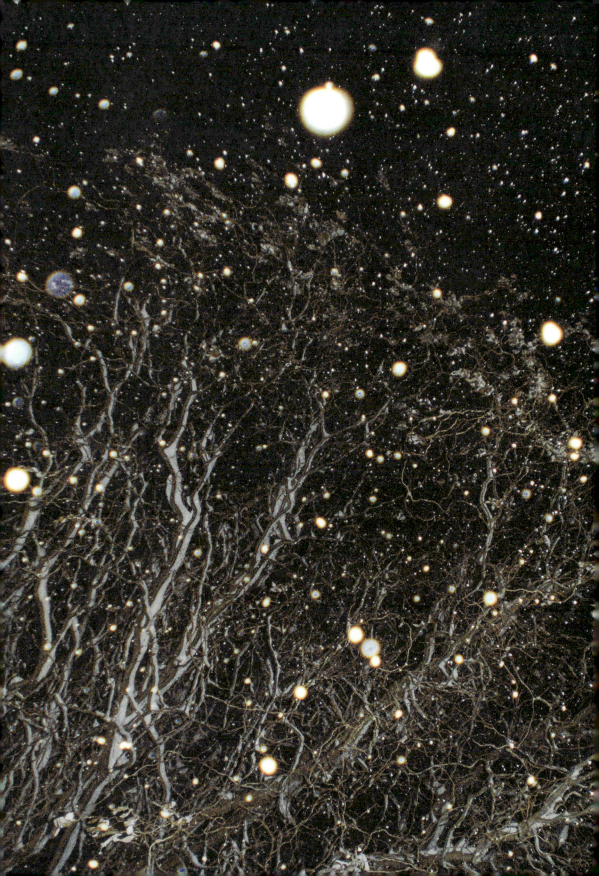

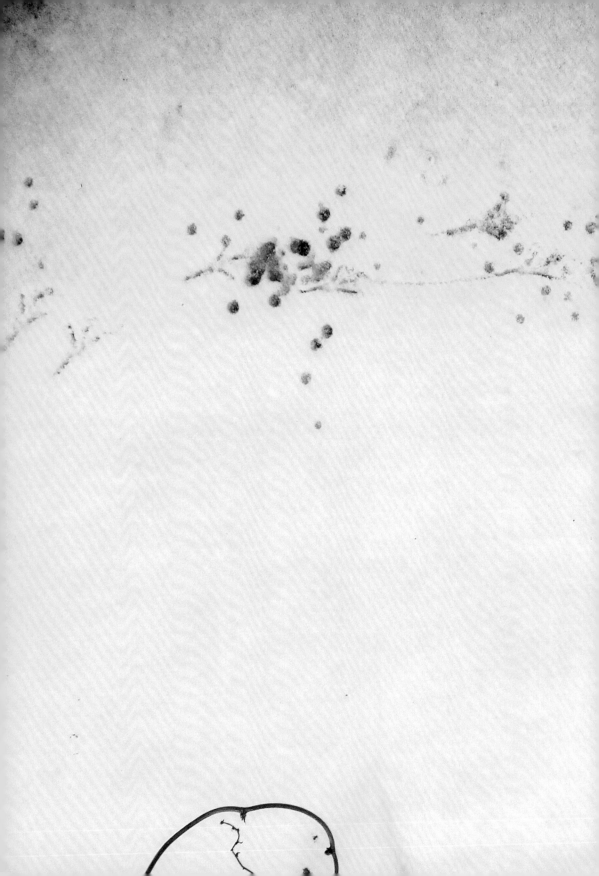

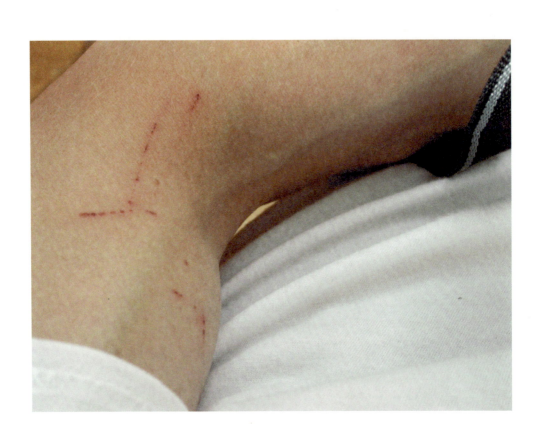

Imprint / Impressum

This two-part publication is published in Bielefeld, Germany, to mark the 30th anniversary of the artists and residency initiative Artists Unlimited / Diese zweiteilige Publikation erscheint anlässlich des 30-jährigen Jubiläums der Künstler*innen- und Residency Initiative Artists Unlimited in Bielefeld

Editors / Herausgeber*innen: Artists Unlimited, Anna Jehle, Paul Buckermann

Kinship in Solitude (Part / Teil 1)
Copy editing / Lektorat: Paul Buckermann, Peter Hermans, Anna Jehle, Anne Koppenburger, Lars Rosenbohm, Juliane Schickedanz
Translations / Übersetzungen: Andreas Förster (English–German / Englisch–Deutsch)
Nathaniel McBride (German–English / Deutsch–Englisch)
Authors / Autor*innen: Jochen Becker, Paul Buckermann, Nanna Heidenreich, Peter Hermans, Rahel Jaeggi, Anna Jehle, Alexander Koch, Ana Teixeira Pinto, Arkadiusz Półtorak, Marcus Steinweg

Archiv Klaus-Dieter Braun (Part / Teil 2)
Image archive / Bildarchiv: Klaus-Dieter Braun
Concept and editing / Konzept und Bildauswahl: Rebecca Butzlaff, Christine Gensheimer, Angelika Höger, Timo Katz, Lotte Reimann, Lars Rosenbohm, Tim Sürken

Design / Gestaltung: Rebecca Butzlaff, Tim Rehm, Tim Sürken
Printing / Druck: druckhaus köthen
Lithography / Lithografie: Heinrich Holtgreve
Binding / Buchbindung: Stein + Lehmann

© 2017 Authors and artists / Autor*innen und Künstler*innen, Artists Unlimited, adocs publishing

ISBN 978-3-943253-19-1
1st edition / 1. Auflage

adocs publishing
Oliver Gemballa
Annenstraße 16
D-20359 Hamburg
adocspublishing.com

Artists Unlimited
August-Bebel-Straße 94
D-33602 Bielefeld
artists-unlimited.de

We want to express our sincere gratitude to Klaus for the trust in making available his personal archive for this project / Großer Dank gilt Klaus für das Vertrauen uns sein persönliches Archiv für dieses Projekt zur Verfügung zu stellen

This publication has been made possible with the kind support of / Diese Publikation wurde ermöglicht mit der freundlichen Unterstützung von